Created and Directed by Hans Höfer

INSIGHT GUIDES
COSTA RICA

Edited by Harvey Haber
Principal Photography by Henry Genthe and others
Editorial Director: Geoffrey Eu

HOUGHTON MIFFLIN COMPANY

APA PUBLICATIONS

CostaRica

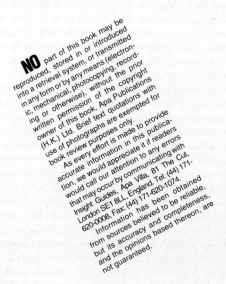

Second Edition (Reprint)
© 1995 APA PUBLICATIONS (HK) LTD
All Rights Reserved
Printed in Singapore by Höfer Press Pte Ltd

Distributed in the United States by:
Houghton Mifflin Company
222 Berkeley Street
Boston, Massachusetts 02116-3764
ISBN: 0-395-66258-3

Distributed in Canada by:
Thomas Allen & Son
390 Steelcase Road East
Markham, Ontario L3R 1G2
ISBN: 0-395-66258-3

Distributed in the UK & Ireland by:
GeoCenter International UK Ltd
The Viables Center, Harrow Way
Basingstoke, Hampshire RG22 4BJ
ISBN: 9-62421-157-4

Worldwide distribution enquiries:
Höfer Communications Pte Ltd
38 Joo Koon Road
Singapore 2262
ISBN: 9-62421-157-4

ABOUT THIS BOOK

Traveling in Southeast Asia in the early 1970s, writers Harvey and Dona Haber discovered the *Insight Guides* series of travel books, and, impressed by the books' uncommon quality, decided that they would one day be the editors of an *Insight Guide*, covering some uncommon, remarkable place.

Fifteen years later, while working on a book project in Central America, the impulse to do an *Insight Guide* was reawakened. Costa Rica, sitting pastorally in the center of the Central American isthmus, had managed not to be touched by a book by Apa Publications; nor had it been noticed by much of the rest of the world.

Two years after receiving the Habers' proposal for *Insight Guide: Costa Rica*, Apa Publications agreed that it was time for the book to join the family of more than 180 *Insight Guides* to destinations around the world. The Habers flew to tropical, frenetic, San José, Costa Rica, and began to assemble the team of specialist writers and photographers necessary to cover this small but complex tropical nation.

The Writers

Harvey Haber has traveled in or lived in 60-some countries but finds himself constantly returning to his favorite place in the sun, Costa Rica. Among other things, he has been a writer, restaurateur, school director and magazine publisher.

Dona Haber is a graduate of the University of California, a former Peace Corps Volunteer, researcher and writer whose two greatest joys in Costa Rica were riding buses and sampling *gallo pinto* at roadside cafés. She could most often be found in the library, researching early Costa Rican history. She also contributed substantially to the Places section, the guide to the country which follows the History and Features sections at the beginning of the book.

Marine biologist **Henry Genthe**, a principal photographer for *Costa Rica,* had spent 15 years traveling, writing about and photographing Central America on various research and educational expeditions. His work has been published in *Omni, Discover, Geo, Smithsonian* and *Natural History,* and in *Time/ Life* books and *National Geographic*.

Cindy Hilbrink left the University of California at Santa Barbara, where she had been teaching English and writing, to report on the rural Costa Rican. Hilbrink has been published in many national magazines.

The fifth person to become a member of the *Insight Guide* team was **Thomas "T" Felkay**. A professional navigator and sailor, "T" contributed invaluably to the investigation of the country and was responsible for the maps and archival research and work on the Travel Tips section.

Answering endless questions and advising the editor and writers of *Costa Rica* on cultural, anthropological and sociological issues, as well as being a major contributor to the People chapter, was Costa Rican **Moisés Leon**. Leon received his doctorate in cultural anthropology at Tulane University, and is a university lecturer on Central American history and contemporary social issues.

John McPhaul, a Costa Rican/American freelance journalist, added to the History section. McPhaul was born in San José, Costa Rica, raised in California, and graduated from Dartmouth College. He writes frequently

Harvey Haber

Dona Haber

Genthe

Hilbrink

Felkay

for Costa Rica's English language newspaper, *The Tico Times*.

Architect **Juan Bernal Ponce** contributed his expertise to the section on San José and the urban Costa Rican. Trained at the Paris Ecole des Beaux Arts, Ponce teaches at the University of Costa Rica and is one of Latin America's leading urban designers.

An important contribution was made by political journalists **Tony Avirgan** and **Martha Honey**, who have lived and worked in Costa Rica for many years. Tony, a keen fisherman, is a reporter for National Public Radio, the BBC, and *The Times* of London.

The Food and Fruits chapter was written by **Marjorie Ross-Cerdas**, a Costa Rican human rights lawyer and journalist, who writes a weekly feature on food and culture in one of Costa Rica's main newspapers.

Botanist **Mary Sheldon** wrote "Wayside Plants". Her work in identifying individual species of flora and fauna among the profusion of species in Costa Rica was unmatched.

Alexander Skutch, the ornithologist and tropical naturalist, contributed a piece on the Resplendent Quetzal. He has lived in the Costa Rican wilderness for over 50 years.

The Photographers

A formidable team of photographers contributed to *Insight Guide:Costa Rica*. San José-based **John Skiffington** delved deep into his vast stock library for many unique shots.

Chip Isenhart and **Jill Bermingham Isenhart** focused their cameras on the many environmental issues and national marvels of the tropical countryside. **Carlos Jinesta** has spent his life growing and photographing the limitless varieties of tropical hardwood trees of Costa Rica. **Michael** and **Patricia Fogden**, contributors to *Insight Guide: Amazon Wildlife*, again showed why they are among the world's top nature and wildlife photographers. Liechtenstein-based **André Bärtschi** is a natural history specialist who spends some time each year working in Central- or South American rainforests.

Nicaraguan **Julio Lainez** is possibly the most congenial photojournalist anywhere.

Insight Guide newcomer **Gary Braasch** provided some superlative shots of national parks and lodges, while Apa stalwart **Carl Purcell** came to the rescue in an hour of need. **Roy Quesada, Carlos Manuel Uribe** and **Miriam Lefkowitz** did field location photography and covered the Limón carnival.

The Costa Rica Institute of Tourism (ICT) contributed invaluable resources and personnel. **Tania D'Ambrosio** and **Susana Orozco** handled the complexities of Costa Rican bureaucracy and worked miracles over the fax and phone, effectively paving the way for *Costa Rica* through seven or eight ecosystems. And perhaps the greatest of unsung heroes was ICT driver **Jorge Chacón**, without whom, as they say....

The impressive staff of *The Tico Times*, particularly editor **Dery Dyer**, and staffers **Karen Cheney** and **Martha Brandt,** proffered time, counsel and expertise to *Costa Rica*'s writers and photographers.

Architect's and hotelier **Julio Garcia** and wife **Lavinia** served as cultural advisors, hosts and best friends. They bestowed the use of an office and invaluable introductions to all the right people at the right time.

Fernando Zumbado, former Costa Rican cabinet member and ambassador to the United States and United Nations, extended rapport, good cheer and discerning words.

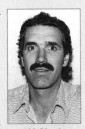    

McPhaul   *Jinesta*   *Chip Isenhart*   *Jill Isenhart*   *Ponce*

CONTENTS

History and People

Features

Places

Maps

TRAVEL TIPS

**For detailed information
see page 271**

A SANCTUARY OF THE MIND

"Costa Rica deserves to be better known. The prevailing idea in Europe and North America as to the Central American Republics is that they are sunk in a state of somnolence and inertia, from which nothing can come. They are represented as the scene of incessant interior wars, and one imagines them as constantly suffering from instability of government and insecurity. Nothing is more false than these suppositions for this little country. It has arrived at a state of culture and civilization that many larger nations might well envy."

- from *Costa Rica and her Future*
by Paul Boitley, London, 1889

Costa Rica is a small, democratic and peaceful country with a level of social development that always seems to surprise first-time visitors. Despite its vulnerable economy and existence in a politically precarious area, wracked by wars, repression, revolutions and economic woes, it continues, sometimes haltingly, to become developed. In many ways, Costa Rica defies definition as a Third World nation.

There are of course, certain images positioned in the mind, waiting to rise up as one considers Latin American countries. It matters little what degree of sophistication one has about these places; they are there, those clichés, and will not go away; they are waiting to define a whole people, even an entire continental region, with a few facile mental pictures: Mexico is Mañana-land. Tequila and tacos, burros and cactus, fiesta and siesta. Peru is llamas, and Indians in baggy white pants, shawls and hats; rosy caramel faces chewing coco leaves. Brazil is Rio, beaches, Carnival and the rain forest, the girl from Ipanema.

But Costa Rica. What and where is it? Who are its icons, how does one label this place?

Not very long ago it was necessary to point at the map to Costa Rica's location between Panamá and Nicaragua in Central America, so that foreigners would not confuse it with Puerto Rico. Panamá was known for its canal. Nicaragua for its revolutions. Costa Rica simply was unknown.

Preceding pages: black sand beach in Limón province; the spreading Cenízero tree dots the grassy plains, Guanacaste; cloud forest of Cerro de la Muerte; the Gaudy Tree Frog. **Left**, Foxgloves along the highway to Dominical.

There are certain qualities about Costa Rica and its people that are unavoidably true: Peaceful. Democratic. At times more European than Latino. Friendly. Educated and predominantly middle class.

An official at the World Bank defines Costa Rica as "the land of the happy medium."

An important national hymn contains the lines:

A love for peace
And respect for law
Has been expressed by your
courageous children.

Perhaps that is where Costa Rica is in the mind: a blessedly peaceful, even pastoral, land. A place where one can return, and sit, and simply be.

In Central America, at the end of the 20th century, amidst an area of regimes, strongmen, revolution, dictatorships, coups, assassinations, we find a people of extraordinary normalcy, seemingly nestled in a lyrical country of magnificent, diverse topography.

There are those observers and travelers who will consider this too simplistic, too idyllic a view to be true. Yet it is there. There is something about this country, something in the land that lends itself to the viewpoint that Costa Rica is a most beautiful, intrinsically safe place: a sanctuary of the mind.

Right: giant philodendrums, a small part of the tropical exuberance.

On 8 September, 1502, Christopher Columbus arrived on the Atlantic Coast of Costa Rica and took refuge in the calm waters just off the coast, between tiny Uvita Island, and what is now the Port of Limón.

The native Indians greeted the Spaniards with interest and brought out goods to trade with them. They swam out to the ship carrying cotton cloth, shirts, tumbago pendants (an alloy made of copper and gold) and weapons such as clubs, bows and arrows. The Spaniards in turn found the Indians friendly, clever and intelligent, and admired the unusual animals of the region. With two Indian guides, the explorers made short excursions along the Atlantic Coast, surveying the land and people and their potential for the Crown of Spain.

The Rich Coast: So impressed was Columbus by the golden mirrors the Indians wore about their necks and by their many stories of gold and gold mines along the coast to the south, that he named the area the Rich Coast of Veragua.

Rich though it seemed to Columbus at the time, the newly discovered area was not to be a great, rich jewel in Spain's crown. In fact, the "Rich Coast" turned out to be one of the poorest of Spain's American colonies. Impassable mountains, impenetrable forests, raging rivers, unbearable heat, floods, disease, swamps, shortages of food, internal rivalries, lack of natural resources and a way to generate wealth, all oppressed the settlers to the point where they were often reduced to living like the savages they had come to conquer: wearing goat hair garments or clothing made of bark, using *cacao* (chocolate beans) for currency, eking out a bare subsistence in the fields, using native methods to cultivate native crops. This bleak reality, in contrast to the Spaniards' great dreams, remained to be discovered by those who followed. Columbus himself naively returned to Spain with dreams of returning to this rich land and requested of the king that he be named the Duke of

Veragua. To this day his descendents use the title.

If Columbus left the Rich Coast with overblown dreams of gold, riches and happily submissive Indians ready to labor for the Crown, fed perhaps by his own personal dreams of wealth and fame, what was life in the newly discovered land really like?

It *was* a rich land; richly diverse, rich in animal and plant life, rich in forests, mountains, rivers, swamps and grasslands. In the Atlantic Watershed area, where much of the

land is flat, navigable rivers and the tributaries were swelled in some areas by more than 400 centimeters (158 inches) of rain per year. In the heavy tropical vegetation grew wild rubber trees, orchids and ferns. Fish, alligators and an occasional shark lived in the rivers. Water fowl, turkeys, iguanas, red monkeys, howler monkeys, boars, peccaries, and jaguars inhabited the forests.

To the north, in the Nicoya region were tropical dry forests, also abundant in plant and animal life: on the broad, seasonally dry plains grew the beautiful wide, green Guanacaste tree, the *javillo* with its poisonous sap and thorny trunk, the *cenizaro* with its flesh-colored flowers, the *guapinol,* and many varieties of cacti and spiny shrubs. White faced monkeys, howler monkeys, red squirrels with grey tails, tapirs, coatis, deer, jaguars, mountain lions, coyotes and numerous other animals lived in the forests; and in the trees, red and yellow macaws, wild turkeys, quail, dove, parrots. Avocadoes, papayas, plums, guavas and countless other fruits grew wild.

And the grasslands and swamps of the southern Pacific region, often called the Diquis region, were lush with life, as were the often misty green hills and valleys of the Central Highlands, where broadleaf evergreen forests, palms and white oaks grew on

Coctu, Corobicí, to name a few. We do not know the names the Indians called themselves, and since some groups were completely wiped out, even before the Spanish came, we do not have names for them, or know what languages they spoke. Because of this, archaeologists usually refer to Indian groups by the areas in which they lived: Guanacaste/Nicoya region, the Atlantic Watershed/Central Highlands region and the Diquis region (or Southern Pacific region).

At the time of Columbus' arrival, the people of the Guanacaste/Nicoya region lived in well-developed settlements, some with populations as large as 20,000. These settlements, supported by the cultivation of

the luxuriant hillsides and harbored innumerable species of birds, animals and plants.

Groups of Indians with diverse languages and cultures lived throughout these areas in small chiefdoms. They were agricultural people, cultivating crops of *yuca*, corn, *pejibaye* (the bright orange fruit of palm), and numerous other plants; supplementing their diets with wild fruits and game from the forests, fish and shrimp from the rivers, and crustaceans and small oysters from the ocean.

The Spanish colonists gave the Indians the names by which we know their descendants today (often the name of the chief at the time): the Chorotega, Huetar, Bribri, Cacebar,

corn, were built around central plazas, marketplaces and religious centers.

In the Atlantic Watershed/Central Highlands area, in the mountains near the present-day city of Turrialba, was a city with wide, cobblestone-paved walkways, freshwater springs bubbling out of stone-lined pools, and a stone aqueduct system carrying fresh water to some of the stone mounds on which houses were built. This ancient city, called Guayabo, flourished and disappeared (approximately 1000 B.C. to A.D.1400) before the arrival of the Spaniards. Other groups within the Atlantic Watershed/Central Highlands region were less settled. They cultivated root crops and hunted what small game was available, and then moved on to new lands when the soil or supply of game became depleted.

In the Diquis region the people also hunted, cultivated root crops and lived in well-fortified villages, which were strategically laid out to protect villagers from enemy attack.

Influenced by some of the other great indigenous cultures of the Americas, the native people of Costa Rica had become skilled in the arts of ceramics, gold and metal work, fine weaving, and stone carving. Costa Rica, it seems, was a kind of mercantile and cultural crossroads of the Americas. Linguistic and cultural influences, not to men-

marines from ancient Ecuador, making ports of call all along the Pacific Coast of Mexico, Central and South America, frequently stopped at sites in Nicoya, bringing the crafts and arts of Mexico, Central and South America to the people of the Nicoya region. Perhaps it was they who introduced Olmec influences to the area—or perhaps the Olmecs (and others) came themselves. Regardless, the influence of the Olmecs is strongly seen in the Pacific Northwest: in an impressive range of pottery styles; in utilitarian articles such as grinding stones; and in the practice of certain customs, such as the filing of a person's teeth into points.

Over the years, the pottery of Nicoya de-

tion a wealth of artifacts and materials, were being exchanged not only within the country but from as far north as Mexico and as far south as Ecuador. The native Costa Ricans were enthusiastic traders and prized jade pieces, ceramic ware, gold and stone carvings from throughout Mesoamerica and South America.

The Nicoya area, with its quiet Pacific bays and safe anchorages, had long been a pre-Columbian commercial port. Merchant

Left: an elated Nicoya figure, with pierced ears. Above: stone female carving, Guayabo. Right: Nicoyan phallic male figure.

veloped into a vigorous hybrid style that for centuries would be traded around Central America and southern Mexico. A collection of such work is available at the National Museum. Lively, bold, colorful, work: large globular jars, and vessels; figures of men and women, some with oversized genitals and physical deformities; animals of all kinds; mysterious effigies of man-birds; haunting funerary masks and some quieter pieces, almost luminously beautiful.

One of the great pre-Columbian mysteries of Costa Rica is the source of jade for the many jade pieces found throughout the country. To date no jade quarries have been located in Costa Rica, yet carved jade pieces have been found throughout the countryside. Guatemala is believed to be the source of most of the jade, although some pieces may have come from Mexico. Many of the jade pieces appear to have been treasured for years, passed down as heirlooms—and others appear to have arrived in one form and to have been re-sculpted to the tastes of their new owners. One interesting theory holds that some of the jade was brought to Costa Rica by pre-Columbian looters of Mayan burial sites, thus explaining the presence of Mayan hieroglyphs on the jade—which apparently had no value nor significance to the Costa Ricans. (The Jade Museum in San José

and extending into the Central Highlands, abounded with gold, which the Indians washed out of rivers, obtained from shallow digs in the savannahs, from under groves of trees on hilltops, or in the plains. They became experts in the art of gold working and employed a variety of different techniques, including the "lost wax" method, to craft a zoological garden of phantasmagoric beasts: a satisfied looking alligator walking off with a small boy-child in his mouth; a male-figure with an oversized, erect penis, surrounded by frogs and other animals; a two-headed figure, each head with a flute at its mouth.

The people of the Diquis region also wove

has an extensive display of pre-Columbian jade pieces of great variety, including a tooth with jade inset and jade breast supports or brassieres, believed to have been worn by high ranking women.)

And gold. The gold which so inflamed the imagination of the Spaniards, the gold which they so coveted. Gold headbands, gold arm and leg bands, gold collars, patens, bracelets, beads, bells. Golden ornaments sewn on clothes. Gold tweezers for plucking away unwanted facial hair. Gold awls, fishooks and needles. Gold sheathing for teeth. Golden masks.

The Diquis region, along the South Pacific

fine, white cotton cloth, which was prized throughout the country. It was often sewn into shirts, perhaps using golden needles, and was worn by both men and women as decoration or for ceremonial occasions. It was also used to wrap the bodies of the dead.

The Diquis region is the site of another great pre-Columbian mystery: great granite spheres, some as small as oranges, some weighing up to 16 tons, measuring up to two meters in diameter and perfectly spherical to within a centimeter or two. Made of granite, andesite and sedimentary stone, these balls, numbering in the thousands, were found along river beds and arranged in cemetery sites. None have been discovered anywhere else in the world. How were they made? How were they shaped, to be so perfectly spherical? How were they transported over 30 kilometers from the source of the stone to the ceremonial sites where they were arranged? And what do they mean? There are no answers: the giant spheres yield none of their secrets. They stand mute in their new locations, at the National Museum and in the gardens of expensive homes throughout the Central Valley. One can also see them, undisturbed in their original habitat, in a place on Isla Caño, near Corcovado National Park.

Archaeological data on the village life, the diet, the arts and commerce of the early Costa Rican people could lead one to believe that life was plentiful, complete and quite idyllic. Except for one thing: war was almost continuous.

In the Guanacaste/Nicoya region, wars were fought between rival groups to obtain captives for human sacrifice (and consumption) and throughout Costa Rica, there were wars to capture women and youths for slaves (who were sacrificed, sometimes brutally, on the deaths of their masters), to obtain the heads of enemies, which were carried as trophies, and to obtain access to new land. Sometimes, as in the Diquis region, men and women warred together.

Artifacts and skeletons found in unearthed graves suggest that the dead were honored; that funerals and burials of high ranking people were important and sometimes elaborate affairs. People of rank were buried with riches—and their slaves were sent after them (killed) to serve them in the other world.

Of their spiritual beliefs little is actually known although much has been speculated. Phallic images and figures in pottery and stone, emphasizing male and female genitalia suggest a religion focused on fertility and the practice of fertility rites, which probably included the music of pottery drums, bone and clay flutes, trumpets, ocarinas, clay and gourd rattles. Large vessels for the fermentation of corn, yuca or pejibaye suggest ritual inebriation. Drug paraphernalia suggest the ritual use of coca. And there were medicine men, shamans, with vast knowledge of the flora of the forests, who cured illness, forecast the future and dealt with supernatural matters.

Beyond the simple conclusions and elaborate speculations drawn from artifacts, little is known about the religions of the early Costa Rican people. The proud pre-Columbian lineages quickly disintegrated with the arrival of the men from across the sea, who captured their leaders, disrupted their communities, enslaved their people and destroyed their ceremonial religious articles.

It happened, looking back through time, in the blinking of an eye: the fine, spirited pre-Columbian artistry gave way to a lackluster

mediocrity as the Indians became an oppressed people. The once fanciful and finely sculptured grinding stones were replaced by river boulders; the elaborately decorated ceremonial vessels, by undecorated cooking pots; the dynamic spiritual beliefs and practices, by a half-hearted hybrid religion.

The rough terrain of Costa Rica, the inclement weather, the resistance of the Indians and the endless feuding among the Spaniards delayed The Conquest, as it is called, but the inevitable took place—and Costa Rica's rich pre-Columbian traditions were all but destroyed by the inexorable forward march of European colonists.

Left: ritual drinking vessel. **Right:** gold breast plate, Diquis region.

The Conquest: When Columbus set sail from Spain in 1492 on his first voyage to the New World, he was planning to find a group of islands near Japan, which he conceived to be about 2,400 nautical miles to the west of Spain. There he would build a great city and trade gold, gems and spices from the Indies, with the cities of Europe. He would be a rich governor, lord of it all. He wasn't trying to prove the world was round: educated people of the time already knew that. He was out to advance his fortunes, to become rich and famous, and it happened that his aims of discovering new lands over which he could rule, coincided with the interests of the Spanish Crown. The wars to oust the Moors

There were four voyages, throughout which Columbus continued to believe he was just a short distance from the great Oriental destinations of his dreams. The first took him to the Bahamas, which he insisted was an island in the Indies near Japan or China. Always a stubborn man, when he reached Cuba, he led an expedition inland, expecting to arrive at the fabled city of Peking. It wasn't until Magellan sailed around the world in 1522, years after Columbus had died, that things were set straight. But if Columbus' calculations of distance were mistaken, especially regarding the width of the Atlantic, it shouldn't detract from his skill and courage as a navigator.

from Spain had depleted the royal treasury. The promise of the wealth of the Indies was attractive indeed.

Thus Columbus so impressed Isabella, Queen of Spain, and her secretary of the treasury that they put up $14,000 to finance and outfit his fleet. Columbus had driven quite a bargain. He would receive three ships, equipped and maintained at the Crown's expense, a large share of the trade from the discovered area, governorship of the islands he might discover, the title of admiral, noble rank—and all of these privileges passed on to his children. No other explorer had asked for so much.

On his first voyage, Columbus also established the first Spanish settlement in the New World, at Hispaniola, today composed of Haiti and the Dominican Republic. One of his ships, the *Santa Maria*, had wrecked on a reef and after a local Indian chief helped him salvage the cargo, Columbus decided to build a fort there and leave 40 men to search for gold while he returned to Spain with several captive Indians. Columbus' return to Spain was triumphant. He was given a grand reception, was named Admiral of the Ocean Sea and was ordered to organize a second voyage to further explore Hispaniola.

The second expedition, outfitted with 17

ships and 1,000 male colonists, reached Hispaniola only to discover that the 40 settlers which had been left there had been killed after mistreating the Indians. Undeterred, Columbus sailed on from that site to the north coast of Hispaniola, where he attempted the establishment of another settlement. Leaving his brother Diego in charge, he went off to explore the area, again in search of gold. But things did not go well in his absence. Settlers fought among themselves and with the Indians. Frustrated gold hunters returned to Spain and grumbled about the disappointingly small amounts of gold and the cruelties of Columbus, (who, it must be said, tended toward arrogance). Things

Indians. But even that failed to satisfy many. Large numbers of men returned to Spain demanding back pay and Columbus' head. The man sent to Hispaniola to quell the disturbances put Columbus in chains and sent him back to Spain. Columbus, however, through the intercession of Isabella and Ferdinand, managed to secure his release and set out on his fourth voyage.

It was on this voyage, sailing up and down the Atlantic Coast looking for a passage to what would later be called the Pacific, that Columbus discovered in Central America the Rich Coast of Veragua. He spent 18 days in what was later to be called Costa Rica, near the present day port of Limón, in a place

were beginning to go bad for Columbus. The talk was affecting his reputation.

Nevertheless a third voyage was planned and approved, and while Columbus was exploring the Atlantic coast of South America and claiming it for Spain, Hispaniola was seething with discontent. "Not enough gold!" was the cry, and "We can't eat this Indian food!" Columbus tried to placate the rebels, as would his successors throughout Central America, by permitting them to enslave the

Left: conquistadores. **Above**: the Pinta flounders in a storm. **Right**: the virgin of the Navigators.

he called Cariari, repairing damages to his ships, the *Captiana, Gallega, Viscaína* and *Santiago de Palos*, while the near tideless ocean lapped on beautiful white and black sand beaches and coconut trees swayed in the gentle breezes. The respite was sorely needed: a violent storm off the coast of Honduras had caused considerable damage to his ships, and his men, one third of whom were between the ages of 13 and 18, were sick and exhausted. Columbus himself, at 51 years of age, was almost prostrate with the pains of arthritis.

And so the story goes, that the Indians of Costa Rica, wearing golden mirrors and necklaces greeted the Spaniards, guided them around the area, and spoke of great mines of gold, pointing south. "I have seen more signs of gold in the first two days than I saw in Hispaniola during four years," Columbus wrote to the king and queen. He had struck it rich. He would be wealthy. He would be titled. His descendents would carry the noble names he won for them. He would return to Spain, reap the benefits of his discoveries and become a rich and titled man.

The return voyage, however, was difficult. His ships had been attacked by worms and foul weather, and were leaking badly. He made it only as far as Jamaica, and spent a year there, marooned, unable to get help

cas and were his spiritual heirs.

One is tempted to characterize the Conquest as a brutal cartoon: greedy, ruthless *conquistadores* bungling explorations, slitting each others' throats for gold, territory or gubernatorial titles, murdering, stealing from and enslaving the peoples of the land. It took 60 years from the time of Columbus' arrival at Limón until the first settlement in Costa Rica was established. The troublesome terrain, the unfriendly oceans, the extreme weather and the Indians, who were not easily subdued, played a large part in the delay — but it must be said that the continuous, jealous feuding among the *conquistadores* themselves was also responsible for the fail-

from the governor of Hispaniola, who was worried that Columbus might usurp his position. There were food shortages and an attempted mutiny, but eventually Columbus and 100 of the original 135 men did return to Spain in 1504, shortly after the death of Queen Isabella.

Columbus spent his final years in failing health, attempting to secure the governorship, trade and other benefits which had been part of his bargain with the queen — but the king refused to even see him, and the struggle to attain title, territory and wealth fell to his sons and their sons — and to the *conquistadores* who followed him to the Ameri-

ure of many colonization attempts.

Gold was consistently the big theme. When the *conquistadores* asked the Indians about gold mines, the Indians pointed South, ever South, to the fabled mines of Veragua. It gave the Spaniards the fever. But if the Indians knew the location of the mines, they never revealed it, and to this day, the great, legendary mines remain undiscovered. The *conquistadores*, spurning the placer gold found in rivers, had to content themselves with taking the Indians' gold, which they did — until there was no more, and then they had to determine how to survive, let alone get rich.

In 1506, two years after Columbus returned to Spain, King Ferdinand sent the Governor Diego de Nicuesa and a group of settlers to establish a colony at Veragua. It was the first of a number of ill-fated attempts to establish settlements. Nicuesa's ship ran aground in Panamá and he and his group set about walking up the coast to their destination. Food shortages and tropical diseases were acute. The terrain was devastating. Indians along the way burned their own crops rather than yield their food. By the time the settlers finally arrived, their numbers had been reduced by one half.

At this time, expeditions from Spain were landing throughout the Atlantic coast of

appeared on the Pacific coast to accommodate would-be explorers who had sailed in to Atlantic ports and walked across the isthmus, ready to set sail on the Pacific and continue their explorations. The Pacific was an attractive prospect. It was unexplored, had better anchorages, and was thought to have more gold.

The second land expedition to Costa Rica occurred in 1522. It was led by Captain Gil González, and it too ended without establishing a settlement. Faulty ships hastily constructed on the Pacific Coast of Panamá took water and forced González and his men to abandon the sea and move forward on foot. González' adventures, which included

Central America. They were capturing Indian slaves and sending them to work in the mines of Hispaniola, stealing the Indians' gold and furiously searching for a passage across the continent to the other ocean.

Finally, in 1513, Vasco Nuñez de Balboa, a young stowaway who was escaping his debts on Hispaniola, led an expedition across the isthmus and discovered the Pacific Ocean. It wasn't long before rudimentary shipyards

Left: Catholic missionaries among the Indians. **Above**: converting the Indians with the power of The Cross. **Right**: Governor de Nicuesa colonizes the tropics.

a walk of 224 leagues (well over 500 miles) from the south Pacific coast of Costa Rica to the north, and into Nicaragua, have a mythic quality to them—at least as they are recorded for the king by the party's accountant. At the age of 65, and suffering from arthritis, which was aggravated by the unceasing rain, González sometimes had to be carried on a litter, but he made the arduous trip, once resting for 15 days in the home of the Terraba chief near Borruca. According to his accounts, he baptized some 32,000 Indians in mass baptisms as he went, collecting golden items of vast value.

If King Carlos I of Spain (who, by the way,

didn't speak Spanish), enjoyed a well-told adventure story, he was certainly pleased with González' account of his travels, which recount some extraordinary meetings with the Indians of northern Costa Rica and Nicaragua. One of González' converts to Christianity was Chief Nicaragua, who, prior to being baptized with his wives and 9,000 of his subjects, put some rather astute questions to González, including: "Where are the souls of people? Once they leave the body, what do they do?" "How was it possible that Jesus could be God and man at the same time and his mother a virgin?" And finally, "Why did so few men want so much gold?"

Another encounter was with Chief days after his visit, returned and attacked the Spaniards, perhaps in attempt to get his gold back. It was an attack that González and less than 20 men, at least according to the story, easily repelled.

González ran into trouble later on with the greedy Pedrarias, governor of Panamá, who was responsible for the deaths of many Spanish *conquistadores*, including Balboa, his son-in-law, whom he had beheaded. Pedrarias' ire was aroused by the enormous amounts of gold González, had collected and by González, refusal to give up his claim on Nicaragua, and the affair ended with González fleeing Panamá with his treasure.

The Indians of Nicoya and Nicaragua were

Diríagen, who showed up one day accompanied by 500 Indians, each carrying one or two turkeys, 17 women covered head to foot in gold disks, 10 men with standards, five trumpeters, and other attendants, bringing 200 golden hatchets. The party stopped in front of the house where González was staying, the trumpeters played their trumpets and then chiefs, women and lords entered. When González asked their business, Diríagen replied that they had come to see the men with beards who rode upon strange beasts. Probably Diríagen had come to ascertain the number and strength of the Spaniards, because he declined to be baptized and three not so fortunate as González, who got away with his life and his treasure: the expedition had brought smallpox, influenza and plague to the area, and tens of thousands of Indians died of the diseases. Survivors of the epidemics faced another danger: impressment into slavery. Indians from the Nicoya region, who then lived in large population centers and were vulnerable to such attacks, were captured, branded with hot irons and shipped off to Panamá and Peru to be sold as slaves.

The second attempted Costa Rican settlement was at Villa Bruselas, near present-day Orotina, not far from the large port city of Puntarenas. It lasted only three years and succumbed to feuding among the settlers and Indian attacks.

During this period, the *conquistadores* who arrived in Central America were free to exploit the Indians in virtually whatever way they wished. The Spanish policy of *requerimiento*, which went into effect in 1510, permitted settlers to make war on (kill) Indians who did not become baptized, a convenient justification for the killing of Indians and plundering of their gold.

Later, *encomienda*, a royal grant from the Crown, gave settlers the right to forced Indian labor without compensation—or to demand goods as tribute. It was, in effect, slavery. The Indians were re-located to live on the land where they worked, and were considered the property of the grant holder. The Church proved to have an uneasy time with the *encomienda* system, however, and after campaigning by many churchmen, including Friar Bartolmé de las Casas, a former *conqusitador*, *encomienda* was abolished in 1542, when it was repealed by the New Laws. Until the Crown had approved the system of *encomienda*, the *conquistadores* could not realize their aspirations of becoming landed aristocracy, with all of the rights and assumed privileges of title, and land without Indians to work it had no real value.

Encomienda was not as widely practiced in Costa Rica as it was in the other Central American colonies. For one thing, the Indian labor force in Costa Rica was smaller. As well, the Costa Rican Indians were not unified and living in large population centers as were, for example, the Mayans of Guatemala. Instead, they lived in smaller, autonomous groups spread throughout the country. The Spaniards weren't able to simply move in and, in a single effort, conquer large numbers, as they had in Mexico. And, too, the Costa Rican Indians did not take well to slavery. Many fought and died avoiding enslavement, and many others fled to the mountains, where they could not be followed. And finally, the practice of *encomienda* was abolished well before large numbers of settlers arrived in Costa Rica. Nevertheless, *encomienda* or enslavement of the Indians by the Spaniards, did occur in

Left: a portrayal of idyllic early Indian life by chronologer, Figueroa. **Above**: a Nicoyan warrior.

Costa Rica, as it did throughout Central America and its repeal set off violent protests among the settlers, who conceived that they could not survive without slave labor. In Nicaragua, feelings ran so high that an armed uprising of colonists murdered the bishop who had supported *encomienda's* repeal. Settlers petitioned the king to revoke the New Laws, stating that they had invested their lives and possessions into settling the new land and the Crown had derived much benefit from their sacrifices, but the king, to his credit, refused to do so.

Still, the Crown had to support the colonists in their need for labor. *Encomienda* was replaced by a system called *repartimiento*

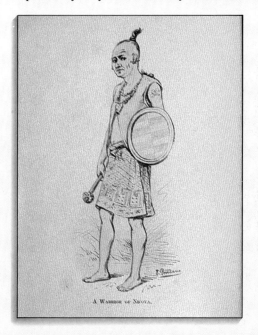

A WARRIOR OF NICOYA.

which required all Indian men between the ages of 16 and 60 to labor one week of each month for private individuals, religious institutions, municipalities and government offices. On paper, the system was supposed to provide Indians with compensation for their labor and leave them free to work their own fields the other three weeks of the month, but in practice, abuses were entered in and the system functioned differently. Indians were required to devote considerably more than a week's labor to the Spaniards as they had to walk long distances, sometimes days, from their villages to their work places, and they were charged for the food and any other goods they consumed—thus using up the token pay they were to have received.

Years passed but little changed. The search continued for the great gold mines of Veragua, to which the Indians had referred, but the mines were never found. Spanish *conquistadores* plundered the coastlines, taking what booty they could find, capturing Indians and enslaving them, fighting all the while among themselves for claims to the new lands. English pirates appeared on the scene, competing for gold and slaves. Spain's Central American colonies were developing and administrative centers grew up in Panamá, Nicaragua and Guatemala. In 1539, officials in Panamá used the name Costa Rica for the of black slaves and "auxillary" Indians from Nicaragua. (Bringing Indians from one area to another was a common practice among the *conquistadores*, as the Indians scarcely ever attempted to escape and return to their homes.) Cavallón also brought horses, cows, goats, pigs, chickens and ducks to enhance the community's chances of success. It was a well-planned and financed expedition—and finally, 60 years after Columbus' arrival at Veragua, the first inland settlement in Costa Rica was established. It was called Garcimuñoz, after Cavallón's place of birth.

The next year, Juan Vásquez de Coronado, called by some historians the true conqueror of Costa Rica, arrived. He moved the

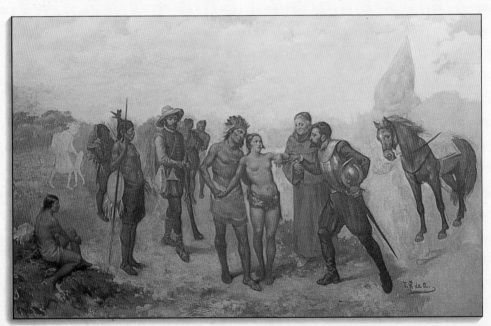

first time, to distinguish the territory between Panamá and Nicaragua, but still, there were no settlements.

In 1546, Luis, the grandson of Christopher Columbus, finally succeeded in being granted the title Duke of Veragua, and set out on an expedition with 130 men to claim the legacy left him by his grandfather, but he was attacked by Indians, lost most of his men, and the expedition was a failure.

In 1559, Phillip II of Spain insisted that Costa Rica be populated, this time well inland, and in 1561, Juan de Cavallón arrived with a group of 90 Spaniards recruited from Guatemala and Nicaragua, along with a team

Garcimunõz settlement to the Cartago Valley at a place called El Guarco, and it was there, for the first time, that a permanent community took root. Coronado's tactics with the Indians of Costa Rica were different from those of his predecessors. While he fully intended to settle their lands, and take what gold he could, he was friendly towards them, treated them with respect and requested, rather than demanded, labor and tribute.

Coronado was pressured by his soldiers and the settlers, who weren't particularly interested in peace, to be more aggressive with the Indians. The settlers wanted food, gold, and labor, or at least the promise of wealth and an easier life. During this time, they were continuously threatening to desert Costa Rica, claiming life was too difficult. Coronado's peaceful strategies were effective, however, and allowed the colony to grow.

Among Coronado's successes was the surrender (pacification, it was called) of a local chief, Quitao, who called a meeting of all the chiefs in the area and announced that he was sick and tired of running around and hiding in the jungles and was ready to submit to the Spaniards. He told the other chiefs they were free to decide for themselves what they would do. The chiefs asked Quitao to decide for them and he replied that he would, but they must be advised that they would have to

serve the king and his representative and those who did not go along would be severely punished. Then, as a token of his submission, he sent 150 Indians to serve the Spanish, an act that was "cause for great admiration among the Spaniards."

Coronado's explorations through Costa Rica are recorded with his keen, almost affectionate observations of the Indians. In the Diquis region, visiting the Coctu, wrote of the well-organized and well-developed vil-

Left: the return of Dulcehe by Coronado. **Above:** Don Juan de Cavallón.

lages, unlike anything he had previously seen. He noted that the people had much gold, which they acquired from tribes on the Atlantic Coast and scooped from the rivers, and much cotton clothing. He described them as a very good looking people, bellicose, skillful in their manners, and very honest, "a thing rarely seen in Indians."

It was among the Coctu that Coronado met the "most good looking Indian" he had ever seen, Chief Corrohore, who asked his assistance in recovering his sister, Dulcehe, who had been kidnapped by a neighboring chief. Coronado's efforts on behalf of Corrohore were successful and Dulcehe was returned.

It was not always peaceful, however. Coronado, known for making peace among some of the warring tribes of Costa Rica, also joined them in their wars against one another. As well, there were Indian uprisings in the colony. On returning after an exploration Coronado found that all the Indians of the area, including Quitao, were at war with the Spanish. (The Spanish had been taking Indian corn.) Indians in Orosi had killed eight Spaniards and their horses, and his old friends, the chiefs Aserri, Currirabá, Yurustí, Quircó and Purirsí, had been made prisoners. In an attempt to calm the situation, Coronado went to speak to the Indians. Unfortunately, he lost his temper and ordered two of them to be dismembered.

The lack of gold and food and the Indian revolts imposed continuous hardships on the settlers. Supplies and new settlers were brought in from Nicaragua, but the life was almost unendurable for the Spaniards. In 1569, settlers demanded Indian slaves, threatening to abandon the colony if their demands weren't met, and Perafán de Ribera, Coronado's successor, an old man of 74 years and in frail health, went against the laws of Spain and permitted the settlers to make slaves of the Indians.

The late 1560s marks the end of the Conquest of Costa Rica. By that time, the indigenous people of the new colony had been killed, had died of diseases, had submitted to the Spaniards or had fled to the forests of Talamanca. The land was now available to the settlers from Spain, to come and make a new life. And come they did, to this poor colony called "the Rich Coast," to work the land with their own hands and forge the future of Costa Rica.

The Costa Rican colony did not grow quickly. In 1573, there was a total of 50 families in Cartago, and a fledgling community that would later become San José. Spanish immigrants arrived from Extremadura, in the west of Spain, from Andalucia, in the south, with its strong Moorish influences, and from Castilla, the heart of old Spain. The Spanish had also founded Espiritú Santo de Esparza and Nicoya on the Pacific Coast, and although the population of Costa Rica was slowly growing, life was anything but easy.

During the Conquest, *conquistadores* had loaded their ships with gold, had lined their pockets with it and had sent their obligatory percentages off to the royal treasury, which had swelled with their contributions. But by the end of the 16th century, the gold was gone, there was little Spanish currency available and it appeared as though there was no way to generate wealth. Cacao beans were used as money and barter became common. Even the few goods the colonists "bought" from Spain were traded for wheat flour, pigs, lard, chickens, tobacco, and the liquor which they produced on their farms. Most families lived on isolated farms on the Central Valley, in a state of grim impoverishment, working their lands as best they could. Farming methods were primitive and social and church life were almost non-existent. People seldom went to town, even on Sundays and festival days, many because they had no clothes to wear nor cloth to make them from. Some wore garments made of goat hair or tree bark.

Church attendance was poor, a fact which concerned the Bishop of León, in Nicaragua, who ordered that the colonists form settlements around churches. Five years later, after nothing had changed, he threatened, again to little avail, that all who failed to comply would be excommunicated. The Bishop of León had little to do with his Costa Rican flock, however. Between 1697 and 1815, the holder of this priestly office only visited Costa Rica 11 times, with intervals

Left: the flambuoyant English pirate Morgan. **Right:** Miskito bandits make light of the colonist's labors.

between visits of up to 33 years.

The influence of the Church was not great in the small colony, nor was the influence of Spain herself, nor that of the colonial governor in Guatemala. It was, after all, a three month trip from Guatemala by horse, and truly, there was little to visit Costa Rica for. The colony was so poor that its governor was financed and paid out of the Crown budget for Nicaragua. Beyond that, Costa Rica was largely ignored.

Many point to this period of Costa Rica's

GENERAL PETER BLAM.

history as an explanation for the Costa Ricans' love of liberty, peace and personal independence. They say the beginning of their great democratic tradition began with the independent yeoman farmer, working his plot of land in the hills. His modest life, in the words of historian Carlos Monge Alfaro, "was dominated by the desperate struggle to subsist, producing in the descendents of the *conquistadores* a human breed quite different from the *criollo* of Chile, Mexico, Peru, Venezuela or Guatemala." (A *criollo* is a person of Spanish descent, born in the New World, as distinguished from a Spaniard born in Spain.) Monge says that because of the economic conditions in Costa Rica, social classes and castes did not arise, that there were no despotic officials who arrogantly kept themselves apart from the populace, no groups of strong and powerful *criollo* landowners, no Indians who hated the Spaniards, no wretched *mestizo* class (those of mixed Spanish and Indian blood) which had to endure the landowner's abuse.

Many modern historians point out that Costa Rica was not as egalitarian and classless as Monge's history suggests, but it was a rare land in which even the governor and his aristocratic friends are said to have lowered their heads to the sun and dirtied their hands in the soil of their own fields. The work was

the Crown set up tobacco processing plants and granted to Costa Rica sole rights within the colonies to grow tobacco. But Costa Rican tobacco was not of good quality, and there was not a large market for it.

On the Atlantic Coast pirateering and slave-trading were the business of the day. The Atlantic waters were continually plundered by English pirates with names like Drake, Mansfield, Morgan, and Owens, and by French, Dutch and Portuguese buccaneers, all attempting to control the territory so they could cross the isthmus, Atlantic to Pacific, and avoid the Spaniards in Panamá.

In 1641 a slave ship wrecked off the coast of Nicaragua/Honduras. The black slaves on

Saqueo y incendio de la Ciudad de Esparza por los piratas ingleses.

A Dn. Miguel Gómez de Lara sucedió como Gobernador y Capitán General el Maestre de campo Dn. Manuel de Bustamante y Vivero, nombrado por Real Cédula de 11 de mayo de 1692. Tomó posesión el 28 de Abril de 1693 y residenció a su antecesor. Este Gobernador era caballero de Santiago. Este Gobernador escribió de Cartago con fecha 6 de Junio de 1693 al Presidente de la Audiencia

hard, but the hilly, green land, irrigated by rivers, was fertile and beautiful and the climate was gentle. Colonists grew wheat, vegetables, sugar, and raised livestock and poultry. Commerce developed slowly.

The first export of the Costa Rican colony was mules. They were walked along the Mule Road, to Panamá, where they were sold to hardy souls who needed the beasts to bear the goods they were carrying from the Atlantic to Pacific Coasts. Later came cacao production on the Atlantic Coast, and then tobacco, in the Central Plateau. In an attempt to give Costa Rica a product to export and a dependable income which could be taxed,

board the ship escaped onto the Atlantic Coast. They were well-liked by the Indians, who intermarried with them, and over the years, they developed an identity and language of their own. They were called the Miskitos. British pirates allied with the Miskitos and together they wreaked havoc on the Atlantic Coast of Costa Rica and on the cacao cultivation which was underway there.

Cacao was being grown in Matina, not far from Limón, on large plantations owned by a few of the wealthy settlers in the Central Valley. Black slaves from Jamaica were brought in to tend the trees, which needed little attention apart from harvesting the fruit. For the Miskitos, the undefended cacao plantations offered little resistance. They simply sailed in for their biannual raids, took the cacao, captured the slaves and set off again. The colonial government was powerless to stop them, as it hadn't the resources to do so.

Finally, in 1742, after many years of devastation led by such Miskito Kings as Anibal, Peter and Talan del Ze, the government built Fort San Fernando in Matina, only to have it destroyed five years later by the pirate Owens and the Miskitos, who were under orders to do so by the Jamaican governor. (The British and the Spanish were at war.) By 1779, things had become so bad that the Miskitos requested tribute of the Costa Rican government—and the government actually began to send them "presents." The Miskitos would visit Matina and, waiting for them would be a Napoleanic coat of bright fabric and shiny buttons, a three-cornered hat, or other attractive gifts.

President Braulio Carrillo, many years later, in 1841, refused to continue paying tribute—or making gifts—to the Miskitos

and threatened to bring the resources of the country to war against them. Probably because cacao production had dwindled greatly by then, the Miskitos stopped raiding Matina. Traces of their influence remain in the Atlantic coast area, however, and many of the place names there come from the Miskito language: Talamanca (Talamalka), Sixoala, Cahuita.

The Talamanca region of Costa Rica, owing to its mountainous terrain and inaccessibility, had escaped the Conquest. Groups of Indians, some of them refugees who had fled oppressive conditions elsewhere in the country, lived there, undisturbed by the invading Spaniards. As more colonists arrived in Costa Rica and began to clear land, build roads and farm, the small size of the available Indian labor force became a serious problem. The solution was to begin raids on Talamanca. After numerous, unsuccessful raids and attempts to conquer Talamanca, with counter attacks and cruel revenges on both sides, hundreds of Indians were "relocated" to the Central Valley by the Indian Resettlement Policies of 1747.

In the central valley, communities were being established and growing. In 1706, the village of Cubujugui, which later became Heredia, was founded; in 1737 Villa Nueva de la Boca del Monte, now San José; and in 1782, Villa Hermosa, now Alajuela. Cartago

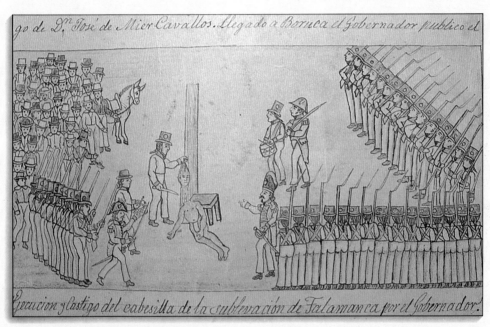

Left: English pirates sack Esparza, near the Pacific. Above: a public beheading in Talamanca.

was the moveable city. Established in 1561 by Juan de Cavallón as Castillo de Garcimuñoz, the city site and name were abandoned when Coronado moved all the inhabitants to El Guarco in the Cartago Valley. Then Perafán de Ribera moved it again, to Mata Redonda, near present day Sabana. Later it returned again to the Cartago Valley, to its present location. In 1723, Irazú Volcano erupted, covering Cartago, which then consisted of 70 adobe houses, a main church, a parish church and two shrines, in layers of ash. In the capital city of the day there was no doctor, no druggist, and no commercial sales of food.

Costa Ricans, with their attention on subsistence and survival, remained largely unaffected by the currents of thought and the conflicts that led to Central America's struggle for independence from Spain. The discord that was brewing elsewhere in Central America, fueled by rigid class distinctions and onerous trade restrictions, did not affect Costa Ricans, whose attention was on today's planting and tomorrow's meal.

Mail Independence: Costa Ricans like to relate that they received their independence from Spain by mail. In fact, a courier aboard a mule arrived in the Central Valley of Costa Rica with the news on October 13, 1821, nearly a month after colonial officials in Guatemala City, then the capital of the Capitancy General of Guatemala, had declared independence from a faltering Spanish Empire.

The news sparked ambivalence, confusion and conflict over what independence meant for the backwater region of Costa Rica. Being the province furthest removed from the colonial capital, Costa Rica came under the least influence of the Spanish crown, the Catholic Church, the colonial bureaucracy and the monopolistic Guatemalan traders who dominated colonial life in the rest of Central America.

Tucked away in the mountain recesses of the country's central highlands, leaders of the four small communities of San José,

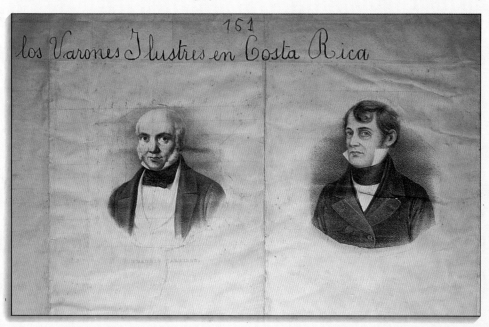

los Varones Ilustres en Costa Rica

Cartago, Heredia and Alajuela began a debate over what to do next.

To Costa Ricans, independence meant less the sloughing off of the shackles of entrenched colonial institutions—than creating from the beginning their own institutions in order to slough off the bone-aching poverty of their recent colonial past.

But the vaguely worded declaration of independence which arrived from Guatemala City provided the Costa Ricans with precious little information as to where to begin the process of nation-building.

Taking their cues from the 1812 Spanish Constitution—written with the distinguished participation of liberal Costa Rican Florencio de Castillo — local leaders drafted their first constitution, the *Pacto de Concordia* on December 1, 1821. A split quickly developed over whether or not to follow the lead of other Central American countries in joining the Mexican Iturbide Empire, or to opt for total independence. Leaders of the towns of San José and Alajuela, inspired by the revolutionary ideas that were then sweeping the world, argued for independence, while those of Cartago and Heredia leaned toward the Empire. There were even those who argued passionately that Costa Rica should become a part of Colombia, then ruled by Simón Bolívar.

strict colonial trading laws, that is, smuggling, and Alajuela developed into an on-the-fringe agricultural center where smuggling of tobacco flourished. Both towns developed more freewheeling, commercial-based liberal attitudes than those of their more stodgy neighbors.

The issue of whether or not Costa Rica would join the Mexican Empire was settled on April 5, 1823, when two armies from the rival cities met in battle on the Continental Divide between San José and Cartago in a skirmish which left 20 men dead. The victorious independence forces, led by a former merchant seaman named Gregorio José Ramírez, took the town of Cartago, assuring

The disagreements reflected the basic disparity in the respective characters of the cities. Cartago, the old capital, and Heredia as well, had been founded to create Catholic congregations out of the early settlers, who were religiously reticent. And so these towns evolved into centers of conservative thought and were more closely linked to the old colonial bureaucracy.

San José was founded by settlers who were banished from Cartago for defying the

Left: 19th century heads of state. Right: early-20th century Nicoya Indians.

independence from the Mexican Empire. As it turned out, the mail was late again. For it was discovered that Augustine I of Mexico had fallen several days before the fateful battle, and there was no longer a Mexican Empire.

Ramírez set a precedent by relinquishing power in order to return to his farm, one that would be followed by other victorious Costa Rican conquerors. He later returned to put down an army coup, establishing civilian dominance over the military at a very early stage in the country's development.

Statehood was conferred upon a rather ambivalent Costa Rica by the Federal Republic of Central America, a noble effort at creating a "United States of Central America" out of the five provinces, with a capital in Guatemala City. It was an effort doomed to failure because of the tenacity with which the elite class clung to the local colonial social order, in other parts of Central America.

As Costa Rica, largely a nation of family farmers, lacked both an elite class and a well defined social order, it offered neither great resistance to, nor enthusiasm for, the Confederation. As a sovereign federal state, the country elected its first Head of State, Juan Mora Fernández, a teacher at one of Costa Rica's two elementary schools, who distinguished himself by conducting the affairs of

social disintegration which had befallen the community as a result of the first modest signs of prosperity brought on by the planting of coffee, near San José. That limited prosperity brought with it prostitution, gambling and the theft of property at levels which had been unknown during the more austere colonial era. A strong, no-nonsense authoritarian hand was called for, and a San José lawyer named Braulio Carrillo fit the description.

Carrillo imposed vagrancy laws, removed Costa Rica from the faltering Central American Federal Republic and enacted a number of liberal reforms such as a civil and penal code. He also outlawed the church's right to tithe and earned the enmity of the other

state with prudence and humility.

To minimize the rivalries between the four main population centers, the *Ley de Ambulancia* was passed, rotating the capital between the towns every four years.

The first printing presses arrived in Costa Rica under Mora Fernández and by the time his successor, another elementary school teacher named José Rafael Gallegos, was elected, against his will in 1833, several newspapers were in print. One of them, *La Tertulia,* published humiliating attacks on Gallegas, who, not much interested in the office to begin with, resigned as Head of State. One of *La Tertulia's* major complaints was the

Central Valley townships by imposing a tax on rural land, using the revenues to build roads and ports. Braulio Carrillo also paid off Costa Rica's share of a debt to British bankers which had been incurred by the founders of the Central American Federation, a debt that other Central American countries would have hanging over them until well into the 20th century. The payback of the so-called "English debt" eventually paid dividends in the form of good credit with which to invest in the country's new found source of wealth: coffee.

Carrillo had, with unabashed autocracy, already ordered public administration around the exigencies of the coffee economy when an English seaman, on his way back to England with a cargo of pelts purchased in Seattle, Washington, stopped in Costa Rica in search of ballast for his ship. He loaded some 500,000 pounds of coffee into his hold and the Costa Rica – Liverpool connection was, inadvertently, made. Thus were the British Isles and, ultimately, the European continent, opened up as a market for Costa Rican coffee.

The domination that coffee gave to the citizens of San José and Carrillo's vigorous action in ordering that the country's administrative institutions be formed around the newly found source of wealth, caused resentment from the other townships. In 1837, Cartago, Alajuela and Heredia joined together to challenge Carrillo and San José in the *Guerra de la Liga*. Emerging victorious from the battle, Carrillo moved the capital permanently to San José.

When his term was up in 1837, Braulio Carrillo left office, only to return in a military coup the following year, after his successor tried to roll back some of his reforms. Continuing to force the country down the road to a coffee fueled progress, he proclaimed himself president-in-perpetuity. But by 1842, the new social order created by Carrillo rose up to overwhelm him. Members of the budding coffee oligarchy, anxious to get their chance at administering the country, called on General Francisco Morazán, the hero of the Central American Federal Republic, who was ousted during a civil war in Guatemala three years earlier, to free them from what they conceived to be Carrillo's despotism. Morazán was welcomed as a liberator when he arrived in Costa Rica, in April of 1842, with an army of 500 mostly Salvadoran volunteers. The head of Carrillo's army, Vicente Villaseñor, met Morazán as the general and his men neared Alajuela on their march from the Pacific port of Caldera and offered to join forces with him. The *Pacto de Jocote* sealed, Carrillo fell and was forced into exile to El Salvador.

A special assembly named Morazán Provisional Head of the State of Costa Rica. The General received a hero's welcome in Heredia and Alajuela, but received a somewhat cooler

reception in San José.

Morazán wore out his welcome when he attempted to use Costa Rica as a base to revive his moribund Confederation. The General sent missives to the other Central American countries calling for a National Constituent Assembly to revive his dream of a unified Central American nation, threatening to impose compliance by force of arms. When Morazán tried to conscript Costa Ricans to enforce his ultimatum, the people of San José revolted. After three days of open insurrection and fierce fighting, Morazán escaped the capital, seeking but not finding refuge in Cartago. There he was captured and returned to San José. On September 15,

ARMS OF THE CITY OF CARTAGO.
Granted by King Philip II., August 11, 1565.

1842, the 21st anniversary of an uncertain Central American independence, General Francisco Morazán, the father of the still-born Central American nation, was executed in San José's Central Park.

Less than three years later, Braulio Carrillo was assassinated in San Vicente, El Salvador.

Today, Costa Ricans have mixed feelings about Braulio Carrillo. He is remembered as both a despot and as a strong, sometimes benevolent leader who, perhaps, was the right man at the right time to force Costa Rica to break with its colonial past, placing the country firmly, if hesitatingly, on the path to nationhood.

Viva Volio! Those two words defined an era of social reformism in Costa Rica which culminated in the broad system of social security enjoyed by the Costa Rican people today.

Jorge Volio Jiménez, one of the most colorful and controversial figures in Costa Rican history, was in turn a Catholic priest, a military leader and zealous reformist politician whose fiery spirit helped fuel mass social movements that challenged the dominance of the country's coffee oligarches.

Beginning in 1889, with the drafting of the country's liberal constitution and the institution of a reliable quadrennial electoral process, Costa Rica entered an era of bucolic prosperity and political stability.

The affairs of state were left in the hands of so-called "Olympian" political plutocrats who administered public affairs with easy assurance. "Let things go; let things happen; the world turns on its own..." summed up the philosophy of such plutocratic liberal leaders as three-time president Ricardo Jiménez.

Periodic dips did engender moments of fiscal crisis, however, as the downward trickle of profits in the coffee economy failed to reach growing numbers of people, especially in the neglected urban centers. Faced with the closing of European coffee markets during World War I, Costa Rica's first reformist president, Alfredo Gonzáles Flores, instituted a tax on coffee. Gonzáles Flores immediately incurred the wrath of the coffee establishment which backed the president's own army chief, Federico Tinoco, in a coup on January 27, 1917. Tinoco assumed the presidency and named his brother Joaquín to head the army.

Popular reaction to the repressive Tinoco dictatorship brought Jorge Volio Jiménez onto the country's political stage with a dramatic flourish. The pious scion of a Cartago coffee family that gave Costa Rica several presidents, Volio began studying for the priesthood at Belgium's Lovaina University in 1903. Heavily influenced by Belgium social Christian thinking, Volio returned to Costa Rica in 1910 to become pastor of the parish of Carmen de Heredia. No simple parish priest, in 1912, Volio denounced the silence of the Costa Rican government over the intervention of U.S. Marines in Nicaragua and backed up his words by leading a group of Nicaraguan revolutionaries into battle. He was seriously wounded in the battle of Paz Centro in southern Nicaragua.

Half a century before Vatican II reforms gave rise to fundamental changes in Latin America, and before such revolutionary priests as Colombia's Camilio Torres began making headlines, Costa Rica had its own particular version of "liberation theology" embodied by Jorge Volio.

For his military adventure, Volio was suspended from the Church, but was later reinstated and assigned to the Santa Ana parish. But his passion for social justice led him to more clashes with the conservative local hierarchy, and in 1915 he left the priesthood to devote himself to working for social change.

When the Tinoco dictatorship became repressive, Volio and a handful of other Costa Ricans formed an armed resistance that plotted against the Tinocos, first from Panamá and then from Nicaragua. The revolutionary forces were defeated by government troops led by army chief Joaquín Tinoco in battles near the Nicaraguan border in early 1919. But the Tinoco dictatorship was brought down not by this armed resistance nor by a military, but rather by school teachers and students who rioted after soldiers marched on them, during a demonstration, in July of 1919.

The rioting included the sacking of the pro-government newspaper *La Informacion*. Future Costa Rican President José (Pepe) Figueres would one day tell a group of students that his political education began with a typewriter — one thrown at him from the window of *La Informacion* during the melee.

On August 9, 1919, Federico Tinoco resigned the presidency. The next day Joaquín Tinoco was gunned down as he walked in the street. The gunman was never identified.

Preceding pages: volunteer militiamen prepare to defend their country. **Left:** young soldiers defend their new republic in a border dispute with Panamá.

His military defeat notwithstanding, Volio received a hero's welcome on his arrival to San José and the cry "Viva Volio!" expressed the hope for change in the country's stodgy political status quo. The title of "General" was subsequently conferred on Volio by the Costa Rican Congress. But much to Volio's consternation, the fall of Tinoco meant a return to business as usual in liberal Costa Rica.

Volio formed the Reformist Party in 1923, which set an agenda for agrarian reform, decent housing, job security and social protections and the General ran for president on the Reformist ticket in that year against Ricardo Jiménez and Alberto Echandi.

cepted in the town of Liberia.

After a gunfight that left two government soldiers and Volio himself wounded, the General was apprehended. He was then brought back to San José where he was examined by the doctors. They diagnosed Volio as suffering from "nervous hypersensitivity." Rather than imprisoning the patriot, Jiménez, in consultation with Volio's family, allowed the General to be taken to Belgium for psychiatric care and Volio's political career came to an ignominious end.

Volio's energy and charisma was such that his Reformist Party could not outlive his influence, an irony considering his constant railing against the *"personalismo"* of Costa

He came in a close third in a vote that gave none of the candidates the required majority. A crisis was averted when Volio agreed to join forces with Jiménez, accepting the vice presidency and a seat in Congress. But Volio did not interpret his pact with Jiménez as one of compromise. Instead, he used his seat in Congress to bewilder his fellow congressmen with withering attacks on the country's upper classes.

When the government once again showed indifference to strife in neighboring Nicaragua, and also to what an increasingly belligerent Volio might do with his force upon return, Jiménez ordered the General inter-

Rica's political parties.

But the reformist movement was important in giving voice to the aspirations of broad sectors of society on the margins of the agro-export economy and in inspiring young intellectuals to action.

One of those intellectuals was Manuel Mora, who, in his own words, "used to follow Volio around like a puppy dog." Disillusioned with Volio's political flirtation with Jiménez, Mora split with the Reformist Party to eventually form the Communist Party in 1931. The Communists immediately made their presence felt in the lowland banana zones. In a strike in the banana zones in 1934, immortalized in the novel *Mamita Yunai* by labor organizer Carlos Luis Fallas, the Communists won wage guarantees and the right to unionize, but only after a torrid and sometimes violent battle with both government troops and the United Fruit Company.

Meanwhile, plummeting coffee prices during the Great Depression had created additional hardship for a great many Costa Ricans. Rafael Angel Calderón Muñoz, a medical doctor, who, like Volio, was inspired by church social teaching as a student in Belgium, gained a reputation as a humanitarian by promoting the first public housing project in a neighborhood south of downtown, which still bears his name.

Another medical doctor, Ricardo Moreno Canas, a healer of near mythic proportions, led a successful effort to nationalize the country's electricity utility in the mid-1930s and was said to have presidential aspirations.

In 1938, a deranged patient who was unhappy with the outcome of an operation to correct a physical deformity, shot and killed Moreno Canas.

The rising tide of reform finally found its champion when, as the economic crisis

A mural in Costa Rica's Museum of Art: Cultivating the wild new country.

reached its breaking point, Costa Ricans elected Dr. Rafael Angel Calderón Guardia to the presidency in 1939. Inheritor of his father's humanitarian legacy and backed by the coffee establishment, Calderón Guardia seemed the perfect choice, as he won the election with more than eighty percent of the vote.

Calderón Guardia, also steeped in Social Christian doctrine at medical school in Belgium, carried out reforms beyond the hopes of even the most fervent reformers and the fears of the most entrenched liberal, creating a social security system, a labor code, and other social guarantees.

But after Costa Rica declared war on Germany and Japan following the attack on Pearl Harbor—a day before even the United States—Calderón Guardia added insult to injury to the coffee barons by using his wartime emergency powers to confiscate the lands of German families, some of whom had been in Costa Rica for generations and who had business dealings and were intermarried within the oligarchy.

Having alienated himself from the traditional source of political power, Calderón Guardia made common cause with Manual Mora and his Communist Party, and the Catholic Church led by the socially minded Archbishop Victor Sanabria. Together they defied the coffee barons and the economic liberals who had dominated Costa Rica since the end of the 19th century, to expand the role of the state in providing for people's needs. The nascent bureaucracies that began to spring up would invariably be headed by a member of the Communist Party. Manuel Mora eventually would be named to head the country's army.

When the worldwide anti-Nazi alliances, which made this peculiar Church-State-Party pact feasible, vanished, so too did popular support for Calderón's leadership. According to Mora, as the government clung to power during the 1948 Civil War to, in his words, "defend the social guarantees won by the people," he was paid a visit by an old friend who offered his support: an elderly and ailing General Jorge Volio Jiménez.

History has shown that the winners of that Civil War, led by José (Pepe) Figueres, had no intention of rolling back the social guarantees, but rather further institutionalized the legacy of nearly 30 years of reformist struggle. It was a legacy summed up by the immortal cry: "Viva Volio!"

Grandfather of Costa Rica: Don Pepe (José) Figueres died in 1990. The sheer outrageousness of his life, the absolute Costa Rican quality of it all, leaves a legacy that will never, ever be equalled. He was, and is, in many ways, the grandfather of the country.

The casual inquirer will know him for his act of abolishing the army; the Costa Rican will know him for the way in which he lived his life, and for the heritage of democracy that he created and solidified and which has become part of the country's psyche.

He was born of Catalán parents, and for

many that somehow explained his ego, his opinionated, self-righteous, impossibly principled, obstinate, courageous, unyielding, unpredictable self. He was self-educated, and as a young man he virtually lived in the Boston Public Library, where he read as if ravenous for the purity of ideas, and became infected with the new and exciting spirit of North American liberalism. He returned to Costa Rica from Boston and New York City, in the 1920s, with a romantic vision and deeply held belief in the nobility of the human spirit, and in a hope for social justice for the people of his native country.

He started a farm high in the mountains

south of San José, and called it *La Lucha Sin Fin* (The Endless Struggle). The farm was successful, and he used the profits to provide schools, libraries, stores, movie houses, soccer fields, and medical clinics to the people of the area. There he learned that it was as he had hoped and believed it would be: that placing social services above his own personal profit offered a far greater reward. At *La Lucha*, Pepe Figueres worked at liberating the *campesino* from the ignorance and poverty that was his natural inheritance, and labored at turning some of the utopian theory of which he had read into workable reality. The day-to-day life at *La Lucha* became a learning process for Figueres; they were lessons which in many ways he was to later apply to all of Costa Rica.

Until 1942, Don Pepe had no real political experience. Then, on July 2nd of that year, the *San Pablo*, a United Fruit Company vessel, was sunk by a German submarine in the Port of Limón. The Costa Ricans aboard were killed, and people everywhere were outraged and screaming for something to be done. The president, Rafael Angel Calderón, responded to the submarine attack and to the excitable flames of hatred that were rising up in the demands of the people, by imprisoning the German and Italian citizens of the Atlantic region. Two days later, on July 4, a celebration planned to honor the U.S. Day of Independence turned into a riot. A gathering of 20,000 people in San José's Central Park turned violent, as the window of a medical doctor who had studied in Germany was smashed. Rioting and looting followed, and the government not only did nothing to control the mob, but, some said, they actually encouraged it. The aftermath of the riots was one of fear and suspicion. Businessmen who had been looted were afraid to speak out and seek redress; instead, cowed by fear of further reprisals, they placed paid ads in the newspapers asserting their loyalty to Costa Rica. Don Pepe Figueres blamed Calderón, whose government, he said, was responsible for the public order and safety.

He decided to express "what everyone felt but was afraid to say," and purchased radio air time on "America Latina." In strident mocking tones he accused the administration of an inability to govern. His acid denouncement of the government was interrupted mid-sentence as the director-general of the police arrived and hauled him away. The result was, perhaps all too predictably, the making of a martyr and national hero out of the imprisoned Don Pepe Figueres.

Figueres spent the next two years in exile in Mexico. There he began to plan his revenge. Force, he was convinced, was the only way to overthrow the government of Rafael Angel Calderón. Always an avid reader, Figueres continued his personal studies, made contacts, mutual help relationships and agreements with exiles, intellectuals and revolutionaries from other countries, and began the stockpiling of arms.

In 1944, after a particularly violent and discreditable presidential election in Costa Rica, with shootings, ballot boxes being stuffed and stolen, and the voting process being degraded to a point well below any previous level, Teodoro Picado, Calderón's political successor, was elected President. Issues of a fraudulent election, the faltering economy, the Communist presence, and widespread official corruption were just too much for Figueres, and he returned to Costa Rica in May of 1944. His apolitical days were over; it was a time for action. Determined to do something about Calderón, he jumped into opposition politics, but felt that the electoral process had been so badly corrupted that he would not run as the opposition candidate. He again insisted that only a violent revolution would bring about the changes that he felt were desperately necessary.

In the fateful 1948 presidential elections, Otilio Ulate, publisher of the *Diario de Costa Rica*, a San José newspaper, ran against Calderón. Ulate won by a substantial margin, but the *calderonistas* maintained control of congress. There were charges and countercharges of fraud. And in the midst of all the violent confrontations, a large number of ballots were set ablaze. The Electoral Tribunal, which had been entrusted to oversee fair elections, and to which the nation was looking for an electoral verdict, failed to issue one, perhaps in the hope that the candidates themselves would reach a compromise-agreement. With no action forthcoming from the Electoral Tribunal and no com-

promise between the candidates, the *calderonista*-controlled Congress, in an unprecedented act, annulled the presidential election. Ulate was arrested by Picado's police colonel, and his closest advisor, Dr. Carlos Luis Valverde, was shot and died the following day. In San José, businesses were closed and storefronts were boarded up. It felt as though a bomb were ready to go off.

Figueres was in the mountains near his ranch, *La Lucha Sin Fin,* planning for the civil war that he had long insisted was necessary and inevitable.

He began the War of National Liberation on March 11, 1948. It consisted of a well-planned, very lucky offensive carried out by

men with no military backgrounds, who were trained by *guerrilleros* from the Dominican Republic and Honduras and armed with guns flown in from Guatemala.

Forty-four days later, 2,000 men, or one in every 300 Costa Ricans, had been killed during the violent, short and sad war of liberation. Figueres' forces were victorious, despite efforts of Nicaraguan dictator Anastasio Somoza, and his invasion of the north of Costa Rica.

President Picado, who had never really believed an armed insurrection would occur, and who really had no heart for conflict, saw that a swiftly negotiated peace was essential.

Left: Don Pepe and Oscar Arias. The country's grandfather and the new Nobel Laureate. Right: a pensive Don Pepe.

Picado announced his surrender.

Don Pepe Figueres, as the acknowledged winner of the battle, and as the head of the victorious junta, entered San José five days after the cease-fire and led a triumphant parade. His National Liberation Army, festooned with flowers, marched up Avenida Central to the International Airport at La Sabana. Figueres addressed the people, outlining his goals and fundamental concepts, which he referred to as "the greatest good for the greatest number." More exactly, he said, the four main objectives of what he called his Second Republic were the re-establishement of civic ethics, elimination of the spoils system in public administration, social progress

United States.

One of Figueres' first acts was to place a 10 percent tax on wealth, a law that was resented, badly administered and, in most cases, evaded by the affluent. He expanded the Social Security system, enacted full voting rights for all women, created a minimum wage, low-cost national health care services for all, legislation on child support, and the nationalization of every bank in the country. The firing of large numbers of bureaucrats and schoolteachers, in an attempt to reorganize government agencies, exacerbated his declining popularity. And then the assets of individuals connected with the Calderón-Picado governments were frozen. Don Pepe's

without communism, and an increased sense of solidarity with other nations.

Figueres' Junta was not universally popular. He had been called a Communist by some and a Nazi by others. His revolution had received funding from very conservative Costa Ricans; he had accepted military aid from the United States; he had also received armaments from a group called the Caribbean Legion, who had given these munitions with the agreement that this revolution was to be the first of a series of revolutions that would re-create Central America and throw out many of the dictatorial regimes that had been put in power with the aid of the

extreme and, to some, arbitrary politics, alienated many. Even the press became hostile to him.

Acceptance of his new vision was extremely difficult in what was then an atmosphere of mis-trust and disharmony. Nevertheless, the Constitution of 1949, when it was finally accepted by the Constitutional Congress, did reflect many of the goals of the Second Republic. It included political and individual freedoms and added new social guarantees. It established the principle of public regulation of private property and enterprise and empowered the state to take actions assuring the widest distribution of wealth possible. It also extended suffrage to women and citizenship to all those born in Costa Rica, of great importance to the Afro-Caribbean people of the Atlantic region, who had earlier been denied the benefits of citizenship.

The new Constitution also abolished the military. This was perhaps Figueres' most celebrated and memorable achievement, and one that he would point to over and over again. In talking of this act he often used an analogy about the general physician: if a member of your family is ill, then the doctor should make a house call. But after the family member is well, it doesn't mean that the doctor has to continue to live with you for the rest of his life.

In a public ceremony, he delivered the keys of the Bella Vista military fortress to the Minister of Public Education, and told him to convert the old fort into a national museum. Don Pepe had a tremendous flair for the dramatic. He also knew how to exploit the moment. With photographers standing by, he took sledgehammer and a symbolic smash at the wall of the fortress. Figueres' supporters consider that dramatic act as a final blow to militarism. His enemies regard the aboliton of the military as a clever move, as, lacking the full backing of the military, he decided to get rid of it.

To ensure that the military and a military sensibility was abolished from Costa Rica for all time, Figueres created policy wherein any high-level police appointee would end his term with the next administration. Such positions of rank became subject to political appointment; they were valid for only a four-year term, and thus a senior police officer in one government could become jobless in the next.

On November 8, 1949 José Figueres voluntarily relinquished his power to the elected president, Otilio Ulate. He then began to prepare for his future political career. He twice served as President of Costa Rica, from 1953-1957 and from 1970-1974 and the National Liberation Party, which he founded, has since achieved many aspects of his program for the Second Republic. In much the same way as the U.S. Democratic party of the Truman and Roosevelt era was for long the standard bearer, and only real political power of the United States, so too was Don Pepe's National Liberation Party.

The traditions of his party, and the heritage of the man himself, has carried many to the presidency of the country. One such president was Oscar Arias, who was awarded the Nobel Peace Prize for his efforts to bring peace to Central America. In December of 1987, during ceremonies just prior to Arias leaving Costa Rica for Europe, to receive the Peace Prize, he walked off of the stage to a small, old man seated toward the front of the cathedral. Helping him to his feet, Arias put his arm around him. As the old man rose, he

began to cry, and the two of them walked down the aisle, down the steps, and out to the crowds gathered outside. Those who witnessed this simple event considered it to be one of the most moving few minutes in the history of the country: the founder of the Second Republic, the grandfather of Costa Rica, Don Pepe Figueres, with tears flowing down his face, walking arm in arm with the brilliant young president whose political intelligence and perseverance had won the Nobel Peace Prize for Costa Rica, and who had, by doing so, trumpeted the existence of this small, supremely democratic country to the world.

Left: politics as Fiesta. Right: President Oscar Arias and family with the Nobel Peace Prize.

COSTA RICA
(THE HEART OF THE AMERICAS)

For further inf
The National Tourist Board, S
or Any Tourist and Travel Ag

WHERE THE WORLD's CHOICEST COFFEE GROWS.

In 1737, authorities ordered constructed, on the flatlands of the Boca del Monte, a thatch-covered hermitage, which was to be surrounded by small houses. Its singular purpose was supposed to be the bringing together of the residents of that area, whose small homes were then scattered widely over the valley, into the form of community. From this inauspicious beginning arose what was later to be the city of San José.

For its first 39 years, San José was a squalid village, with mud covered streets and miserable little houses. Then an official ordered the construction of a tobacco factory. It was from this building that the tobacco industry monopoly was administered. It proved to be an activity that brought a certain degree of prosperity to the town.

Years later, when the cacao and tobacco exports declined, there was experimentation with a new crop: coffee. It grew with such ease and it bore fruit with such abundance, that this once-small Central American colony very quickly left behind, for all time, the misery and squalor that it had known.

England was interested in not only buying this coffee, but also in loaning funds, on account, against the next harvest. The surrounding areas filled quickly with orderly rows of coffee plantations and the people, with their new wealth, sought the life of San José, thus transforming it to a prosperous coffee-growing center.

By the town square there was at first only the Church of Mercy and the Town Council building. But other conveniences, created to service the foreigners that were beginning to arrive, were soon set up.

At the end of the 18th century, the Education Building was erected, as was a cathedral, at the front of which stood a beautiful central park, where the Indians and farmers held their weekly fairs. Money was minted at the Currency House, and, in order to support the militia, the Military Quarters were erected.

In 1821 Costa Rica gained its independence from the Spanish Empire and became a republic. The small village of San José soon grew into a city, a capital city, and its newly installed authorities struggled to improve the streets, build bridges and open roads to the ports. Guards, armed with rusty muskets, patrolled the brick-layered streets, which at night were illuminated by the light of kerosene lamps.

In the dance parlors of the bourgeoisie, the quadrille was in vogue. An actor would recite poetry and a young lady would play Chopin ballads amidst conversations concerning the price of coffee in London.

Social and economic life was rigidly defined. While blacks and Indians lived in the neighborhood of La Puebla, near Cartago, and performed manual labor, the descendants of the Spanish lived in the central part of town where they built their large adobe houses with corridors opening onto enclosed vegetable gardens.

Cultural life centered around the Mora Theater, where fourth-rate companies would perform along with jugglers and an occasional virtuoso musician. The ladies would sit and listen, dressed in their regal dresses, while the gentlemen stood around, robed in their Spanish capes, and smoked and engaged in small-talk concerning politics. Foreign visitors would stay in a rooming house and from there would make visits through the town; some considered the possibility of entering the coffee export business and others idly took notes for their travel diaries.

Wagner and Scherzer, two German scientists who visited Costa Rica during the mid-19th century, wrote:

"There is not a single building that calls attention for its beauty. The government buildings, the garrison and its gallery, the university and the theater are insignificant structures. The cathedral has an air of negligence and economy. There aren't even any chairs. The president of the republic has to sit with his followers on a wooden bench. . ."

Less critical was Felix Belly, a distinguished French journalist:

"I showed up in the presidential palace, an enchanting square building with an internal yard paved in cement surrounded by a double gallery. And at the bottom of this half-Spanish, half-Arab patio, a circular stairway led to the congressional room where President Mora staged a ball for me."

Earnings from the exportation of coffee

engendered an illustrious bourgeoisie. The members of this class traveled to France to have their children educated in Europe. When home in San José, the children missed the theaters, the boulevards, the cafes and the fine architecture of Europe. They were insistent on improving the appearance of their native capital city. As coffee production engendered greater prosperity, the leading planter families increased their investments, which led to rivalries among them. Ever grander plantations were created in an effort to stay ahead of those whom they felt were their competitors.

Costa Rican architects visited the Universal Exposition of Paris and, along with other

through which the brilliant tropical sun shone.

Towards the end of the 19th century, Monsieur Amon Faiseleau Duplantier, who received the concession to establish the streetcar system, divided his farm on the sunny slopes of the Torres River and there began the business of real estate sales. He was successful and the best of San José society fought for the urban lots. Soon the coffee plantations were replaced with tree-shaded streets and stately residences with large gardens. Meanwhile, Minor Keith, who was occupied with developing The United Fruit Company and the railroad system to the Atlantic Coast, finished the Atlantic Railroad station in San José. And at the same time, Mother Superior

new and imported ideas, brought back metal buildings for schools. They imported finely wrought metal plates for walls, steel columns, crests for the buildings and Italian mosaics. The homes of the coffee growers soon began to look like the mansions of New Orleans and Jamaica. French adobe walls, wide, inclined roofs, ornate verandas with white balustrades and woodwork cut in the style of gingerbread. Jalousies and shades protected the windows of colored glass

Preceding pages: an early attempt to lure the tourists. **Above:** a 19th century mud and wattle home, Meseta Central.

Barthelemy Rich was opening her prestigious girls' high school, Colegio de Sión, where the daughters of the bourgeoisie received their education.

On October 19, 1897, the president and a select, finely dressed audience entered the wide doors of the National Theater to inaugurate the building. That opening night featured a magnificent presentation of the opera *Faust*. The sumptuous building with its four levels and a floor plan in the shape of a horseshoe was financed from the national budget and by a contribution from the coffee growers.

By the turn of the century, the village had

given way to a warm and glowing city, which, even if it did not attain the elegant, urbane layout to which it aspired, developed a comfortable lifestyle permitted by its growing prosperity,

If early European critics of Costa Rica had been able to predict the amenities of a turn-of-the-century San José, they would have remained. In front of the theater was the elegant Hotel Francais. Nearby, the Petite Trianon was a coffee house favored by high society, artists and diplomats; a little beyond, the windows of the Golden Eagle were filled with French wine and liquors and Spanish preserves and fine oils. *Talabarteria Inglesa* and *La Tiendita* satisfied the most demand-

of the working population. The Society of *Casas Baratas* began the construction of workers' housing units of the type known as *puerta ventana* where several families would cram in narrow and poorly-ventilated rooms. To the South where there used to be a sector for blacks, and near the railroad station to the Pacific, there soon appeared barracks, warehouses and factories where soap and candles were made. An industrial zone with beer factories, ice-making factories, printing presses, mechanics' shops, and lumber mills slowly began to surround and envelop the elegant urban center.

With the advent of cement structures, the arrival of the new rich, and the industrializa-

ing tastes in matters of decoration and leatherwork. The Ford agency exhibited its 1912 model, priced at $975. It competed with a number of other import agencies as well as real estate businesses, which offered farms, lots, beaches and Victorian residences. The streetcar ran to the limits of the city carrying great numbers of merchants, employees and office workers.

Not all members of the San José society enjoyed a rose-colored life. The city had expanded, too quickly, into vast, obscure and sad suburbs. The War of 1914 and the coffee crisis brought unemployment and below-poverty-level salaries to wide sectors

tion of the city, there also came the desire to modernize and to destroy the past.

Under the pick and sledgehammer disappeared the magnificent National Palace, the Garrison, the National Library, the Union Club and many lovely residences. The city extended its arms beyond the suburbs, the inner city lost its sense of identity and was invaded by mediocre commercial constructions. Fast highways opened up and North American influence began to replace leisurely, elegant European ideals.

San José spilled over and outward in a random fashion. By the 1960s, several neighborhood centers evolved, resembling the style of suburban North America.

Certainly, San José today would no longer win a prize as the most beautiful Central American city. But even so, it still possesses a certain charm that is there to be discovered by the sensitive and curious. Here one will not find the monumental scale of Guatemala City nor the cosmopolitan quality of Panamá City; yet there is a vital quality to the hustle and sheer movement of the place, and very definitely something remains of the coffee-growing bourgeoisie and their Neo-classic architecture and whimsical Caribbean-colonial styles.

In the downtown section today are found an unpredictable montage of commerce, his-

Rohrmoser. But what is special is to be found further out, immersed in the exuberant vegetation that surrounds the city, in the neighborhoods of the original colonial villages such as Escazú, or Santo Domingo de Heredia. Here large tracts of land are covered with trees and vast gardens.

In these suburban towns are *campesinos* in rural houses, residing comfortably next to large homes of diplomats and international politicians.

Some kilometers to the north of San José is beautiful Santo Domingo de Heredia, where amateur antique collectors will enjoy exploring. This region started as a coffee and tobacco growing area and the rural workers

torical buildings, government buildings and banks. There are museums, places of recreation and entertainment, theaters, art galleries and eateries. The inner city is noisy and disorganized.

Automobiles permitted the wealthy classes to move their residences from what had become the inner city to the suburbs. In the first such ring of satellite suburbs are the neighborhoods of Escalante, Los Yoses, Curridabat, Paseo Colón, Sabana and

Left: San José, circa 1928. **Above**: the leisure class at home.

built their white adobe and tile roof houses, made of wood and bark and formed in the classic "L"-shape.

Beyond Santo Domingo is the town of Heredia where, in the central park, one can admire the church with its massive walls of stone, built to resist earthquakes. It is the best example in Costa Rica of the style known as "seismic baroque", which was then fashionable from Guatemala all the way to Panamá.

Near the Barva Volcano is the town of Barva, whose main attraction is its central park and church which was recently restored, faithfully keeping to the parsimonious and simple manner of a rural Costa Rica.

"To our door comes calling the outcast, the fallen, the pursued...

Costa Rica has always been the sacred and secure asylum for all of those who suffer ostracism, be they who they may, and on this soil they have found protection, friendship and homes."

This observation was made by a prominent Costa Rican in 1865, advising then-President Jesus Jiménez to not extradite the deposed Salvadoran President Gerardo Barrios even though this had been requested

"Heretics" fleeing the Spanish Inquisition sought refuge in Costa Rica. Some historians have advanced the theory that some of Costa Rica's earliest European settlers were Sephardic Jews who fled Spain for Central America when the Inquisition began, in 1492. It seems that people have always been fleeing to Costa Rica.

Early pioneers forced to work their own land lived in far-flung, self-reliant family homesteads dotted around the country's Central Valley, a situation that gave rise to a

by other Central American countries.

Jiménez heeded the advice. The Costa Rican government formally rejected the extradition request and thereby all but institutionalized its time-honored tradition of social and political leniency.

Costa Rica's long and honorable history of political tolerance can be traced back to the country's colonial experience, or, more precisely, the lack of a colonial experience. As a virtually forgotten backwater of the Spanish empire, the not-so-long arm of the Crown and the Catholic church centered in distant Guatemala, and barely reached into Costa Rica.

"live and let live" mentality among colonial Costa Ricans and also made them deeply suspicious of centralized authority.

The Church's determination to create congregations of their wayward flocks resulted in the founding of Cartago, and later, the city of Heredia. Efforts by the Crown to use these towns as political and bureaucratic centers from which to control commerce, however, were poorly rewarded.

After independence, the Josefinos' (citizens of San José) defiant nature made fertile ground for the seeds of revolutionary ideas sown by the Enlightenment, something further stimulated throughout the 19th century by the arrival of waves of European immigrants. Some of these immigrants brought capital and technology and contributed greatly to the development of the coffee industry. Others brought education and helped develop a strong tradition of literacy and fine arts.

Costa Rica first had occasion to offer refuge to Central American political exiles following the 1840 civil war in Guatemala, in which members of the fallen government fled to Costa Rica. The many subsequent revolutions throughout the region in ensuing years made for a steady flow of political exiles to Costa Rica, through the remainder of the 19th century.

This century, following that tradition, the list of political exiles includes deposed Venezuelan dictator Matute Gomez, who escaped to Costa Rica aboard an airplane with his family, household staff, and a good portion of gold bullion from the Venezuelan national treasury. As with many of Costa Rica's more infamous refugees, Ticos love stories about Matute Gomez: It seems that during his flight to Costa Rica, Gomez had overloaded the plane with plundered gold and his personal staff. The pilot had to inform him that they would have to jettison some weight in order to gain the altitude necessary for the rest of the flight. Without hesitating, Matute Gomez threw one of his staff out of the plane. And, Gomez was such an outrageous ladies' man, that a woman's reputation could be slurred by association with him: "She is the kind of woman you would see in the car of Matute Gomez..." His ostentatious red house remains a local landmark and a popular geographical reference point.

More reputable beneficiaries of the asylum tradition include Rómulo Bentacur, founder of modern Venezuelan democracy, who spent several years exiled in Costa Rica, along with his protogé, Venezuelan President Carlos Andres Pérez and Cuban revolutionary Huber Matos, who lived in Costa Rica for many years following his ouster from the Caribbean island by his one-time comrade-in-arms, Fidel Castro.

Numerous exiles from neighboring Nicaragua have been granted refuge over the

years, including the leadership of the Sandinista National Liberation Front. A few years after the Sandinistas took power in 1979, Costa Rica began granting asylum to political opponents of the Sandinista Government. During the so-called "Contra war", hundreds of thousands of refugees flooded into Costa Rica from Nicaragua.

In recent years, Costa Ricans have found it necessary to more strictly define the terms of its hospitality as the country became a haven for international criminals of all castes.

Costa Rica's fame as a hide-out for crooks began to grow with the arrival, in 1973, of fugitive financier Robert Vesco, who was taken under the wing of President José (Pepe)

Figueres. Though Vesco was given the boot in 1978, the word was out among international crooks, that the attitude of the Costa Ricans was generally one of receptiveness.

The growth of the international drug trafficking business has caused local officials to adopt stricter immigration and extradition policies, and scores of accused drug traffickers have found their luck drying up in Costa Rica in recent years and have been handed back to authorities in their home countries. But, even as officialdom struggles to define boundaries of hospitality, few believe that the tradition of Costa Rica's open doors will fundamentally change.

Left: international drug lords on the lam. Right: super crook Robert Vesco in repose.

THE PEOPLE OF COSTA RICA

"The blood that flows in the veins of the people of this Republic is too generous. The Costa Ricans are a people of such excellent mettle; ardently patriotic, they are very proud of their independence, their autonomy, and of a prosperity due almost wholly to industry.

The country is one of flourishing villages half hidden with plantations. There it is that the population of Costa Rica dwells, since it is there that are found the hardy toilers who wrest from the earth the products which form the wealth of the land. An air of ease combined with antique simplicity characterizes the majority of these villages, superior they are in many respects to those of Europe..."

by A.S. Calvert, 1901
-from *A Year of Costa Rica*

Costa Ricans are both narcissistic and chauvinistic. And because of this they have acquired the curious art of being poor and not showing it. By any international standards, the Costa Rican is predominantly poor, but he does a good job of not letting anyone take note of his poverty. There aren't the screamingly visible cardboard shanty towns that dominate the cityscape of other developing countries. People seen on the streets of the towns and cities are well-dressed. The homeless, the street people, are not omnipresent and evident as they are in Latin and Asian countries, and, indeed, in all of the large cities of North America.

The Costa Rican has a graceful sense of the universal corruption that surrounds him. He shakes his head, lamentably acknowledging it. He knows that there are problems abounding, both within and without. Almost endless problems beyond resolution. But there is not the nagging, complaining of the hopelessness. He actually believes that it can and will get better.

Travelers to Costa Rica find it difficult to identify the feeling, the sense, that Costa Ricans are somehow different from those in other Central and South American countries. Visitors notice it in subtle ways.

The street vendors in San José are a case in point. In Mexico and other Latin countries, street vendors loudly offer unclean enchantments. In Costa Rica, the vendor displays artful pyramids of avocado, apples, mango, cashew fruit, papaya, and dozens of fruits that are never seen in the United States. In Costa Rica one can drink water from a public tap and not have to constantly be listening for

that first telltale intestinal rumble. In Costa Rica the water is safe. And, in the same way, one usually knows that Costa Ricans are safe.

Costa Ricans are not perfect. Though they are essentially democratic, benevolent and peaceful, the cities are greatly affecting their character. Cities teach people to live separately, apart. In the small towns of Costa Rica there is a connectedness, a familial unity that is tangible to all of one's senses. Perhaps that is why San José can feel unreal at times, as though it is out of place and time, because it is a basic contradiction to the terms of Costa Rica. San José is not a small

Preceding pages: it's Carnival time in Limón!
Left: *Campesino* on the slopes of Irazú volcano cultivating onions. **Right:** Gringa and friend.

town, yet the Costa Rican is essentially at home only in the terms of a small town. He is fundamentally a *campesino*, rural, even pastoral. The Costa Rican takes comfort in his friends and family, he only dips in and out of the city, as a hummingbird tasting colored sugar water from a hanging plastic feeder—and then, whenever he can, darts back to his village, to his town.

To fly to Costa Rica, leaving behind the numbing babble of Los Angeles or Miami, and to head for a small town there, is to leap backwards, stunningly, to an earlier time. But it is not an earlier time in North American or even European lives, it is somewhere else, somewhere more idealized and more

ports of the country defenseless against their traffic. Yet one feels that she will endure, that there is strength in the fragility, and that people all over the world will do whatever they can to ensure the survival and intelligent growth of this vulnerable country and its people.

Costa Ricans call themselves Ticos. It is a reference to their common use of the diminutive ending: "Un momentico, por favor." There is a formal kindness, even a sweetness to the way in which they speak Spanish.

Ticos are politically temperate, shy and not aggressive. They are a prudent people. The Costa Rican, today more than ever, is

precious. Like treasured remembrances of things past, one wants to protect it, to shield it from the gross intrusion of foreign influence. The visitor wants to shut off the television set that is beaming satellite-relayed shows and commercials from the cities of the United States. Costa Rica at times feels fragile, surrounded by Nicaragua and Panamá, with questionable advice and political succor from the U.S. Agency for International Development, with Japanese investors buying whatever appears profitable, with political and economic refugees coming in from other parts of Central America, with drug dealers finding the shores and

actively democratic. And so is his belief in democracy. Earlier it was only the game of democracy; more of a pretense, an aberrant love of the rules and trappings of democracy. The parades, the festive honking of car horns, the shouting, "Hey, look! I voted!" Today it is stronger, more involved, more functional, even more passionate. The demonstrations, protests, strikes, rallies, caucuses are relentless. Yet the people remain mostly prudent, respectful, discreet.

One need only go to Guatemala, Panamá or El Salvador, and observe the differences. And yet these other countries are only short distances away, only miles apart. The Costa

Rican is as different from these other Latin people as, say, the Swiss is to the Italian, or as the German is to the French. And the Costa Rican revels in the difference and is unabashedly proud of it.

The Costa Rican invites foreigners. There one finds duty free zones, tax free incentives to retired emigrants, tax free incentives to foreigners setting up industry, other incentives to those creating tourist facilities. There are institutions created by the government to encourage people to come and view the marvels of the country, and to settle and live there.

Because the United States is by far the richest neighbor in the hemisphere, and

"The problem is that the Costa Rican looks too much to the North. He should be looking to the South." But even if he did, the Tico would insist that he is different from most Latinos because of what he calls his "whiteness," his European heritage. And, too, the Tico of the Central Valley of Costa Rica easily forgets, or rather dismisses, the complex ethnic and racial makeup of the Costa Rican people.

Racially, Costa Rica is not a simple place. The blacks of the Atlantic Coast speak English and talk with pride of their blackness and their Jamaican heritage. The gregarious people of Guanacaste have dark skin, resemble their Nicaraguan neighbors in manner and

therefore the most powerful broadcaster of image and ideology, Costa Rica knows a great deal more about the United States than the United States knows about Costa Rica. Ticos know the names of sports figures, actors and actresses, musicians and politicians from the U.S.A., and they know the strange collection of fact and fallacy that one derives from watching television and going to movies made in Hollywood.

A Latin American writer recently observed,

Left: *pipas*, drinking coconuts for sale at a roadside stand, Limón province. **Above**: Puntarenas schoolboys.

accent, and refer to the majority residents of the Central Valley as Cartagans. The Indians of Costa Rica belong to six linguistic groups, though they increasingly use Spanish, and debate as to whether it is more important to retain their indigenous cultural identity or to assimilate more into the main Costa Rican culture. The Chinese-Costa Ricans are called *Chinos*; and in some of the smaller towns they are ubiquitous and seem to own many of the bars, restaurants, and retail stores. The persistent myth of Costa Rica as a classless democracy, with no conscious awareness of race nor color, is not reality, it is just that: a myth. Yet somehow they are all

Costarricense, and much of the time they swagger with superiority over their Central American neighbors. They like being Tico, and they believe in this rare place, this Costa Rica.

A Complex Blend: For the Costa Rican, historical reality is often in conflict with cherished myths. Tradition holds that almost all Costa Ricans descended from hard-working rural Spanish yeoman farmers; that they came from good, simple, unpretentious, egalitarian stock. Yet among colonial immigrants to Costa Rica from the Iberian peninsula there were Spanish Jews and Arabs, Catalans and Basques, and a great many people from the Middle East.

pany were English, Irish and North Americans. The largest group, however, were the workers, West Indian blacks, who built the tracks, the endless numbers of bridges, the docks and the wide, rectangular streets of the Port City of Limón. Blacks remained along the isolated Atlantic Coast, and they continue their lives there today, enriching those coastal communities with a distinct Afro-Caribbean flavor.

Chinese laborers from southern China joined the blacks on the railroad project in 1873, essentially as slaves, or what was referred to as "indentured workers," but escaped this labor as soon as they figured out how to do so, to work as domestic servants,

Immigrants began to arrive in large numbers during the second half of the 19th century, attracted by the promise of prosperity generated from the developing coffee industry and the Costa Rican government's open door policies. German and English settlers became involved in the import-export trade, while Lebanese, Turks and Polish Jews became powerful local merchants. These were not simple agrarian folk.

As well, the construction of the railway to the Atlantic Coast, during the later part of the 19th century, brought new waves of immigrants: among the builders, managers and technicians of the Northern Railway Com-

cooks and grocers in developing rural areas and port cities.

The management of the railroad company had serious difficulties with the Chinese. In an attempt to try an alternative working force, they imported several hundred Italian rural laborers. But the disagreeable working conditions soon led the Italians to leave the railroad project, as had the Chinese before them. Many of them remained in Costa Rica, and in 1959 they were joined by other Italian farmers who settled in a government- sponsored colony, San Vito, in the Southern Pacific region of Costa Rica.

During the last couple of decades, onerous

political conditions and deteriorating economic circumstances in their home countries have brought significant numbers of South Americans to Costa Rica: middle-class, educated Chileans, Argentinians and Uruguayans. These groups have greatly enhanced Costa Rica's cultural sensibilities over the last twenty years. The exceptional T*eatro El Angel*, as an example, was virtually transplanted to San José, along with numerous dissidents, all fleeing the Pinochet dictatorship of Chile.

The prospect of the British Colony of Hong Kong being transfered to Chinese hands has engendered a steady flow of Asian immigrants from Hong Kong since the 1970s. In

country's environmental awareness.

Historically, it has been and will apparently continue to be an exotic assortment of arrivals to the warm and inviting shores of this small Central American nation. The story of Costa Rica's immigrants is not entirely unlike that of the "melting pot" of foreign arrivals that, often against seemingly impossible conditions and odds, crossed the borders of North America. During Costa Rica's history, as well, the treatment of immigrants has often been inexcusable, even shameful. But in Costa Rica it has had a distinctly Tico flavor.

Blacks in Costa Rica: As early as 1825, Afro-Caribbeans came to Costa Rica to fish, hunt

1986 a survey reported that there were over one hundred Asian restaurants in San José and the surrounding districts.

Since the 1960s, Costa Rican laws favoring North American and European retirees, have led to the establishment of a large number of comparatively wealthy gringos in the Central Valley area. And even more recently, the arrival in Costa Rica of many ecologically concerned North Americans and Europeans has stimulated some major changes in the

Left: ubiquitous *pulperia* (neighborhood store) and proud owner. **Above**: bus stop lovers in the park.

turtles, and market coconuts. These immigrants were part of a sizable migration from the West Indies to the Central American Atlantic Coast. From Panamá to Honduras, they came looking for work to support themselves and their families. Many were transient. One man might harvest cacao in Limón, then find employment on the barges in Nicaragua and next labor on the construction of the Panamá Canal. They went where there was work.

In 1872, under contract from Minor C. Keith, who was later to become the founder of the United Fruit Company, blacks from the West Indies came to work on the construction of the Atlantic Railroad. They proved more successful than previous laborers imported by Keith, in their ability to tolerate the working conditions, which included exposure to yellow fever, malaria, and poisonous snakes, as well as very severe physical labor and oppressive management. But they were not invulnerable. After some 4,000 West-Indians had died during the construction of the first 20 miles of track between 1881 and 1891, Keith imported an additional 10,000 laborers from the West Indies. Others came to the Atlantic Coast on their own, looking for any kind of work available and to escape the poverty of their native islands. Some ultimately were given land along the nana fields of the Atlantic United Fruit Company is well-documented. And when United Fruit left the Atlantic region and moved to the Pacific Coast, the unemployed blacks were left behind. Many emigrated out and away from Costa Rica, for much the same reason that had motivated their parents to immigrate to the country in the first place: They were again seeking work. Those who stayed behind lived for the most part at subsistence level, often just producing what they could from the small plots of land that they had settled on. They retained their English language and their Protestant religion, remaining proudly separate from the Hispanic Costa Ricans.

railroad right-of-way and others rose from the ranks of laborers to become managers in the banana business. Most originally planned to earn whatever money they could and then to return to their islands; yet many remained in Costa Rica.

The blacks of Costa Rica are the country's largest and certainly the most visible minority. They were for many years subject to racist immigration and residency laws that restricted their movement from the Atlantic Coast to the Central Valley. With the abandonment of these laws, many of them moved to the San José area and entered professional fields.

The maltreatment of workers in the ba-

When the new Constitution of 1949 declared that anyone born in Costa Rica had automatic citizenship, doors finally opened for blacks. They began to send their children to public schools, to enter politics. When, in the 1950s, the value of cacao soared on the international market, many of the squatter-farmers were able to achieve a certain prosperity. And in an ironic reversal of historical patterns, they hired Hispanics to work their fields. Many of the subsequent generation of blacks were well-educated and, preferring the professions to farming, left the Limón area. Indeed, many left Costa Rica entirely, to find jobs in Panamá, the United States or elsewhere. Those middle class, educated blacks who have remained in Costa Rica have many times married Hispanics, but their assimilation into Costa Rican society is not a complete one, due mostly to a curious two-sided racism that exists. The blacks usually consider themselves more civilized and superior to the Hispanic Costa Ricans, and the Hispanic Costa Ricans usually insist that blacks are racially inferior. Today less than five percent of the Costa Rican population, and less than 25% of the population of the Atlantic Coast of Costa Rica, is black.

Chinese Immigrants in Costa Rica: The first Chinese to set foot in Costa Rica were 77 indentured servants, in 1855. Almost twenty

liquor stores. A steady trickle of Chinese immigrant laborers followed, the newcomers getting assistance from those who were already established. Through work contracts and credit assistance from other Chinese, they set up commercial ventures along the railway system, the port cities and in growing rural communities throughout the country. Their small scale businesses required little capital investment, only a minimal acquaintance with the language, and allowed all members of the growing family network to become involved in tending the business. Chinese family traditions upheld the authority of elders and reinforced a strong generational hierarchy and well-defined di-

years later, despite the existence of a law against the permanent settlement in Costa Rica of African and Asian races, contractors for the Atlantic Railroad imported "one thousand healthy, robust Chinese of good customs and addicted to work." These two groups were to become the founding fathers of the Chinese Colony of Costa Rica

Those contracted by the railroad quickly left that work, and, as their fortunes improved, set up small eateries, grocery and

Left: shimmering beauty queens at the Hotel Cariari. **Above**: shining devotion at a town fair in Guanacaste province.

vision of labor, plus a strong work ethic. Because of this, their businesses almost inevitably flourished.

Chinese colonies headed by businessmen associations similar to those established in California and elsewhere, evolved into strong business groups in the cities and towns of Costa Rica. By the turn of the century, a number of Chinese immigrants had become wealthy businessmen, who then sponsored the immigration of other family members and acquaintances.

Among the first generations to settle in Costa Rica, many male immigrants began living with local Costa Rican women, white women, while retaining marriages established in China, with childhood brides. Money which they sent to China was often used to finance family enterprises back home and contribute to the development of their home communities. The successful Costa Rican-Chinese traveled to China to oversee his holdings, raise a family and invest towards retirement in the home of his ancestors. During his absence from Costa Rica, his business was managed by close younger kin. To the Costa Ricans, it seemed as though these older Chinese did not die, but simply disappeared, leaving in their place younger replacements who, more than likely, also took on their legal identity.

the value of devoted persistence and discipline, necessary to succeed in the face of a difficult task. The school finally had to close down, due to dwindling numbers, but it did succeed in reinforcing respect and admiration for ancestral traditions.

Those Chinese born of Costa Rican mothers and raised in Costa Rica consider themselves full members of Costa Rican society, identifying heartily with its ways and traditions, while, at the same time, expressing a strong sense of devotion to their immigrant forefathers. Although many among them have married Hispanics, much against the overwhelming and loud opposition of their parents and the foreboding ostracism of the

Since the Communist takeover in 1949, return to their Chinese homeland has become less attractive, and most Costa Rican Chinese have forsaken hope of a permanent return to China.

Eventually, the Chinese Colony in Costa Rica came to include generations of mixed descendants of Chinese men and Hispanic women. In an effort to conserve and strengthen Chinese cultural values among them, a Chinese School was established in Puerto Limón in the 1950s, where language, writing and Chinese history and culture were taught. The practice of writing in Chinese calligraphy prepared students to understand

Chinese community, they have, nevertheless, retained venerable family traditions that express Chinese values of ancestral wisdom and family solidarity. Many young Costa Rican-Chinese have joined the ranks of the professionally educated; yet, as doctors, lawyers, engineers, business administrators and university professors, they continue to contribute to and oversee the family businesses that allowed their ancestors to achieve economic success in Costa Rica.

Chinese participation in the social life of the towns in which they settled is wonderfully evidenced during Limón's annual Carnival. Here the traditional, sinuous Chinese dragon snakes its way through the crowded streets to the beat of steel drums, alongside of flamboyantly-costumed Caribbean dance troupes.

The Indians of Costa Rica: Cherished historical tradition holds that there were few Indians in Costa Rica when Columbus arrived, and so, lacking an indigenous people to enslave and then use as a labor force to colonize the country, the conquistadors, and then the colonists, had to work the land themselves. And thus began Costa Rica's lengthy tradition of small independent farmers working their own land and taking care of themselves. Yet archaeologists have recently estimated that some 60,000 native people

The history of the Indians of Costa Rica is much like that of the other indigenous peoples of the American continent. The Europeans brought diseases to which the native populations had no immunity. Entire tribes were obliterated before they had even seen a white man.

The Chorotegas, cousins of the Nicarao, inhabited Guanacaste and the Nicoya Peninsula in pre-Columbian times. They lived in patrimonial groups, grew corn and were culturally similar to groups of Southern Mexico. These peoples were decimated during the Conquest by disease and by slave traders who carried them into Panamá and Peru. Their descendents are today mostly inte-

were in Costa Rica when Columbus arrived. In one location, a developed culture of approximately 10,000 indigenous inhabitants lived in the area that is now under research at the Guayabo National Monument, in the mountains above Turrialba. Concentrations of people in the Guanacaste region were believed to be equally great or larger. Today less than 15,000 native people remain in the entire country.

Left to right: heady blossoms off to market; melons and vendor at the 10th Avenue open air market, San José; and *Boyero*, brahma oxen and painted car, in San Antonio de Escazú.

grated into contemporary Costa Rican life.

Other Indian groups, today spread over much of Costa Rican spoke dialects originating in Colombia, and were divided into clans: the Guaymi, the Terrabas, the Borucas and, in the Talamanca mountains, the Bribri and Cabecares. These people lived in matrilineal societies in clearings in the jungles. With the coming of the Europeans, many of them fled their villages and moved further into the almost inaccessible jungle regions of the southern mountains and thus were not easily found and subdued. Much of their culture has been preserved by their descendents who still speak their original language and live in the remote regions of the Talamanca Mountains. Despite the influence of Christian missionaries, they have not forsaken their animistic religious traditions. The Bribri call their deity "Sibu" and use shamans, with their vast knowledge of the rainforest's medicinal herbs, to cure illnesses. They refer to the white man as "*hormiga*," or ant, a being who wipes out everything in his path.

Further south, along the Panamá border, the Guaymi Indians live in their traditional areas, which span political boundaries.

No matter how remote their jungle reserves, the Indians are not isolated from contemporary culture. Battery-powered televisions bring pressure to consume soft drinks

and junk food, as well as images of the First World to these people who are living without electricity and running water. The cultural imperialism of the airwaves is persistently penetrating the sanctuary of those who for five hundred years have resisted the conquistadors. And among the young, the temptations of the world are great and the desire to assimilate strong.

Today the indigenous peoples live on reserves authorized for them in 1971. By law, non-Indians cannot own land inside these areas, but the law has been difficult to enforce and non-Indians have moved into these territories which, perhaps unfortunately for the Indians, contain a great deal of the country's mineral wealth.

Many Indians complain bitterly of the encroachment of the contemporary society which threatens their language, their cultural identity and their way of life. Caught in time between two worlds, slowly relinquishing the old, but not yet embracing the new, they are vulnerable. In the 500 years since the Conquest, little has changed for the aboriginal Costa Rican people. The stranger still dominates things and the choice between isolation and assimilation is still painful.

The Gringo: They are unmistakable in San José, standing out amidst the dense, crazy streets and violently crowded sidewalks, their blonde heads rising above everyone else's. They are as enormous crane-like birds, searching for something. These gringos, so highly visible, easily catch the eye in Costa Rica. They have been coming to Costa Rica for a long time.

In 1888, fifteen hundred "good, humble, thrifty Italians of a superior race," were brought here to work the Atlantic Railways, and later settled on the southern peninsula.

Early in the 19th century, attracted by the promise of wealth from coffee, the French, Germans and English came to Costa Rica. Many married Costa Rican women, and became thoroughly assimilated into the aggregate of Tico culture.

Quakers from the United States came seeking a place of peace and found it in the cloud forest of Monteverde, where they formed a community dedicated to a life of harmony with the land as well as their fellow man. From the United States and Europe recently have come fairly large numbers of retirees and others, more idealistic in their visions. The *pensionado* is a non-national living in Costa Rica with a guaranteed monthly income. Most often these people are retired North Americans who have come to Costa Rica simply for the higher standard of living their dollar affords them. Often, too, there are the young and environmentally concerned who view Costa Rica as a laboratory, a place in the world where the viability of living in harmony with the environment can be demonstrated to the world at large.

Left: first cellist of the renowned National Symphony Orchestra. Right: disciples of the golden arches in San José.

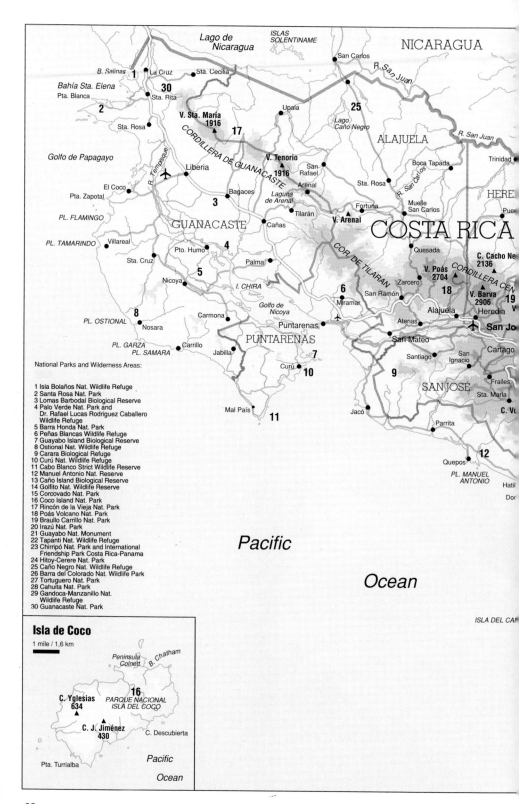

National Parks and Wilderness Areas:

1 Isla Bolaños Nat. Wildlife Refuge
2 Santa Rosa Nat. Park
3 Lomas Barbodal Biological Reserve
4 Palo Verde Nat. Park and
  Dr. Rafael Lucas Rodriguez Caballero
  Wildlife Refuge
5 Barra Honda Nat. Park
6 Peñas Blancas Wildlife Refuge
7 Guayabo Island Biological Reserve
8 Ostional Nat. Wildlife Refuge
9 Carara Biological Refuge
10 Curú Nat. Wildlife Refuge
11 Cabo Blanco Strict Wildlife Reserve
12 Manuel Antonio Nat. Reserve
13 Caño Island Biological Reserve
14 Golfito Nat. Wildlife Reserve
15 Corcovado Nat. Park
16 Coco Island Nat. Park
17 Rincón de la Vieja Nat. Park
18 Poás Volcano Nat. Park
19 Braullo Carrillo Nat. Park
20 Irazú Nat. Park
21 Guayabo Nat. Monument
22 Tapanti Nat. Wildlife Refuge
23 Chirripó Nat. Park and International
  Friendship Park Costa Rica-Panama
24 Hitoy-Cerere Nat. Park
25 Caño Negro Nat. Wildlife Refuge
26 Barra del Colorado Nat. Wildlife Park
27 Tortuguero Nat. Park
28 Cahuita Nat. Park
29 Gandoca-Manzanillo Nat.
  Wildlife Refuge
30 Guanacaste Nat. Park

Isla de Coco

1 mile / 1,6 km

Peninsula Colnett
B. Chatham
16
PARQUE NACIONAL
ISLA DEL COCO
C. Yglesias
634
C. J. Jiménez
430
C. Descubierta
Pta. Turrialba

Pacific
Ocean

Pacific

Ocean

Costa Rica National Parks

20 miles / 32 km

Caribbean

Sea

Boca del Rio San Juan

Tortuguero

27

LIMÓN

R. Pacuare

Siquerres

Matina   Bahía
          Moin
                  Puerto
                  Limón

21

C. Matama
▲
Chirripó Abajo   2251   **24**   Cahuita   **28**
ARTAGO   **23**   Bribri   Pto. Viejo   **29**
                          Shiroles
                    R. Telire   Sixaola
Cerro Chirripó
3820   **23**   **23**
Muerte CORDILLERA
23   DE TALAMANCA

Cajón   C. Kámuk
                   3549
Buenos Aires   R. Sini   PANAMÁ

                  23   C. Echandi
                            3167
              Potrero Grande   ▲

Palmar Norte
Cortés   R. Gr. de Térraba   Coto Brus
                PUNTARENAS
de   San Vito
ado
PL   R. Chiriquí Viejo
ADA
San   Rincón   **14**   Neily
Pedrillo   Golfito   San Andrés
      Golfo Dulce
15
    PENINSULA
      DE
      OSA   La Cuesta
Carate
        Cabo   Río Claro
        Matapalo
                          Pto. Armuelles

                    Bahía de
                    Charco Azul
                    o de David

              Pta. Burica

NATIONAL PARKS, RESERVES AND REFUGES

Twenty-seven percent of Costa Rica is designated as national park, biological reserve, wildlife refuge or some other category of protected area, both private and public. That is, more than a quarter of the country has been set aside in some capacity or other by human beings to protect it from the potential exploitation and ravages of other human beings. No other country in the world even comes close to such a statistic.

There are other astounding statistics concerning Costa Rica: somewhere between 500,000 and a million total species of flora and fauna, 50,000 species of insects, 2,000 species of orchids, 208 species of mammals, 850 species of birds, endless thousands of species of moths and butterflies. In a space that occupies less than three ten-thousands of the earth's surface are 5 percent of all of the plant and animal species on the planet. Yet these numbers are for most of us only abstractions.

The story of the creation of Costa Rica's parks and protected areas is one of drama, ideals and sacrifice. One of the earliest in an international lineage of protectors was Nils Olaf Wessberg, who, with his wife, Karen, came to Costa Rica from Sweden in 1955 and bought a farm in Nicoya near Montezuma. Fervent naturalists, they built a home of palm leaves, determined to live in harmony with the land. Yet even in this removed corner of the world they did not escape what many call progress, and they watched, dismayed, as the destruction of virgin forest took place at Cabo Blanco, on the Nicoya peninsula. Nils became an activist, working ardently to raise money to purchase the property and thereby preserve it. After 1,000 pages of letters and three years he raised the $30,000 he needed to purchase the 2,930 acres (1,172 hectares) that today constitutes the Cabo Blanco Strict Nature Reserve. Today, a plaque inside the park is a grateful memorial to Nils, who, while trying to es-

Preceding pages: dusk at Braulio Carrillo National Park; heliconia amidst the eternal green of the jungle floor; Páramo, an unusual ecosystem seen on the summit of Chirripó; and another day, another beach on the Atlantic coast.

tablish another park in the Osa Peninsula, was killed by those who were not in agreement with his work.

Another individual, Mario Boza, a student of Costa Rican forestry, was able to put his conservation ideas to work in the creation of Santa Rosa, the country's first national park. In 1969, the Forestry Law trumpeted the creation of the Santa Rosa National Monument and established the National Parks Department. But of course with little funding and personnel to enforce it, the new law went unrecognized and the land continued to be used as it had been in the past, as grazing pasture for the cattle of nearby ranchers and as homesteads of squatters who cleared the land by slashing and burning it.

Unable to halt the destruction through bureaucratic channels, Boza went to the people through the press. "Santa Rosa in Flames; National Park Being Ruined," read the headlines. The public was outraged and park authorities were duly authorized to move out the squatters and protect the land from the encroachment of livestock and agriculture.

Of the national parks system, Rodrigo Carazo, president of Costa Rica from 1978-82, said: the parks are ". . . splendid natural laboratories which we offer to the international scientific community and also to children, young people and adults who should not be denied the joy of direct contact with nature in its pristine state. All of this represents the contribution of the Costa Rican people to peace among men and good will among nations."

The work in the massive natural laboratory that is composed of Santa Rosa and Guanacaste National Parks is on a scale that transcends nations and generations. Here, in Guanacaste, an experiment in natural reforestation conceived and implemented by North American biologist, Dan Janzen, has implications for the future of all of planet Earth. To Janzen it is painfully obvious that reforesting devastated areas is not as simple as it has seemed. Careful study of areas as large as Costa Rica's parks is teaching that the fabric of life is infinitely elaborate and that to reweave what has been torn is not just a matter of planting trees.

As admirable as Costa Rica's conservation initiatives may be, the economic development of this Third World country is counter to its environmental efforts. Parks, after all, are expensive. Urban sprawl resulting from the concentration of 60 percent of Costa Rica's population in the most fertile area of the country, the Central Valley, covers the land with concrete and asphalt and it continues at a frenzied pace. Extensive soil erosion, an effect of the rapid deforestation of the country by the destructive use of land for cattle grazing, causes a phenomenal loss of topsoil. Threats to the watershed as well as the nation's extensive hydroelectric system also result. Uncontrolled dumping of toxic wastes from banana, coffee and fertilizer industries have contaminated coastal and inland waters. Agricultural chemicals used in pesticides, once employed only on the traditional export crops of bananas and sugar, are now being used by vegetable and flower growers and result in, among other things, the virtual elimination of large species such as armadillos and crocodiles along the Tempisque River. The crazed rush to feed the demands for exotic plywood by the First World is resulting in the deforestation of the land surrounding the magnificent Tortuguero canals. And so it goes.

In its attempts to imitate much of North America and the First World, there is the inevitable conflict between consumption and conservation.

The gringos, tourists, *machos* (as Ticos refer to the North Americans and Europeans) are carriers, across the border, through the airport and into Costa Rica, and through the incessant medium of satellite television, of everything the Costa Rican wants and fears and hates and covets and rejects: the gringo brings the AIDS virus and imposes his concepts of cleanliness and medicine on the people of Costa Rica. The gringo brings luxury beach hotels, consumerism, and a Coca Cola bottling company. He also brings a vision of progress to a people that want to join the 21st century. It is, to say the least, a mixed blessing.

Attempting to balance these forces are the armies of international naturalists. Environmentalists and ecologists from all over the world come to Costa Rica to join the side of "the good guys." Today, Costa Rica has

Left: birders in heaven, Monteverde.

environmental experts in abundance, and dozens of international conservation organizations work on behalf of the country's ecological efforts.

Believing that true conservation can only be accomplished by the will of the people, the national parks system has made a great effort to educate the Ticos most affected by the transfer of land into parks. The co-operation of these people is necessary for the parks' survival. For example, the custom of hunting species for whom the parks is a refuge often must be changed. Large animals, such as pumas and jaguars, require an extensive amount of free territory in order to survive. Convincing people not to kill them, a joint effort with Nicaragua along the San Juan River, which comprises the border between the two nations, are examples of the potential for national parks to engender cooperative international relations.

Yet is this good news enough? The fact that Costa Rica is thought of as a safe, quiet democratic place is perhaps both Costa Rica's great blessing and her problem. The world will not be continually moved to donate aid and attention and media coverage to such a gentle democratic place.

It is not clear yet as to which side will prevail, the conservationists or the economic development-at-all-costs forces; it is not predictable whether Costa Rica will become

despite the fact that the cats are a constant threat to livestock, is an enormous and often thankless task.

Eco tourists and traditional travelers to Costa Rica support the national parks system by coming to visit them: by staying at the private reserves, by viewing and understanding something of the national parks, and through their work and contributions to the many foundations working to preserve Costa Rica.

Costa Rica's La Amistad National Park spans the border of Panamá, and will soon be extended into a park system within that country; and the proposed Peace Park, to be a successful environmental model for the nations of the world or another failed experiment in idealism.

The National Parks: The purpose of the National Parks is to preserve areas of particular beauty and ecological significance before they are destroyed.

Every ecosystem of Costa Rica is represented in the park system. The parks encourage scientific studies and environmental research. There are some important though seemingly simplistic rules governing the parks: while hunting is prohibited, fishing is allowed. Recreational use (swimming, surfing, birdwatching, etc.) and educational facilities are permitted, while hotels are not. Lodges are available in several parks.

Santa Rosa National Park

Santa Rosa National Park (122,350 acres/ 49,515 hectares), located in Guanacaste, is the site of of one of Costa Rica's most famous battles—and an important and interesting experiment in reforestation involving the local families of the region. It has become an international research center for studying the ecology of the tropical dry forest and two of its beaches, Nancite and Naranjo, are important turtle nesting sites. Many

the park offer accommodations, some quite rustic, for tourists and well as researchers. Horses are available. Camping is permitted. Call the Guanacaste Regional Conservation Unit for information. Tel: 69 5598.

Rincón de la Vieja National Park

Rincón de la Vieja (34,799 acres/14,083 hectares) is an active volcano with nine identified craters on the summit as well as hot springs and steam and gas vents. Two days are required to ascend the summit. Hiking is excellent but trails are not marked. Rainfall can be heavy. April and May are the best times to visit. Guides and horses for rent are

mammals, including monkeys, peccaries, birds and 22 species of bats live in the park. Camping is allowed and water is available.

Guanacaste National Park

Guanacaste National Park, adjacent to Santa Rosa National Park, was created in 1989 to protect the migratory paths of animals living in Santa Rosa. Three different biological stations in different regions inside

Left: Hummingbird and Passion Flower. Above: a Turquoise-browed Mot Mot waits for the perfect fly.

available. Camping is permitted, although there are no facilities. Bring water, warm clothing, good hiking boots and rain-resistant gear. Lodging is available near the park at Albergue Rincón de la Vieja. Call first for reservations. Tel: 66 0473.

Volcán Poás National Park

Poás Volcano National Park (13,835 acres/ 5,599 hectares) is one of the most developed of the national parks and one of the few active volcanoes on the continent which is easily accessible by a good road. Well marked trails weave around the craters and offer spectacular views of steaming fumaroles. Camping is not permitted. There are restrooms, a picnic area, potable water, educational displays and guides available. Audiovisual presentations are offered in the auditorium on Sundays, the park's busiest day.

Braulio Carrillo National Park

Braulio Carrillo (108,969 acres/44,099 hectares), located in the highlands between San José and the Atlantic Coast, contains steep mountains, dense forests, rivers and innumberable waterfalls. Two extinct volcanoes and two small lakes are located within the park. Birds are especially plentiful: 347

hike. (Irazú last erupted in 1965 and now only emits thin streams of gas and steam.) The summit offers wonderful views of the Atlantic and Pacific coasts. Camping is permitted, but there are no facilities. There are picnic areas and lookouts, and guides are available. Take warm clothing, food and water, and be prepared for rain. Irazú is only 90 minutes drive from San José.

Tortuguero National Park

Tortuguero (46,815 acres/18,946 hectares) is the most important nesting area for the Green sea turtle in the western Caribbean, an area of vast, open, windswept beaches. It is

species have been identified there. Views of the park are stunning as one drives through it on the highway to Limón. Camping and hiking are permitted. It's a good idea to wear boots, as there are snakes. Potable water and guides are available. Go early in the day for the best views and birdwatching. Fog often moves in later in the day.

Volcán Irazú National Park

Irazú Volcano (5,705 acres/2,309 hectares), at over 11,000 feet (3,432 meters), is the highest volcano in the country, with four presently dormant craters, where one may

arrived at by an extraordinary system of inland waterways, which provides an excellent opportunity for observing the plant, animal—and human life of the region. Rustic lodging is available in the village of Tortuguero. Camping and hiking are permitted in the park. Just outside the park are several lodges, some with many amenities, which provide package tours; transportation, lodging, meals and guides.

Cahuita National Park

On the Caribbean, Cahuita (2,637 acres/ 1,067 hectares) is one of the most beautiful regions in Costa Rica. The park has long, white sandy beaches and a large coral reef which spreads out like a fan in front of a point. The area is rich with marine and terrestrial life. Camping is permitted: facilities include showers, restrooms, picnic area, potable water, guides and a field station. Lodging, restaurants, glass bottom boat tours and equipment rental are available in nearby Cahuita town.

Palo Verde National Park

Palo Verde National Park (14,095 acres/5,704 hectares) is a large park encompassing lakes, swamps, grasslands, woodlands and forest, a major sanctuary for migrating waterfowl in Central America. During the rainy season, rainfall in the park is heavy and flooding of the plains is widespread. The dry season is hot and windy. Access by road is difficult. Camping is permitted at the administrative center. Rustic lodging and meals are available in the park if it is not full of researchers. Contact OTS at Apartado 675-2050, San Pedro Montes de Oca. Tel: 36 6696. Several tour companies offer natural history visits.

La Amistad National Park

Immense Amistad National Park (479,199 acres/193,929 hectares) is also an international park, sharing a border with Panamá. It has been declared by UNESCO a "Reserve of the Biosphere" and a "World Patrimony Site," in recognition of the diversity of its flora and fauna and because of its scientific value. Over half of La Amistad National Park has yet to be explored. It is an enormous region in the mountains of Talamanca, protecting the largest virgin forest in the country and encompassing an extraordinary number of habitats. Nearly 400 species of birds and over130 species of orchids have been seen there. Camping is permitted but there are no facilities. Water in the streams is potable. Hiking near the Las Tablas Forest Reserve is safe and rewarding, but hiking into the interior of the park should be undertaken only by experienced tropical trekkers. Contact the

Left: nature's camouflage. **Right**: caterpillar on a leaf, one of the surprises of a walk in the National Parks.

National Parks Service (Tel: 33 5284) to inquire about hiring a local guide or horses.

Chirripó National Park

Mount Chirripó (123,919 acres/50,150 hectares), at 12,606 feet (3,842 meters) is the highest mountain in Costa Rica. On the summit are crystal clear glacial lakes surrounded by stunted vegetation. Chrirripó National Park, also named a Reserve of the Biosphere and World Patrimony Site, surrounds the mountain and is contiguous with La Amistad. The flora and fauna are diverse with several endangered species represented. Temperatures at the summit can drop sud-

denly to below freezing. Camping is permited and there are rustic huts available, although no other facilities. Hiking trails are marked and lead to the summit.

Barra Honda National Park

The major feature of Barra Honda National Park (5,671 acres/2,295 hectares), located in the Nicoya Peninsula, is an extensive and magnificent network of caves, some which have not yet been explored. Within the caves, an entire habitat lives: bats, insects, birds, blind salamanders and fish. Hiking trails exist throughout the park and a visit is rewarding even if one doesn't descend into the caves. Camping is permitted and potable water is available. To visit the caves, call the National Parks Service (Tel: 33 4070) to make arrangements.

Cocos Island National Park

Cocos Island or Isla del Coco National Park (5,930 acres land, 45,898 acres sea/ 2,400 hectares land, 18,575 hectares sea) is the largest uninhabited island in the world, with many endemic species of plants, birds, lizards and insects. Located 364 miles (586 km) west of Costa Rica, it has over 200 waterfalls, dense vegetation and underwater caves, and receives an average of 276 inches of rain per year. Cocos' history is full of pirate stories. Many insist that there is pirate treasure hidden there still. Camping is not permitted on the island: you must sleep on your boat. There is potable water, however; and hiking, although the trails are not marked. Contact the National Parks Service for current information and permission to enter. Tel: 33 5284. Some tour companies offer tours to Cocos. Cocos Island requires additional attention here in this review of national reserves, in that it is the largest uninhabited island in the world, the richest in endemic species, and certainly the most unique of Costa Rica's National Parks.

Cocos Island is a robust, wild and vigorous place, rising abruptly out of the open sea, some 100 meters high, as if out of nowhere. As its crown is a thick coniferous forest, full of springs and rivers. The cliffs along the sea are covered with incredibly thick tropical vegetation, with glimpses of magnificent waterfalls plummeting straight down to the sea. Sailing around the island, one sees rocky crags and wondrously formed islets that have been shaped by the wind and water.

Two bays, Wafer and Chatham, offer a way to tie up and gain entry to explore the island. Chatham is small, with a rocky beach. In this area, one senses the past explorers and visitors, of pirates, treasure hunters, whalers, artists and environmentalists, who have in years past jumped ashore from this bay.

To the west of Chatham is Wafer. Most consider this to be the best access route to the island. After anchoring and reaching the shoreline, the traveler has to climb steep cliffs, going up and down ancient natural paths, leaping from rocks across rivers all the way to the highest part of the humid forest. Here there are bountiful bromiliads, giant ferns, orchids, unnamed flowering plants, mosses and ferns covering almost everything. And from a high peak, one can see the view of an unbelievably blue sea above an impossibly green landscape, with white, angel-like doves moving gently, hovering and fluttering in the air. Every natural path, every river, every waterfall, every beach has some rare treasure. The peace is astounding and deafening. And the views of the coral reef, the crisp clarity of the water, the lushness of the landscape, all somehow put one in a mental state that is receptive to the mysterious legends of pirates and treasure that seem inherently a part of the place itself.

Lionel Wafer, a pirate physician who visited the island in the late 1600s, wrote about Cocos Island, and his 300 year-old description remains accurate today: "There is a steep mountain that crosses the center of the island, around which there is a plain that extends to the sea. This plain is coversed with coconut trees which flourish marvelously because of the rich soil. But what most contributes to the loveliness of the place is the number of clear, fresh water springs that fill the entire lower part of the island. The water overflows in several places, forming other little springs. Furthermore, when the rocks advance over the plain, there are waterfalls that form a kind of archway. All of this, together with beauty of the landscape, the view of the coconut trees and the freshness of the air, create a delicious and satisfying state for the senses. It is for reason that our sailors so enjoy the attractions of this island when they fill their water jugs with the sweet water that descends the mountains and forms a small river."

Manuel Antonio National Park

Miles of sandy white beaches shaded by the trees of the jungle at the sand's edge, Manuel Antonio (1,685 acres/682 hectares) is one of the most popular parks in the national parks system. Abundant birds, marine life and wildlife, especially monkeys,

A mature green iguana looking positively prehistoric.

which often play in the trees on the beach. Good snorkeling. Hiking trails are marked. Horses are available for rent. Camping is not permitted but there is plenty of lodging adjacent to the park and in nearby Quepos.

Corcovado National Park

Located on the Osa Peninsula, Corcovado National Park (103,257 acres/41,788 hectares) is a remote and biologically diverse park, rich in flora and fauna, encompassing virgin rainforest and beautiful beaches. Over 500 species of trees are found within the park. Many species of animals that are on the worldwide endangered species lists inhabit the park: ocelots, cougars, jaguars and Baird's tapir. The largest population of scarlet macaws in the country live there. Trails are well-defined. Get a permit to visit the park from the park's administration office in Puerto Jiménez. Tel: 78 5036. Camping is permitted but must be arranged for beforehand. Facilities include restrooms, potable water and showers. Remember to bring food, good boots, mosquito repellent and netting. Sometimes there is space available in the park stations. In addition, there are cabinas in Puerto Jiménez and several lodges in the area offer accommodations, meals and guides.

Guayabo National Monument

Guayabo National Monument (536 acres/ 217 hectares), in the highlands above Turrialba, protects the remains of a sophisticated pre-Columbian city that flourished in the years between 1000B.C. and 1400A.D. Petroglyphs, stone paved walkways, waterways and other stone structures of great archaeological significance in a beautiful site amidst wild impatiens, guava trees and clusters of hanging oropendula nests. Visitors to the ruins must be accompanied by a park ranger, who can turn out to be a good source of interesting information. The park also has educational displays. For thosewho become enamoured and wish to stay longer, there is a camping and picnic area with running water and latrines. Guayabo Na-

Poison Dart frogs, used by indigenous people to poison tip their arrows.

tional Monument is open on weekends only, from 8 a.m. to 4 p.m.

Arenal National Park
(Eternal Children's Forest)

Arenal National Park is Costa Rica's newest national park, having been conferred park status on 22 April 1990.

Marino Ballena National Park

This is also a relatively new park, having been decreed a park on 6 April 1990. The area is actually an island off the coast of the Pacific, in Puntarenas Province between Punta Piñuela and Punta Uvita.

Biological Reserves: Biological Reserves are similar to parks but may not be as scenic nor as desirable for recreation. The reserves are untouched areas containing whole ecosystems with a marked diversity of plant and animal life. They are established to protect, conserve and maintain natural processes for study and scientific research. Fishing and hunting are prohibited as is any activity that might modify the biological equilibrium.

Carara Biological Reserve

Located near Orotina, 68 miles (110 km) from San José, Carara (11,614 acres/4,700 hectares) is easily accessible and offers good wildlife sighting opportunities. Scarlet macaws, roseate spoonbills, boat billed herons, wood storks, blue-gray tannagers, and many other birds inhabit the reserve. Camping is not permitted. Call the National Parks Service (Tel: 33 5284) to arrange for a guide (It is recommended that you go with a guide.) and to get information regarding the conditon of the roads and trails.

Monteverde Cloud Forest Reserve

Monteverde Cloud Forest Reserve (26,116 acres/10,569 hectares), a hard 4-hour-plus ride from San José, is of interest for its abundant life, its very walkable trails through the forest and for its adjacent community, Monteverde, which was founded in the 1950s by a group of Quakers from Alabama.
Within the reserve are 400 species of birds, including the quetzal, 490 species of butter-

flies, 100 species of mammals and 2,500 species of plants, to mention a few. Monteverde is the only known home of the Golden Toad. Maps and checklists of birds and mammals available at the Visitor Center. Guides are available by calling the reserve (Tel: 61 2655) or naturalists Gary Diller (Tel: 61 0903) or Meg Laval (Tel: 61 0952). The reserve is open from 7 a.m. to 4 p.m. daily except on October 6 and 7. Bring rain gear and rubber boots. Lodging in the reserve is available, although limited. There are, however, excellent accommodations in the town of Monteverde and in nearby Santa Elena. Reservations are essential during the dry season.

there are no camping facilities. Bring your own supplies.

Hitoy Cerere Biological Reserve

Hitoy Cerere Biological Reserve (22,619 acres/9,154 hectares) is located in the mountains of Talamanca, in rugged, wet terrain. It rains over 138 inches (3,500 mm) a year and there is no defined dry season. Innumerable rocky streams, whitewater rivers and spectacular waterfalls are found throughout the reserve. The forests are thick with evergreen trees cloaked by mosses and lichen, orchids and epiphytes. The wildlife is abundant but difficult to see as most of it is either nocturnal

Lomas Barbudal Biological Reserve

Sometimes called the Insect Park because so many insects reside there, Lomas Barbudal Biological Reserve (5,621 acres/2,279 hectares) is located on the northern border of Rafael Lucas Rodríquez Caballero National Wildlife Refuge. Some 250 species of bees live in the reserve. Some of the impressive birdlife to look out for in the reserve are the Scarlet Macaw, Great Curassow and the Keel-billed Toucan. There are year-round rivers and springs, and excellent swimming holes to cool off in. Hiking is very good during the dry season and camping is allowed, although

or lives in the treetops. The reserve is home of the Jesus Christ lizards, which earned the name by being able to walk on water. Few biological studies have been made in the reserve, and there are areas which have not yet been explored. Camping is not permitted in the park. Hiking is permitted, although trails are not marked and can be steep and extremely rigorous. Bring water.

Isla Guayabo, Isla Negritos and Isla Pájaros Biological Reserve

Located in the sunny, scenic Gulf of Nicoya, Guayabo, Negritos and Pájaros Islands are nesting sites of many seabirds including the brown pelican. Guayabo Island (16.8 acres/6.8 hectares) is a large, rocky mound, about 164 feet (50 meters) high with tall cliffs. Access is difficult, by means of a small, pebbly beach formed by a landslide. Several medium-sized caves can be seen on the northwest side of the island at low tide. In addition to brown pelicans, frigatebirds, laughing gulls and brown boobys nest on Guayabo. The peregrine falcon winters there.

The two Negritos Islands (198 acres/80 hectares) are covered in semi-deciduous forest, rich in frangipani, spiny cedar and the gumbo-limbo tree. Racoons, parrots and mainly pelicans. Permission must be obtained from the National Parks Service before visiting any of these islands. Camping is not permitted and there are no facilities.

Caño Island Biological Reserve

Caño Island (741 acres land, 1,433 hectares sea/300 hectares land, 5,800 hectares sea), located 12 miles (20 km) west of the Osa Peninsula, is an important archaeolgical site. It was a pre-Columbian burial ground and one of the main attractions there are the stone spheres made by pre-Columbian people. Wildlife is scarce on the island, but for lovers of marine life, there are several coral

doves live on the islands and in the waters surrounding them are giant conch, oysters, tripletail, dolphin and mackerel. The birds found on Guayabo also inhabit the Negritos Islands.

The beaches of Pájaros Island (9.4 acres/3.8 hectares), the smallest island in the reserve, are rocky and covered with mollusks, rock oysters, crustaceans and small barnacles. The wild guava is the most predominant tree, and of course, there are many seabirds, reefs offering very good snorkeling. Hiking and camping are permitted and potable water is available. Contact officials at Corcovado National Park to arrange for a visit.

Cabo Blanco Strict Nature Reserve

Cabo Blanco (2,896 acres/1,172 hectares), encompasses a wet, tropical forest on the tip of the Nicoya Peninsula. One of the most scenic spots along the Pacific coast, it contains a large population of marine and shore birds and mammals. There is a small museum, picnic area, latrines and well-maintained trails. The sea is rich in marine life.

<u>Left</u>: brown-throated three-toed sloth. (Perezoso de tres dedos.) <u>Above</u>: Kinkajou (Martilla).

Access to Cabo Blanco is via the ferry across the Gulf of Nicoya, from Puntarenas, and then several tortuous hour on unpaved road through Montezuma. Permission to visit from the park ranger is required before entering the reserve. Swimming is permitted, but snorkeling is not. Camping is not permitted in the reserve, but lodging is available about 7 miles (11 km) away in Montezuma and some neighbors to the reserve permit camping on their land.

National Wildlife Refuges: Wildlife Refuges are established to protect wildlife habitats and thus the existence of certain species. They exist where protection is essential for

of Nicaragua. It was established to protect nesting colonies of brown pelicans, American oystercatchers and frigatebirds. The region becomes very windy during the dry season. Camping is not permitted. No facilities available.

Ostional National Wildlife Refuge

An important nesting site for the Pacific Ridley sea turtles, Ostional National Wildlife Refuge (400 acres land, 1,450 acres sea/ 162 hectares land, 587 hectares sea) is located in the Pacific dry zone amongst deciduous forest and encompasses beautiful stretches of coastline. *Arribadas*, massive

the perpetuation of certain wildlife. Generally these reserves do not have outstanding scenic or recreational value. They include private land in some places. Scientific and recreational uses are permitted when they don't threaten the protected species. Administered by the National Wildlife Directorate. Tel: 33 8112 or 21 9533.

Isla Bolaños National Wildlife Refuge

Isla Bolaños Wildlife Refuge (62 acres/25 hectares), an oval-shaped rocky mound in the Pacific, is located only a few miles north of Santa Rosa National Park near the border

arrivals of the nesting turtles, occur from July to December. Camping is permitted but there are no facilities. Hiking throughout the refuge is allowed, but trails are not marked. Lodging is available in new, simple cabinas in Ostional and meals can be purchased from local families. Call the village grocery store (Tel: 68 0467) to reserve a cabina and find out if the turtles are active.

Tapantí National Wildlife Refuge

Tapantí National Widlife Refuge (11,651 acres/4,715 hectares) is located in the rugged Talamanca Mountains, and biologically is not very well known. The reserve is criss-crossed by 150 rivers, canyons and water-falls. It is rainy and humid and vegetation is dense. Although there is a great variety of wildlife, animals are difficult to see, with the exception of birds and butterflies. Two hundred eleven species of birds have been counted, including the quetzal, which nests there in the late spring. Hiking and camping are permitted and there are facilities for picnics and outdoor cooking. Cabins near the entrance to the refuge are sometimes available. Call ahead to request a guide or to ask about the cabins. (Dirreción de Vida Silvestre has radio contact with Tapantí. Tel: 55 0192) The refuge is open daily except

refuge, is an excellent place to view the nesting Leatherbacks as well as a variety of other wildlife. Camping is not permitted, although hiking is. Accommodations are available in Tamarindo.

Dr. Rafael Lucas Rodríquez Caballero National Wildlife Refuge

An extension of Palo Verde National Park, Dr. Rafael Lucas Rodríquez Caballero Wild-life Refuge (18,172 acres/7,354 hectares) is located in the heart of the hottest, driest basin in the country. Dry season (January through March) is considered by some to be the best time to visit, because access roads are then

Thursday and Friday from 6 a.m. to 4 p.m.

Tamarindo National Wildlife Refuge

Tamarindo National Wildlife Refuge (1,038 acres/420 hectares) on the northwest Pacific is important for its mangrove swamps and its beaches, which are one of the most important nesting sites in the world for the Leatherback turtle, the largest of the sea turtles. Playa Grande, located within the

<u>Left</u>: eyelash viper. <u>Above</u>: Mexican Hairy porcupine.

more passable, and visitors can more easily view the abundant water birds. Hiking and camping are permitted but there are no faciliites.

Peñas Blancas National Wildlife Refuge

Peñas Blancas National Wildlife Refuge (5,930 acres/2,400 hectares) protects an im-portant watershed site. Located northwest of Puntarenas, its steep terrain is covered by forests. Wildlife is scarce, but there are abundant birds and butterflies. Hiking the steep slopes is for those who are in good physical condition. Camping is permitted, but there are no facilties. Bring water. For information about access and camping, call the Wildlife Office. Tel: 33 8112.

Barra del Colorado National Wildlife Refuge

Located along the inland waterways of northeastern Costa Rica and extending to the Nicaraguan border, Barra del Colorado (227,329 acres/92,000 hectares) is one of the most pristine rainforests in the country, accessible only by boat or plane. Rainfall ranges from 158 inches to 236 inches (4,000 mm to 6,000 mm) per year, resulting in the forma-

acres/1,309 hectares), in the Osa Peninsula, is a lengthy 8-hour bus trip from San José. The refuge is important for its wet, tropical virgin forests, which have many trees in danger of extinction, including purple heart, plomo, butternut and manwood. Golfito also boasts 11 species of heliconia, 31 species of orchids and more than 12 species of fern. Trails are slippery during the wet season, but it is still a lovely time to visit. Hiking and camping are permitted but there are no facilities. Bring boots and rain gear. Check with the Wildlife Office (Tel: 33 8112) about camping in the refuge and information on access. A variety of lodging is available in the nearby town of Golfito.

tion of diverse wetlands, which can be visited by navigating its rivers, channels and lakes—the best way to observe the wildlife which inhabits the banks and shores. Much of the refuge is unexplored. Few marked trails exist. Camping is permitted but there are no facilities Lodging is available inside the reserve at private hotels near the town of Barra del Colorado. A visit to Barra del Colorado could be combined with a visit to Tortuguero National Park.

Golfito National Wildlife Refuge

Golfito National Wildlife Refuge (3,235

Gondoca y Manzanillo National Wildlife Reserve

Gondoca y Manzanillo National Wildlife Reserve (12,387 acres land, 10,961 sea/5,013 hectares land, 4,436 sea) is one of the most beautiful coastal regions in the country. Located south of Puerto Viejo on the Atlantic, it extends along the coast to the border with Panamá. The beaches are white sand, fringed with coconut palms and offer gentle waves and a coral reef of about 2 square miles (5 square km), rich with tropical marine life. Most of the refuge is flat or has gently rolling hills, covered with forest, grasslands and some farms. Many animals and birds live in the refuge, including some which are in danger of extinction, such as the crocodile, tapir, caiman and paca. Camping is permitted although there are no facilities. Bring water. Hiking is limited to the coast.

Curú National Wildlife Reserve

Curú Wildlife Reserve (208 acres/84 hectares) is located in the Gulf of Nicoya and has three beautiful beaches, ideal for swimming and diving. Although small in size, it encompasses 5 habitats and offers sanctuary to a surprisingly large and diverse number of animals, birds, and plants, including over

Caño Negro National Wildlife Reserve

Caño Negro National Wildlife Reserve (24,633 acres/9,969 hectares) is located in the northern part of Costa Rica, not far from the Nicaraguan border, and is comprised of swamp and marshlands. Lake Caño Negro covers about 1,977 acres (800 hectares) during the wet season, but almost disappears completely during the dry season. The reserve provides excellent birdwatching opportunities, including extremely large flocks of Anhinga, Roseate Spoonbill, White Ibis, and Jabiru, the largest bird of the region, which is in great danger of extinction. There are also several species of mammals, includ-

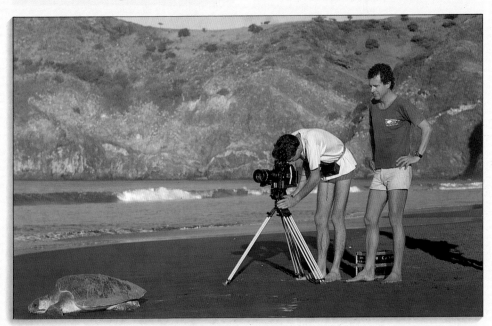

110 species of land and sea birds and the white-faced Capuchin Monkey.

The refuge is private property, belonging to the Schultz family, who request that visitors call before coming. (Tel: 61-2392 or 61-6392) Rustic cabins along the beach, built for researchers, are occasionally available. Family style meals are served. Camping is not permitted and there are no facilities, but the hiking is excellent.

Left: spotting wildlife along the Atlantic waterways. **Above**: photographing Green Turtles, Santa Rosa.

ing the large cats. Camping is allowed and there is limited space in a rustic environment. During the wet season, plan to rent a dugout canoe or boat for birdwatching. In the dry season, one may hike or rent horses. Contact the Wildlife Office or try the public telephone at Caño Negro (Tel: 46 1301) to make inquiries.

Other Protected Areas: In addition to the National Parks and Wildlife Reserves, there are several other categories of protected areas which constitute an integral part of the immense nature reserve system of Costa Rica:

Resource Reserves or Forest Reserves have been established to protect natural resources for future use. They are generally located in largely unpopulated areas and are difficult to reach. Hunting is prohibited and recreational uses strictly regulated. The Robert & Catherine Wilson Botanical Garden is adjacent to a forest reserve belonging to the Organization for Tropical Studies. Here, orchids, palms and heliconia grow in their natural habitat. Some forest reserves: Arenal Lake, San Ramon, Juan Castro Blanca, Grecia, Cordillera Volcanica Central, Taboga, Matina, Río Machos, Los Santos, Golfo Dulce.

Regional parks, often located near urban centers, provide recreation and environmental

education. They vary in size, but each has exceptional scenery meriting conservation, but not of national or international importance. Agriculture, logging and hunting are not permitted. Camping is. Regional parks would correspond to state or city parks of the United States. Regional parks in the San José area include: El Parque Metropolitano, La Sabana, Parque del Este, Parque de la Paz.

Anthropological Reserves or Indigenous Reserves are large, remote forest areas free from the influence of modern technology, inhabited generally by indigenous people or societies. The reserves have been established to protect the lifestyles of these peoples and

to allow them to pursue their lifestyles without the influence of modern technology. The ecosystem is thus also preserved. Modern technology and foreign cultures and individuals are not permitted in the reserve, though this regulation has been difficult to enforce. The Talamanca Indian Reserve or territory, on the Atlantic Coast, remains the home of the Talamanca Indians. They continue to practice there their tribal ways, maintaining traditional systems of religion and healing. In addition to Talamanca, Costa Rica has the following Indigenous Reserves: Ujarras-Salitre-Cabagra, Osas, Cocles, Tayni, Telire and Chirripó.

Cultural Monuments protect one or more cultural, historical or archeological sites of national importance. They may provide recreational, educational and scientific activities. For example, the Guayabo National Monument houses the largest archeological project in the country.

Biosphere Reserves contain samples of important animal or plant communities or a unique natural phenomenon. Established to conserve genetic diversity and the preservation of the main ecosystem in the area, they allow the natural evolution of species to occur. These Reserves are managed to perpetuate the existing use of the land, which may be private property. If it is, though, strict regulations govern its use and esthetic maintenance. Individual property owners are sometimes given subsidies for their participation in the reserve. In 1982 Chirripó and La Amistad National Parks were declared "Reserves of the Biosphere" by UNESCO.

World Patrimony or Heritage Sites are established by the UNESCO to protect portions of the earth considered important on an international scale. These sites may contain features of evolutionary periods or significant geological processes. These sites may harbor an endangered plant or animal, or are considered to have great cultural, social, scientific or artistic value. These areas are fully protected and may or may not be open to the public. In 1983 UNESCO declared Chirripó and La Amistad World Patrimony Sites and in 1991, Cocos Island was proposed as a patrimony site.

Above: thankfully, animal trophies are now prohibited. **Right:** pondering their future?

106

Learning about Costa Rica's plants is learning about Costa Rica. Knowing which plants are which, is one way to become more in touch with the country. Identifying them can become an enjoyable game as you travel along the way.

Coconut Palm: Smooth single trunk. Large feather-like fronds. Yellow or green clusters of coconuts. Water in immature nuts, called *"pipas,"* good for drinking. Meat and milk from mature nuts are used for cooking.

Pejibaye Palm: Spine-covered trunk with feathery fronds. Large clusters of small heart-shaped orange nuts. Nuts are popular and common in San José street markets. Heart of palm, or *palmito* taken from small suckers at base of tree, used in salads.

Almond Tree: Single trunk tree with branches forming a platform. Commonly used as shade tree. Rounded reddish or green leaves. Located along beaches. Not related to almond tree in United States, but nut tastes similar.

Mango: Large tree with asymmetrical fruits in clusters. Eaten green with chili powder or red when ripe. Same family as poison ivy. Allergic individuals may develop a rash from eating fruit or contacting the wood.

Figs: Many different species in the tropics. Fruit eaten only by animals. The strangler fig or *matapalo* sends roots around trunk of host tree, which may ultimately be killed. Often used as living fence posts.

Gumbo Limbo: Often called "tourist tree" because of the reddish, peeling papery bark which resembles sunburned skin.

African Tulip Tree: Large, deep green-leaved tree, with brilliant red-orange blossoms tinged with yellow at the end of branches.

Jacaranda: Large open-crowned tree which loses leaves but remains covered with deep blue-purple blossoms during the dry season.

Erythrina: Medium size grey-barked tree, belonging to pea family. Used to shade coffee plants on coffee *fincas*. Bright orange flowers.

Sensitive Plant or Mimosa: Low growing ground cover, visible all along roadsides. Blooms are lavender puff balls. When touched, water pressure in cells of plant drops, causing leaves to instantly fold up.

Living Fenceposts: Several kinds of trees are used for fenceposts, including Gumbo Limbo, Erythrina, Figs, Madre Raton, and Madre de Cacao. Cuttings from all of these take root and develop into trees.

Cacao: It is from this fruit that chocolate is made. Seeds in large oval pods that grow directly off of the trunk. Small trees with large leaves.

Bananas: First introduced to the New World in 1516. Fruit forms in suspended bunches on drooping stalk. Commercially covered

with pesticide impregnated blue plastic bags. Many varieties used by local people, including plantains, which are cooked green or ripe.

Coffee: Small tree-like shrub with glossy dark green leaves. White flowers. Red berry-like fruit contains two coffee beans, which are harvested November through March. Related to the Gardenia.

Sugar Cane: Introduced here. Large grass-like plant growing to 15 feet in height. Feathery blossoms. Used for its sugar or squeezed for sugar cane juice.

Wild Cane: Similar in appearance to sugar cane but smaller and grows wild. Used for wall-building material in rural houses.

Poor Man's Umbrella: Huge, up to five-foot diameter leaves. Located at cooler higher elevations, such as along the highway in Braulio Carrillo Park. It is used as an emergency umbrella.

Papaya: Long-stemmed, with hand-shaped leaves on straight trunk. Grows to 15-feet. Seen around houses or on plantations. Here both small yellow Hawaiian variety and large green Central American variety with dark orange flesh, are grown. Latex from unripe fruit, collected by scoring the skin, is used to manufacture meat tenderizer.

Philodendrum, or Monstera: Large-leaved vine, with large heart-shaped leaves with

a fence shrub, seen around houses.

Heliconia: Large, strap-shaped leaves on long stems growing directly from the soil in clumps. Lobster claw-like hanging flowers. Popular with birds and photographers.

Ginger: Clumps of thick-stemmed plants. Crowned by fragrant white, red or yellow flower clusters. Torch ginger has pink flowers on a single stalk. Showy flowered forms are not used for cooking ginger.

Mangroves: Collective term for unrelated tree-like shrubs growing in brackish water or muddy, silty soil. Red mangrove on prop roots grows along river estuaries and calm coastal shores. Nurseries for young fish and shrimp. Stabilizes shorelines, traps detritus

holes. If it looks like a houseplant that is grown out of control, it is probably a Philodendrum or Monstera.

Dracena: Single-stalked shrub with striped chartreuse strap-shaped leaves. Often planted as fences in coffee plantations. Seen in large fields where cuttings are harvested for ornamental plants.

Hibiscus: Medium sized dark green shrub with trumpet-shaped flowers in many sizes and colors. The red hibiscus is often used as

Left to right: the national flower; the banana flower; and passion flowers along the forest path.

and creates new landmass.

Jaragua Grass: Introduced from Africa. Common in Guanacaste and other pastureland areas. Has alternating light and dark stems, growing to six feet.

Bromeliads: Large family of plants with many epiphytic species seen on trees, telephone lines, etc. Sprays of strap-shaped leaves, with purple and red flowers in stalks.

Orchids: Usually difficult to spot in forests. Most are epiphytic, on rain forest trees. Small leaves. Flowers are borne in clusters on long spikes. Look for them in downed branches and in rain forest trees, flowering during February through April.

Bakeries and dessert shops compete for attention on every block of San José, and a white fudge, called *cajeta*, is a national passion. Yet somehow Ticos are obsessed with physical fitness. Surprisingly trim figures, usually clad in the latest neon-colored sporting togs and athletic footware, are commonly seen jogging along the highways and exercising and vigorously playing in the parks of every town.

On the pot-holed highways, cyclists in bright lycra tights compete in a life-threatening game with fatalistic drivers for the few patches of smooth asphalt. Joggers, drenched in sweat in the warm midday sun, gulp thin mountain air as they run up volcanic slopes. Every village, regardless of size, has at least one soccer field, and it is always in use. On weekends, the enormous La Sabana Park, on the west side of San José, is filled with thousands of athletes: soccer teams, basketball players, swimmers, volleyball players, roller blade teams, and baseball enthusiasts. On the Central Valley plateau, private golf and tennis clubs with complete health spas cater to wealthy suburbanites who want a modern, fashionably trim profile.

In this country of spectacular natural wonders, and comfortable climate, outdoor sports have clearly become very, very popular with Costa Ricans and tourists alike. The Ticos love all aspects of their sports: playing them, watching them, and celebrating their heroes. A 48-page daily newspaper can have 30 of its pages devoted to sports. On any Sunday, Costa Rica feels like a nation caught in a crazed frenzy of athletic activity. While soccer continues to fire passions in a way in which no other sport ever will, the Ticos are discovering and becoming active in every athletic endeavor imaginable. And visitors are coming in increasingly greater numbers to Costa Rica to surf isolated beaches, to windsurf on magnificent Lake Arenal, and to enjoy some of the best whitewater river rafting in the world.

Preceding pages: rafters hit a hole on the Reventazón gorge. Left: …on any Sunday. Right: Ticos celebrate an international soccer cup victory.

Whitewater Rafting: The brightly-colored inflatable raft rushes down a chute of cascading whitewater, then plunges over and through waves that are nearly six feet (two meters) high. Those in the raft gleefully dig their paddles into the frothing water, and then shriek with delight as they maneuver the raft between boulders the size of cars. After a while, a calm spot on the river is reached, an eddy, and from there the raft passengers take pause and look up from the roaring river course, to inhale and appreciate the beauty of

the Reventazón Gorge. The scenery includes the colossally broad panorama of the canyon, and rolling fields of coffee, sugar cane, wild grasses and radiant flowers blooming unexpectedly in the canopy of trees that lean over the river.

Whitewater rafting is new to Costa Rica, and it is rapidly growing in popularity, for Costa Rica has more accessible whitewater rivers and rapids than any place else in the world. It is, of course, the unique geography of the country that makes it one of the world's great destinations for rafters. To have the right kind of rapids it is necessary to have a river that descends in a fairly steep gradient.

The four mountain chains which wind down the axis of Costa Rica provide the basis for these conditions perfectly. The Talamanca Range and the Cordillera Central have many steep, wide, magnificent and perennial rivers which are regularly supplied with bounteous rainfall.

Despite its perilous appearance, whitewater rafting is a very safe sport. And it offers anyone in moderately good health an exhilarating way to observe the scenery and wildlife of the country. Three professional outfitters provide all of the necessities: life preservers, helmets and rafts, and their guides have been through training in the classroom and on the rivers. Most Costa Rican head

year by Michael Kaye of the United States, who established Costa Rica Expeditions. Ríos Tropicales, founded by Rafael Gallo and Fernando Esquivel in 1985, pioneered rafting on the Sarapiquí and Sucio Rivers. Local graduates of their kayaking school have represented Costa Rica at the World Championships of Whitewater Racing. Aventuras Naturales, the third company to enter the field here, became a Costa Rican whitewater outfitter in 1988. Between the three companies, thousands of participants have experienced the rapids, whitewater and scenery of Costa Rica's rivers.

The variety of these rivers provides an enormous range of wilderness experiences.

guides have been trained at whitewater schools in the U.S.A. and many have worked with the world's best.

The first white-water exploration of Costa Rican rivers was made by Costa Rica Expeditions on the Reventazón River in 1978. The Pacuare and Reventazón Rivers, both drain from the eastern slope of the central volcanic cordillera to the east of San José, and reports of exceptional whitewater conditions, as well as ideal weather and scenery, had other groups hurrying to explore the rivers of Costa Rica.

Commercial whitewater rafting in Central America was pioneered during the following

Some offer idyllic float trips through luscious landscapes with abundant wildlife, while others contain explosive whitewater and raging rapids which challenge the most experienced rafter.

The Sarpiquí River flows through the lowlands of Heredia, providing stunning scenery and exceptional whitewater. About a two-hour drive from San José, the upper portion of the Sarapiquí contains moderate rapids which are suitable for novice paddlers. On the calm, lower section of the river, the jungle closes in and gives rafters the opportunity to view the monkeys, otters and extensive water fowl of the area.

The Reventazón River is a one and half hour drive from San José and offers some of Costa Rica's most challenging whitewater and spectacular scenery. Rafting companies run four sections of the river. The first, which is just below the hydro-electric power plant of Cachí, is steep and contains continuous rapids of moderate to high difficulty. The second section, from Tucurrique to Angostura, is suited to novice paddlers and provides splendid views of the surrounding volcanoes. The final two sections of the Reventazón, from Angostura to Siquirres, contain some of the most challenging whitewater in the world.

Many consider Costa Rica's most famous

allowing time for exploring the waterfalls and for relaxing in camp.

For rafters who are also bird watchers, the Corobicí River is legendary. In the adjacent Palo Verde National Park, over 300 species of birds have been observed and most can be seen from rafts on the Corobicí. Because the river's perennial flow is controlled by a dam on Lake Arenal, it becomes an oasis which attracts birds, monkeys and lizards during the dry season in Guanacaste.

Surfing: During the last few years, Costa Rica's unending beaches have been discovered by surfers from North America, Australia, and Europe. They generally concur that the quality of Costa Rica's surf is in the

whitewater river to be the Pacuare. It passes through a deep gorge in dense jungle that contains rich flora and wildlife. Most groups spend two or more days in the descent on this river from Tres Equis to Siquirres, and camp in riverside sites within view of thundering waterfalls and great flocks of birds.

On the Pacific side of Costa Rica, the river system offers the longest uninterrupted stretches of whitewater in Costa Rica. Most rafting parties take four days to travel the 50 miles (80 kilometers) from Chiles to Crujo,

Left: a well-shaped Pacific wave. **Above:** wave jumping on Lake Arenal.

top four—along with California, Hawaii and Australia. As well, they find that the surf in Costa Rica is plentiful and uncrowded, the water temperature is around 80 degrees Fahrenheit throughout the year, and that there is still the rare experience of having a wave all to oneself, just offshore of a beach that is pristine and empty.

A map of Costa Rica reveals what may not be too obvious from just driving on the highway up or down the coasts: there are a lot of beaches and, often, few access roads to many of them. In fact, there are some 132 miles (212 km) of Atlantic Coast and 635 miles (1,022 km) of Pacific shore, sculpted with sandy beaches, rocky headlands, off-shore reefs and river mouths near coastal jungles. There are also a great number of open beaches which are exposed to ocean swells coming from many directions. Much of the coastline is removed from civilization, and there may be no facilities, food or emergency services within many miles. A four-wheel drive vehicle is often essential to get to many of the beaches, especially during the rainy season.

The wave-making conditions are complex in Costa Rica. On the Pacific Coast, swells originating from storms in the north and central Pacific Ocean occur frequently from November through March. South swells from

Jacó, a Pacific beach town located southeast of the Gulf of Nicoya, is less than two hours by car or bus from San José. It is a long silty beach trapped between two jungle-covered rocky points, with waves that are particularly good for body surfing or boogie boarding. The surf is easily accessible, just beyond the patios of many of the hotels and cabinas. At Jacó, the beach is not particularly beautiful and the currents and riptides are strong.

Jacó is often used as a base for trips to other surfing areas nearby. Just under two miles (three km) to the south is Playa Hermosa. It is possible to hitchhike, rent a bike, or take a bus with a surfboard around the point south of Jacó, to this beach. South from Jacó to

distant storms prevail for the remainder of the year. Pacific beaches are shaped by sediment which is carried to the sea by major rivers. The silt migrates up and down the coast on strong onshore currents. Sand bars produce beach breaks with long and fast right and left rides along much of the coast. Sand spits form at the river mouths, and create long, and often clean point breaks. But because the sand bottom is unstable, bars and sandspits change with the season. Tides and winds also strongly influence wave shape.

With hundreds of miles of coastline, there are many undiscovered, nameless surfing beaches. Some popular spots are:

Playa Panamá are many undiscovered and unexploited surfing spots.

North of Jacó, near Puntarenas, the sandspit at the mouth of the Barranca River produces what is reputed to be one of the longest left-breaking waves in the world.

Far to the north, the beaches of Guanacaste Province have some of the best surf anywhere, particularly during the dry season when steady offshore winds help to create the waves. The break near Witch's Rock at Playa Naranjo, in the Santa Rosa National Park, is one of the best known and most spectacular waves. Getting there requires a very long, bumpy, journey in a four-wheel drive vehicle along nearly impassable roads, but the sight is worth the discomfort.

The Nicoya Peninsula to the south of Guanacaste is scalloped with one beach after another, and many of them, such as Nosara, have rideable waves.

From December through April, large swells engendered by winds and storms originating in the Caribbean, arrive at Costa Rica's east coast beaches. The steep, fast-moving waves break over shallow coral reefs, often in shapes and sizes which rival those of the north shore of Oahu, in Hawaii. Smaller west swells from tradewinds originating in the West Indies prevail from June through August. The only months when there is generally little or no surf on the east coast are September through November.

Near Limón, some two and a half hours east of San José, are Playa Blanca and Playa Portete. Both are good, popular surfing beaches. Approximately one hour south of Limón, Puerto Viejo, a tranquil Caribbean village, is the site of the sometimes wicked Salsa Brava, a surf break that now seems to have an international reputation. From December through March, consistent, large north swells hit the coral reef in Puerto Viejo with tremendous force.

On arriving at the International airport outside of San José, one can inquire at any of the auto rental agencies for a free surf guide pamphlet.

Windsurfing: In January, 1991 a television sports network hosted and filmed Costa Rica's first windsurfing contest. The event served as an announcement to the world that Costa Rica warranted recognition as an outstanding destination for international windsurfers. During the competition, strong tradewinds whipped the picturesque Lake Arenal into a sea of white water and waves, creating ideal conditions for European and North American windsurfers. The few pioneers who have sailed Arenal favorably compare this lake with the world's best windsurfing locations, such as the Columbia River Gorge in Oregon and Maui in the Hawaiian Islands.

On approximately 50 percent of the days between January and April, consistent winds

between 25 and 50 knots blow along the length of Arenal, creating excellent short board sailing conditions. For the remainder of the season, lighter winds predominate and are ideal for longboard sailing.

Sideshore winds are consistent and blow across the full width of the lake. During high winds, steep swells provide the right conditions to practise acrobatic speed runs, jumps and loops.

In addition to a notable lack of crowds and excellent windsurfing conditions, the scenery surrounding Arenal is stunning: the classic, conical form of Arenal Volcano, often blowing fiery ash against a backdrop of lush rolling hills, and the sparkling shores and

azure blue waters of Lake Arenal itself.

Costa Rica's Lake Arenal is on the edge of the windsurfing boom. But Tilarán, on the shore of the lake, is yet a sleepy mountain town, with only a church, a park, and a few small hotels. Local windsurfing entrepreneurs are concerned about the effects that their sport may have on the town and environment, and are working with officials from the municipality to restrict the development of large hotels and resorts along the lake shore, and to promote the construction of small lodges which will complement and not overwhelm the exceptional environment surrounding the lake.

The king of game fish swims leisurely towards Costa Rica's Caribbean Coast. At 150 pounds, he fears no predators except sharks as he cruises towards the mouth of the Colorado River.

Where the tarpon has been is a mystery to man. He could be coming from Florida, South America, or West Africa. He might have been in local waters the entire time.

But now he is with an ocean school of 100 fish of the same size. Suddenly they spot a school of *titi*, a small sardine-like fish, and

be suspended or reversed, or there's no chance of success. The first rule that goes against all that you've ever learned is to retrieve the lure with the rod tip low—at water level or, better yet, in the water. That way, when it's time to set the hook, the rod tip can be brought up and backwards in a long arc. The maneuver must be repeated rapidly at least three times with a force that would tear the hook out of the mouth of almost any other fish.

If you react fast enough, and if you're lucky, the tarpon will be hooked before it

chase them to the surface. The tarpon cause an acre of the Caribbean to explode as they churn the water and devour the *titi*.

If a fishing person from one of the nearby lodges at Costa Rica's Barro Colorado is lucky enough to witness this scene, it's simply a matter of casting into the chaos to get into contact with what many consider the most exciting aquatic quarry on earth.

Tarpon sometimes strike like a rocket, hurtling 15 feet straight up as they hit the plug. At other times they inhale the lure so gently that it's hard to tell whether or not one of the giant fish is even on the hook.

In tarpon fishing, the rules of angling must

makes its first jump. If you're not so lucky, you'll see your lure thrown into the air as the great silver fish seems to explode out of the water and reach for the clouds. A tarpon's jump is like no other in fishing. They reach incredibly high; twist right, twist left, flip over, fall back on the line and do everything possible and impossible to get free. Usually the tarpon succeeds. Usually you lose. The success rate of experts is to land approximately one out of every 10 hooked.

Few tarpon are killed by fishing people in Costa Rica. Their flesh is bony and a high respect is developed between angler and this magnificent fighter fish. Today, most tarpon hooked and landed are lip gaffed and released.

Tarpon are one of the few fishes capable of taking in air directly through the mouth rather than by filtering water through their gills. This ability is necessary because these big active fish need more oxygen than they can get from the waters that they sometimes inhabit. The direct breathing accounts for their "rolling," when they come to the surface and flop on their side while gulping air. It also makes it possible for tarpon to swim freely between salt and fresh, even oxygen depleted, water.

Tarpon enter the river mouths all along the Caribbean Coast of Costa Rica, from the Colorado River in the north, to the Sixaola River, which forms the border with Panamá. In most rivers, they swim a few hundred meters upstream in search of food and return to the sea.

Only in the Río Colorado do they keep going up river, following the *titi*, in an incredible freshwater journey of more than 124 miles (200 km) to Lake Nicaragua, close to the Pacific Ocean.

As the tarpon begin their long swim, they pass a series of thin fingers of water stretching northward almost to the border with Nicaragua. These freshwater "lakes" are full of a variety of exotic fish that make great sport on light tackle. One of the most fascinating is the alligator gar, known in Costa Rica as "*gaspar.*" Looking like a holdover from pre-historic times, this fish has a long, narrow snout as full of sharp teeth as an alligator's. Its coffee-colored body is covered with tough skin and large scales. It's tail is broad and powerful. The meat of the alligator gar is white, firm and sweet, not unlike that of shrimp. The eggs, however, should never be eaten as they are highly toxic.

As the tarpon continues his swim westward, he soon leaves the Colorado River and enters the Río San Juan, which forms the border between Costa Rica and Nicaragua.

The tarpon is not alone in his upriver swims. Snook also make the long journey following the *titi*. And following them all are bull sharks.

Left to right: everyone lands a sailfish; Guapote, caught in Lake Arenal; and Mahi-mahi, dolphin fish, off the Nicoya coast.

The sharks, like the tarpon, continue all the way to Lake Nicaragua. Their presence in the lake has led many people to believe that there are "fresh water sharks" in the lake. Actually, they are just visitors from the faraway Caribbean.

Snook are the mainstay of sport fishing in Costa Rica. Large snook are plentiful in all parts of the Caribbean and Pacific Coasts, as well as in rivers throughout the country.

All along the Río San Juan, there are lesser rivers flowing into it from Costa Rica. The confluence of the San Juan with the Colorado, Sarapiquí, San Carlos, Infernito, Pocosol, Medio Queso and Frío Rivers, all offer excellent angling for tarpon and snook.

None are heavily fished and all require a bit of enterprise to reach. But those who make the effort are well rewarded.

An exception to this rule of relative inaccessibility is the Río Frío which passes right through "downtown" Los Chiles, which is a three-hour drive on paved roads from San José.

The Río Frío is full of tarpon, snook, white drum, gar and other exotic species. Some people fish right from the municipal landing in Los Chiles. Others, who have boats, launch them there and venture north or south. For those who don't have a boat, it is possible to rent a *panga*, driven by a knowledgeable local person who also acts as a guide. These *pangas* can be found at the municipal landing.

Some tarpon, as they swim up the Río San Juan, apparently take diversions far into the side rivers. This is the case with the Río Frío. Thirty minutes by boat, south of Los Chiles, is the convergence of the Río Frío and the Río Sabogal. Here tarpon, up to 100 pounds, seem to be present at all times.

Every morning and every evening the giant fish, too big to be in a narrow river, leap high into the air, reentering the water with a thundering splash. It is a sight every fishing enthusiast would love to see. It can also be one of the most frustrating experi-

ences imaginable, because there are days when these fish just won't take a lure. However, just the sight is well worth the effort—and there's always a good chance of hooking into one of them.

The Río Frío, as well as most of the other rivers of Costa Rica, is full of a fish often overlooked by sport fishing people. The *machacha*, a silvery speedster, is an unusual fish in that is primarily a vegetarian. They can often be found under the overhang of chile*mate* trees waiting for ripe fruit to fall into the water. Costa Ricans often fish for them using pieces of banana or tomato. But *machacha* will also take small lures or flies

running, changing directions, diving and leaping into the air. *Machacha* can run up to 20 pounds and two to five pounders are common and offer great sport. Their flesh is bony but tasteful.

Up a few of the rivers that feed into the San Juan, particularly the Sarapiquí, can be found the *bobo*, a difficult but rewarding quarry. These fish, which run up to 30 pounds, feed on shallow, fast-moving water. They are relatives of the salt water mullet and are pure vegetarians. But they can be taken on small spinners and they offer great sport as they fight hard through the rapids.

In these Atlantic slope rivers can be found other exotic species including the *mojarra*, a strong sharp-toothed, brightly-colored pan fish resembling a perch on steroids.

Fishing off of the Pacific coast of Costa Rica for most means angling for sail fish, marlin and tuna. All along the Pacific coast there are sport fishing operations springing up and all are finding success.

Operators in the Gulf of Papagayo were the first, and the area was shown to be the most productive sail fishing in the world. Sails here are not the scrawny Atlantic variety. They are hefty, healthy Pacific sailfish averaging over 100 pounds. Fought on 15-pound line or less, they offer fantastic sport and a spectacular show full of graceful jumps. Sails are always released in Costa Rica.

In recent years, marlin have been discovered throughout most of the Pacific coast. Dolphin, tuna and rainbow runner are plentiful off shore and the spectacular rooster fish and snook can be found close to land.

Off shore reefs offer great fishing for snapper, including the prized *cubbera*.

Often overlooked are the fishing possibilities from the Pacific beaches. Every beach on the Pacific coast offers the chance to take various types of jack and drum as well as trophy size snook from the surf. Mouths of rivers and streams often attract congregations of snook. Casting from rocks often locates snapper and rooster fish.

Roosters abound on Costa Rica's Pacific coast. The wide-bodied powerful fish with the long, spiky dorsal fin which gives it it's name, is particularly plentiful around the rocks in Puntarenas or the nearby Pacific port of Caldera. Once hooked, the rooster fish raises it's comb and speeds away across the surface, offering a unique show and fight.

Trout have never done well in Costa Rica. Despite numerous attempts to stock them in high mountain streams, they have never really thrived. Trout fishing is possible in the breathtaking mountains between San José and San Isidro General, such as in the San Gerardo de Dota valley area, and, even if the fish are somewhat small, the scenery more than makes the day worthwhile.

A worthy substitute for trout is the *machin*, which can be found in rivers where trout would be expected, and which puts up a vigorous fight, similar to that of a trout.

The star of Costa Rica's few lakes is the *guapote*. Some people call this fish the "rainbow bass", although genealogically it has

The *guapote* is a spectacular looking fish. It "lights up" displaying many colors on its flank. A breeding male has large bulbous protrusions above the eyes that make it look as though it summers in the Love Canal. *Guapote* in Lake Arenal, the main place where they are fished, can run up to twenty pounds or more, although a 15-pounder is about all that a mortal can handle.

There is a second type of guapote, the *guapote pinto*, or painted *guapote*, which can be found in rivers which flow into the San Juan.

Costa Rica is truly a paradise for fresh and salt water fish—an unusual place, where the distinction between fresh and salt water is often blurred.

nothing to do with bass. The main similarity to bass is in the way it is fished, casting or flipping plugs or spinner baits. Deep jigging is often productive as well.

Once hooked, the similarity to bass is soon forgotten. The *guapote* is to a bass what a diesel is to an HO model train. The *guapote* is not a light tackle fish. Once hooked, it heads for cover with the force of a rhino. If it makes it, it is lost and will almost surely cut the line on underbrush.

Left: the fish market offers some surprises. **Above**: fishing for trout and *machín* in the high mountains.

And Costa Rica is one of the few places left on earth where you can maintain a feeling of exploration while fishing. You'll only run into other fishing people if you want to.

A license is required to fish in Costa Rica and there are seasons for many species and locations.

Keko's and Gilca's fishing stores in San José will arrange licenses and gladly give advice (in Spanish). Peter Gorinsky speaks English, German, Spanish and a few other languages and is the country's foremost fishing guide, specializing in fly and light tackle fishing. Peter is happy to give fishing advice and can be reached at 28-0267.

COSTA RICAN FOOD AND FRUITS

It's been a long time since the Chorotegas inhabited the northern part of Costa Rica. At the time of the Spanish conquest, these native tribes planted their maize only during a new moon because they believed that as the moon grew, so did their crop. Their life was very much centered around corn, and the rules they had to follow were very strict. From sowing time until the harvest, husband and wife had to sleep apart, and the sowers could not eat any chili or salt nor drink any fermented beverages. Today, farming techniques have changed, but corn is still present in almost every meal in most households, and so is the influence of the aboriginal people.

With cornmeal, the Chorotegas prepared a very thin unleavened pancake, the *tortilla*. It is the main ingredient of Costa Rican *gallitos,* a type of hors d'oeuvre made by wrapping them around mashed black beans, spicy meat, a spoonful of vegetable stew, pork rinds, or, really, almost anything. Chorotegas also prepared *tamales,* rectangular pieces of dough (ground corn beaten with lard and certain spices), with different fillings, wrapped in corn husks and steamed. This food, of Aztec origin, is still eaten in Mexico and in the whole of Central America, but it is almost never the same in any two countries. Chorotegas put tomato, pumpkin seeds, sweet pepper, and deer or turkey meat in their *tamales*. The sauce, which contained tomato, chili and pumpkin seeds, was called *pipian*, and is still, today, prepared in a very similar way. *Tamales* are traditionally eaten during the Christmas holidays. So, if you visit the country during the holiday season, be sure to order a warm, hearty *tamal*, and a cup of excellent Costa Rican coffee. Stuffed turkey is also present at the Christmas table. Turkeys (*chompipes*) were here before Columbus and were taken to Europe by the Spaniards.

In like manner, Spanish conquerors brought animals such as cattle, lambs, goats and pigs from their homeland to Central America, enriching the already abundant variety of foods they found here, which included melons, cucumbers, mint, lettuce, cabbage and an enormous variety of other fruits and vegetables. The mixture of indigenous and imported food produced an interesting amalgam of flavors, which in years to come would constitute what we today call traditional Costa Rican food.

Fruits, fresh vegetables, beef, abundant salads, rice and beans have been the trademarks of Costa Rican cooking. *Picadillos* are found in every Tico home. Diced potatoes, *chayotes* (cho-chos or vegetable pears) or string beans are mixed with finely chopped meat, tomatoes, onions, fresh coriander, bell peppers, (and whatever the cook feels may add flavor to the pot). Leftover *picadillos*, fried with rice, are served for breakfast, usually with hot *tortillas*, and are called *amanecido*.

Gallo pinto, a dish made of black beans and rice, well-seasoned with onions, sweet pepper and fresh coriander, is perhaps the most ubiquitous and typical of Costa Rican dishes. It is eaten mainly for breakfast, accompanied by fried eggs, cheese, sour cream and hot *tortillas*.

Rice is an important ingredient of many Costa Rican dishes. Ticos eat rice and shrimp, rice and squid, rice and octopus, rice and lobster and, at every country festival, rice and chicken. All of the dishes are well-seasoned and are usually served in a natural tomato sauce that is the trademark of the cooking of this land.

Though these recipes are prepared in a way that is uniquely Costa Rican, here the Spanish influence is also present. An exceptional soup is *olla de carne*, a hearty meat and vegetable stew, the origins of which can be traced back to Cervantes' master novel, *Don Quixote*. The *olla podrida* is the great-grandparent of the soup the people in Costa Rica love the most. What gives the distinct flavor to the Costa Rican version is the mixture of vegetables cooked in it: yucca, green plantain, sweet potato, tannia, *tacacos*, taro, pumpkin, carrot, cho-cho, onion, cabbage, etc. Another very interesting soup, and one available at neighborhood restaurants throughout the country, is *sopa negra*, made with black beans, onions, fresh coriander and hard-boiled eggs.

Costa Ricans season their food with a mixture of dry spices called *condimentos mixtos* (mixed seasoning), that are readily available at the markets. There are many different brands of liquid sauces as well. Most often these contain corn flour, salt, garlic, black pepper, onion, coriander, paprika, and a small amount of hot chili. "English sauce," the native version of the Worcestershire sauce, is also used sparingly by most cooks, perhaps as often as is fresh coriander. Jalapeño chiles, from the mountain towns of Zarcero and Cervantes, are very good and not quite as hot as the Mexican varieties.

Costa Rican coffee is surely among the best in the world. No dinner is complete in this country if not followed by a *tacita de café* (a small cup of coffee). Brewed traditionally,

twenty grams of powdered coffee for each cup are placed in a cotton bag, and boiling water slowly poured through it. All the varieties are good, but "Café de San Isidro de El General" is certainly one of the very best anywhere in the world.

In addition to drinking coffee, the Costa Rican people also drink a lot of alcohol. The national beer is very popular. But it is rare for someone to have a drink without a *boquita*, tidbits ranging from small portions of hot beef broth to *ceviche*, small *tamales* or *tortillas con queso* (*tortillas* with cheese). This practice is strictly followed both at public establishments and private homes. Don't be

Preceding pages: a harvest color among Costa Rica's hundreds of fruits and vegetables. Left: the busy San José restaurant scene. Right: *Picante!* Sliced red and green chilis for a sauce.

surprised if, invited for dinner, you are overwhelmed with *tragos* and *boquitas* (drinks and snacks) before the meal is even served.

Regional cooking: Costa Rica is only 20,000 square miles (51,000 square kilometers) in size, and yet there exist several clearly differentiated regional cuisines.

If Costa Rica as a whole is tropical and natural, the foods of Limón, the beautiful Caribbean province, are even more exotically tropical and flavorful. The area offers a wide diversity of dishes influenced by African and West Indian cooking. The names of the ingredients have the beat of Calypso and reggae: *haki, yokotaw, bami, calaloo* as do the names of the dishes themselves: *tie-a-leave,*

dokunu, johnny cake. You will also find strong traces of Chinese cuisine, as there are many Chinese living in the area. The trademark of the cooking of Limón is coconut. Coconut oil and milk are used generously in most recipes, including the traditional rice-and-beans. For this popular dish, rice is cooked in a pot filled with red beans, coconut milk and aromatic herbs. This dish is the regional variation of the traditional *Gallo pinto*, but in Limón it's served on Sundays and festive occasions.

From their African heritage, the *Limonenses* have kept the original names of many ingredients, the privileged use of some

tubers, such as the yam, and wide use of green leaves in soups and stews. Their African heritage also influences their use of herbal teas made with an infinite variety of plants. From their ancestors' hard lives in the sugar plantations of the West Indies, the *Limonenses* have inherited many products that were included in the daily rations of the slaves: breadfruit, salted cod, mangoes, cassava, plantains, and a great variety of tropical fruits. From their United Kingdom influence they have retained several recipes for cakes, pastries and breads which, from the days of slavery, they had to prepare for their British masters. All of these influences enrich Limón's cuisine and make its cookery very special.

In Guanacaste, to the North, pre-Columbian traditions in cooking are very much alive. A larger variety of corn dishes are cooked there than in the rest of the country, including delicious pastries and desserts. *Tamales, chorreadas, tanelas* and many other regional delicacies can still be found throughout Guanacaste, and some beach hotels there are now starting to include them on their menus. Since cattle is one of the area's main industry and resources, milk products there are often very good. Bagaces cheese (a hard, slated cheese, used shredded and added to other recipes) has been, since the last century, an important portion of the salary of the *peones* on the haciendas. *Cuajadas* (fresh cheese balls) are usually present at breakfast, to be eaten with hot *tortillas Guanacastecas,* which are larger than the ones eaten in the rest of the country.

African slave women were brought to the region during colonial times to work in the kitchens of the haciendas. They also left their mark on many exotic recipes still cooked in that province. *Ajiaco* and *bajo,* stews made with a mixture of meats and vegetables, maintain their African origins.

On the Pacific coast, Puntarenas presents a variety of recipes using ingredients from the sea, *guiso de cambute* (conch stew), and dishes featuring different combinations of fresh shrimp, lobster and squid. *Patacones,* crisp green plantain sliced and topped with black mashed beans, are a necessary accompaniment to fresh *ceviche de corvina* (marinated white fish).

Easter fare: Since colonial times, the Easter meal has been a traditional one. The Catholic

Church's prohibition on eating red meat during Lent explains why fish, pastries and sweets are so available for the Easter celebration. Since the last century, *bacalao con papas* (salted cod and potatoes) has been traditionally prepared for Easter. Huge quantities of salted cod are imported from Europe especially for this occasion.

Just before Easter week, especially in and around Cartago, a type of fruit similar to the pumpkin, but oval and quite large, is sold in the streets. These are *chiverres,* and a preserve made with them, called *cabellito de angel* (angel's hair), is eaten during Easter throughout of the Central Valley.

Costa Rican *ceviche,* prepared especially and using coriander freely to perfume the fish. Fresh *palmito* (heart of palm) is also traditionally eaten during Lent, but can be bought any time pickled in vinegar. *Palmito* and rice is an elegant, festive dish served with grated cheese on top.

Flor de Itabo is the flower of a plant often used in the fences of the coffee farms. It is a very white bunch of lily-like flowers that are also eaten for Easter, stewed in butter with eggs and tomato.

El casado: You will find *casado* (married man) listed on the menus of many restaurants in all seven provinces of Costa Rica. Its name, an example of Tico humor, derives from the ordinary daily fare a man suppos-

at Easter, but available all year long at any neighborhood *cevicheria,* is similar to the Mexican dish because both show the influence of the Aztecs. It is nevertheless a bit different from any other *ceviche* prepared in Latin America. Here it is prepared by marinating small cubes of white fresh fish in a sauce made with lime juice, olive oil, fresh coriander, onions and bell peppers, for at least 12 hours. Most Costa Rican cooks believe in keeping the lime juice to a minimum

edly receives after he has been caught and married. *Casado* consists of a combination of rice, beans, meat, fried or scrambled eggs, spaghetti, some vegetable *picadillo,* and a salad, all served on the same large plate. It is a favorite lunch of bureaucrats and employees who don't have time to go home. Listed as "typical" food in some restaurants, tourists like to order it because it gives them the opportunity to sample many dishes, the portions usually being very generous.

Costa Rican Nouvelle-cuisine: Increasing exportation of food has stirred new interest in Costa Rican vegetables and fruits. As a result, new recipes have been conceived, as

<u>Left</u>: Typical country fair food: *empanadas*. <u>Above</u>: the national dish, *gallo pinto*, all dressed up.

well as imaginative ways of rewriting traditional ones. *Pejibaye* soup, a delicate orange creamy broth, when correctly made, has been lately served at banquets for foreign dignitaries and ambassadors. The common, but never ordinary, mashed black beans, well-seasoned with onions, sweet peppers and coriander, are now served at formal dinners as proud hors d'oeuvres. Posh restaurants are starting to feature native cooking nights, introducing such delicacies as plantain soufflé or pork-filled cassava pastries. Restaurants called *típicos* are not always a good choice for trying native cuisine, though, because some of them feature, shall we say, unsavory, overcooked stews and watery desserts.

Of course, the best place to taste Costa Rican food is in the friendly home of a Costa Rican middle-class family. This is essentially a land of mountain people, shy but proud. So, to find the true gems of Costa Rican food, you must defeat the host's efforts to pamper you with international dishes. Don't hesitate to ask for local food.

Fruits of Costa Rica: Fernandez de Oviedo, a Spanish writer, came to Costa Rica in the l6th century and immediately fell in love with the astounding variety of tropical fruits that were everywhere available. Enthusiastic at every new discovery, he pronounced the pineapple the "best looking, most wonderful lady in the vegetable world."

De Oviedo probably didn't get to try all of Costa Rica's different fruit, however. There were simply too many. Among the hundreds that you might adventure forward and try is the mombin (*jocote*). The *tronador* is the best variety. The Spaniards said the mombin was a type of plum when they first saw it, but it really has nothing in common with the plum. This fruit is juicy and spicy, unlike any other. Street vendors sell brown paper bags full of mombins from August through October, the color varying from dark green to bright red, depending on ripeness. Mombin is usually eaten fresh, as is its cousin, the yellow mombin. Some refer to the yellow mombin as the hogplum because hogs are very fond of it and fatten on the fruit that falls to the ground from wild trees in the forest. The coco-plum (*icaco*), on the other hand, is never eaten fresh, but its white flesh is made into a sweet preserve, called *miel de icaco*. Another cousin, the *ambarella*, (*yuplon*), was brought to Jamaica by Captain Bligh, of the *Bounty*. It came to Costa Rica in the hands of English-speaking Jamaican immigrants, to the Port of Limón. It is eaten uncooked, with a little salt, or made into a preserve.

A book about the Colombian writer Gabriel García Marquez, a bestseller in Latin America, has the provocative title *The Guava's Perfume.* You will better understand how the title elicits the Latin American experience if you visit a home when the woman of the house is making guava jelly. The entire house fills with the aroma of this wonderful fruit. But one may, of course, simply eat the guavas as raw fruit and enjoy them right away.

Another fruit, called in English "Costa Rican guava" (*cas*), is yellow in color, round, and has soft white flesh. It is acidic, but highly valued for jelly-making and for drinks. If you see it on a menu, under *"naturales,"* try a *jugo de cas* (cas juice).

The fragrance of the guava is only rivaled by that of the rose-apple (*manzana rosa*), a beautiful round fruit, whitish green to apricot-yellow in color, perfumed with the aroma of the rose. The flesh is crisp, juicy and sweet. As a preserve or crystallized, it is delicious. If you eat it fresh, don't overdo it. Rose-apples must be eaten in small quantities. A relative of the rose-apple, the *ohia* or mountain-apple (*manzana de agua*), is a beautiful oval fruit, white to crimson in color. Its flesh is apple-like: crisp, white and juicy. *Ohia* jam is exquisite.

The fragrance of the nanzi (*nance*) is more controversial. This small, round yellow fruit has been popular among Costa Ricans since pre-Columbian times, but foreigners tend to find its smell too strong. It is used for preserves, wines and jellies. *Nances en guaro* (nanzis in liqueur) are very good. Bottled in a strong liqueur and left to ferment for nine months, they take on an amber-brown color. Nanzi sherbets are also very popular.

The loquat (*níspero*), an oval-shaped, small fruit, with a large seed, pale-yellow to orange in color, is also called the Japanese meddlar.

flesh is usually eaten fresh, but in Limón you can still find it made into a mixture somewhat cryptically called "matrimony," prepared by scooping out the pulp and adding it to a glass of sour orange juice.

Carambolas, which also look like beautiful stars when cut in thin slices crosswise, are used as garnish for desserts. This shiny, five-sided fruit is about two to three inches long, with a translucent, pinkish-yellow color.

Alajuela's Central Park, where young and old gather to enjoy the good weather and each other, is full of mango trees, with their tempting fragrance, and that is why the town, second in importance only to San José, is called Mango City. Alajuela's mangoes are

The flesh, firm and meaty in some varieties, melting in others, is juicy and of a sprightly acid flavor. Although commonly eaten fresh, it can also be used in cooking.

You will also find edible stars in this surprising constellation of fruits. Yes, Costa Rican star apples (*caimitos*), when halved transversely, look like stars, similar to the mangosteen (an exotic fruit found in Malaysia and Thailand). This glossy fruit varies in shade from purple to light green. The sweet

Left: Marañon, cashew apples. The gray part is the edible nut. Above: a papaya orchard near Turrialba.

sweet, firm and delicate. The male mangoes (*mangos*) are sweeter and spicier, but smaller and softer than the females (*mangas*). The mango aroma is spicy and alluring. Few other fruits have a historical background as developed as the mango, and few others are so inextricably connected with religious beliefs. Buddha himself is said to have been presented with a mango grove, so that he might find rest beneath its graceful shade. Besides eating them as dessert fruits, Costa Ricans make mangoes into chutney—that spicy sauce well-known to those who enjoy East Indian food—as well as preserves, sauces and pies. For many people, mangoes are the very definition of summer.

Mangoes have an even more exotic cousin, the cashew fruit, best known for the kidney-shaped nut attached to its lower end. The fleshy portion, or apple, varying in color from brilliant yellow to flame-scarlet, is eaten fresh in Costa Rica. Its brilliant color and penetrating, almost pungent aroma make this one of the most delectable of all tropical fruits. The flesh is yellow, soft, very juicy and zesty. It is also used to make a jam, a wine and a refreshing beverage somewhat similar to lemonade, which retains the special aroma and flavor of the unique cashew fruit. In the late 1970s, the Costa Rican government decided to plant acres and acres

fruits, sometimes called "hairy lychees," look like gooseberries covered in fleshy spines. To eat them, simply cut the leathery rind with a sharp knife and pull it back from the pulp.

Certainly among the most exotic fruits is the sweet *granadilla* , a favorite among the people of Central America. This fruit is oval in shape, orange to orange-brown in color. Within the hard crisp skin a bundle of seeds is surrounded by an almost liquid, translucent and wonderfully tasteful pulp. Use a spoon to eat this extraordinary fruit.

Also strange-looking is "the bullock's heart," called *anona*, a heart-shaped fruit which changes from green to a dark, reddish-brown as it ripens. The sweet pulp is milk

with cashews, meant to be exported abroad. The venture was a financial failure, but the trees are still there, and there was a wonderful side effect: parakeets and parrots adore the fruit, and many species that were almost extinct are now increasing their numbers while dining on abundant cashew apples.

Paw-paw (papaya) grows almost everywhere in the country, and British tourists, in particular, are enamored with a drink called *papaya en leche*, a sort of papaya milk shake. Papaya is also excellent as a meat tenderizer.

The most exotic sight in a fruit market in Costa Rica has to be the rambutan (*mamon chino*) stand. The bunches of red and orange

white and contains several large black seeds. After cutting it in half, eat it with a spoon, using the skin as a bowl.

The *anona* is related to the custard-apple (*anona chirimoya*) found in the northern part of the country. It has a delicate sweetness and a delightful fragrance like rose-water. Mark Twain remarked that it was "deliciousness itself."

Still another fruit in this amazing family, the *guanabana*, is unrivaled for its use in sherbets and refreshing beverages. Foreigners find the flavor somewhat suggestive of a combination of pineapple and the mango, but Costa Ricans consider that to be heresy.

One of the best fruits of Tropical America from the province of Guanacaste, is the *sapodilla* or naseberry, here called *chicozapote* or *níspero*. It is a dessert fruit, rarely cooked or preserved in any way. The French botanist Descourtilz described it as having the "sweet perfumes of honey, jasmine and lily of the valley."

A relative of the *sapodilla*, the mammee-sapota or marmalade-plum (*zapote*), kept Cortés and his army alive on their famous march from Mexico City to Honduras. The bright salmon-red color of the pulp catches the eyes of tourists walking the Avenida Central in San José. Street vendors, knowing the sales appeal of the beautiful color, cut the marmalade-plums in halves. To one not used to the very sweet fruits of the tropics, the flavor of the *zapote* may be at first somewhat cloying. Very ripe *zapotes* can be used to make wonderful ice creams and sherbets.

While Cortés and his men survived on mammee-sapotas, many a Spaniard who came to Costa Rica learned to live on *pejibaye* a treasured food of the aboriginal Indians. You will surely see it on the fruit stands, with its glossy orange skin and black stripes. Cooked and peeled, its yellow pulp tastes very good when a little mayonnaise is added to it to soften its rather dry texture. It cannot be eaten fresh. Pejibaye soup is one of the most exceptional dishes of Costa Rican nouveau cuisine.

Breadfruit, like bananas, is grown in the Atlantic region of Costa Rica. This fruit of Polynesian origin was also introduced to the West Indies by Captain Bligh, and the Jamaicans planted it in Limón. The breadfruit is an attractive, ornamental tree with large leaves, and the fruit is a regular ingredient in many Caribbean dishes.

Refreshing fruit drinks such as *fresco de maracuyá* (passion-fruit) accompany every Costa Rican meal, and the variety is really amazing. One of the favorite and most nourishing is made from *mora* or blackberries. The berries are blended, strained and added to sugar water or milk. And, as mentioned earlier, one of the more refreshing fruit drinks is made from *cas*. A *tamarindo refresco* is similar in color and taste to apple juice. It is

made from the seed pod of the tamarind tree. Balls of *tamarindo* seeds and pulp wrapped into balls the size of oranges are available at every market. The seeds are put in hot water to wash off the sticky *tamarindo* and then are mixed with sugar and diluted with cold water. Most Costa Rican fruits, and there are hundreds of them, are good for making drinks in water or in milk.

Fruits are also the main ingredient of many traditional desserts. Since early colonial times, cooks in these territories have pampered family and friends with candied fruit cores, pumpkins in syrup, all sorts of jellies and a variety of delicious fudges.

Costa Rican fruit are available for every

possible taste preference, throughout the year. It's only necessary that one be a little adventurous. Get up early some morning and visit the Mercado Borbón, or the produce market off of 10th Avenue, or the dozenz of fruit stalls near the Coca Cola bus station. Or go to the open-air produce and fruit markets on Saturday morning, held in almost every town on the Central Plateau, to see and taste the season's harvest. Along the highways and main roads will be vendors of fruit and fruit drinks that have not even been mentioned here. Pause and take a look at what is available the next time you pass a *frutería* or fruit stand and try a taste of Costa Rica.

Left: mountains of melons, Cartago. **Right**: a *pejibaye* vendor, Central Market, San José.

Ticos call it Costa Rican snow when the white coffee blossoms blanket the fields of the Central Valley and the sweet jasmine-like fragrance of the bloom fills the air. Since coffee grows best above 4,000 feet (1,200 meters), where temperatures average between 59 and 82 degrees Fahrenheit (15 and 28 degrees Celsius), the Central Valley seems ideal for the raising of coffee.

One might surmise that coffee is indigenous to Costa Rica, but it's not. The Spanish, French and Portuguese brought coffee turned out, was a simple matter. The climate and the soil conditions seemed created for coffee cultivation. Coffee *fincas* quickly occupied much of the land, except for that needed to graze oxen. As the only Costa Rican export, the country's financial resources supported it. By 1840, coffee had become big business, carried by oxcart through mountains to the Pacific port at Puntarenas, and from there by ship to Chile from where it was transported to Europe. By the mid-1800s Costa Rica's oligarchy of

beans to the New World from Ethiopia and Arabia. In the early 1800s, when seeds were first planted in Costa Rica, coffee plants were merely ornamental, grown to decorate patios and courtyards with their glossy green leaves, seasonal white flowers and red berries. Costa Ricans had to be persuaded, even coerced, into growing them so the country might have a national export crop. Every Tico family was required by law to have at least a couple of bushes in the yard. The government awarded free plants to the poor and grants of land to anyone who was willing to plant coffee on it.

Growing coffee in the Central Valley, as it coffee barons had risen to positions of power and wealth, for the most part through processing and exporting the golden bean, rather than in growing it.

In 1843, an English sea captain, William Le Lacheur, on a return voyage to England from the West coast of the United States, stopped in at Costa Rica's Pacific port of Puntarenas, in need of ballast for his empty ship. As it happened, 1843 was an exceptional year for coffee production and the farmers had more of the beans than they could sell. They took a chance with Le Lacheur and loaded up the holds of his ship with coffee, allowing him to use the heavy sacks as ballast. He made the trip to England, around the Cape, and 2 years later he returned to pay the coffee planters their profit. And thus was made the Costa Rican connection with the English and European markets.

Costa Rica was fortunate in its early development of the coffee industry. But coffee has not always been a blessing. Ironically, it was the very success of coffee production that was responsible for Costa Rica's first international debt. The country borrowed 3 million dollars from England to finance the Atlantic Railroad so coffee could be exported from the Atlantic port of Limón. And when coffee hit bottom on the international market in 1900, the result was a severe shortage of basic foods in Costa Rica that year.

This dependency on an overseas market beyond their control has left the Costa Ricans vulnerable on many occasions. Throughout the 20th century, coffee prices have fluctuated and the economy of Costa Rica has varied accordingly.

Traditionally, banana, citrus and poro trees were planted in the coffee fields to provide some shade for the coffee plants. Later coffee hybrids were developed that did not need shade and treeless fields allowed more yield per acre. These varieties, however, were found to deplete the soil more rapidly and required fertilizer to enrich it, adding to the cost of production. Today many coffee-growers have returned to the traditional shade-loving plants.

The coffee plant itself is grown in nurseries until it's a year old, at which time it is transplanted to the field. Two years later it bears harvestable berries and, with care, will continue to bear for the next 30 to 40 years.

As coffee grows best in a mountainous climate, many of the hillsides in the Central Valley are covered with rows of the bright green bushes, reflecting the sun with their shiny, luxuriant leaves. Some of the fields are virtually vertical and one cannot imagine how pickers keep from tumbling down the slopes as they collect the berries. An ingenious solution of planting the trees directly behind one another so that the trunk of the downhill tree serves as a foothold, allows workers to harvest the red berries. Coffee is harvested from November to January, dur-

ing school vacation and Christmas holidays, and it is traditional for entire families in rural areas to to pick coffee together, some of the money earned going for Christmas presents and new Christmas outfits.

Certainly the best way to partake in the Costa Rica coffee experience is to take Cafe Britt's exceptional coffee tour. Located about 1 kilometer north of Heredia, just outside of San José, this theatrical happening takes visitors through the entire coffee process, from growing the coffee cherry to correctly tasting the final product. Combining elements of professional theater, a multimedia show, a farm visit, plant tour and tasting session, Cafe Britt whirls the visitor through

an education into the universe of coffee in about an hour. It is not to be missed. Phone 60-BRIT for information.

Costa Rican coffee has been traditionally mixed with other coffees to upgrade blends that are destined for worldwide export, to give them a liveliness and body. But increasingly today, consumers are demanding the unadulterated stuff: 100 percent pure Costa Rican coffee. All of the elements seemed to combine miraculously to produce what *aficionados* consider to be the best of these best coffees, perhaps superior to any in the world, in the highland regions around Poas, Barva de Heredia, Tres Rios and Tarrazu.

Left: coffee pickers, circa 1920. Right: selectively harvesting the reddest coffee berries.

EL CONDON

UNA EFICAZ MEDIDA
DE LA QUE PUEDE DEPENDER SU

Téngalo siempre a mano

COMISION NACIONAL DEL SIDA   DEPARTAMENTO DE CONTROL DEL SID
MINISTERIO DE SALU

Preceding pages: earrings for sale, Plaza de la Cultura; a section of ceiling, the National Theater; always have one on hand!; and the Basilica de Nuestra Señora de Los Angeles in Cartago. **Left:** stone sphere, origin and significance unknown, Osa peninsula.

Costa Rica is definitely not an island in the Caribbean; it is in the center of the Central American isthmus. Traveling around the countryside, one has the sense of being in a large country; geophysically there are so many things going on. There is the feeling that it would take months to really explore it all. Yet it is, in terms of physical size, a small country. With less than 20,000 square miles, it is one of the smallest countries in Latin America. It is bounded on the north by Nicaragua, and to the south by Panamá; two countries often in the international news, and two countries profoundly different from this usually benevolent and prosaic land. To the east is the tranquil Caribbean Sea and to the west is the tumultuous Pacific Ocean. Costa Rica is as complex and perhaps more diverse than any place of its size on earth; divided into several distinct regions, each of them looks and feels as an entirely separate place.

Perhaps it is the hot coastal plains in the tropical zones, with its rolling wild grasses and plantations of palm and banana, or the thickly-forested valleys and coastlines, fringed with beaches of every description, that drew many of the early travelers here; or perhaps it is the fertile central plateau in the temperate zone, higher, at 3,200 to 6,500 feet, with its rich fecund cloud forests and magical tropical jungles, which has attracted an international community of conservationists, biologists, birdwatchers, environmentalists,

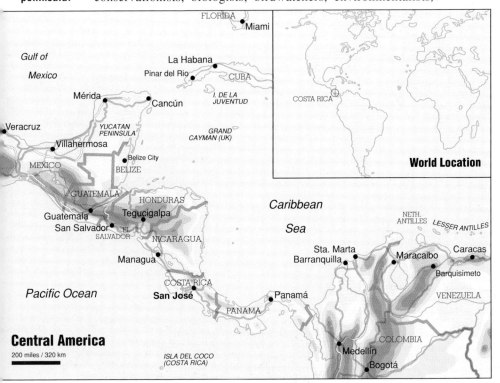

Central America

200 miles / 320 km

World Location

naturalists and the ecologically attuned; and many a Northern European or *gringo* from the midwestern or northern United States or Canada, has found Costa Rica's cool highlands, consisting of gently rolling, wooded pastureland, reminiscent more of Switzerland than a banana republic, to be an ideal place.

The highland mountains traverse Costa Rica, from the northwest to the southeast, in three ranges, rising to more than 12,500 feet. These are the magnificent Guanacaste, Central and Talamanca ranges.

Never far away, is the coastline. Indeed, there are many easily accessible points throughout this country from where you can simultaneously view both the Atlantic and the Pacific oceans. The Atlantic Coast measures only 135 miles in length, while the Pacific Coast of Costa Rica, with its deep gulfs and indentations, is several times that length. On the Pacific there is the Nicoya peninsula to the north, and the Osa Peninsula to the south. Each of these large peninsulas harbor numerous small islands. And, remote and mysterious, many miles off of the Pacific Coast, is the exceptionally beautiful and still pristine Cocos Island.

Running as veins of a precious ore through the body of the country is a network of waterways and rivers. They rise and fall through the mountains, flow to the sea on both coasts, and provide a seemingly endless source of fresh water, and hydraulic power.

The soil of the Central Valley is exceptionally fertile, due primarily to the volcanic ash which has fallen through the centuries. This rich, drainable soil is ideal for producing Costa Rica's coffee, and traveling through the high country, one can view seemingly endless coffee *fincas* with their deep green, jewel-like foliage, flowing up impossibly steep ridges, and across the floor of great alluvial valleys.

Although most of Costa Rica's volcanoes are extinct, there are some which are still active. Póas Volcano, at 8,900 feet (2,705 meters), is located not far from the town of Alajuela, and has what may be the world's largest crater, measuring more than a mile in diameter; and Irazú volcano, at 11,322 feet (3,440 meters), not far from the city of Cartago, is active, and can be viewed at relatively close range. On some nights, Irazú provides a fiery show, but it pales in comparison to the rumbling, explosive spectacle of Arenal Volcano, at 5,358 feet (1,635 meters) in height, which is the most consistently active of Costa Rica's volcanoes. Other mountains are Chirripó Grande, at 12,532 feet (3,810 meters), and Terbi, at 12,512 feet (3,800 meters), the highest elevation points in the country.

Although geographically situated in what earlier travelers used to call the "torrid zone," the great majority of Costa Rica's population are never really torrid at any time of the year, living as they do, for the most part, on the Central Plateau, at elevations between around 1,500 feet (456 meters) and 4,500 feet (1,370 meters), in very

Left: prehistoric stone ball, discovered in the high mountains.

acceptable, "perennial spring-time" temperatures of between 68 and 78 degrees Fahrenheit, morning, noon and night.

However, near the coasts the temperatures are indeed tropical and there are distinct alternating wet and dry seasons, at different times of year, for both the Atlantic and Pacific; and for those people that do live the year around at the ocean's edge, there are certain times when they will be overwhelmed by the too-sensuous hot and humid mid-day air and be driven, as most species are, to seek shade and, hopefully, onshore trade breezes, for a two or three hour *siesta*. The tropical downpours, usually arriving with great predictability in the afternoons during the wet seasons along the coasts, can best be described as "awesome." Certainly millions of words have already been written about these extraordinary dramas of lightning, thunder and torrential rains; and, if you have never experienced it, well, it just isn't Kansas. After an evening of being humbled by these nightly displays, you'll know you're not in Dublin, Munich, or Tokyo, either.

Away from the tropical coasts, the climate is, of course, greatly determined by the altitude above sea level. At each level, temperatures are amazingly constant throughout a 24-hour cycle, regardless of the season, or time of year, from the heat of the coastal plains to the chilliness of the great volcanos and slopes of the mountain ranges.

From the edge of the almost tideless Caribbean sea and the pounding Pacific coast; up and across the volcanic mountainous *cordilleras* ; up, up to the highest peak, to cold and brittle Chirripó, it is all, amazingly, the Republic of Costa Rica.

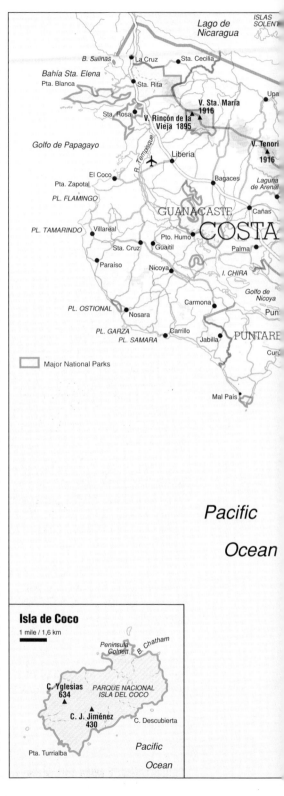

146

NICARAGUA

Carlos

R. San Juan

Negro

Boca del Rio San Juan

San Juan del Norte

ALAJUELA

R. San Juan

Boca Tapada

Trinidad

R. Colorado

Sta. Rosa

R. San Carlos

Caribbean

Sea

Muelle
San Carlos

HEREDIA

Tortuguero

Fortuna

Puerto Viejo

Aguas Zarcas

LIMÓN

RICA

Quesada

San Miguel

Cariari

V. Poás
2704 ▲

C. Cacho Negro
▲ 2136

Guápiles

R. Pacuare

Zarcero

Siquerres

San Ramón

V. Barva
2906 ▲

V. Turrialba
3328 ▲

Matina

Bahia
Moin

Alajuela

Heredia

V. Irazú
▲ 3432

Limón

Atenas

San
José

Cartago

Turrialba

Barranca

Santiago

San
Ignacio

La Suiza

San Mateo

R. Tárcoles

Chirripó Abajo

C. Matama
▲ 2251

Túfares

SAN JOSÉ

Frailes

CARTAGO

R. Chirripó Atlántico

Bribri

Pto. Viejo

Jacó

Sta. Maria

C. Vueltas
3156 ▲

R. Telire

Shiroles

Sixaola

Parrita

C. La Muerte
3491 ▲

Cerro Chirripó 3820 ▲

R. Chirripó del Pacífico

R. Térebé

Quepos

San
Isidro

Cajón

C. Kámuk
▲ 3549

PANAMÁ

PL. MANUEL ANTONIO

Hatillo

R. Sini

C. Echandi
3167 ▲

Dominical

Buenos Aires

Potrero Grande

Palmar Norte

Cortés

R. Gr. de Térraba

Coto Brus

Bahia de
Coronado

PUNTARENAS

San Vito

R. Chiriquí Viejo

ISLA DEL CAÑO

PL.
COLORADA

Rincón

Golfito

Neily

San
Pedrillo

Golfo Dulce

San Andrés

Pta.
Llorana

Canoas

La Cuesta

Carate

Río Claro

Cabo
Matapalo

Pto. Armuelles

Bahia de Charco Azul
o de David

Pta. Burica

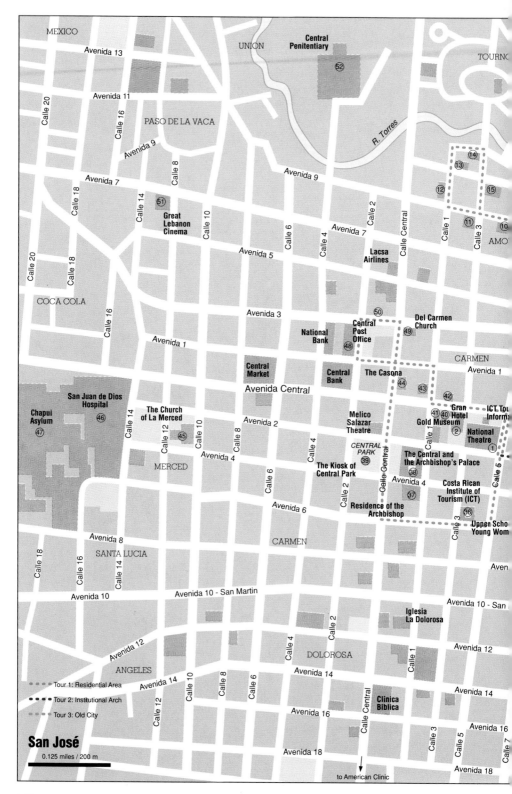

MEXICO

Avenida 13

UNION

Central
Penitentiary

52

TOURNO

Avenida 11

Calle 20

Calle 16

PASO DE LA VACA

R. Torres

Avenida 9

Avenida 9

14

13

Calle 8

12

15

Avenida 7

Calle 18

Calle 14

51

Great
Lebanon
Cinema

Calle 10

Avenida 7

Calle 2

Calle Central

Calle 1

Calle 3

11

10

Avenida 5

Calle 6

Calle 4

Lacsa
Airlines

AMO

Calle 20

Calle 18

COCA COLA

Calle 16

Avenida 3

50

Central
Post
Office

Del Carmen
Church

49

Avenida 1

National
Bank

48

CARMEN

Avenida 1

Central
Market

Central
Bank

The Casona

44

43

42

Avenida Central

41

40

Gran
Hotel

ICT Tou
Inform:

San Juan de Dios
Hospital

46

The Church
of La Merced

Calle 14

Calle 12

45

Calle 10

Avenida 2

Calle 8

Melico
Salazar
Theatre

Gold Museum

2

National
Theatre

Chapui
Asylum

47

CENTRAL
PARK

39

The Central and
the Archbishop's Palace

1

MERCED

Calle 4

Calle Central

38

Avenida 4

Costa Rican
Institute of
Tourism (ICT)

The Kiosk of
Central Park

Avenida 4

Calle 6

Calle 2

37

Avenida 6

Residence of the
Archbishop

36

Upper Scho
Young Wom

Calle 3

Avenida 8

CARMEN

Aven

Calle 18

Calle 16

Calle 14

SANTA LUCIA

Avenida 10

Avenida 10 - San Martin

Calle 2

Iglesia
La Dolorosa

Avenida 10 - San

Calle 4

Calle 1

Avenida 12

Avenida 12

DOLOROSA

ANGELES

Avenida 14

Calle 10

Calle 8

Calle 6

Avenida 14

Avenida 14

Calle Central

Calle 12

Avenida 16

Clinica
Biblica

Calle 3

Calle 5

Avenida 16

Calle 7

San José

0.125 miles / 200 m

● ● ● Tour 1: Residential Area
● ● ● Tour 2: Institutional Arch
● ● ● Tour 3: Old City

Avenida 18

to American Clinic

Avenida 18

148

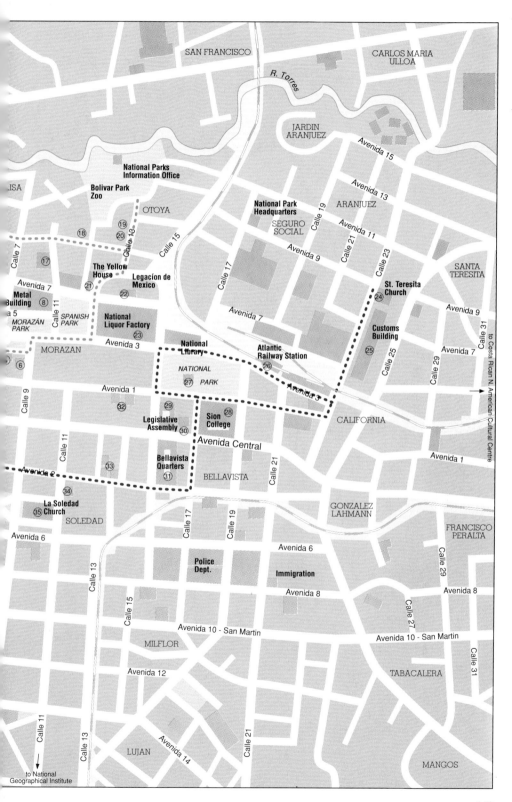

SAN FRANCISCO

CARLOS MARIA
ULLOA

R. Torres

JARDIN
ARANJUEZ

Avenida 15

National Parks
Information Office

Avenida 13

Bolivar Park
Zoo

ARANJUEZ

OTOYA

Calle 19

National Park
Headquarters

Avenida 11

SEGURO
SOCIAL

19

Calle 13

Avenida 9

18

Calle 21

20

Calle 15

Calle 23

Calle 7

SANTA
TERESITA

17

Calle 17

St. Teresita
Church

The Yellow
House

Avenida 7

24

21

Legación de
Mexico

Avenida 9

Metal
Building

8

22

Customs
Building

Calle 31

Calle 11

SPANISH
PARK

National
Liquor Factory

Avenida 7

Avenida 7

MORAZÁN
PARK

23

25

Calle 25

Avenida 3

6

MORAZAN

Avenida 3

National
Library

Atlantic
Railway Station

26

Calle 29

to Costa Rican N. American Cultural Centre

NATIONAL

27

PARK

Calle 9

Avenida 1

32

29

28

CALIFORNIA

Legislative
Assembly

Sion
College

30

Calle 11

33

Avenida Central

Calle 21

Bellavista
Quarters

Avenida 1

Avenida 2

31

BELLAVISTA

34

La Soledad
35 Church

SOLEDAD

GONZALEZ
LAHMANN

Calle 17

Calle 19

FRANCISCO
PERALTA

Avenida 6

Avenida 6

Calle 29

Police
Dept.

Immigration

Calle 13

Avenida 8

Avenida 8

Calle 15

Calle 27

Avenida 10 - San Martin

Avenida 10 - San Martin

MILFLOR

Calle 31

Avenida 12

TABACALERA

Calle 11

Calle 13

Avenida 14

Calle 21

to National
Geographical Institute

LUJAN

MANGOS

149

SAN JOSÉ

The growth, some might say the flowering, of San José, began on that day, sometime during the first half of the 19th century, when Europe decided to have its daily cup of coffee.

By the 1850s, San José was racing into a transformation that was unstoppable. Everything had to be the best, the most modern, the most European. With every bag of coffee that was exported there was a proportionate enrichment of the economic, social and cultural life of the Josefinos. As the city became wealthy, so did the needs of its inhabitants to become refined, sophisticated, worldly.

By the end of the 19th century, San José was buoyant and booming from the profits of its coffee exports. It was the third city in the world to have public electric lighting, one of the first to have public telephones, the first in Central America, perhaps in all of Latin America, to initiate free and compulsory public education to all of its citizens, and the first to allow women to attend high school. Admittedly, the roads were unpaved, but most homes of the upper classes had pianos.

Through much of the first part of the 20th century, San José continued to prosper and build: a national library, schools, bank buildings, parks and plazas, ministries, hotels, theaters, a sumptuous post office building, bookstores, hospitals, churches, a magnificent Palace of Justice, an international airport. And then, in 1956, Costa Rica's population passed the one million mark. The international focus of influence had shifted and the people ceased coveting things European and became heavily influenced by North American standards and sensibilities. Cars and trucks began to appear where there had only been the gentle horse and buggy, ox carts, pedestrians and bicycles. The population doubled over the next two decades, and by the mid-1970s, the air in San José was noticeably dirty and the once civilized, narrow streets be-

came overwhelmed with a relentless rush of cars and people who were in a hurry to get somewhere. Graceful, ornate old buildings were torn down to be replaced with harsh, brutally ugly copies of North American modern architecture. San José, the 19th century civilized city, could not adapt its physical limitations to meet the demands of its raucous 20th century people. And today the realization of this conflict is a city that, by any standards, is dense, polluted and unattractive.

Certain islands of repose remain, places to refresh and renew oneself during the struggle to find the heart of this city. There are a couple of good museums: the National Museum, located in an old military fortress between Avenida Central and Avenida Segunda, off of Calle 15; the Gold Museum, located below the Plaza de la Cultura. On Avenida Segunda, adjacent to the Plaza de la Cultura, is the National Theater, probably the most beautiful building in the country. The coffee shop in the National Theater is a favorite

Left: learning about Democracy at a political rally. *Right*: the National Youth Symphonic Orchestra.

place; quiet, elegant, yet alive. And to sit and have a *refresco natural* on the veranda of the Gran Hotel, while listening to marimba bands and the burble of 20 different languages as people from everywhere rush around the Plaza, should not be missed.

There are souvenir shops, many good theaters, many decent, but unremarkable restaurants, an abundance of cabarets and night clubs, a few surprisingly intelligent art galleries. There are also, tucked here and there, some extraordinary remnants of old San José, hints of what a handsome, delightful place this used to be, not very long ago.

And so, for those with the inclination and willingness to seek out this fallen beauty, she is still there, hiding from the stench of black diesel exhaust and the impact of too many people.

A Walking Tour: The best time to take this architectural tour, or any part of it, is on a Sunday morning, when the least amount of traffic will be found on the streets. Lacking a free Sunday morning, go early or late in the day, perhaps just before twilight, when the rush and roar of the city has quieted down. (The numbers correspond to the San José city map on pages 148-9.)

1. **The National Theater**

Neoclassic in style, with four levels, and a very well equipped stage system. Modeled after the grand Paris Opera House. Its main audience seating floor is adjustable to different heights. The floor plan is in the form of a horseshoe, and the acoustics are excellent. The detailing was done by Spanish and Italian artisans. Its construction was financed by 19th-century coffee barons, who, chagrined that there was no appropriate venue for the world renowned opera star, Adelina Patti, to perform in Costa Rica, offered to pay a tax on every bag of coffee exported, and thus ensure that one would be built. The product of this coffee tax, the National Theater, was inaugurated in 1897.

2. **The Gran Hotel**

This was originally the old French Hotel. Its original location was in the Central Park.

The crowded streets of downtown San José.

152

3. Teatro Variedades

Built in 1891 and remodeled in 1893. This was the most popular theater in San José. The first movies were shown here.

4. Residence of Jiménez de la Guardia

A perfect example of modernist style, showing sculptural elements.

5. Casa Lines

A commercial building, inspired by European models.

6. Key Largo

A very early residence built in a precise neoclassic style. Its roof is crowned with a metallic crest. Inside, the craftsmanship of its ceiling is notable.

7. Music Chapel

Ornamental architectural work; this building was constructed in 39 days. It is one of the first constructions to use pre-stressed concrete.

8. Metal Building

This enormous all-metal building was brought here by boat, in 1892, for the purpose of housing 1,000 students.

9. Alliance Francés

Originally a private home, its style is a variety of "Caribbean Victorian" architecture.

10. Casa Morisca

This eclectic residence was done in a Moorish style, which was considered the height of fashion at the beginning of this century.

11. Urban Residence

This is a particularly fine example of an early-20th century Caribbean-style building.

12. Urban Residence

Most notable in this home is the fine detailing around the windows, and the extensive decorative ceiling work.

13. Wooden Houses

These houses are notable for their well preserved condition, and for the harmonious way in which they have been adapted to the slope of the street.

14. Urban Residence

This particular residence is distinguished because of its fine treatment of the veranda.

15. House of Monseñor Rodriguez

The residence of this prelate is built in a Moorish style, and is noteworthy for

A quiet Sunday morning on the Paseo Colon, San José.

its intricate glasswork and complex plaster decoration.

16. Le Chambord
This is the best example of residential Caribbean style, with its fine treatment of the verandas, windows and columns.

17. Hotel Don Carlos
This building is exemplary because of the way in which it successfully combines the stylistic mannerisms of art deco with neoclassic forms.

18. Wooden House
This turn-of-the-century residence is very well preserved and is a beautiful example of the Caribbean style.

19. Urban Residence
This well preserved neoclassic building serves as the home of the National Dance Company.

20. L'Ambiance
This beautiful manor house has an interior patio with a corridor and fountain. Notable is some of the fine detailing with precious woods in the flooring, ceilings and baseboards. It has been converted into a hotel and restaurant.

21. The Yellow House
Originally it was the seat of the Central American Court of Justice; today it is the Ministry of External Relations. Its style is Colonial Neo-baroque.

22. Legación de México
Perfect example of Neoclassical architecture, beautifully preserved.

23. National Liquor Factory
A complete quadrant. The facade which faces Spanish Park, with its overly decorative stonework, and the east facade, are exemplary.

24. Santa Teresita Church
This church was designed in a classical style, unusual for this area.

25. Custom House
This is a somber building, made of stone and brick with a metal roof, completed shortly after the Atlantic Train Station.

26. Atlantic Train Station
After lengthy delay, which provoked great public indignation, the Costa Rica Railroad Company met its obligation and built a new train

Before the onslaught of cars, San José in the early 1930s.

terminal for the city of San José. It is built in a French style, with attic-roofing and some sculptural treatment of its balustrades.

27. National Monument

Inaugurated in 1885, this notable sculpture represents the heroic act of Juan Santamaría against the *Filibusteros* of William Walker. It was cast in France, and was shipped by steam freighter to Puerto Limón.

28. Sion College

In 1878, a French religious group arrived in Costa Rica. They founded the College of Sion, in order to educate young society women. The College building is two stories, circumscribed by corridors with Neoclassic arches and rectangular patios.

29. Legislative Assembly

This colonial style building was constructed in 1939 as a presidential house. It has been drastically transformed.

30. El Palacio Azul

This is one of the best remaining examples of residential architecture. It used to be the North American legation.

31. Bellavista Quarters

The central part of the building was built in 1870. It later became a residence and then served as barracks for the military. It was finally abandoned when the national army was abolished. Today, it serves as the National Museum.

32. Residences

This is a contiguous group of beautiful homes which are entered by means of bridges.

33. Urban Residences

This group of houses is an excellent example of urban homes of the middle class at the beginning of the century. The small lots do not allow room for front gardens. They were renovated in 1988, after the Plaza de la Democracia was built.

34. Wooden House

This is simply a lovely example of a well-constructed, well-proportioned wooden house.

35. La Soledad Church

This church was built in 1909. Its ec-

The National Theater.

lectic design is characterized by an atrium which is flanked by two symmetrical towers. In front is a small plaza where fairs were once held.

36. Upper School for Young Women
This school displays a facade which is of a harmonic neoclassical style, utilizing three kinds of windows. It has been beautifully restored by the Ministry of Culture.

37. Residence of the Archbishop
This house and the structure next to it on the corner are of a very sober, yet elegant design.

38. Cathedral and the Archbishop's Palace
The cathedral was begun during the early-18th century. Unfortunately, it was destroyed by an earthquake in 1821 and its reconstruction was only completed in 1871. Of the original structure, only the outside walls remain.

39. The Kiosk of Central Park
The kiosk represents an eclectic style.

40. Banco Anglo Bank
A solid example of commercial architecture at the turn-of-the- century.

41. The Juan Knorr Structure
This structure, built in 1914, is built in a sober Neoclassical style. It shows curved frontal structures, large cornerstones and tiled pillars. It is representative of early 20th century commercial architecture.

42. Lehmann Bookstore
Interesting structure, of a similar vintage with the Juan Knorr building.

43. Steinworth Building
A nice example of modernism, despite the fact that it is today in a somewhat dilapidated state.

44. The Casona
The Casona was formerly known as the Macaya hardware store. It is another example of exceptional commercial architecture.

45. The Church of La Merced
The church represents the Gothic style which its architect employed simultaneously with the Neoclassic.

46. San Juan de Díos Hospital
The third hospital built on this location. Its style is one of functional sobriety without superfluous ornamentation. Built in 1895.

47. Chapui Asylum
It served as a hospital for the mentally ill. Its ground plan contains pavilions and hints of the medieval Gothic.

48. Post Office Building
Its architect combined elements of lyrical French classicism and modernism. It is was built by an English construction company in 1914.

49. Del Carmen Church
The extreme nature of its facade is unusual. Also of note is its outstanding corner detailing.

50. Commercial Structure
Coming from the turn-of-the-century with characteristics similar to those of Casa Lines (Number 5), but with more simple decoration.

51. Great Lebanon Cinema
It is an excellent example of the art deco style which led the way to modern architecture, with its rectilinear decoration and cement work.

52. Central Penitentiary
This eclectic design combines medieval and military architecture. Its floorplan allows the structure to be overseen from a central vantage point.

Stacks above the Gold Museum, Plaza de la Cultura.

CITY BUSES

Buses are ubiquitous in San José. They go everywhere throughout the city and its surrounding areas. Some downtown streets are choked and clogged with them: shiny new Mercedes models, freshly washed and festively painted with murals on their rear windows; sooty, rusty wrecks emitting thick black, smoky stuff; recycled school buses from the U.S., scrupulously cared for and graced with fanciful names to give them new life.

Whether new and slick or decrepit and smoky, the buses have a common trait. They are wonderful windows into Costa Rican life. Most everyone uses them: students on their way to classes, women in heels, dressy clothes and impeccable make-up on their way to work, country folk in country clothes coming into town to do business of one kind or another, young mothers taking children to doctors' appointments at the social security hospital, men with briefcases and neat slacks and shirts. They're all on the bus, heading this way or that.

And for ten or so colones, you can climb aboard and join in the great comings and goings of life on the Central Valley. A bus ride in San José is not particularly comfortable, especially during peak hours, but there's no better or more enjoyable way to make quick and often delicious observations on Tico life and character. For one thing, chivalry is still alive. Or is it a simple sense of decency, of caring for others, a quiet courtesy? Young men will assist older men or women up the steps, a seated passenger will offer to hold your packages while you stand, someone will always offer his or her seat to an older person or a pregnant woman. The bus driver will wait for someone making a last minute dash.

Brief vignettes of Tico life on the buses:

A retarded young boy, known to the bus driver by name, boards on Paseo Colón, and for a few stops, become the bus' official door-opener. Then the boy tires of the game and, saying goodbye to the driver, leaps off at the next stop.

A very old *campesino*, returning a trip to the city, takes a long time to board. He carries a heavy burlap bag, redolent of coffee and pejibaye.

A small girl in a rumpled pink dress enters the parked bus, waiting for its scheduled departure at the Coca Cola bus stop. She speaks to the driver, then stands at the front of the bus, singing a mournful song about love. When she finishes, she moves down the aisle with an open hand, into which we drop our small change.

Take at least one bus ride in San José. Board near the beginning of the line, when you can still get a seat, and watch the rush of humanity come aboard, pausing to place their fare in the driver's hand, pushing past the turnstile, greeting friends and neighbors as they make their way down the aisle, more passengers stop after stop, until it isn't possible to squeeze another body on.

Or take a bus in the middle of the day, when things are somewhat less harried and you can observe the city passing by. Catch a bus downtown, on one of the streets near the National Theatre and ride it to wherever it goes and back. Or if you speak a little Spanish, ask people on the street or bus drivers for a little direction, and catch a bus to wherever you're heading. ∎

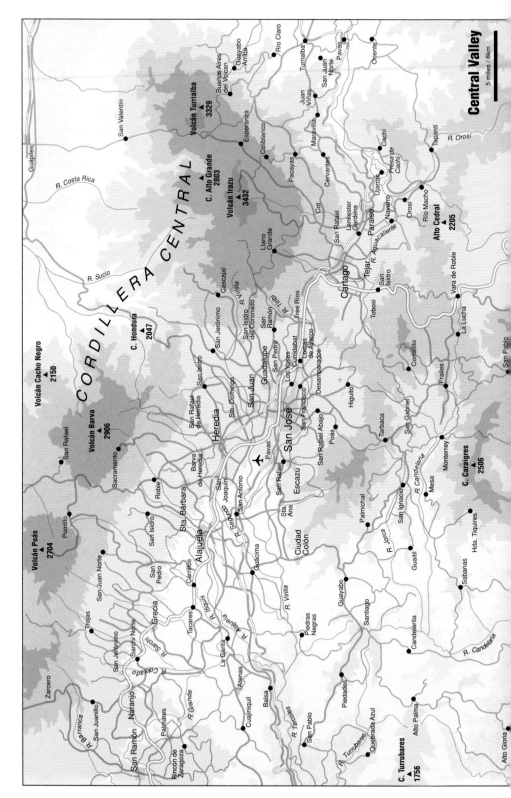

Central Valley

5 miles / 8km

THE CENTRAL VALLEY

The Central Valley is the heart of Costa Rica. It is here, high in the temperate, green highlands, that 60 percent of the country's population lives. In the Central Valley is located the seat of government, the agricultural and commercial centers, the oldest cities, the coffee farms which put Costa Rica on the map, the architectural treasures, the churches, the theaters, the universities and the high cultural life of the country.

The Central Valley *(Valle Central)* or Central Plateau *(Mesteta Central)* as it often called, is neither, strictly speaking, a valley nor a plateau, as it contains both valleys and plateaus. Central Highlands might be a more apt name for this area, only 15 miles by 40 miles, where two major mountain ranges meet, an area of of rich volcanic hills and river-filled valleys where altitudes range from 2,600 to 4,000 feet (800 to 1,500 meters).

The countryside is unsurpassingly beautiful and variable. The climate is salubrious. The air is sweet and soft. The people are friendly, dignified and independent. Volcanoes, some still active and smoking, others dormant or extinct, rise up above the hills around the valley, and above them, a big sky, constantly changing, as dark, charcoal rain clouds, intense, searing patches of blue, fluffy white cumulus, and occasional rainbows, come and go.

There are misty, almost enchanted places like the Orosi Valley or dusty farm towns like Santa Ana, adobe villages that sing of old Costa Rica, such as Barva, and crowded, noisy, relentlessly vital cities, like San José or Cartago. And they're all easily accessible. Daytrips by bus or rented car, or with tour groups can be easily arranged.

Passing through the small, highland towns and villages, one sees what in Central America is an impressive sight: people living in small houses on plots of land which they themselves own and farm. Neighborhoods are often a hodgepodge of larger, fancy homes and small, humble ones. Housewives in housedresses and aprons chat in front yards as they watch their babies. Children in school uniforms talk and play together as they walk up the road for lunch at home. Produce from back yard fruit trees and gardens is for sale on little tables or stands in front of houses: strawberries and berry preserves, homemade farmer's cheese and sour cream, oranges, candied, stuffed grapefruit, mangoes and tomatoes. Visitors to shops and stands, restaurants and parks, are accepted with a mild, easy curiosity. No one seems especially surprised to have a gringo walk into the local *soda* and order *arroz con pollo* (chicken and rice).

San José, Alajuela, Cartago and Heredia are the largest and most important cities of the Central Valley. San José, the capital, is the premier city of the country, a sophisticated and vital center, noted for its national symphony orchestra and highly respected dance and theater companies. It has a vibrant

night life, flourishing markets, impressive museums and galleries, and many international restaurants and hotels, some with spas, workout facilities and casinos. Surprises attesting to the internationality of Josefinos are found throughout the city: delicious German dark and wholegrain breads, Italian cheeses, afalfa sprouts and baby vegetables are available in supermarkets, a radio station plays American and British favorites of the 1950s, 60s and 70s, vegetarian restaurants and "health food" stores, a sushi bar, and an art movie theater showing international films.

Radiating out from San José are busy Central Valley towns and suburbs, each with its own flavor and identity: historic Escazú, bland Rohrmoser, exclusive Los Yoses with its lovely old residences, San Pedro, home of the University of Costa Rica and many good restaurants. There are also 4 national parks to explore, several volcanoes to climb and one of the country's most important archaeological sites to visit. Most of these places of interest in the Central

Valley are reachable from San José in an hour or two.

Though most travelers come here between December and March, to escape the winter chill of North America and Europe, these months are Costa Rica's dry season, its "summer." Frequent travelers to the area know that it is the rainy season in Costa Rica, with its afternoon downpours and dramatic displays of lightning, when the Central Valley is at is magnificent best: lush, green, bursting with life and color, and best of all, the air and the city itself is kept clean by a daily bath.

Day Trip to Poás Volcano: Poás Volcano National Park, the most developed of all the parks, is a popular attraction. It is only 25 miles (37 km) from San José on good roads leading through the city of Alajuela. Poás can become crowded and cloudy, so it's best to visit early in the day when views are better and before the crowds arrive. The cool freshness of the air as one ascends the mountain is invigorating, but it can get chilly, rainy or breezy, so dress appropriately.

A map of the nature trails is available at the Visitor's Center. Audio-visual presentations are given in the auditorium on Sundays. From a lookout point above the crater, there is an overview of the volcano, which in May of 1989, shot ash a mile into the air. The main crater, which is 1 mile wide (1.5 km) and 984 feet deep (300 meters), is one of the largest in the world. Poás, unlike Irazú and Arenal Volcanoes, does not today have violent eruptions and is one of the more accessible active volcanoes on the continent. She is active in 40-year cycles and is currently producing acid-like rain and sulphurous gases. When the sulfur gas emissions become too strong, the park is closed. Even when open, the park recommends that visitors not stay more than 20 minutes near the crater.

Well-maintained trails take one through a vivid landscape rich with wildflowers and a great variety of mosses, bromeliads and ferns. Many frogs and toads live in the park and some, especially the tree frogs, are extremely colorful. After wandering through this wonderland, descend from the park to one of the restaurants for lunch and enjoy typical Costa Rican food, including *fresas en leche,* local strawberries blended with milk and a bit of ice, or stop at one of the many roadside stands to buy strawberry preserves and cookies made by local women. To spend more time in the fresh, mountain air, consider an overnight at **Albergue Volcán Poás.**

As one descends 200 meters into **Alajuela**, population 127,772, it becomes warmer. Join old-timers in the central park, amidst an orchard of mango and other mature trees, while they engage in their favorite pastime of assigning not always flattering nicknames to passersby. Here the Festival of Mangoes is held for 9 days in July. Alajuela is the birthplace of Juan Santamaría, the young Costa Rican whose courage was responsible for the routing of William Walker and his *fillibusteros* from Costa Rica in 1856. **The Juan Santamaría Museum** in the former jail, one block from the central park, tells his story.

East of Hacienda Los Reyes in La Guacima in Alajuela, is **The Butterfly Farm.** This 4 acre enterprise is a breeding farm for over 500 different kinds of exotic butterflies, which are exported by the tens of thousands to a waiting market in Europe. The Butterfly Farm is full of wonder, with its waterfall, extensive tropical plantings, and the endless color variations of the butterflies themselves. Open to the public every day of the week. Tours are at 9:00 a.m., noon and 3 p.m.

From Alajuela, take the old highway towards the Pacific to reach La Garita, which, among several other places in Costa Rica, boasts the best climate in the country. **La Garita** is expansive and green, filled with lovely homes and gardens, fields of dark green coffee bushes and plant nurseries *(viveros)* where visitors are very welcome. Stop at a nursery and walk through rows of magnificent ferns, palms, ficus and flowering plants. The restaurant **La Fiesta del Máiz,** open on weekends, is something of an anthropological experience. It features the near-endless variety of

Poas volcano, in an active phase.

dishes that Ticos make from corn. Customers can sample them all. Nearby are **Zoo-Ave**, an aviary of birds indigenous to Costa Rica, and **Bosque Encantado**, which encompasses a lake surrounded by a medieval castle, fairy tale figures, playhouses and horseback riding trails.

On the way back to San José is the *Ojo de Agua* (Eye of Water), where a subterranean river gushes a staggering amount of water through the earth, filling several swimming pools on its way to becoming drinking water for the town of Puntarenas. Painted in faded pinks and aquas, with the grassy areas, pools and lakes not quite as well maintained as one might wish, Ojo de Agua gives the impression of having seen better days; still, it is a pleasant place to stop for a swim or a walk, and on weekends, when it is very crowded, to get a great glimpse of San José's working class at leisure. Ojo de Agua has served as a barometer for the effects of deforestation in Costa Rica: the water table has been dramatically low at the end of recent dry seasons.

Day Trip to Heredia: A day trip to the province of Heredia, the center of Costa Rica's coffee production, quickly takes one out of the heat and clatter of San José. Without going more than 15 miles (24 km) from the city, one can walk in an evergreen forest or cloud forest reserve rivaling those of much more remote and inaccessible areas.

Santo Domingo de Heredia, midway between San José and the city of Heredia, has been designated by the United Nations as one of the best places in the world to live, although it is difficult to ascertain what criteria were used. Here many of the colonial houses have been restored.

Heredia, population 55,000, and just 6 miles (9 km) from San José, has been called *La Cuidad de los Flores* (The City of Flowers). The city was first settled in 1706 by Spaniards, and is famous for having the largest number of blue-eyed people in Costa Rica. The newer section of Heredia looks like many Third World cities, with dangling wires and electrical signs advertising Lucky Strike and

A Sunday soccer match brings out the town.

Pepsi hanging across the streets. Many stores full of merchandise suggest that this coffee-rich area is affluent, and indeed, by Costa Rican standards, it is. **The National University** is located in Heredia; it turns out the nation's teachers and has one of the best veterinarian schools in Latin America. The old town center, with an adobe museum building and lovely church, is being partially restored and is a pleasant place to stroll.

The **basilica**, constructed in 1796, is adorned with bells brought from Cuzco, Peru. Inside, a statue of the Virgin Mary stands surrounded by neon stars and a crescent moon. In contrast, stained glass from Europe depicts scenes from the life of Christ, the faces of the apostles delicately painted, their passions illuminated by natural light.

In the park in front of the basilica, surrounded by several historic adobes, a kiosk provides a concert hall for the local band which twice a week offers selections of the music of John Philip Souza and various European composers.

Take the road to **San Rafael** and be-gin the ascent into the mountains from there. Villas above the town are architecturally Swiss Alpine, often down to Tyrolean paintings on the shutters. Driving through here, there is the feeling of having suddenly entered into an Austrian watercolor landscape. Wealthy Ticos of earlier generations were traditionally educated in Europe and returned to their country with a great appreciation for the architecture of Northern Europe, which one often sees expressed in this cool, mountain area. Now, many young Ticos go to graduate schools in North American universities, and cultural affinities are changing.

The temperature drops dramatically above San Rafael, where **El Castillo Country Club**, another surprise, is open to all who pay the admission fee. It offers the only ice skating rink in Central America, a large indoor pool, a gym, go-carts, and a miniature train. A large restaurant with impressive views over a cypress forest to San José and the Central Valley and mountains beyond, serves lunch and dinner. Huge fireplaces in the

Planting new coffee bushes, near Alajuela.

dining room further the impression that one has wandered beyond equatorial regions and into northern Europe. A castle on the grounds was built by a past Costa Rican Minister of Foreign Affairs.

The road beyond El Castillo continues to **Monte de la Cruz,** where a small shrine sits in a private forest reserve. For Sunday hikers from San Rafael, far below, this is a favorite destination .

Proceed downhill to the fork and turn back uphill to El Tirol. People stroll the roads of Costa Rica, especially on Sundays, the traditional day for visiting with family. Bus service is reduced on Sundays, further necessitating walking. Tico drivers are used to sharing the roads with pedestrians, but foreigners in rental cars can find these driving conditions difficult.

Tell the Guard at El Tirol gatehouse that you are going to **Hotel Chalet Tirol** and drive through a residential area of weekend cottages and retirement homes set in alpine fields. A good road leads through a cypress forest where sun fil-ters warmly through branches and dapples meadow wild flowers.

Hotel Chalet Tirol sits in the middle of a cloud forest reserve bordering Braulio Carrillo National Park. A fern-choked trail winding under orchid and bromeliad-laden old trees allows visitors to hike several hours through the cloud reserve to the border of the national park. Back at the hotel, hewn wooden steps, lovely water colors, a charming bar, European furniture and a menu in French welcome the weary hiker. Among the restaurant's specialties are baked camembert cheese with wild blackberry sauce, and Norwegian smoked salmon. A grove of A-frame wooden cottages await those who choose to spend the night.

Descending, the warmth of the valley below is welcome. The road to S**an José de las Montañas** is lined with flowers grown for export. On the road above San José de las Montañas in wonderfully fresh, cool mountain air, is **El Pórtico Hotel**, offering conference rooms, a tv and game room, pool, jacuzzi, sauna, a comfortable

Inside the Basilica de Nuestra Señora de Los Angeles.

bar and dining room and acres of green hills with hiking trails.

In **Barva de Heredia**, founded in 1561, colonial-era adobes surrounding the central park are being restored, giving the entire area the feeling of a colonial town. Standing on the steps in front of the adobe **Basilica de Barva** (1797) and looking out over the red tile-roofed adobe houses to the mountains beyond, one gets a sense of Central Valley life in the 1700s. At the **Coffee Museum** one can learn about coffee production. If you have a chance during your travels in coffee country, taste the ripe, red fruit which surrounds the coffee bean. It is surprisingly sweet and good.

Beyond the cathedral is the small **Grotto of the Virgin of Lourdes** (1913). Artisans from Barva produce bamboo and palm market baskets, baskets used by coffee pickers, and fruit and bread baskets, which they often sell by the roadsides.

There is a road to **Barva Volcano**, that runs just above the town of Barva de Heredia, and then through San José de la Montaña and on towards Sacramento. This volcano is actually on the western side of Braulio Carrillo National Park. Camping facilities are located near the park entrance, and from there its a good hike to the crater lake.

Take a short detour before heading back to San José and have a meal in **Santa Barbara de Heredia** at **El Banco de Mariscos**, a popular seafood restaurant. The family of El Banco owns its own fishing boat and brings the day's catch up the mountains in iced trucks. Offering good seafood at reasonable prices, the restaurant fills quickly at mealtimes and becomes noisy and cheerful. There is often a line outside the front door. Best to arrive early unless you enjoy the hubbub. Servings are large: you might want to order half-portions (*medianos*).

Not far from El Banco is the exceptional **Finca Rosa Blanca Inn**, considered by many the best small hotel in Costa Rica. It is certainly the most extraordinary, and the resident owners' attention to detail and care of their guests

The volcanic fields on the slopes of Irazú.

is a model for Costa Rica and the rest of the world.

The roads in this area criss-cross and are not at all well-marked. Even Josefinos taking Sunday drives have to stop passersby and ask, "Is this the road to ____?" Asking directions is part of the process of driving in Costa Rica and puts one in touch with people on the street. Their responsiveness and helpfulness is impressive.

Gardens and Valley: Another interesting day trip takes one to Lankester Gardens and the Orosi Valley via **Cartago** (population 87,125). Cartago, located 14 miles from San José, was the capital of Costa Rica until 1823, when it lost capital-city status to San José. Its illustrious colonial past is obscured, though, since repeated earthquakes and eruptions of Irazú Volcano have destroyed most of the colonial buildings. Throughout their history, Cartagans have attempted to build a temple to Saint James the Apostle, patron saint of Spain. The first church, begun in 1562 was finished in 1570,

and was one of 2 churches in the entire country. When it was destroyed, a stronger building was built in 1580 on the same site. This too was leveled by the trembling earth. Subsequent churches met the same fate and when Cartago's massive cathedral, begun early in the 20th century, was toppled by the 1910 earthquake, all efforts to rebuild were abandoned. The roofless walls with their empty Gothic windows still stand. The site, called **Las Ruinas** (The Ruins) is now a garden with a small pond and is a popular and romantic spot.

Cartago, once the center of Costa Rican culture, is still her religious center. The enormous **Basilica de Nuestra Señora de los Angeles** (Basilica of Our Lady of the Angels), a Byzantine structure that dominates the landscape for miles, was built in honor of Costa Rica's patron saint, *La Negrita*. The origins of the basilica are rooted in the miraculous. In 1635, a young girl walking through the forest that once grew on the site of the basilica discovered a dark-skinned

The ruins at Ujarrás.

statue of the Virgin Mary. A priest carried the statue, called *La Negrita*, to the parish church, but it mysteriously returned, twice, to its location in the forest. In 1926 the Catholic Church built a basilica on the spot to house the statue. A room full of abandoned crutches, plaster casts and other paraphernalia testify to the cures effected by *La Negrita.* Water from the spring behind the church is also said to have healing powers: the faithful go there to fill bottles and jars. On the saint's day, August second, thousands of pilgrims gather at the basilica. Many walk from San José, making the last part of the journey on their knees. Some walk from Panamá and Nicaragua. On that day, the image of the black virgin is carried to another church in Cartago and then, in a solemn procession, through the city and back to its shrine in the basilica.

From Cartago it is a short trip to the **Lankester Gardens** in **Paraíso de Cartago**. It is said that Paraíso (Paradise) was named by weary Spaniards moving inland from the Atlantic coast

The Atlantic Railway winds through Cartago.

who found Paraíso's cooler weather and lack of malarial mosquitoes paradisiacal. English botanist Charles Lankester, sent to Costa Rica by a British company to work with coffee planting, arrived in 1900 at the age of 21, and when the coffee venture failed, he decided to stay. He bought 37 acres (15 hectares) of land to preserve local flora, especially orchids and bromeliads, and to regenerate a natural forest. Today Lankester Gardens is run by the University of Costa Rica, where hundreds of species of orchids attract large numbers of species of birds. February through April are peak flowering months. The gardens are open daily from 9:30 a.m. to 3:30 p.m.

South of Cartago the landscape becomes green, misty and almost magical, especially during the verdant rainy season. At **Ujarrás**, in a beautiful site, are the ruins of a 17th-century church with an interesting history:

The first place of worship constructed in this region was not the church, but a shrine in honor of the Virgin del Rescate de Ujarrás, who, in 1565 appeared to an

Indian fishing on the banks of the Reventazón River. The apparition came from inside a small trunk. The Indian carried the trunk to the center of Ujarrás, but by the time he got there, the trunk had become so heavy that even a dozen men could not lift it. The phenomenon was interpreted by the Franciscan fathers as a sign that the virgin wanted them to construct a shrine on that spot, to be used by the Indians and the Spanish, and so it was constructed.

A hundred years later, in 1666, the story goes, a band of pirates led by the notorious Mansfield and Morgan landed on the Atlantic Coast of Costa Rica with the intention of sacking the country. The Spanish governor, Juan Lopez de la Flor, assembled all available fighting men and sent everyone else to the mission to pray. The pirates came inland as far as Turrialba and then, mysteriously, abruptly turned back. Some say the pirates were tricked by de la Flor, who had posted the few men and guns they were in possession of at strategic points in the hills and then leaked the word that

there was an ambush awaiting the pirates. A few gunshots from different points caused them to believe the ruse and retreat. Other accounts say their retreat was a miracle worked by the Virgin. The grateful townspeople built the church of Ujarrás to commemorate the miracle. The church was destroyed a hundred years later by an earthquake. Its remains stand among gardens and trees with hanging streamers of Spanish moss.

A few kilometers beyond Orosi, the **Cachí Hydroelectric Dam** channels waters from a reservoir on the Reventazón and Orosi Rivers, into an immense spillway. A curtain of water slides down a vertical face, and out with an astonishing explosion of foam and spray into a heavily forested gorge in the Reventazón River. The concrete dam structure itself contrasts sharply with the lush natural terrain around it, and the power of the rushing water with the peace of river. **Charrarra**, near the dam, is a recreational site with a pool, restaurant, lakeside trails and boating on the lake.

Just up the road towards Orosi, some three miles (5 km) north of the Motel Río restaurant, on the bank of the river, is a simple, two-story cane house surrounded by primitive wooden sculpture. Macedonio Quesada, a sparkling, 64-year old sculptor, with absolutely no teeth filling his enormous grin, lives and works there in the beautiful countryside. As a visiting artist/professor at the University of Costa Rica, Macedonio took university classes, received an honorary degree and taught students for many years. His work can be seen in galleries around San José, and a large collection of it can be viewed at his studio/home where visitors are cordially welcomed.

The town of **Orosi**, untouched by the earthquakes which have leveled the colonial structures of Cartago, retains the look of an earlier Costa Rica. Visit the colonial church, take a walk around town, have a snack at one of the *sodas* or go to the **Los Patios Thermal Baths** for a therapeutic soak in the warm, mineral waters.

Just above the valley, there is a look-

The spillway at Cachí dam.

out site *(mirador)* and park, maintained by the ICT (Costan Rican Institute of Tourism). Its 3 acres of sloping, well-trimmed lawns provide spectacular views of the Reventazón River with Cachí to the left and Orosi to the right. It is a perfect spot to pause for a picnic and a walk.

Tapantí Wildlife Refuge: The upper part of the **Orosi Valley** has enormous rainfall, rendering it unsuited for agriculture: thus it still has magnificent virgin rainforest. **Tapantí Wildlife Refuge** protects the rivers which supply San José with water and electricity. It also offers great birdwatching, fishing and river swimming. Birdwatchers will want to get an early start and arrive in Tapantí when the park opens at 6 a.m. The drive from San José takes about 1.5 hours and is especially beautiful in the dawn.

Trails are well-marked in the lower part of the refuge. Oropendulas, black, raven-sized birds with yellow tail feathers and stout ivory-colored bills, nest in colonies within the refuge. Clusters of 30 or more pendulous nests hang from branches high in the trees. Two eggs are laid by the oropendula females, but parasitic giant cowbirds, like the cuckoo, steal a spot in the nest for their own eggs, letting oropendula females raise their chicks. An exchange is effected, however, as the baby cowbirds, which feed on botflies, keep the baby oropendulas free from these parasites. One usually hears oropendulas before seeing them. The males let out a gurgling, liquid song and bow to the females in courtship displays.

The creek paralleling **Oropendula** Trail is filled with smooth, warm boulders which invite hikers to sit, cool their feet in the water, and perhaps lie back for a mid-morning snooze in the sun. Tapantí is open every day except Thursday and Friday. It is always advisable to have a guide on the trails. Call ahead to make arrangements with one of the refuge guards to accompany you on your walk.

Turrialba, CATIE and Guayabo National Monument: Turrialba is an active town,

Sculptor Macedonio Quesada laughs at life.

its streets and parks bustling with people of all ages, talking, yelling, buying, selling. The open fruit and vegetable market which lines the sidewalk in front of the railroad station features some of the freshest and best-looking produce available in Costa Rica, most of it grown in the hills above town. Turrialba's reputation as a whitewater river rafting center is growing and rafters and kayakers from all over the world are discovering the Reventazón and Pacuare Rivers. Just a few miles beyond the town of Turrialba on the highway is **CATIE**, the **Centro Agronómico Tropical de Investigación y Enseñanza** (Center for Tropical Agronomy Research and Teaching). On this 2,000 acre (808 hectare) research plantation, scientists are experimenting with the introduction of more than 5,000 varieties of 335 species of crops with economic potential. Over 2,500 varieties of coffee, 450 varieties of cacao, as well as many varieties of bananas and pejibaye palms are part of the seed bank of CATIE. Additionally, work is being done here on the critical problems of deforestation, overgrazing and the sensitive ecology of the river basins. They prefer that visitors come with a group. Guides demonstrate the cultivation, processing and care of palms, coffee, cacao, and orchids.

There are not many accommodations in Turrialba valley, but visitors to CATIE and the surrounding areas usually stay at the **Hotel Wagelia** or at the basic **Hotel Interamericano**. In the mountains above the valley, not far away, is the **Turrialtico**, with a couple of rooms with private bath, and the **Pochotel**, which has cabins with views to the Caribbean Coast.

Guayabo National Monument, the site of a large pre-Columbian city, is located on the slopes of Turrialba Volcano. Although only 11 miles (19 km) from Turrialba, it's a 40-minute trip, the last part of it on unpaved roads. It is thought that 10,000 people lived at the Guayabo site from 1000 B.C. to A.D. 1400, when they abandoned it for some unknown reason. A park ranger at the

Symbiosis of oxen and egret.

entrance provides a guide to take visitors through the excavated area, which contains a complex system of stone aqueducts, house foundations and roadways amidst a setting of guava trees, wild impatiens and clusters of oropendula nests. The guide will point out stone-lined graves, now empty, which served as the first indication to archaeologists that a city site was nearby. As well, there are several large petrographs, the significance of which can only be speculated upon.

Display rooms in the park show archaeologists' conceptions of what Guayabo looked like when it was a flourishing city.

As do many of the parks of Costa Rica, Guayabo suffers a shortage of funds for its conservation and excavation work. Some funding comes from a special one-colon tax on each box of bananas exported from Costa Rica.

Guayabo National Monument is open on weekends from 9 a.m. to 4 p.m., but if one calls during the week, the ranger may be able to arrange for a guide to show visitors through the site. All visitors to the excavation site must be accompanied by a guide. Bring sweaters and raingear, as rains and cool mists are frequent. Camping is permitted in the park, but not at the archaeological site.

Not far from the park is **La Calzada,** a restaurant and small hotel which accommodates visitors who wish to spend more than an afternoon at Guayabo.

On the way back to Cartago stop for rest and refreshment in the village of **Cervantes** at **La Posada de la Luna**. Hernan Luna, the *simpático* owner of La Posada, has an eclectic collection of rare artifacts, curiosities and plain old junk stored in glass cases and hanging from the walls of the restaurant: pre-Columbian jade beads, copper and gold pieces, carved stone heads, rusty old swords, two-man saws, antique kitchen utensils and early transistor radios. Buy some cookies fresh from the oven, or try a fruit drink and a large, handmade tortilla with local sour cream.

This area of the Costa Rica is known for growing the best pejibayes in the

Farmlands on the Meseta Central.

country; if you pass a house with clusters of plum-sized orange fruit hanging outside for sale, stop and see if the seller has a few cooked ones for sale. (Pejibayes must be boiled for some time before eating.) Peel the skin and eat the fruit. Many people like to dip them in mayonnaise, like artichoke hearts.

Day Trip to Irazú Volcano: Irazú Volcano National Park is accessible from Cartago. From the 11,000 foot (3,800 meters) summit, it is possible on a clear day, to see both the Atlantic and the Pacific. Irazú last erupted on 19 March, 1963, the day of the arrival of President John F. Kennedy in Costa Rica on an official visit, one of his last visits to a foreign country before his assassination. For 2 years, Irazú continued to shower ash over much of the Central Valley. People carried umbrellas to protect themselves. Ash piled up on the Reventazón River causing it to flood and destroy 300 homes. Roofs caved in from the weight of the ash. San José was black.

A visit to Irazú is a relatively easy half-day journey. Visitors can go to the top ridge, walk along the rim of the main crater and look across an other-worldly landscape consisting of a brilliant green lake, black and gray slopes punctuated here and there with white steam jetting into the air, from fissures in the rock.

Day Trip to Braulio Carrillo National Park: **Braulio Carrillo National Park** can be reached only 45 minutes from downtown San José. Take the highway to Limón and turn off before the Zurqui tunnel at signs to the park. Or take the entrance 11 miles (17 kms) beyond the tunnel at La Botella trail, where the grade is not so steep and strenuous. Trails are often muddy and snakes have been sighted. Wear boots and bug repellent.

Braulio Carrillo National Park, 172 square miles of mostly primary forest, was founded in 1978 at the urging of environmentalists who feared that the opening of a highway between San José and Guápiles would provide loggers and developers with access to rapidly vanishing virgin forest. Deforestation

Overlooking Irazú's crater.

had followed the opening of many other roads throughout the country. A compromise was reached: the road would go through, but the 80,000 acres (32,320 hectares) of virgin forest surrounding the highway would be preserved in a park. The park thus embodies some ideals of enlightened progress.

Braulio Carrillo contains 5 distinctly separate forest habitats, dominated by the wet tropical forest. Hundreds of varieties of orchids and ferns and almost every variety of bird native to Costa Rica are found here. In order to understand the life cycles, and to spot the camouflaged wildlife and avoid missing hidden spectacular vistas, before going arrange for a guide through the National Parks service or an eco-tourism agency. A 1½ hour circular trail begins behind the kiosk. Here there is a chance, albeit a small one, of seeing the Resplendent Quetzal, the neotropics' most spectacular bird. Odds of a sighting are improved by going between March and May, the mating season, and entering the park at dawn. The lingering impression of

Braulio Carrillo is of vastness: huge canyons, misty mountains and the ubiquitous broad-leaf plant, the Poor Man's Umbrella, covering the hillsides.

A pleasant and refreshing few hours can be spent hiking along the **Carretera Carrillo**, an abandoned highway built in 1881, and paved in stone, connecting the Central Valley with the Atlantic Railway. Today after running for 6 miles (9 km) the road terminates at Braulio Carrillo, to which there is no entrance at this point. Its worn stones carried a stream of oxcarts loaded with coffee to the train to be taken to Limón and then abroad. From San José take the road through Moravia and then beyond to San Jeronimo, where you will find the cobblestones that indicate the Carretera Carrillo.

The Western Suburbs Of San José: On the west side of San José are the suburbs of Pavas, Rohrmoser, Escazú, Santa Ana and a large metropolitan park with sports facilities called La Sabana.

La Sabana Park is on the site of San Jose's outgrown international airport.

In the Sabana is the **National Stadium**, a small lake, the **National Art Museum**, an Olympic-sized swimming pool, well-used tennis, volleyball and basketball courts, jogging and walking paths, and several soccer and baseball fields. La Sabana is alive with thousands of Ticos every Sunday. During the week it can be a quiet place for walks. Across from the National Art Museum is Soda *Tapia*, a good place for typical Costa Rican food and fruit drinks.

The rather colorless, modern suburbs of **Rohrmoser** and **Pavas** are distinguished by the presence of the United States Embassy and AID Building. Many diplomatic personnel live along the wide, nearly treeless streets of Rohrmoser, in modern houses protected by wrought iron grillwork. Plaza Mayor, a new shopping center in Rohrmoser is especially slick and well stocked and serves the community which lives there.

Escazú was originally a crossroads on trails between Indian villages. Because water was abundant there, the Indians found it a good place to spend the night on their journeys, and gave it its name, which in their language meant "resting place."

Spanish settlers were also attracted to Escazú: they settled in the hills and began farming. It was during these early days that Escazú became known as the city of the witches and many say there are witches living there still, who will, for a fee, tell one's fortune or concoct a love potion.

Today Escazú is an interesting if sometimes chaotic blend of Old Costa Rica and a modern, international community. The town center has adobe buildings, a nice church and soccer field and the feeling of a sleepy, *campesino* town where neighbors have known each other for generations. Just outside of town, however, are enclaves of fancy homes owned by North Americans and Europeans, drawn to Escazú by the agreeable climate and beautiful views. Here new BMWs zoom past painted oxcarts pulled by stately pairs of oxen. Horses and cows, broken loose from their tethers, wander in the highway

A *campesino* awaits the bus to town.

crowded with buses and cars. High tech buildings of white plaster and shiny metal stand next to funky *sodas* and small fruit stands.

Above the town of Escazú is a smaller village, **San Antonio de Escazú**, which, every March, holds an oxcart festival, called the *Dia de los Boyeros*. Almost 100 painted carts, some nearly a century old, and the great oxen which haul them, plus hundreds of *campesinos*, and thousands of visitors, gather on the San Antonio soccer field in front of the church for this annual festival.

A splendidly theatrical hotel, **The Tara**, with its tall white columns and architecture straight from the pages of *Gone With the Wind*, suggests another time and place, as it sits on a hillside above San Antonio de Escazú. Also high in these hills is the more modest **Pico Blanco Inn**, with its own impressive views of the Central Valley.

San Rafael de Escazú is a newer section of town along the highway to Santa Ana. It has several shiny commercial centers with international stores, supermarkets, restaurants and glitzy interior decor shops. Outside of San Rafael on the road to Santa Ana, there is a large walled compound with lights, guards and surveillance paraphernalia. It isn't a high security penitentiary. It's the residence of the United States ambassador to Costa Rica.

There is a distinctly rural atmosphere in **Santa Ana**, a town famous for its onions, which hang braided on the lintels and eaves of restaurants and stands along the road. On the downward grade leading into town, **El Estribo,** an Argentine open-air restaurant specializes in beef, roasted onions and strolling mariachi musicians.

A walk around the outskirts of the downtown take one past traditional adobes in various states of decay and old wooden houses covered with bouganvillia and lush tropical foliage. Enormous trees grow in yards. Dogs sleep in the middle of the roads. Across from the church, next to the bank in a small, open-front *fruteria*, a pleasant man sells fruit, baked goodies and a delicious fresh fruit punch. On the other side of town, toward the freeway entrance, are stands selling pottery, baskets, local fruit and onions.

Above Santa Ana is the small village of **Salitral**, where mineral spring water, once bottled and sold, still bubbles up through a pipe in the ground.

Cuidad Colón can be reached by backroads from Santa Ana, through rolling hills, or by way of the freeway. It's best known perhaps to those who have come to inspect La Universidad para la Paz, **the University for Peace,** which is on a well-marked road not far out of town. The University for Peace, sponsored by the United Nations to study the ways of peace, and to offer a counter to the teachings of the war colleges, offers graduate courses to students from all over the world.

Returning to Santa Ana via back roads, one passes **La Cabriola,** a popular weekend restaurant and picnic site where horses can be rented. The food at La Cabriola is nothing special, but the gently rolling hills above it are beautiful and perfect for riding.

The building of the Atlantic Railway, described by knowledgeable railroad engineers as "the most difficult damned piece of railroading in the world," was quite a story; and it was one that, in many ways, would affect the life of Costa Rica, for a very long time.

By 1850, coffee in Costa Rica was big business and was becoming the most important source of income for the small nation. The government, composed primarily of members of the coffee oligarchy, knew that it would have to find a way to more easily get its coffee to ships in deepwater ports, if it was to enter fully into competition for international markets. At the time, Costa Rica's coffee could only reach its buyers in Europe by first being hauled to the Pacific Coast port of Puntarenas, and from there shipped around Cape Horn, on the southern tip of South America. Just transporting it from the Central Valley plateau by burro and cart to the seaport was difficult enough. Finally, a railway was built toward the Pacific, but it was a public joke, a cartoon train that could barely make it over its 10 mile run, and it was dubbed the "*burro-carril*." It was, nonetheless, a time when everyone was in love with trains, and one of Chief-of-State Tomás Guardia's most significant acts, in 1871, was to award a contract to someone who would build a railway to the Atlantic.

The job of building the 120-mile long railway was ultimately awarded to a U.S. citizen, Minor Cooper Keith. Though he was young and had but a grade school education, Minor Keith was charismatic, a "wheeler-dealer," tough, persistent, somewhat larcenous, a capitalist adventurer: he was, perhaps, uniquely qualified to do the job. It was said that he had the "heart of a benevolent pirate," and many felt that that was requisite to get the seemingly impossible task done.

This railroad construction project from the Central Valley to the Caribbean coast, along a rugged mountainous route through some of the country's most formidable jungle, was to connect Alajuela and Limón. Its construction overburdened the Costa Rican government with an enormous debt. The world was watching, and it had to be completed. To continue the development of the railway, more than eight million dollars were borrowed from British banks. The bankers took obvious advantage of the financially unsophisticated Central Americans, and the resultant strain on the Costa Rican economy lasted for over 40 years.

Completed in 1890, in the construction of its first 20 miles alone, it cost the lives of more than 4,000 workers. Decimated by disease and impossible working conditions, the Costa Rican railway workers finally refused to work outside of the Central Valley and so Keith began to recruit first Chinese and Italian laborers for his work crews, and then blacks from the West Indies. The West Indian workers, mostly Jamaicans, were thought to be immune to the malaria and yellow fever that

were then raging out of control in the tropical lowlands.

Keith renegotiated the bank debts with the British bankers, and, in gratitude, was given the concessions to the railway and an outright grant of 800,000 acres of land, adjoining the railway route between the Central Valley and the Atlantic Coast. It was nearly seven percent of the entire national territory. In exchange for this extraordinary grant, Keith was to cultivate the land, and mortgage some of it, thereby raising additional capital with which to complete the Atlantic Railroad. He succeeded in establishing banana plantations along the right-of-way adjacent to the tracks, and in so doing, he created the beginning of Costa Rica's banana industry. Some of the first freight to be rolled along what was then Keith's own privately owned new railroad line, were crops from his own banana plantation holdings. The easy success of the banana venture quickly attracted foreign capital and exports of the fruit increased rapidly. Furthermore, the government imposed no export tax on the fruit company until 1903.

In 1889 he merged his company with the Boston Fruit Company and formed the giant United Fruit Company. The infamous company has often been commemorated in song and political tale as "La Yunai". Gabriel García Marquéz in *One Hundred Years of Solitude*, writes of the effects of the Atlantic railway on the mythical town of Macondo.

The Atlantic Railroad continued thereafter to transform the country from small subsistence farms to a highly specialized commercial-agricultural economy that was largely dependent on nations vastly more powerful than Costa Rica: England and the United States.

This railroad also introduced a new element into the Costa Rican socio-cultural structure. Many of the black, English-speaking Jamaicans brought in by Keith to work the railways remained after its completion, to live along the Atlantic Coast as railroad employees, dockworkers and banana plantation laborers.

Keith's Atlantic Railway was finally completed in 1890, having required 19 long and difficult years to build. Until early 1970, it was the only

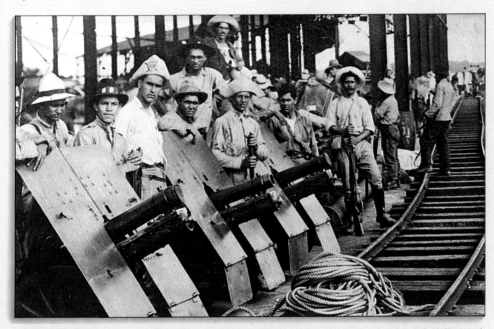

The United Fruit Company opened Costa Rica to powerful foreign investment and management, and in so doing it came to symbolize the evils of foreign domination and control.

Thus the coffee barons who ran this small Central American nation inadvertently helped create the banana industry, the country's other leading agricultural export. It was never an ideal situation, for both coffee and banana were ultimately to produce enormous social and economic problems, in addition to massive profits for those very few at the top.

Left: gliding to one of the 78 stops enroute from San José to the Atlantic coast. **Above**: protecting the railway from Panamanian incursion, 1917.

existing route between the Central Valley and Puerto Limón. It is not known how many millions have ridden in its cars, between San José and Limón, over the last hundred years of service. But the last passenger rode on the Atlantic Railroad, which later came to be known as the "Jungle Train", on November 20, 1990, just days short of its 100th birthday. Service on the original railroad cars was suspended because of continued financial losses and landslides along the rail lines. Today a diesel powered "railbus" runs on the Atlantic railway tracks between Turrialba and Limón, and there is optimistic talk of again opening up the glorious seven-hour trip on the original Atlantic Railroad, all the way from San José to Limón. ■

THE CENTRAL PACIFIC

Should the chaos of San José, with buses belching black clouds of diesel exhaust at eye level, and every pedestrian attempting to be a *torero*; with streets that have no names, hotels with no addresses, and no one confused by it all but you—should it finally become just a bit too much—then consider a day trip to the **Pacific Coast** and the tranquility of the beach. The nearest beaches are Jacó and Puntarenas, each a little less than 2 hours away. You can, of course, drive, heading out and past the International Airport toward the Pacific, or you can catch a bus, from the **Coca Cola bus station** in downtown San José.

More than just a bus station, Coca Cola is an animated area of lively, small shops; of people and things crammed too tightly together. It can have that underworldly, discomforting sense which places like the *medina* in Tangiers and the *barrio chino* in Barcelona have: tiny stalls jammed with stuff, street vendors hawking, the poor just surviving in any way they can. Cheap furniture, cheap clothing, cheap food, repair shops repairing small broken things; with kids that come aboard the buses and sing plaintive songs in exchange for a small coin. It's a Latin translation of a Dickens novel. Here one senses that feeling of things being on the edge, of pickpockets, drunks, and people wounded by the streets and by life. But it shouldn't be feared, this cacophony of sights and smells. One need only be advised to keep an eye on valuables and then to go, preferably early in the day, and catch a bus to the beaches.

The reverse side of the ICT Road Map lists phone numbers of bus companies, time in transit and frequency of departures and returns. Bus fare from San José to Jacó is approximately $2.

If you go by car, use the old road turning off of the highway towards Atenas, past the Juan Santamaría International Airport, and then head through **La Garita de Alajuela**. On this route, one of the first lowland towns that you'll approach is **Orotina**. The road to Orotina winds through coffee farms built on precariously steep slopes. Driving along the ledge of these mountains, the views are often of rich green farms and rolling valleys; and looking up at the almost horizontal fincas, you will find it difficult to imagine how the coffee can be harvested here.

For several months out of the year, small stands along this road advertise *toronjas rellenas* for sale. These candied grapefruit, stuffed with white milk fudge, are beyond the most extreme edge of *dulce*.

Orotina is a very quiet place, but perhaps not for much longer, as it is the projected site of the new airport that will soon serve Puntarenas, the capital of the large and remote province of the same name.

Near Orotina, Dagmar Werner, a German herpetologist, has an iguana ranch. Here, brilliantly colored baby iguanas seem to be everywhere; the ranch is a surrealistic dream, with the

*Preceding pages: the beach at midday, near Nosara. **Left:** an unnamed waterfall, near the highway to Orotina. **Right:** Scarlet Macaw, Carara Reserve.*

turquoise green lizards sitting in rows, silently observing you. It is said that they taste much like chicken, and are referred to as *pollo de arbol*, or tree chickens. They grow faster, consume less and produce a much higher yield of meat per acre than beef. Werner, and the Pro Green Iguana Foundation, are hoping that the iguanas which they release will give local people a source of food and income that will encourage them to maintain the forest, or to reforest it, rather than slashing and burning their land and clearing it for cattle grazing.

The **Carara Biological Reserve** straddles the highway between Playa Jacó and Puntarenas. One of the closest reserves to San José, Carara lies in a transitional zone between humid and dry land forest, and sustains wildlife from mountainous terrain, primary and secondary forests, lagoons, and marshlands of the Tárcoles River. Guides, available by advance request (call The National Parks Service), are an asset in interpreting the ecological complexity of this reserve.

Nearly 100 scarlet macaws are the great glory of Carara. These enormous red, yellow and blue parrots mate for life and live for over 30 years. Over 40 pairs were counted in Carara in 1991. A small staff patrols the park and is continually on the lookout for poachers of these valuable birds. The macaw nests in December and by January the young are strong but still in their nests. They make easy prey at this point for thieves who sell them on the black market. Only 1,000 macaws are left in the wild, while there are some 1,500 in captivity, in Costa Rica.

During the evenings when the lowlands cool, pairs of macaws fly down from their daytime feeding areas in the mountains. At sunset, park your car near the bridge along the highway outside of the park entrance and listen for their racous squawking as they fly over the highway to their roosting areas in the nearby coastal mangroves. And while waiting for the macaws to fly by, watch for shorebirds and waders which frequent the estuary. Roseate spoonbills,

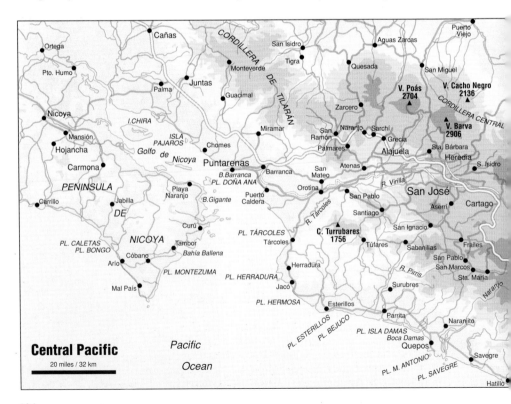

Central Pacific

20 miles / 32 km

Pacific Ocean

with their pink colors, are spectacular at sunset. Crocodiles look like inanimate logs on the river banks, lying motionless, waiting for such a prize as one of the spoonbills.

The **Central Pacific Coast beaches** could be something of a disappointment, if you are anticipating the white talcum powder beaches of tourist brochures. The attraction of these places is their proximity to San José, not their picture-postcard perfection. With a bit of exploration off of the main road, and once away from the density and hustle of the central beach scene, however you will easily find some clean and appealing beaches and secluded coves. Explore Tárcoles, Herradura, Hermosa, and Esterillos beaches.

From San José, the first beach is Playa Jacó. It has a party-time, beach town ambience, with plenty of cold beer and hammocks in coconut palms. Cabinas are readily available, and cost around $10 per day per person. They are usually clean and often situated on the beach. In addition, there have recently been con-structed first class hotels with swimming pools, full bars, air conditioning and tour packages to other points of interest in this coastal province.

Hotel meals in towns such as Jacó can be good, but don't miss some of the small seafood restaurants (*marisquerias*). Excellent ones are easily found on a dead end road at the upper end of Jacó, only a short walk from the hotels and cabinas.

A meal might begin with a *ceviche* cocktail and proceed to a *pescado entero*, a freshly caught whole fish, or perhaps a *filete de corvina a la plancha,* grilled sea bass, or *pulpo al ajo*, octopus in garlic sauce. Also available everywhere are excellent jumbo shrimp and lobster, from the Gulf of Nicoya.

Two miles (3 kms) down the coast from Playa Jacó is **Playa Hermosa**, one of the best surfing spots on the coast. Rent a bike, or take a bus to get there. Turn right off of the highway onto a dirt road which passes through the gate of a cattle ranch. The road runs between the beach on the right and beautiful

Iguanas are nicknamed "tree chickens," because of their taste.

marshland on the left. Continue on this dirt road to the large almond tree on the beach and Playa Hermosa. It is an easily accessible place where one can observe a variety of wading birds: great white herons and snowy egrets, great blue, little blue, tricolor and little green herons. You may also see *jacanas*, the lily pad walkers with the huge yellow feet, and black-bellied whistling ducks.

Driving south towards Quepos are arrows pointing to **Esterillos Beach**. Esterillos lies just off of the highway, and is usually empty, usually very quiet. It is a seven-mile long expanse of sand, almond and palm trees. Signs on the beach indicate **Esterillos Oeste** and **Esterillos Este**. To the northwest, Esterillos Oeste has the calmest waters. A few houses and cabinas, for the most part owned by North Americans, are scattered along this end of the beach, but people are seen only infrequently.

To the southeast, on Esterillos Este is the **El Delfín Hotel**, with balconies catching the breeze, and its large open dining area right on the sand. Camping

is permitted on Esterillos and turtles still come here to lay their eggs. Basic cabinas are available, as are some of the private homes, especially during off-season.

The drive south on the highway here is peaceful, passing through cattle country to the small plantation town of **Parrita**, dominated by an enormous 1,700 hectare (4,200 acre) African oil palm development, which was established in 1985 by United Brands Fruit Company. Oil palms do very well here. Unfortunately, palm oil is much higher than other oils in saturated fats, and thus is declining in popularity.

Palm oil workers live next to the highway, in plantation villages of 2-story, brightly painted homes, set in a "U" around what is the focal point of every Tico village: the soccer field.

Manuel Antonio National Park is composed of 3 long strands of magnificent white sandy beach fringed by jungle on one side, and on the other, by the Pacific. The beaches are clean and wide. Above them are tall cliffs covered in thick jungle vegetation.

To get to the park, leave the beach tourist community of **Manuel Antonio** and wade across the estuary at the south end of the beach. At high tide this stretch of water can be up to your neck, so try to time the crossing at low tide. The white sand beach here is called **Espadilla Sur**. Crossing over through the strip of forest leads to **Manuel Antonio Beach**.

There are trails in the park for hiking and wildlife sighting, but it is usually not necessary to go in search of monkeys: they will find you, especially if you are in a sharing mood, with your lunch.

Within the 1,685 acres (680 hectares) of the park are primary forest, swamps and tropical woodlands, with hundreds of surprisingly beautiful species of plants.

Just outside the park to the north, in the hills which rise up above the beach, and on the beach itself, are every class of hotel, cabina and restaurant. The **Mariposa Hotel** is perhaps the queen of them all. Located high on a cliff overlooking the beach, it is an elegant hideaway. The **Barba Roja**, not far from

Morning street scene, Quepos.

the Mariposa, offers good, gringo style food, seafood, and magnificent views of the Pacific; European-owned **Hotel Plinio** has delicious Italian cuisine and the **Hotel Vela** offers vegetarian food with a Spanish touch as well as seafood and chicken. Two recent additions to the many hotel offerings are **El Salto**, with its own private biological reserve, pleasant hilltop cabins and the sense of being a retreat from the world; and the **Hotel Costa Verde**, an exceptional place, with beautifully designed, complete apartment facilities. Down on the beach, **Cabinas Manuel Antonio** offer basic cabinas, and **Mar y Sol** and **Memo's** offer basic cold beer and Tico specialties.

There is also lodging in **Quepos**, 4 miles (7 km) away, with regular bus service to Manuel Antonio. Quepos has very acceptable accommodations and the flavor of an old-time Costa Rican fishing and banana town. Generally, one can save a great deal, if money is a consideration, by staying in Quepos at night and traveling the few miles to the park and beaches of Manuel Antonio during the day. **Hotel Ceciliano** is recommended. Regardless of where one stays, reservations are essential during the holiday season at Manuel Antonio and Quepos: it is a popular destination and becomes crowded quickly.

Few people know that the first mission in Costa Rica was established in the area here, in 1570, and was abandoned in 1751. Ruins of the mission are located up the Naranjo River. The cemetery is still visible, as are remnants of the fruit orchard, which has regenerated from the original stumps. Don Melton, and Anita Myketuk, at the **Buena Nota** gift shop, long time residents of the area, can provide information concerning the mission, as well as most things related to Manuel Antonio.

There is a lot to see and do at Manuel Antonio. One may hike the park trails, walk the beach, sun, surf, swim, snorkel or perhaps rent horses and go on a jungle trail horseback ride. Jesse Biesanz, at Unicorn Adverntures, offers guided horseback tours on a private jungle trail.

The beach at Quepos.

Along the way he will reveal some of the secrets of the jungle: which vines to cut for a drink of sweet, fresh water, the best technique for eating lemon-honey ants (before they nip you on the tongue), the names and lore of trees and plants along the way. Other options include mountain biking or sea kayaking tours, available from Ríos Tropicales. One can get to Manuel Antonio by car, bus or plane. It's about a 3½ hour trip by car through some beautiful countryside and stretches of unpaved road, about 4 hours by bus and 20 minutes by plane. The SANSA flight costs approximately $9.

Puntarenas: For many, Puntarenas, (population 35,000) is a place to pass through; just some place to go so that you can get somewhere else: you pass through Puntarenas enroute to the islands of the Gulf of Nicoya, or when taking the ferry to Bahía Ballenas, Tambor and Montezuma. Consider slowing down a bit and take some time to explore this port town.

Puntarenas used to be a bustling, noisy place, filled with longshoremen, sailors on leave, prostitutes, businessmen. Wealthy merchants from San José had homes here where they went to conduct business and escape the city. But the growth of the port of Limón and, more recently, the opening of modern **Puerto Caldera**, have made Puntarenas something of an anachronism.

The new deepwater port of Puerto Caldera lies between Orotina and Puntarenas on the coast. Caldera handles the cargo of over 360 major ships a year. It is Costa Rica's second largest port, after Puerto Limón. Cars from Japan, rice and corn from the United States, and coffee, bananas and pineapples from Costa Rica pass through here. Cruise ships dock to allow passengers their parsimonious one day in Costa Rica.

Today fishing is Puntarenas' main industry. The tourism industry is small, though large new hotels, such as the **Fiesta**, are opening south of town. The beach along the gulf appears beautiful, with its view of the long arching coastline, and the sun setting over Nicoya is heartwrenching. But, though you will find the water here full of swimmers, the ocean is polluted and not recommended for swimming by the Costa Rican Ministry of Health. Plans are being made to clean up the estuary and to cease dumping the city's waste into the ocean. If these needed actions do come about, and soon, then Puntarenas may become a vital center of tourism.

The crowded center of Puntarenas, three blocks back from the beach, bustles in the morning as Puntareneans conduct business. Everyone seems in a hurry, perhaps to accomplish what they need to before the onset of the afternoon heat. Though, like San José, an architectural victim of excessive concrete, Puntarenas still retains many of its older buildings: plank structures with latticework below the roof to permit the breeze. The wooden buildings are painted in such color combinations as bright turquoise and red, and together with the few remaining mansions of the merchants and the Church, they convey the flavor of a Puntarenas in its prime.

Have a light lunch at the **Hotel Cayuga**, spend the afternoon at the clean

Ocean view from the Mariposa Hotel, Manuel Antonio.

and ample public pool along the beach, and talk with locals. The new pool is the pride of Puntarenas.

Evening is perhaps the best time here. Enjoy a late afternoon *refresco* at one of the *sodas* on the **Paseo de Cortes** and watch the sun sink below the mountains of Nicoya across the bay. The *sodas* offer a chance to try some native Costa Rican drinks. This is perhaps the only place in the country to get *maté,* a type of milkshake with a lingering, nostalgic aftertaste. Try a cold, creamy *pinolillo* made with toasted, ground corn. After dinner you might want to return for desert and to linger awhile longer with the sweet wind from the estuary. Then a *granizado con fruta* is refreshing. Or try *granizado con todo*, shaved ice topped with a sweet red syrup and ice cream, served with a tiny can of sweetened condensed milk!

Seafood restaurants and hotels line the oceanfront. Most are air-conditioned or adjusted to catch the ocean breezes. The **Tioga** and **Las Brisas** are decent places. On the estuary is the **Portobello**, a good hotel, which offers privacy, gardens and birds. The hotels along the estuary also offer free mooring and facilities to cruising sailboats. The **Yacht Club** here is extensive, well protected, professionally managed, and one of the very first stops a trans-oceanic yacht makes on the first leg of a trip from the West Coast of the U.S. to more distant ports-of-call.

Stroll through town after dark, and you will see Ticos here at their leisure. In the warm still night, children play in the streets, riding bikes, playing ball, darting in and out of their open front doors. There are few cars on the streets. Old folks rock on the porch or bring chairs to the sidewalk to converse with neighbors. In the downtown, the bars and the poolhalls are full.

Calypso Tours offers a cruise on their boat and visits to the islands in the Gulf of Nicoya. They cross the waters of the Gulf and visit **Tortuga Island** and there, in an idyllic white sand and turquoise water setting, provide what is perhaps the best seafood buffet in the country, as

Manuel Antonio's three beaches.

well as folkloric music and entertainment. There is also adequate time for swimming and beach play. The Pacific Island Cruise is a very professionally managed one-day tour, with round-trip transportation from San José. Other tours, including fishing, rafting and visits to Carara, are also offered by Calypso, one of the first and best of such companies in Coast Rica.

A short ways South, down the coast, at **Playa Doña Ana**, the Tourist Institute (ICT) has developed a beach resort with bar, restaurant, showers and good parking, on a cove between two spectacular rock headlands. Doña Ana is the site of the Costa Rican world invitational surfing championships, which hosts teams from all over the world.

A ferry crosses from Puntarenas to Playa Naranjo and the **Nicoya Peninsula**. The 2-hour trip across the **Gulf of Nicoya** passes among small lush islands. The ferry leaves Puntarenas at 7 am and 4 p.m. and returns from Playa Naranjo at 9 am and 6 pm, on Monday through Sunday. On Friday, Saturday and Sunday, an additional ferry leaves Puntarenas for Playa Naranjo at 11 am, and departs Playa Naranjo for Puntarenas at 2 pm. Arrive at the ferry landing well ahead of the scheduled departure as the line can get very long and only a limited number of vehicles are allowed aboard. You must purchase a ticket for the vehicle and one for each passenger. Sit on the top deck for the best views. Refreshments are available at a snack bar.

Arriving by ferry to Nicoya brings one to a different world from that of the area around Puntarenas. It is one of seasonally dry grasslands, gigantic spreading trees, rolling cattle ranches, memorable bays and beautiful beaches.

The trip up to and across the Gulf is the easy part of the journey to Tambor, Montezuma and Cabo Blanco. From there onward, the road is rough, long and unpaved. During the rainy season it is muddy and a few of the rivers and creeks without bridges can become impassable without a four-wheel drive vehicle. And during the dry season, along the roadway a fine, brown dust coats **Clothing vendor, Puntarenas.**

190

THE RESPLENDENT QUETZAL

A cclaimed as the most magnificent bird in the Western Hemisphere, the Resplendent Quetzal is worthy of this high praise. The pigeon-sized male owes his elegance to the intensity and brilliant contrasts of his colors, the sheen and glitter of his plumage, the beauty of his adornments, and the noble dignity of his posture. The rich crimson of his underparts contrasts with the shining, iridescent green of his head, chest, and upperparts. His head is crowned with a narrow crest of upstanding feathers that extends from his small yellow bill to his nape. The pointed tips of the long, loose-barbed coverts of his wings project over the crimson of his sides in beautiful contrast. Most notable are his central tail coverts, which stretch far beyond his tail and, like two slender green pendants, undulate gracefully when he flies. When viewed from below, the pure white outer tail feathers contrast with the crimson of his belly.

As may be seen on many an ancient sculpture and modern painting, the long tail coverts were highly valued as personal adornments by the Aztec and Mayan nobility. As Guatemala's national bird, the peaceful quetzal contrasts refreshingly with the fierce predators and fire-breathing monsters that other nations have chosen for their emblems. Years ago, Guatemalans assured me that their symbol of liberty would die if deprived of freedom, but modern aviculturists have learned how to keep it alive—a hard negation of a beautiful myth.

The quetzal's notes are eminently worthy of a bird so splendidly attired. Fuller and deeper than those of any other trogon, they are not distinctly separated but slurred and fused into a flow of soft and mellow sound that is unforgettably beautiful.

Monogamous pairs of quetzals nest in the holes of trees located in mountain forests or in nearby clearings. The hole, like that of a woodpecker, extends straight downwards from the opening at the top. Usually it is deep enough to conceal all of the sitting birds except the ends of the male's train.

On the unlined bottom of the chamber, the female lays two light blue eggs. She incubates through the night and the middle of the day. The male takes a long turn on the eggs in the morning and again in the afternoon. His train arches over his back and projects through the doorway, fluttering in the breeze. On an epiphyte-burdened trunk, the ends might be mistaken for two green fern fronds. Sometimes, when his partner arrives to relieve him of his long spell in the nest, he soars straight upward, above the treetops, loudly shouting a phrase that sounds like "very-good very-good." At the summit of his ascent he circles around and dives down into sheltering foliage. These "joy flights" appear to be another expression of the abounding vitality that produces his elegant plumes.

Hardy Resplendent Quetzal are still abundant in ample tracts of unspoiled montane forests, where they are neither shot nor captured for sale as cage birds. So long as such forests are preserved, they are in no danger of becoming extinct, but if all such forests are destroyed, Central America will lose its most magnificent bird.

-Renowned ornithologist Alexander Skutch has lived in the tropical rain forest of southern Costa Rica for more than 50 years. ■

The Quetzal with its favorite food, young avocado.

plants and road travelers.

From the ferry landing at Playa Naranjo, Tambor is about a two-hour drive, and Montezuma is just under three hours. There are no road signs along the way, but local people are gracious and accustomed to guiding visitors. There are no buses leaving from Playa Naranjo; however in Paquera, one can catch a bus and continue on to Cóbano, the last stop before Montezuma.

At Playa Naranjo is the **Hotel Oasis del Pacífico**, which offers sportfishing, horses, a pool, tennis and hammocks by the water. The beaches are not much for surfing or swimming. Oasis del Pacífico offers a special low rate for day usage of its pool and facilities.

The drive along the peninsula, although rough, is rewarding. It traverses through small towns and villages, miles of vast pastureland, past dwellings of every description, people on horseback, and every now and again startling views of the blue bays of the Pacific.

Hotel Bahía Gigante sits on a bluff above **Bahia Gigante**, offering cabinas and condos and a pool fed by warm spring water. Surrounding the hotel are 9 miles (14 km) of road and trails for hiking. Horses and fishing equipment can be rented at the hotel, and they will arrange transportation from San José or pick up guests at the ferry. Beyond the town of Paquera is **Curú National Wildlife Refuge** and **Bahía Ballena** (Whale Bay), a wide, large bay of surprising beauty and tranquility. The waters are gentle and warm, with large flocks of pelicans diving into waters that are rich with fish. January is an especially good time for sighting whales. **Hotel La Hacienda**, located on a large cattle ranch, is a peaceful resort with pleasant rooms, well kept grounds, swimming pool, croquet lawn and its own private landing strip. Guided horseback tours, fishing and a variety of tours to the area are available, including a day trip to Cabo Blanco or Curú Wildlife Refuge.

Down the beach from La Hacienda is the small village of **Tambor**, where more basic lodging, local-style meals and a

Holiday beachgoers a Puntarenas.

view of life as it was lived before tourism arrived, are available. After Tambor, is the **Tango Mar Surf and Saddle Club**, a new luxury resort offering a variety of amenities.

Continuing southeast, one arrives at the town of **Cóbano**, and from there, the road leads to **Montezuma**. Arriving in Montezuma, in many ways, feels like arriving at the end of the line. The dirt road rolls bumpily down a hill and ends abruptly in front of a row of funky hotels and cantinas on the beachfront. Here, young North American and European travelers outnumber the local people, who have accepted them with seeming good grace, building a variety of small, inexpensive cabinas, sodas, extra bedrooms and camping places to accommodate visitors.

Downtown, the **Hotel Montezuma** overlooks the beach, and serves cold beer, loud music and good fish casados. **Chico's Bar** serves local food and drinks, and the shiny white **El Sano Banano** features great fruit drinks, hearty, vegetarian fare and big screen

videos of popular films 3 nights a week. Lenny and Patricia Iocona, owners of El Sano Banano, also offer cabins in the woods just off a beautiful white sand beach. Exceptional people with great affinity for Montezuma, they are involved in a number of community improvement projects.

In the center of the village are **Cabinas Mar y Cielo**, **Cabinas Las Arenas** and **Cabinas Karen**. Cabinas Karen is the stark, white house just next door to the Sano Banano. Doña Karen also rents simple cabins with shared kitchens, in the forest, off the beach on the north end of town.

South of town a short ways is the **Hotel Lucy**, **Casa de Huéspedes Alfaro** and a number of other cabinas and *sodas* and camping sites along the beach. To the north, is **El Pargo Feliz**, which has good fish and lobster dinners, and small cabinas. Places fill up quickly during the dry season, and reservations are advised.

While most lodging and dining in Montezuma ranges from basic to ac-

odge
versees the
acific.

ceptable, the beach-going is exceptional. To the north of town, there are wide, sandy beaches, with beautiful clear water, some with great shelling. A walk up a scenic path leads to a dramatic waterfall and river. To the south are beaches with surf crashing against volcanic rock— and, a short hike away, another waterfall.

Bikes and boogie boards can be rented at the Sano Banano, and horses through the Hotel Moctezuma or Cabinas Mar y Cielo, but most visitors to Montezuma seem to spend their time swimming, sunning or simply hanging out in this laid-back place that seems expressly designed for the youthful, low budget traveler.

It is almost 7 miles (11 km) from Montezuma to **Cabo Blanco Strict Nature Reserve**, along a little-used, unpaved road which parallels the beach. One can drive, bike, walk (if ambitious) or ride a horse to get there, although horses are not allowed in the reserve. Cabo Blanco Strict Nature Reserve was established on October 21, 1963, and is Costa Rica's oldest protected wildlife region. It was through the inspiration and tireless efforts of Nils Olaf Wessberg, a Swedish immigrant to this area of Costa Rica, that the reserve was established. Wessberg was killed by an assassin while trying to establish a similar reserve in the Osa Peninsula and is fondly recalled as an important pioneer of the parks system in Costa Rica.

Originally Cabo Blanco allowed no public access: all life there was to be protected, without any interference from Man. Today however, approximately one third of the reserve is open to visitors, and strict rules guide the behavior of those who enter, beginning with registration and a briefing at the reserve's administration center. It is open from 7 am to 5 pm daily.

Camping is not permitted in the reserve, nor are radios, loud noises, usage of drugs, masks, snorkels, nor the removal of any shells, rocks or marine life from the beaches. Guarding the reserve becomes more difficult, a ranger says sadly, as foreigners move into this now **Sunrise mist rises above the forest canopy.**

194

very desirable area and buy land for vacation homes or touristic developments. This crowds out local people who have traditionally used these open spaces adjacent to the reserve for hunting and fishing, to supplement their subsistence-level existence. As the local people get squeezed out, they begin pushing in on the reserve lands, and so begins an ugly cycle of enforcement of reserve rules against those who have lived in the area for generations.

For the time being, however, Cabo Blanco is there in all her glory, with lyrical hiking trails amidst rivers, creeks, and waterfalls, and a stunning, rocky coastline.

Monteverde: The **Monteverde Cloud Forest** lies atop the Continental Divide, some 110 miles (182 km) from San José. More visitors are attracted to this private reserve than to any other in Costa Rica, and usually for one purpose: to sight the Resplendent Quetzal, the most spectacular bird in the tropics.

Mayan kings prized the quetzal's irridescent green tail feathers more than they did gold. And because the Mayans believed the quetzal, "the bird of life" would not live in captivity, it symbolized to them a supreme freedom. To the 20th-century naturalist, perhaps the quetzal in the Cloud Forest of Monteverde does not represent freedom in that ancient sense, but sighting one is always a profound event.

Here the rising air cools quickly, and dense clouds form and swirl. Moisture condenses on leaf surfaces and drips to the perpetually muddy forest floor. Patches of brilliant sunlight burst through, then disappear abruptly behind clouds, plunging all color into deep shade. Monteverde is an almost theatrical environment of swamps, waterfalls, dense old growth woodlands and wind-pruned forests. It seems a likely environment for the quetzal.

Though listed as an endangered species throughout Central America, it is estimated that nearly 1,000 quetzals make their home in Monteverde. It is a difficult bird to spot. Cloaked in radiant green plumage, they can, except for

Hummingbird and orchid in the Monteverde cloud forest.

their almost luminous crimson breast, virtually disappear among the rich colors of the cloud forest.

It is not easy to get to Monteverde. Twenty-two miles (36 km) past the turnoff to Puntarenas, on the Inter-American highway, just before crossing the Lagarto River, are signs directing the traveler to Monteverde. Turn right at kilometer marker 149 and continue on the gravel road into the Cordillera de Tilarán mountain range for 26 miles (43 km) of poor road conditions, all the way to **Santa Elena** and then Monteverde. Allow between 3 and 4 hours driving time from San José.

It was a group of Quakers who, in the 1950s, in conjunction with biologists of the Tropical Science Center, had Monteverde designated as a biological reserve. These North American Quakers, searching for a place free from militarism, settled in the mountains of Monteverde. To support themselves, they began making cheese from milk brought to their primitive processing plant each morning by Tico dairy farm-

ers. Today the Quakers produce tons of cheese daily, and it can be found in markets throughout Central America. Enroute to the reserve, stop in at their **cheese processing plant** for a tour. They are open from 8:30 a.m. to 5:00 p.m., Monday through Friday, and half-day on Saturdays.

In 1987, a group of Swedish elementrary school children raised and donated enough money to purchase 15 acres of forest. Now, with support from young people in the United States, England, Japan, Canada and Costa Rica, the **Children's Eternal Forest**, being saved by and for children, covers some 20,000 acres (8,000 hectares) adjacent to Monteverde Cloud Forest Preserve. The Children's International Theater for the Environment also develops young people's environmental awareness through both local and international production of plays by children.

Accommodations in Monteverde range from basic to plush. There are many, as Monteverde is a primary destination for naturalists, and several places are personal hotels named for cloud forest plants and animals. One such exemplary place is the **Sapo Dorado**. In each of its 10 "mountain suites" a fireplace is made ready to warm you after a day on the damp trails. The **Pensíon Heliconia** is a newer inn, with a very nice, southern European atmosphere. The **Hotel de Montaña Monteverde** has views of the Gulf of Nicoya from its rooms, and offers more deluxe accommodations than others in Monteverde. The **Belmar** is chalet-style and homey. One of the first inns in the area, the **Pensíon Quetzal**, has a woodsy, pleasant feeling. Regardless of where you stay, plan on a minimum of 2 days. And it is always necessary to make reservations in advance. Monteverde is a very popular destination.

Before leaving the forest, visit the **Hummingbird Gallery**, across the road from the administration center. Owners Michael and Patricia Fogden, biologists and pre-eminent nature photographers, have spent two decades shooting the fauna of Monteverde and their remarkable work is shown here.

Left: elephant ears in the eternal forest. **Right**: this pavoncillo flower is pollinated by hummingbirds

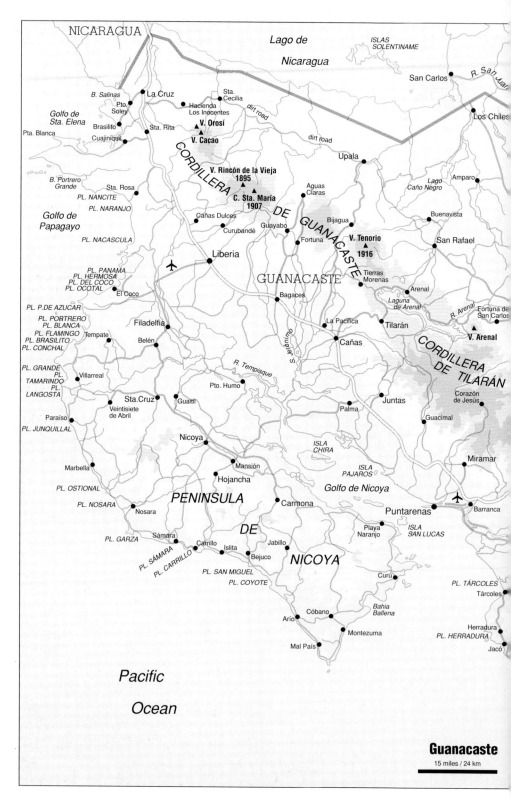

NICARAGUA

Lago de
Nicaragua

ISLAS
SOLENTINAME

R. San Juan

San Carlos

Los Chiles

B. Salinas
La Cruz
Pto.
Soley
Golfo de
Sta. Elena
Brasilito
Pta. Blanca
Cuajiniquil
Sta. Rita

Sta.
Cecilia
Hacienda
Los Inocentes
V. Orosí
V. Cacao

dirt road

dirt road

Upala

Lago
Caño Negro

Amparo

B. Portrero
Grande
Sta. Rosa
PL. NANCITE

CORDILLERA

V. Rincón de la Vieja
1895
C. Sta. María
1907

Aguas
Claras

Buenavista

PL. NARANJO
Golfo de
Papagayo

PL. NACASCULA

Cañas Dulces

Curubandé

Guayabo

Bijagua

Fortuna

V. Tenorio
1916

San Rafael

DE GUANACASTE

Liberia

GUANACASTE

Bagaces

Tierras
Morenas

Arenal

Laguna
de Arenal

R. Arenal

Fortuna de
San Carlos

PL. PANAMA
PL. HERMOSA
PL. DEL COCO
PL. OCOTAL
El Coco

La Pacífica

Tilarán

V. Arenal

PL. P.DE AZUCAR
PL. PORTRERO
PL. BLANCA
PL. FLAMINGO
PL. BRASILITO
PL. CONCHAL

Filadelfia

Tempate
Belén

Cañas

CORDILLERA
DE TILARÁN

PL. GRANDE
PL.
TAMARINDO
PL.
LANGOSTA

Villarreal

R. Tempisque

Pto. Humo

Juntas

Corazón
de Jesús

Paraíso
PL. JUNQUILLAL

Sta.Cruz
Veintisiete
de Abril

Guaitil

Palma

Guacimal

Nicoya

ISLA
CHIRA

Marbella

Mansión

Hojancha

ISLA
PAJAROS

Golfo de Nicoya

Miramar

PL. OSTIONAL

PENINSULA

Carmona

Puntarenas

Barranca

PL. NOSARA

Nosara

DE

Playa
Naranjo

ISLA
SAN LUCAS

PL. GARZA
Sámara
Carrillo
Islita
Jabillo

NICOYA

PL. SÁMARA
PL. CARRILLO
Bejuco
PL. SAN MIGUEL
PL. COYOTE

Curú

PL. TÁRCOLES
Tárcoles

Bahía
Ballena

Córbano
Ario
Mal País

Montezuma

Herradura
PL. HERRADURA

Jacó

Pacific

Ocean

Guanacaste

15 miles / 24 km

GUANACASTE

Guanacaste stretches endlessly towards the horizon. During the dry season much of it is covered in wild savanna grasses that float over the land, like lakes of gold. During the rainy season the land itself appears to be alive with thick, green tropical forest growth. It is Central America's Texas, the big country, where vast grasslands are punctuated by huge, spreading trees and white brahma cattle.

Had the residents of Guanacaste voted in 1858 to be a part of Nicaragua instead of Costa Rica, Costa Rica today would not be as rich and diverse as it is. From 1570 to 1821, Costa Rica was part of the Captaincy General of Guatemala, a collection of Spanish Central American provinces. In 1787 the government in Guatemala decided that Guanacaste was too small a province to exist independently, and awarded it to Nicaragua. Twenty-five years later, in an effort to give Costa Rica sufficient population to be represented in the Captaincy General, Guanacaste was made a part of Costa Rica. Then, in 1821, the Captaincy General was dissolved and the nations of Central America became autonomous. Guanacaste's national identity came into question. The *Guanacastecos*, as the residents of this province are called, were divided: the Northerners around Liberia wishing to be a part of Nicaragua and the Southerners on the Nicoyan peninsula wishing to remain in Costa Rica. A vote of the residents was held and they elected to be a part of Costa Rica. They are an independent people, proud of their heritage, naming their capital city Liberia, from their love of freedom and their role in the rout of the slave trader William Walker in 1856. Many are descended from the dark-skinned Chorotega Indians with skin the color of tortoise shell, eyes a warm brown, black wavy hair, and an easy, friendly grace.

In **Cañas** one first has the sense that this part of immense Guanacaste is more like a separate country, caught somewhere between Costa Rica and Nicaragua than it is a province of Costa Rica. Cañas provides a central location from which to visit Lake Arenal, Rodríguez Caballero and Palo Verde parks.

Cañas, which was named for the fields of white flowered wild cane which covered the countryside, is a pleasant cowboy town, with a frontier feeling, not unlike a village in Mexico. There is a fine hermitage a few kilometers north, just before the highway crosses the Corobicí River.

Four kilometers north of Cañas on the highway is **La Pacífica Ecological Center**. This private reserve with comfortable cabins, beautiful pool and grounds, has extensive trails paralleling the Corobicí River, which provide excellent vantage points for bird watching. Over 220 different species have been identified there. One of them is the boat-billed heron, an exotic-looking bird with a wide, ungainly bill, the use of which has never been scientifically explained.

The **Rincón Corobicí Restaurant**,

Preceding pages: the Tabebria tree blossoms during the dry season. **Right**: inseparable: Guanacaste horse and owner.

overlooking the Corobicí River on the highway adjacent to La Pacífica, is a pleasant place to rest and take refreshment. Listen to marimba players and watch great flocks of white cattle egrets fly past on their way to evening roosts in nearby trees, lining the river banks. Settled in for the night, the egrets resemble thousands of white blossoms on flowering trees.

Wildlife Areas:Palo Verde and **Rodríguez Caballero** are contiguous protected wildlife areas near the mouth of the Tempisque River. To reach these two areas, take the road from Bagaces to the west, off of the Inter-American highway. Four-wheel drive is recommended, especially during the rainy season. The southern entrance to the Park, from Cañas, may be closed. Call the National Parks Service office to find out which of the routes are open and are most navigable.

Tidal fluctuations, seasonally overflowing rivers and unique topography attract 300 species of terrestrial and water birds, including herons, whistling ducks, ibises and the immense jabiru storks, to these two protected areas. Large mammals and reptiles are also abundant and can be easily seen during the dry season when they gather at water holes. Deer, coatimundis, armadillos, iguanas and crocodiles up to 15 feet long are not uncommon here.

Only 20 years ago, currents and sediment runoff from Guanacaste formed a sand bar, which then became stabilized as an island. Today it is known as **Isla de Pájaros.** From Rodríguez Caballero Wildlife Refuge, a boat and guide can be chartered to this island, located in the middle of the **Tempisque River** near the head of the Gulf of Nicoya. And often one can request to go along with the park rangers, on their visits to Pájaros. This quiet place provides the isolation favored by many water birds. While the white ibis and a species of egret are the only birds which regularly nest here, roseate spoonbills, wood storks and snake birds also nest on Isla de Pájaros.

Liberia, the capital city of Guanacaste province, established over 200 years

Cattle egrets roosting at sunset.

ago, is centrally located along the Inter-American highway. It is also known as *Ciudad Blanca*, the White City. Original residents carried white volcanic earth and gravel on foot from the nearby slopes of Rincón de la Vieja and Miravalles Volcanoes and constructed traditional white adobe homes in the unique "Doorway of the Sun" style. Doorways on both sides of the northeast corner of the houses catch the morning and afternoon sun. Many of these lovely old adobe homes can be seen, just south of the park, off of the narrow streets of Liberia. Some of them are being restored, and the owners often welcome visitors to see the work in progress. Inside the houses are classical courtyards, and grand rooms with high ceilings and 19th century murals. The kitchens, to the rear of the houses, open onto courtyards, where corn and other grains were dried.

Continuing up-country from the city of Liberia is **Rincón de La Vieja National Park**, with four complete ecosystems contained within its 34,801 acres (14,084 hectares). The park is named for the volcano it protects, which name derives from the legend of an old woman who once lived on its slopes. Her house was referred to as the old woman's corner — hence Rincón de la Vieja. Access is difficult because of poor roads, but the adventurous will find it virtually untouched. Certainly the most extraordinary area, located at the foot of the volcano, is "**Las Pailas**" or the Kitchen Stoves. Here 20 acres of hot springs, boiling mud pots, sulfur lakes and vapor geysers that color the surrounding rocks red, green and vivid yellow, offer a bizarre geological phenomenon unique in Costa Rica. It is rumored that the mud from the **Sala de Belleza** (Beauty Salon) boiling pots, like that from the Dead Sea, when cooled, makes an excellent facial beauty mask. Visitors must exercise caution, however, since breaking through the brittle ground surface of the area can result in severe burns. It is much wiser to go with a guide. Lodging is available at **Albergue Rincón de la Vieja,** and this very pleasant hostel makes a good base

Naturally bubbling mud pots at Rincón de la Vieja.

from which to explore different areas of the park. Call in advance to let the owner know that you are coming. Then go north from Liberia, approximately 3 miles, and turn right onto the gravel road which leads to the village of Curubandé. From there go approximately one mile to the entrance to Hacienda Guachipelín, then enter through the gate and continue until you see a sign saying "Albergue."

Another road, the "official access road" to the park station at Rincón de la Vieja, winds bumpily 17 miles (27 km) east out of Liberia. Appearing strangely snow-covered, it traverses an area of white chalky earth that gives Liberia the name of White City. At the ranger station at the end of the road, you can climb to a lookout point for a view down the slopes of the volcano, across grassy plains, to the ocean. The station offers a bunkhouse and a good campsite next to the ruins of an old sugarcane-processing plant. It is a 2½ hour walk from there to the hot springs, which offer a place to soak weary bones. A cool pond nearby

THE MINI-ZOO

Walking along the wide dirt paths of La Pacífica Ecological Center, adjacent to the Corobicí River, one sees, in the midst of a grassy field, a small sign advertising "Mini Zoo."

Had it not been for Javier, a biologist at La Pacífica, we might have ignored the sign. But Javier had made a point mentioning the mini zoo, and had referred to its caretaker as "a beautiful person."

So we followed the sign, across the field and through a barnyard full of goats, sheep, rabbits, guinea pigs and chickens to a "Mini Zoo." We are hardly prepared to find an impressive collection of Costa Rica's big cats living quietly, almost as family pets, on the farm—or the mini zoo—of Lily Hagnauer and her husband, Swiss-born farmers and environmentalists, who are themselves rare breeds.

Two large, feisty, adolescent cougars in a large, chain-link enclosure come to the gate as Lily approaches. When she enters the enclo-

sure, they rub against her legs and purr loudly, like giant housecats. One of them leaps towards her and she staggers back, laughing and pushing it down. The other rises on its hind legs, placing its forepaws on Lily's shoulders to lick her face and hair. A wildlife inspector brought the cougar orphans to Lily when they were 3-weeks old, shivering with cold and fear. She took them to bed with her to keep them warm and bottle-fed them every 2 hours with baby formula and chamomile tea. Unfortunately, they cannot now be returned to the wild, as they have no fear of man.

A crochety, 23-year-old ocelot, exceeding its life expectancy by 7 years, whines a litany of complaints to Lily. She releases the door of its wooden box and coos to him in Swiss-German, scratching its head all the while. Two beautiful young female ocelots, its descendents, nap in their enclosure, below.

A large, adult jaguar lies amidst the foliage in its cage. Brought to Lily's from the overcrowded zoo in San José, it lies in a bathtub sized hole it has dug in the cool earth. He is enormous and it is sobering to view its green eyes and powerful body from inches away, a chain link fence the only barrier. Lily estimates there are only 250 jaguars remaining in Costa Rica.

The cages are not especially pretty places: they were not built so much with the idea of displaying the cats to the public as with the idea of providing adequate and secure enclosures for them. Each animal has its story: how it was injured and nursed back to health, how it was orphaned and found, how it once escaped its cage and went for a walk in the countryside. There are also macaws, lovebirds, and hundreds of brightly-colored parakeets which Lily breeds to help raise revenue to feed the cats.

The Hagnauers came to Costa Rica from Switzerland in the1950s when Mr. Hagnauer, an agronomist, was assigned here to test and promote pesticides. Having come a long way since those days, the Hagnauers ended up purchasing the experimental farm owned by the pesticide company and turned it into a model of ecology for cattle farmers all over the world. Now retired, the Hagnauers live quietly on a nearby farm where they garden, care for the cats, birds and dogs and do what work they can to further environmental causes in their adopted country. ∎

Lily and friend.

is refreshing afterwards. Horses can be rented from the ranger station, but permits must have been secured in advance from Cigifredo Marin, head ranger at Santa Rosa Park. Santa Rosa, Guanacaste, and Rincón de la Vieja parks are all administered from Santa Rosa Park.

At the junction of the Inter-American highway just outside of Liberia, is the Bramadero Restaurant. The air is rich with the smells of leather tack hanging on the walls and beef cooking in the kitchen. Dark, tanned cowboys or *sabaneros*, with broad-brimmed hats, sit at heavy wooden tables drinking beer. Outside, trucks roll through the intersection on the Inter-American highway, carrying cargoes of cattle. The intersection is the major truck stop between Nicaragua and San José, where three gas stations, repair shops, bars and restaurants provide travelers with 24-hour services.

To explore the area from here to the Nicaraguan border, one might use as a base the **Hotel Hacienda Los Inocentes**, a working ranch and traveler's lodge off the Inter-American highway on the road to Santa Cecilia. This scenic byway is bordered by streams with waterfalls and acres of saplings being used in reforestation programs. Los Inocentes is 25 minutes by car from Santa Rosa and Guanacaste parks, and approximately 40 minutes from the nearest beach.

The Hacienda Los Inocentes has been remodeled, with care to the preservation of the original architecture, to accommodate guests. Here, after a day in the field, one can relax in hammocks or in wicker chairs, viewing the ranch and Orosi Volcano while taking tea or a cup of Costa Rican coffee.

The great offering of the hacienda is its horseback rides. Fifty well-trained horses are available for visitors and the *sabanero* guides will match one to a guest's riding ability. Along streambeds, through forests and fields at the base of Orosi Volcano, the guides point out monkeys and sloths, iguanas and rare birds, enriching your experience considerably.

Costa Rican bullfights, where only the *torero* gets hurt.

At the end of a day in this region, consider making a short trip east to the village of **Santa Cecilia** to watch the sun set over **Lake Nicaragua**.

During the recent war in neighboring Nicaragua, many of the local young men from this area were drawn into the battle, either for or against the U.S.-backed Contra forces who were trying to overthrow the ruling Sandinistas. Near here, in the northern addition to Santa Rosa National Park, a clandestine CIA airstrip was constructed to bring in supplies to aid the Contra effort, in violation of Costa Rica's neutrality laws. Built with the blessing of ex-president Alberto Monge, it was torn up under the administration of Oscar Arias. Arias' destruction of the CIA airstrip caused great chagrin to the Reagan administration, and resulted in a drastic decrease in U.S. aid money for Costa Rica.

As a result of that Contra-Sandinista war, many women in this region raise children alone. On Saturday evenings, as the sun is setting and the dirt roads and hills glow with a burnt orange hue, the surrounding country roads fill with old men, women and children, walking to town. They wear their best clothes, to promenade in the town square and to socialize with their neighbors.

A rise in the bumpy road about 5 miles (8 km) beyond the center of Santa Cecilia brings the vast inland sea that is Lake Nicaragua into view. The lake figured into William Walker's plan to conquer Nicaragua and to use the Nicaraguans as a labor force to build canals from Lake Nicaragua to the Pacific. He envisioned a waterway to transport goods by boat across the isthmus from the Pacific to the Atlantic. Wealthy investors in the United States backed this plan. But the defeat of Walker in Costa Rica, and later in Nicaragua and Honduras, put an end to the idea.

A trip to the bay at **Puerto Soley**, the northernmost Pacific beach of Costa Rica, passes through the small town of **La Cruz**, a stopping place for those traveling north through Central America, and for migrant laborers from Nicaragua crossing back and forth, seeking

A Guanacasteco farm family.

work in Costa Rica. The town is often full, especially at night, and, like border towns everywhere, offers excellent people-watching. A left turn in the center of La Cruz goes to the mirador built by the Costa Rican Tourist Institute, a pleasant place to rest and view the valley and bay below. Winding down the hill, past a ranch established by Somoza, the ex-dictator of Nicaragua, is serene Puerto Soley. The beach here is empty and breathtakingly beautiful.

In the bay, the National Wildlife Refuge of **Isla Bolaños** thrusts its rocky ledges 267 feet (81 meters) above the surface of the sea. An almost vertical island, it is the only nesting site in Costa Rica for the frigatebird and one of very few for the brown pelican. One can visit Isla Bolaños by asking for Gustavo, almost surely to be found among the houses near Puerto Soley, as he has been for the last 12 years. He will take 5 people to the island and guide them around it. The 25-minute ride in his fishing boat gives a magnificent view of the shore. As the boat approaches the

island, the frigatebirds rise from the giant rocky mass and circle eerily above it, hanging in the sky, etching their forms against the clear blue. Gustavo will escort you over the ledges and rocks, and with his intimate knowledge of the sea and land there, will answer questions.

The frigatebirds make nests in the dense thickets of woody vines on cliffs 131 feet (40 meters) above the sea. It's not for the isolation and protection of the remote island that they nest here. Because of their wide wingspan and small bodies and feet, they find it difficult to take off from a standing or running start like other birds, and have to throw themselves into the air from a high ledge to catch the wind updrafts. In the dry season, when the frigatebirds mate, you can see the males puffing out brilliant scarlet sacs on their throats to attract the females.

It is an enjoyable walk around Isla Bolaños and then, at the end of the day, an enjoyable return to Puerto Soley, over transparent blue water, watching the magenta sun setting behind evening

Brahma cattle under the shade of a Guanacaste tree.

clouds.

Guanacaste and Santa Rosa National Parks: South of here are Guanacaste and Santa Rosa National Parks. **Guanacaste National Park**, purchased and created in 1989 with foreign funds donated to Costa Rica's Neotropica and National Park foundations, has added over 280 square miles (108 square km) to the nearby protected lands of Santa Rosa National Park.

Guanacaste Park encompasses a wide band of largely deforested land which extends from Orosi and Cacao Volcanos to the Pacific Coast. Dry tropical forest dominates this vast land, but habitats ranging from mangrove swamps and beaches to rain and cloud forest are also within the park's boundaries. Over the past several hundred years, complex patterns of cutting, grazing, burning and farming have dissected Guanacaste into a complex mosaic of life zones.

Dan Janzen, the visionary ecologist whose life work is the preservation and reforestation of Guanacaste, feels that this park will ultimately be restored to its original state. "Dry forests have been destroyed," Janzen says, "but they are tough, able to withstand six months of drought a year and are very regenerable." With the acquisition of Guanacaste National Park, the large tracts of land necessary for successful forest regeneration are now protected and under national park management. The park sustains large populations of many animal species which are able to find refuge during summer droughts and migrate freely between "islands" of forested areas.

Animals eat and disperse seeds from the trees, and have created these forest islands. Rain forest insects, important in pollinating dry forest plants, are attracted from nearby mountain slopes. In 20 years, significant canopy forest will have developed. And, in 200 or 300 years, full-grown tropical dry forests may again dominate Guanacaste.

During 20 years of scientific work at Santa Rosa, Janzen has taught two generations of local people an intelligent appreciation of the forest. Through his

La Casona, site of William Walker's defeat.

work, residents of Guanacaste now have experience and expertise in fire fighting, maintaining horses and managing cattle, identifying plants and dealing with "biotic challenges" like ticks, diseases, thirst and wounds. Jobs as research assistants, guides and reserve caretakers provide many with skills and a stable, long term source of income. Above all, the charismatic Janzen has given them a kind of inspiration which should ensure the future protection of Guanacaste.

Hotel Las Espuelas bills itself as the "Center of Guanacaste's Ecological System" and it is indeed strategically located on the Inter-American highway just south of Liberia. Las Espuelas provides tours, has a swimming pool and all of the amenities—serious considerations in cowboy country.

Santa Rosa National Park, where much scientific research is being done, encompasses nearly all of the environmental habitats of the region. A nearly infinite system of trails takes visitors through zones of deciduous tropical hardwoods, to arid mountains with deserts of cactus and thorny shrubs, and along rivers lined with forests to mangrove swamp estuaries near the beach.

Along Santa Rosa's **Naked Indian Path**, gumbo limbo trees with peeling red bark have the appearance of sunburned skin, and are nicknamed "tourist trees." Like many of Santa Rosa's trails, this walkway passes through forest which, during the dry season, loses many of its leaves, making wildlife viewing easier for the tropical naturalist. Enormous multi-colored iguanas are commonly seen in the trees bordering the trail. Hiking toward Duende Creek and the bat cave, look for them sunning on tree branches. Their tails often hang straight down, revealing their presence.

Santa Rosa's significance as the location of the historic battle against William Walker, was a primary factor in the government's decision to make it a national park. In 1856, some 9,000 Costa Ricans, from all social classes, fought to oust Walker from their country, and half of them lost their lives in

A traditional grain husker.

the fight. A final battle against Walker was held at the hacienda **La Casona** (The Big House). The three times that Costa Rica has been invaded, it has been here that the invaders were turned back.

Today, a different kind of battle is fought in Santa Rosa. The rangers at the station tell of their encounters with hunters. Though hunting is outlawed in the park, the law is virtually unenforceable due to inadequate numbers of rangers. Armed hunters coming into the park are frequently met by unarmed park rangers who often must fight them to remove them from park boundaries. The low-paid rangers often risk their lives in these skirmishes.

The beautifully restored hacienda La Casona is open to the public and provides a window into the life of Costa Ricans during the Colonial Period. The stone corrals are 300 years old. The house itself, with its beautiful weathered wood, has on display original pieces of furniture and artifacts. A trail leads to a memorial to the heroes and martyrs of the battle, and a historic plaque contains President Juan Rafael Mora's famous speech in which he exhorts his countrymen to defend Costa Rica against William Walker, and not to leave their "noble tasks, but to prepare weapons."

The latest addition to Santa Rosa National Park is the northern section, formerly the ranch of ousted Nicaraguan dictator Somoza, who lived there so he could go easily and clandestinely back and forth across the border. The Costa Rican government was interested in expanding Santa Rosa Park to make possible a stable population for some of the park's species. It also felt that its best interests were not served by the presence of an ousted military dictator near its border. For those reasons, in 1979 the **Murcíelago Hacienda**, owned by the Somoza family, was expropriated and made part of the national parks system.

The hacienda, on **Saint Elena Bay** with access to **Playa Blanca** and its untouched white sand beach, is now a part of Santa Rosa Park. It can be reached **On the trail to Witch's Rock.**

from the entrance at the northern end of the park. A sign on the Inter-American highway past the main entrance to Santa Rosa indicates the way.

A rugged, 8 mile (13 km) kilometer hiking trail, or four-wheel drive road during the dry season, leads from the Santa Rosa ranger station to **Naranjo Beach**. White sand and clear water with excellent surf breaking near **Witch's Rock**, a monolith one mile offshore, make Naranjo a popular, though remote, surfing destination. Primitive campsites at Argelia House and Estero Real have outhouses and a windmill pumping fresh water for showers. Campers should, nonetheless, bring their own fresh drinking water.

Nancite, one of Costa Rica's most pristine beaches, is northwest from Naranjo. Each month, usually on a waxing three-quarter moon, turtles come ashore here to nest. Tens of thousands may participate in the event, called an *arribada*, one of Costa Rica's grandest natural spectacles. Exact times are unpredictable, as they are with most bio-

logical phenomena. Even though a full scale *arribada* may not be taking place, solitary turtles can usually be seen nesting on Nancite and Naranjo Beaches.

Beaches of Guanacaste: Though traditionally cattle country, Guanacaste today is known by most for its beaches, many of which are in the process of being developed into major resort destinations. An international airport scheduled to be built outside of Liberia will bring sun-starved tourists from Canada, the northern and eastern United States more directly to these beaches.

Playas Panamá, Hermosa, Coco and Ocotal are beaches some 30 to 40 kilometers from Liberia, at the end of winding roads, most of which are paved, but pocked with mudholes and ruts during the rainy season.

The first view of the ocean is of **Coco Beach**, a honky-tonk little town of open-air bars, tiny restaurants, beachfront hotels, boardwalks, and teenagers on vacation. The large cove and wide sandy beach bustle with activity. Skiffs filled with fish are brought ashore and

A ranger patrols Nancite beach.

offloaded onto trucks parked on the sand. Radios from the seafood restaurants help to put people in the mood with infectious Latin *salsa* and raucous rock 'n roll.

Just up the coast, **Playa Hermosa**, a sparkling cove with gentle surf, has a small hotel in a setting of beach almond trees. The Italian owner of the **Cabinas Playa Hermosa** runs the resort with a European elegance. Homemade pasta with fresh, grilled fish is served with a decent bottle of wine, on a white table cloth with a tropical flower centerpiece. The meal, served under a thatched palapa surrounded by rustling palms and cooled by an afternoon sea breeze, represents a delightful synthesis of the Mediterranean and Central American cultures.

Next door to the Cabinas Playa Hermosa, on the sand, are campesino-run restaurants that usually offer a fresh fish dinner for a dollar or so. And at the other end of the cove and the economic spectrum is the **Condovac** luxury hotel and condominiums, which entertains its guests with toys ranging from jet skis to

windsurfers, a discotheque and tennis courts, water skis and golf carts that transport guests up and down the hill to the beach.

Playa Panamá, the site of a future Costa Rica Tourist Institute (ICT) development lies at the end of the road, on a beautiful, undeveloped bay ringed by coastal woodlands. For the present, it is a peaceful spot conducive to leisurely strolls on the beach and searches for shells and sea birds. There are no hotels or restaurants, but there are bars and a *pulperia* at the south end of the bay. By asking around for a fisherman with an available boat, one can get away from it all, by going across Bahia Culebra to Playa Nagascola. Camping is allowed at both Playa Panamá and **Playa Nagascola**.

South of Coco Beach, **El Ocotal**, a luxury hotel rests serenely on a hilltop overlooking the pounding surf, sandy coves, rocky capes and islands of the Nicoya coast. El Ocotal commands incredible views. Its circular restaurant perched on the edge of the cliffs is open to the general public. There is an unpaved road to quiet Ocotal beach, near the entrance to the hotel.

Though difficult to drive to, **Bahía Pez Vela** has a nice black-sand beach and a big game fishing resort, offering excitement in the form of world record-breaking blue marlin and sailfish. It is bit on the pricey side, at $3,850 per person for a three day package. One can, for somewhat less – approximately $100 per day – fish the same waters with local guides and boats.

Continuing south there are other pleasant, less-visited beaches. It may seem as though it is an impossibly complicated maze of dirt and gravel roads. Recalling that the ocean is to the west and the highway to the east should ease one's fears of becoming hopelessly lost.

Turn off of the highway at Comunidad and then head toward Belén. From there it is a short distance to **Playas Brasilito** and **Potrero**. Or you can backtrack from Ocotal to Playa Coco and then drive on for another 9 miles (15 kilometers) to the main highway. From there, turn right to Filadelfia. Three miles (5 km) south

Pacific brown pelican.

of there, head right toward the coast and follow the signs to Flamingo. You may want to relax and go for a quiet swim at **Playa Conchal**, before heading up the coast to Flamingo. To get to Conchal beach, go to Brasilito, and then south a short way, to the end of the road. Walk along the beach to the small hill and then find the path that proceeds over the hill to Conchal, and onto the bottomless drifts of sea shells which make up the beach. The endless trillions of pink, orange, mauve and sunset-colored shells will massage your feet, and reawaken childhood beach fantasies.

Head back again to Brasilito, past the blaring jukebox in the bar across the road from the Mi Posada Hotel, and on to Flamingo.

Several kilometers up the coast, just inside Punta Salinas, **Flamingo Beach Resort** dominates a spectacular, white sand beach, and looks out on rocks and islands dotting the horizon a few miles from shore. Wildlife, such as caimans, monkeys and wading birds have not yet deserted the nearby estuary, but they

soon may. The largest yacht harbor from Acapulco to Panamá is under construction at Flamingo. Due for completion in the mid 1990s, it will accommodate over 300 boats, open the coast to cruising yachtsmen, and have a profound effect on the development of the Nicoya Peninsula.

The balconies of the Presidential Suites at the **Flamingo Condos** look north to **Potrero**, a cove of coconut palms and calm water, with excellent potential for picnics and secluded dips in the ocean. The views get better, and the roads get worse, as you continue north along this picturesque coastline toward **Playa Pan de Azúcar**. When you arrive at Pan de Azucar, it is obviously the last resort. Stop in at the **Hotel Sugar Beach** for incredible views, loud guffaws from the pet macaw, and enjoy a drink, lunch or a swim in the cove. But do not expect to find overnight accommodations between December and April without advance reservations. There is an acute shortage of hotel accommodations anywhere in the country during

these months, and this is especially so at Guanacaste's beaches.

Go through Brasilito, to Huacas and continue for 8 miles (13 km) south, where you will make a right turn for **Tamarindo**. One would scarcely realize that Tamarindo is a national wildlife refuge. The wild life seems more concentrated at Henry's Third World Bar on the south end of town, than it is in the nearby forest.

The **Tamarindo Diría,** a large resort hotel, has two swimming pools, a spacious bar and restaurant and offers tours to every possible destination in Guanacaste. Spend some time walking on the wide expanse of beach here, preferably early in the morning after the tide has ebbed. Patterns of black, grey and brown sand grains turn the beach into a work of art. When the tide is out, life on the wet sand proceeds at a frenzied pace with mobs of hermit crabs busily investigating everything, ghost crabs darting about in a frenzy, and snails bulldozing the sand for food. Look for tiny, flamboyant fish in the intertidal rocky pools at the south end of the beach.

Should you have worked up an appetite for breakfast, try **Johan's Bakery**, a few hundred meters up the road from the Tamarindo Diría. Fresh baked cinnamon rolls, croissants and butter cookies come out of the oven early in the morning. The clientele is, for the most part, North American and European travelers, longing for an alternative to the the predictable Tico breakfast of *gallo pinto con huevos.*

Relatively inexpensive and friendly lodging is available in the village of Tamarindo, at the **Cabinas Zullymar**, **Pozo Azul**, and other small hotels and pensions.

Playa Grande, a 20-minute walk north on the beach, or a one hour drive over dirt road, has excellent surf. Playa Grande is also a major leatherback turtle nesting habitat, and the site of environmental conflicts between conservationists and developers which, when ultimately resolved, may help to define Costa Rica's policies of ecotourism.

Broad smiles greet the visitor at Tamarindo.

VAMPIRE BATS
OF GUANACASTE

There are over one hundred kinds of bats in Costa Rica. From the shrilling flutterings of millions of these creatures, which rises up from the deep caves of Barra Honda, to a quiet few hanging in the cool, darkened corners of La Casona in Santa Rosa Park, they are to be found throughout Costa Rica. Most of them are benevolent, curious-looking animals, who feed on nectar, fruit and insects.

But within Santa Rosa Park, in Guanacaste, inside of a cave near Naked Indian Path, live a group of *Desmodex Rotundum*, or vampire bats. They feed largely on cows. Their habits feed our imagination. It is the stuff from which Dracula was created.

Bats are beneficial, even necessary, as significant pollinators and disseminators of seeds, especially in deforested areas in Costa Rica. Researchers know them to be clean, docile—even friendly. Nectar bats are gregarious and hang from the ceilings of caves in tight clusters. In the evening they feed on insects along roads or dry river beds. At night they search for nectar from white, night-blooming flowers which they pollinate. Bats do much to control insect populations; it is reported that a colony of one million bats would consume over 10,000 pounds of insects each night.

Three of the species drink blood. Hollywood and Victorian novelists have done their part in creating the myth of the vampire who lives on the blood of innocent humans. And there are certain other factors which contribute to the legends that surround this creature: The vampire bat has large thumbs which protrude from the wings, appendages used for stealthy crawling towards the prey. A flat, red, pig-like nose, large eyes, prominent front teeth and relatively small and pointed ears make this one of the least appealing creatures of the night. The caped and fanged black-haired fictional figure from Transylvania no doubt rose up, fully formed, in the imagination of early movie makers who had heard of the nocturnal activities of these animals. For it is true that this species feeds mainly during the darkest hours, before the moon is out, quietly alighting upon a sleeping victim and making a painless incision with razor sharp teeth.

The unfortunate subject of many horror films.

Contrary to the myth, however, the blood of the victim is not then sucked out, but rather lapped up, much as a cat drinks milk.

A bat does not drink its victim dry. Instead, rabies and other infections, introduced through the wounds, kill the prey. Over a million animals a year die this way. Humans are sometimes prey as well, and sleeping people have been infected by the bat with the dreaded paralytic rabies.

Cattle ranchers are striking back against the vampire bat, but not with wooden stakes and crucifixes. Methods of extermination have included gassing their caves with toxic substances and dynamiting. Such methods, often born of an irrational aversion to the bat, of course, do not specifically target the vampire bat. Anything and everything in the area is harmed or killed. One innovative but extreme system involves trappers undergoing rabies vaccinations and then trapping individual bats in fine nets, using thick leather gloves to avoid infection-causing bites. The trappers then coat the bats with poisons and release them to take the poison back to the group of these highly social animals, each treated bat infecting up to twenty others. ∎

Playa Grande has been subdivided into an "urbanization" zone of homesites set back over 50 meters from the mean high tide line, most of which have been sold, but not yet built upon. Conservationists would like to see the entire area protected as a national park. Ecotourism advocates would like to limit development to small educational "ecocenters," and involve both landowners and people from nearby villages in the protection and management of the land, estuary, beach, and turtles. Difficult legal and social decisions lie ahead for tourism policy makers.

But the turtles continue nesting at Playa Grande. During the long nesting season from August to February, as many as 80 turtles a night are counted. **Playa Langosta**, immediately south of Tamarindo across an estuary which is chest deep at high tide, is also frequented by turtles, and by surfers who ride waves just in front of the estuary.

Eleven miles (18 kms) inland from Tamarindo, at the junction of the "27 de Abril" School, turn toward the coast and proceed for approximately 8 miles (12 km) to lovely **Junquillal Beach**. Junquillal is a paradisal, wide, usually tranquil beach which gives one the sense of having found a secret place. **Villa Serena** facing the beach and **Hotel Antumalal**, farther south, are two exceptional hotels, both European owned.

Artist Inga Sperling has chosen Junquillal to celebrate the gentleness and beauty of this part of Guanacaste, and is part of a small international community here. **Playa Negra**, 25-minutes north by foot along the beach is a beautiful walk, ending at a small beach, which, like many unnamed beaches on the Nicoya Peninsula, has as yet escaped the eyes of developers.

Inland from the coast at Paraíso, few populated areas disturb the unbroken beauty of the rolling hills and valleys. An occasional cluster of three or four houses indicates a village. Here chickens, ducks and the lone bicyclist claim the road. The miles are marked by the infrequent passage of herds of Brahma cows, turning traffic into a cattle drive,

A deserted Pacific Coast beach.

216

followed in their leisurely journey by *sabaneros* on horseback. These *Guanacasteco* cowboys don't direct the animals out of the road; they let the automobile wend its way through them. The cattle, with their sensitive faces, seem neither concerned nor curious.

Santa Cruz (population 15,000) is a friendly town located somewhere between the old and the new. In the central plaza the very modern church, built when the old one was destroyed by an earthquake in 1950, stands beside the original colonial clock tower. A video bar greets visitors who walk the cobblestone streets. Chinese restaurants offer fried rice as an alternative to *gallo pinto*. Murals on the school walls portray the evils of drugs and alcohol. The central park is a quiet shady place for sitting and viewing the life of a Guanacaste town.

Hungry visitors to Santa Cruz should not miss the experience of eating indigenous food at the **Coopetortilla**, located beyond the central plaza. In a huge single-room building of tin and screen, an open wood fire is used to prepare the large, hand-made *tortillas Guanacastecas,* rice and beans and other local dishes. A sign says "*ambiente familiar*," or family atmosphere. The excellent regional food is prepared and served by women in immaculate, starched pink and white uniforms and hats.

For those wishing to spend the night in Santa Cruz, the **Sharatoga Hotel** provides air conditioned rooms and a pool; and many cabinas around the town offer the basics.

One of the main attractions to the traveler in this part of Guanacaste is the small town of **Guaitil** where a former potters' co-op offers ceramic pots in the style of the pre-Columbian inhabitants of this part of Costa Rica. After the Conquest, pottery-making died out here, possibly because the images adorning pots were considered pagan by the Catholic church. The popularity of these giant, luscious ceramic pots is obvious from their presence in the lobbies and dining rooms of many hotels in Guanacaste.

Enjoying the glorious Guanacaste sunset.

It seems as though almost every house in the neighborhood of Guaitil has a kiln and pots for sale in the yard. The widest selection, however, will be found next to the soccer field in front of the church. One may possibly see so-called pre-Columbian pottery for sale, though these pieces, if in fact they are pre-Columbian and not fakes, are taken from Indian burial grounds and as historical artifacts are prohibited by the 1982 Patrimonial Law of National Archaeology from being taken from Costa Rica. Their purchase also creates a market, which encourages desecration of burial sites.

From Guaitil it is a scenic, bumpy 50-minute drive on the old road to the town of Nicoya, considered the cultural capital of Guanacaste. An alternative is to return to Santa Cruz and make the twenty minute drive on the highway. The pride of the town is its central park and colonial church, now undergoing restoration.

On the road to the beaches south of Nicoya, the **Hotel Curime** has a pool and *cabinas* with all of the amenities.

Three hours off of the Inter-American highway towards the Pacific from Nicoya, and 7 hours from San José, on bad, bumpy roads, is the seldom-visited **Ostional National Wildlife Refuge,** created to protect the endangered Olive Ridley turtle. The Ridleys prefer Ostional and come there by the tens of thousands, in what is called an *arribada*, to lay their eggs, at certain unpredictable times. Presently there is a controversial program for egg collecting at Ostional, which gives the people of the village of Ostional the right to legally gather as many of the Ridley turtle eggs as they can during the first 36 hours of every *arribada*. It is estimated that during brief egg-laying periods, as many as 100,000 Olive Ridleys may come ashore to this isolated beach, and leave behind over ten million eggs. Most travelers will not find it of adequate interest to travel to remote Ostional to view these thousands of creatures relentlessly and laboriously coming ashore to thump the sand with their flippers and dig their incubation holes to lay their eggs. But those few that do choose to come are asked to check in at the guard station before going to the beach, and then, to view the activities with as little intervention as possible.

Two major beach areas are reachable from Nicoya, and, though the roads are nearly impassable during the rainy season, they are becoming increasingly popular destinations for North Americans and Europeans. These are Sámara and Nosara beaches, with light sand, wide, sweeping expanses of beach, and, usually, gentle waters for swimming. Many of the hundred or so residents of the **Nosara Beach** community are willing to rent out their homes by the week or month. Drive through the windy roads of this striking international community, along the lush, wooded hillsides above the beaches, and look for "Se Alquila" signs. One is often surprised to find that $700 a month, including utilities and maid service, is the going rate for a house with a view of the beaches. A large part of the area here is protected as wildlife reserve, and as a result it is more forested and richer in wildlife than

A Guaitil potter.

other parts of the region. Coatimundis, armadillos, parrots, toucans and monkeys are plentiful. There is also excellent snorkeling, tide pool exploring, and camping in the area. The **Hotel Playa Nosara** is on a point above the beach, and offers inspiring views from its cabins, overlooking **Playa Guiones** and **Playa Pelada**. The small seafood restaurant at Playa Pelada is inexpensive and good. Chat with locals about the beach scene at Las Playas de Nosara, at **La Lechuza Restaurant** near the village of Nosara.

The **Villaggio la Guaria Morada** is south of Nosara a few kilometers, and is an extensive place with nicely designed cabins, pool and guided horseback tours.

Playa Sámara, nearly an hour south of Nosara, has a beautiful white sand beach and a good reef for snorkeling, which also protects the beach from direct waves. Swimming is safe in crystalline, warm, shallow waters with minimal surf. Windsurfers have recently discovered this area, but there is little activity. Off season, one has a feeling of dramatic isolation and escape that is unavoidable on this white sand beach. During the high season, Playa Sámara is favored by Costa Ricans; many Ticos have summer homes here. On the south side of the beach is the exceptional **Hotel Las Brisas del Pacífico**, with a pool fronting the ocean. The German restaurant manager astounds guests with impossibly rich food. To the north of the beach are smaller, basic *cabinas* and hostels, with camping permitted. SANSA airlines flies to Sámara regularly from San José, and provides an alternative to the drive there, which requires the crossing of a shallow river between Nosara and Sámara.

Continuing south from Sámara one arrives at **Playa Carrillo**, yet another near-flawless white sand beach with offshore reef. The **Guanamar** fishing facility is located here, as are a few very basic cabinas. Driving to Playa Carrillo also requires crossing a river, which is impassable if the tide is high. Beyond Carrillo are other extraordinary beaches, isolated, lonely places, sometimes with

"It is prohibited to collect turtle eggs."

fresh water available, sometimes not. **Playa Caletas,** not too far south of Carrillo on unpaved, nearly non-existent roads has large surf with offshore breezes.

About 10 miles from the town of Nicoya is **Barra Honda National Park,** a vast network of caves. Along the road to the Tempisque Ferry are national park signs showing the way to this seldom-visited place. On the flat ridgeline, 1,000 feet (305 meters) above the caves, is a *mirador* (look-out) that one can reach via marked paths. Standing there along the high ridge, with the sounds of an enormous waterfall, amongst screeching tropical birds, howler monkeys, and iguanas in the trees, looking out across the vast Nicoya peninsula can be a humbling experience. To gain entrance to the caves requires calling the National Parks offices in San José and requesting a park ranger guide, usually a week in advance. It is worth the effort. One does not have to be a dedicated spelunker to enjoy Barra Honda, though some of the caves are quite deep and require steep vertical drops to enter. With names such

as *La Trampa* (The Trap), and *Terciopelo* (Fer-de-Lance viper), they may not sound inviting, but the fragile cave formations are dazzling. One such formation, called The Organ, produces melodic tones when gently touched. Ancient human remains, blind salamanders, vampire bats and strange birds share the world of darkness in the Barra Honda caves, which, because they lack an easily accessible horizontal entrance, have escaped vandalism and exploitation.

The ferry across the **Tempisque River** is the preferred passage back to the highway to San José. Pedestrians and hitchhikers are always grateful for a ride to the ferry, and the exchange will often be a good story, a bit of local lore not to be found elsewhere.

The Tempisque ferry is able to carry 40 cars and innumerable passengers for the 20-minute ride across the river. On Sundays, the wait to board it can be a long one, as Ticos from San José return home after a weekend at the beaches near Liberia and Santa Cruz. Small restaurants selling food and beer line the road near the ferry crossing. Vendors near the gate to the ferry sell hot tortillas, shish-kabobs, and peeled oranges.

When the ferry arrives, the cars and buses roll aboard, laden with souvenirs of the weekend: stalks of coconuts and bananas fill rooftop luggage carriers. And, in season, children and adults alike carry home bags of the eggs of endangered species of turtles, still considered by many to be aphrodisiacs. Some of the eggs have been excavated by adventurers, others have been purchased at *sodas* near the beach and are the product of *hueveros,* who make a business of raiding the turtles' nests; others are part of a cache of eggs taken legally by those who are given permits by the government to take the eggs during the first 36 hours of an *arribada.*

It is another 115 miles (185 km) up the coast and through the mountains back to San José. Along the highway, dozens of fruit stands offer an opportunity to load up on tropical fruit, honey, and homemade candies before returning to home or hotel.

Left: protective coloration; false "eyes." **Right:** a Barra Honda cave and explorers.

THE ATLANTIC COAST

Puerto Limón is the Caribbean, with its rich, ripe jumble of sights and sounds and smells. It is a hot, steamy, laid-back place. Most middle class Ticos who live in the Central Valley consider it something of a disgrace, and most young European and North American travelers are enamored, at least with the idea of Limón, if not the place itself.

For many, Limón's annual Carnival is the reason to visit. The week-long jubilant event is held in Limón every October. Carnival first began in 1949, under the leadership of Mr. Alfred Henry King, a barber, who timed the festivities to coincide with the anniversary of Columbus' landing near Limón on 18 October, 1502. El Día de la Raza, the Day of the People, also falls during Carnival Week and includes in the festivities the many indigenous people who live in the region, and who certainly could not view Columbus' landing with any great enthusiasm

The highlight of Carnival Week is the parade, when local people and thousands of visitors take to the street to join in a glorious music and dance spectacle. The drums, the heat, the beat, the shining bodies of dancers and drummers in bright costumes, urge spectators to abandon their inhibitions and to surrender to the Caribbean magic. And so they do, *Limonenses*, and tourists alike, filling the streets, shimmying, shaking, singing and carousing while the irresistible rhythms of steel drums fill the warm, humid air.

The 2½-hour drive from San José to the Atlantic Coast is on a good highway winding through the canyons, mountains, waterfalls and virgin forests of Braulio Carrillo National Park. Descending from the cool cloudiness of Braulio Carrillo into the tropical lowland forests of the Atlantic, the temperature rises and the air becomes heavy.

On the way, stop at the **Guacimo** truck-stop for a snack, a cold drink or a great *gallo pinto* breakfast before proceeding on to the banana plantations of the lowland countryside.

In the center of Limón, there is no cathedral or soccer field facing a plaza, such as one finds in all the towns of the Central Valley. **Vargas Park,** named for a local governor much concerned with the progress of the area, is filled with huge banyan trees with buttress roots which the townspeople use for bus stop seats. If you notice cab drivers and children looking up, they are probably watching the family of *perezosos*, three-toed sloths, which live in the trees of the park. Resting in Vargas Park, on the concrete benches and tables under the palms, watch the remarkable parade of ethnic diversity. Visit the newly opened **Ethnohistorical Museum of Limón.** Displays and lectures illustrate the contributions in literature, education, art, sports and politics that the *Limonense* have made to Costa Rica.

In the 17th century there were cacao plantations on the Atlantic Coast which were worked by black slaves. The Miskitos, and their allies, English pirates from Jamaica, continually raided the ca-

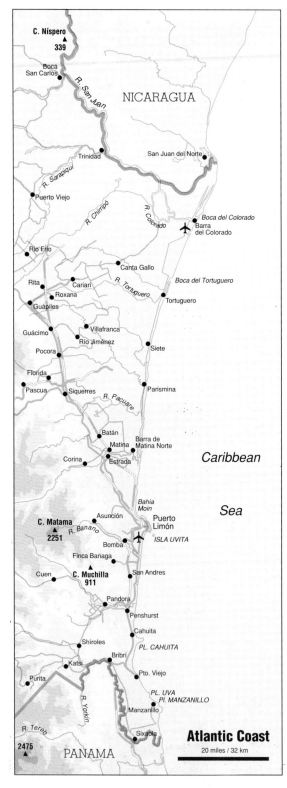

C. Níspero
▲
339

Boca
San Carlos

NICARAGUA

R. San Juan

Trinidad

San Juan del Norte

R. Sarapiquí

Puerto Viejo

R. Chirripó

R. Colorado

Boca del Colorado
Barra
del Colorado

Río Frío

Canta Gallo

Rita   Cariari   R. Tortuguero   Boca del Tortuguero
        Roxana
Guápiles   Tortuguero

Guácimo   Villafranca
        Río Jiménez
Pocora   Siete

Florida

Pascua   Siquerres   Parismina
        R. Pacuare

        Batán
        Matina   Barra de
                        Matina Norte   Caribbean
Corina   Estrada

                Bahía
                Moín
C. Matama   Asunción   Puerto   Sea
▲   R. Banano   Limón
2251
        Bomba   ISLA UVITA

Finca Banaga
▲
Cuen   C. Muchilla   San Andres
        911

        Pandora

        Penshurst

        Cahuita
Shíroles
        PL. CAHUITA
        Bribrí
Katsi
        Pto. Viejo
Purita
        PL. UVA
        Pl. MANZANILLO
R. Yorkín   Manzanillo

R. Telire
        Sixaola   **Atlantic Coast**
2475
▲   20 miles / 32 km
PANAMA

cao plantations until cacao production was finally abandoned in the early 1800s, and the region, which was impossibly hot, humid and swampy, was once again forgotten.

The growth of the coffee market set the Costa Rican government searching for an Atlantic port to facilitate getting the coffee to England and Europe. In 1871, the government decided to establish a port on the site of "El Limón" a migrant black fishermen's village of five huts. That same year, the government contracted the construction of the Atlantic Railroad, which was to go from San José to the Atlantic Coast. Laborers from Jamaica, Italy and China were brought in to work on the railroad, many of whom made permanent homes in the area.

Minor Keith, the North American responsible for building the railroad, began the planting and cultivation of banana along the railway's right-of-way, in order to raise additional funds for the ever-increasing costs of constructing of the Atlantic railroad.

Limón thus became a railroad and banana town, populated largely by black Afro-Caribbean and Chinese immigrants who had come to Costa Rica looking for work. Since 1872, Limón and the banana industry have experienced great booms and busts: bumper banana crops, exceeding the value of Costa Rica's coffee exports; labor troubles and violent strikes; and lean, hard times of no employment at all when United Fruit abandoned the Atlantic Coast.

Limón was effectively ignored by the Central Valley government of Costa Rica for all these years. The black workers and their families had no rights of citizenship; they were not permitted to work in the Pacific Zone nor in the Central Valley. Since the Civil War of 1948, things have improved somewhat for the black residents of Limón. Today they are full-fledged citizens of Costa Rica, and can travel and work anywhere they wish.

In the town of Limón, most travelers who spend the night there stay at the **Hotel Acón** or in one of the cheap, clean and basic hotels near the park. Outside of town is the **Maribú Caribe**, a nice place with a resort atmosphere, on the cliff overlooking the ocean. To the north, past the busy beaches of **Playa Portete** and **Playa Bonita**, is the **Hotel Las Olas**, built over the ocean above a coral reef. There are several other new hotels, rising up in this area, which herald the beginnings of a rapidly growing tourist market just north of Limón.

Tortuguero: Travel on the canals of **Tortuguero**, up through the area north of Limón, has been likened to a trip on the *African Queen*, or to floating dreamily down the Amazon, and even to coasting through a veritable Venice in the jungle. Whatever. It is certainly one of the most wonderfully lyrical 5 hour trips to be taken anywhere. There is a tranquility that soothes the most savage, as one floats dreamily amidst the fragrance of white ginger blossoms, lavender water hyacinths, and the *Ilan Ilan* flower, through the jungles, lagoons and canals of Tortuguero, catching occasional glimpses of sloths, crocodiles, basking fresh-water turtles, green macaws, parrots, and howler monkeys flit-ting and shaking branches high in the exuberant vegetation above you.

There are several ways to go up and through **Tortuguero National Park**, including hitching a ride on a cargo boat, or on the Port Authority's launch, or by renting a dugout canoe, or speedboat, or by taking one of the pleasant boats made available by tour companies and the "jungle lodges" that provide accommodations in Tortuguero. Arranging a package tour is certainly the least complicated way, and this package should include a lodge room, meals, naturalist guides, and the trip through the canals. Some hotels and agencies also include in their tour package a small plane to pick you up near your lodge, for the return to Pavas airport near San José.

Tortuguero is the main nesting area in the Caribbean for the green sea turtle. The **Caribbean Conservation Corporation** has long been established there, for the purpose of studying and protecting the sea turtles that come there to nest and lay their eggs. The area has been

Pulsating rhythms in Limón.

known as turtle hunting grounds since at least the mid-16th century, and the turtles there were randomly exploited for their meat, shells and eggs until 1970, when the area was established as a national park, largely due to the work of Dr. Archie Carr. His work, and that of thousands of volunteers has led, in some degree, to the protection of the Green sea turtles and the Leatherbacks.

If possible, go to Tortuguero during the turtle nesting season. And insist on having a knowledgeable naturalist guide to advise you of things to do and things to avoid, in the spirit of understanding the habits and sensitivities of these magnificent creatures, which have been listed as endangered since the 1950s. Between July and October is the best time to view the prehistoric ritual of the nesting of the Green turtles, and between February and July for the Leatherback. The enormous tractor tread trails, which they leave in the sand as they laboriously make their way up the beaches to dig their nests, are easily visible even at night under a thick stormy sky. And following these freshly-made trails, to observe the nesting of one of these turtles, is an experience which profoundly affects even the most sophisticated traveler.

Launches going up Tortuguero depart from **Moín**, just a few miles north of Limón. SANSA has short flights from San José to **Barra del Colorado**, which is north of Tortuguero, up by the Nicaraguan border. From there one can hire boats to go through the canals. The Guide in Brief lists accommodations. Be advised that this is a very rainy area, and though camping is permitted near the village of Tortuguero, it wouldn't be a good idea. There is, however, inexpensive, basic lodging available in the village.

Talamanca: Most travelers who come to the Atlantic Coast spend a little time in Limón, and then quickly head south to the **Talamanca Coast.**

The drive south parallels the Atlantic, with glimpses of the Tortuguero canals, appearing intermittently off to the right. On this highway, some 20 miles (32 km)

Tortuga Lodge along the Tortuguero canals.

228

south of Puerto Limón is **Aviarios Río Estrella**, an enchanting bird and wildlife refuge located amidst tranquil canals and islands. Here, in a rented canoe, or on their sightseeing pontoon boat, the owners will enthusiastically introduce you to the complex flora and fauna of this part of Talamanca.

Somewhere near **Tuba Creek** begins the Talamanca region of Costa Rica, extending from the Atlantic Coast and reaching into the mountains which run from the Central Valley southeast into Panamá. This area was the refuge of many indigenous people who fled the Spaniards—and the last area of the country to be conquered by them. One story has it that the name Talamanca comes from *Talamalka*, "place of the blood" in the language of the Miskito Indians, and was so named after a battle between the Miskitos and migrant turtle fisherman fishing off the coast of Cahuita.

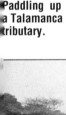
Paddling up a Talamanca tributary.

Until the 1970's, the Talamanca region was populated mainly by the Bribri and Cabécar Indians who lived in the mountains, and by the descendents of English-speaking black immigrants from the Caribbean Islands, who settled along the coast. The blacks lived as farmers and fisherman, following the old ways brought from Jamaica, most affectionately described in their own words in Paula Palmer's folk history, *What Happen*. (This book is a great read for anyone interested in the history of this region.) The blacks planted the coconut trees which line the beaches, developed a local cuisine based on the foods they grew, and sold coconut oil, hawksbill turtle shells and cassava starch for the little money they needed.

They spoke a Creole English, played cricket, danced quadrilles, carved dugout canoes from local trees, and recited Shakespeare for amusement. Isolated by the sea and the mountains, there were no roads connecting these people with the rest of Spanish-speaking Costa Rica, and their life continued quite peacefully and independently. All that has changed now, with the opening of a slick new highway and other roads con-

necting the sleepy coastal towns of Talamanca with San José and the rest of the world.

Most Black residents of the coast now speak both English and Spanish, although, if speaking English, one has to listen carefully and know a few of the local expressions: "Wh'appen," ("What's happening") is the common form of greeting, replacing the "Adios," of the Central Valley. "How de morning?" is "Good morning," and "Go good," is "Take care." The courteous form of address, especially towards an older person, is to use his or her first name preceded by Mr. or Miss.

The indigenous people of the region now, for the most part, speak Spanish in addition to their own native languages, and take part in regional political and economic life, although many maintain ancient beliefs and customs. There are three indigenous reserves in Talamanca: the large Talamanca-Bribri Reserve, the Talamanca-Cabécar Reserve, and the smaller KékoLdi Reserve. Access to the reserves by non-indigenous people is limited: one must have permission from the boards of the reserve associations to enter. Mauricio Salazar of Puerto Viejo's Cabinas Chimuri, however, is authorized to take visitors on horseback trips through the Kékoldi Reserve and can provide information about access to the Talamaca-Bribri Reserve.

Cahuita: Local legend has it that in 1828, William Smith, or Old Smith, a turtle fisherman, rowed and sailed north from his home in Panamá to fish for turtles, and, finding a beautiful calm bay protected by a coral reef near Cahuita Point, decided to settle there with his family. In those early days, Green and Hawksbill turtles were plentiful and so unaccustomed to harassment from man that they were unafraid and an easy strike. Old Smith is said to be the first English-speaking Afro-Caribbean settler to the area, which at that time, was populated with Indians, and frequently visited by pirates.

Cahuita is the largest and most developed of the Talamanca towns. Faded but dignified looking wooden houses,

Life on the coast has its relaxing moments.

once painted bright colors that are now soft pastels, and with a touch of Caribbean whimsy in the gingerbread details, look out over dusty streets. Young travelers from Europe, Canada and the USA, oblivious to local sensibilities, amble along the beaches and roadways in bright beachwear, sometimes displaying a shocking amount of flesh, and new cabinas and small hotels are cropping up all around town.

To the immediate south of Cahuita is **Cahuita National Park**, famous for its fine, sandy beach and coral reef. The reef extends 500 meters out to sea from **Cahuita Point** and offers great snorkeling. There are many species of tropical fish, crabs, lobsters, sea fans, anemones, sponges, seaweed and innumerable other marine creatures to observe amidst the coral formations. The beautiful warm water, in hues of blue and blue-green, the radiant sunshine and coconut trees whispering in the gentle breezes are unmistakably Caribbean.

Camping is permitted in the park; to get to the **Puerto Vargas** camping area, enter from the south side of the park, 3 miles from Cahuita. Coatis and raccoons frequent the campgrounds looking for fruit and other edibles and are not above overturning a tent to get them. Fresh water, outhouses and picnic tables are available.

From Puerto Vargas, one can hike a nature trail in the jungle or explore the wreck of a British slave galleon from which cannons, cannon balls, swords, and copper and bronze manacles and arm bands have been recovered.

Cahuita Tours, on Cahuita's main street, rents snorkeling equipment, bikes, binoculars and scuba diving equipment. As well, they offer a glass-bottomed boat ride to some of the better snorkeling spots. There is also a place near El Típico Restaurant which rents surfboards and snorkeling gear.

José McCloud, a knowledgeable guide, may be available to talk about the flora and fauna of the area.

Hotel Cahuita is located adjacent to the north end of the park (the south side of town), as are cabinas and eateries.

Cabinas Black Beach is located north of town, where waters are gentler and better for swimming. Good food is available at **Cabinas Algebra**, also on the north end of town, and at **Miss Edith's**. Just ask anyone where Miss Edith's is: she has an enviable reputation for her good, down-home Caribbean cooking.

Reservations are essential during Christmas, Easter and during Carnival, the second week in October. Biologists studying the rainfall and weather say the best time to visit Cahuita is from February to April and in October.

The Road to Puerto Viejo: Heading south towards Puerto Viejo, or Old Harbor, along a pretty paved road paralleling the beach, one passes houses of all styles and economic levels; but there is something magical about the Caribbean air and even the humblest shack has a picturesque quality, a friendly appeal, in this setting amidst tall coconut trees. Along the way are roadside stands offering green drinking coconuts for sale: *"Hay pipas,"* the signs say. Stop

Waiting for the bus to Puerto Limón.

and enjoy a *pipa*. Someone will come out of the house carrying a machete and cut the coconuts open for you. They are much more refreshing than a sugary soft drink, and good for your kidneys, too, or so they say.

In many yards are low, wooden dryers with tin roofs, used for drying cacao and coconut. The roofs are opened to the bright sun on clear days, and closed in the rain.

Just before the turnoff to Puerto Viejo, is **Hone Creek**. Hone is the name of a short palm with large roots. The palm bears a fruit, also called hone, from which the local Indians made cooking oil. When the Jamaicans came to the Talamanca Coast to work on the railroad in the 1890's, they began calling it "Home Creek," and today there are official-looking road signs in the area, announcing both "Hone Creek" and "Home Creek."

There is usually a checkpoint with a guard at Hone Creek, seeking to stem the flow of contraband goods from Panamá. To get to Puerto Viejo, take the gravel road to the left. Watch for cacao trees in the now-abandoned cacao plantations along the sides of the road. The fruit grows from the trunk of the tree and turns wonderful colors as it ripens: some become a soft turquoise color, others a brilliant coral. The seeds of the ripe fruit are slightly sweet and undeniably chocolatey, even before they are processed.

Puerto Viejo: **Puerto Viejo**, in contrast to Cahuita's shabby dignity, is a tumbledown Caribbean town. It is a hodgepodge of small, dilapidated wooden houses amidst tall grass and occasional piles of garbage. At the entrance to the town, after one passes the rusted-out barge permanently anchored just off the black sand beach, there's a hurricane-wracked green tin building with a halfway gone roof where the local shoe repair man works in front of a large, open window.

It wasn't long ago that there were no roads to Puerto Viejo; no cars, no tourists, no money. But things have changed. Puerto Viejo's beautiful, undeveloped beaches and easy-going ways have been discovered. New, though small, cabinas, hotels, and developments throughout the area proclaim the arrival of tourism.

North of town is the road to **Cabinas Chimuri**, cabinas constructed of thatch over bamboo in the traditional Bribri Indian style. Chimuri's owner, Mauricio, is wise in the way of the jungles and gives guided horseback tours. **El Pizote Surf Lodge**, located on the right just before town, offers lovely cabins and rooms, well-groomed grounds with trails and good, California-Tico style meals. They also rent bikes, diving gear and horses.

Soda Támara offers some of the best food in town: Caribbean style fish or chicken served with tasty beans and rice and a good selection of fruit drinks. **Stanford's** on the beach is famous for its night life and fish dinners. **The Coral** has what is easily the best breakfast in town, maybe in all of Costa Rica, and excellent pizza.

The **Salsa Brava** breaks over the reef in front of Stanford's. It's a hot, fast, explosive wave which happens from

After a storm, the beach near Punta Uva.

December to April and brings surfers from all over the world. Their influence on local young men is unmistakable: one sees them sporting the latest surf fashions as they walk with their boards to the beach.

There are cabinas along the road to the south of town across from beautiful stretches of white sand beaches edged by palm and beach almond trees. Rivers are bridged by precarious-looking wooden arrangements, which can become slippery in the rain. Signs advertise bicycles for rent, a great way to get around Puerto Viejo and to the nearby beaches.

Along this road is the newly opened **Condotel Playa Chiquita** development. The exceptional Condotel offers complete condominium units, located on an alluring white sand beach with a coral reef, ideal for snorkeling, just offshore. Guided fishing trips are led by local fishermen who will show you the traditional methods of fishing the Talamanca coast, as well as their best-kept secret: the location of the fishing spots. Addi-

tionally, Condotel has such niceties as a traditional, painted oxcart offering rides for kids, and their own organic gardens.

To the south of Puerto Viejo is heavenly **Punta Uva**, where crystalline, aqua water laps quietly on palm lined beaches. Both the air and water temperature seem fixed at a constant, perfect 80 degrees. Further south still on the beach is **Manzanillo**, a tiny coastal village which can be reached by walking along the sand for about two hours from Punta Uva, or by the dirt and gravel road which abruptly stops when it reaches Manzanillo. Here one finds a cluster of houses, a restaurant, a bar, a grocery store, lovely, empty beaches and some very inexpensive cabinas. Local children play in the waves or bathe in the river, men fish in dugout canoes, elders sit around and talk quietly in the shade, and not much more goes on. It's a perfect early morning or late afternoon walk from Punto Uva, along deserted beaches, and once there and resting in the shade of a beach almond tree, the cares of the world tend to fall away.

Josefinas on holiday.

Local women such as Miss Marva, Miss Alfonsina, Miss Edith and doña Cipriana will prepare meals for visitors in their homes if asked, and fisherman and farmers are often happy to chat about their work and the land.

The **Manzanillo-Gandoca Wildlife Refuge,** which protects swamp lands, coral reefs, turtle nesting grounds and the only mangrove forest on Costa Rica's Atlantic Coast, is south of the village of Manzanillo. The **Gandoca River Estuary** is a nursery for tarpon. Most of the refuge is flat or has gently rolling hills, covered with forest, grasslands and some farms. Hiking is limited to the coast. Bring water. Information about the refuge can be obtained from Benson and Florentino Grenald in Manzanillo. A list of the area's birds is also available.

The Road to Sixaola: Sixaola is a border town on the **Panamá-Costa Rica border**. To reach Sixaola, continue along the paved road from Hone Creek to the south, instead of turning off to Puerto Viejo and Manzanillo. The road is paved until just outside of Bribri: the rest of the way it is gravel, in fair condition.

In the early 1900's the United Fruit Company sought to expand its successful banana plantations on the Panamá side of the Sixaola River into Costa Rica. They acquired land, began planting bananas, built a bridge across the Sixaola River, constructed a railroad and built banana processing plants along the tracks.

From just outside the village of Bribri to the border at Sixaola, it is Banana Land. The road is lined on both sides with acre after acre of banana trees as far as the eye can see, the ripening fruit wrapped in blue plastic bags which are impregnated with insecticide. Small banana villages and settlements, some consisting of only a few unpainted company houses, a company store and bar, interrupt the sea of banana leaves, and blue plastic.

Banana processing plants occur at intervals along the road: it's interesting to stop for a break at one of the open air plants to watch the workers handling

Creating a Banana Republic, United Fruit, circa 1916.

the large bunches, called *raicimos*, pulling the dried flowers off the ends of individual bananas, cutting bunches of bananas off the stalks, sorting, washing and putting them in boxes which no longer say "United Fruit" but "Chiquita". You may be invited to load up, for free, from the mountain of green bananas, which look perfectly acceptable, but don't meet the exacting specifications of Chiquita's North American and European consumers.

Mountains of such bananas are formed next to the sorting area. They are used for animal feed, given away or allowed to rot. The smell of fermenting bananas is not an unfamiliar one in this part of the country, and even though bananas are used in an uncanny number of resourceful ways, from green banana ceviche, to banana vinegar compresses, a folk remedy for sprained muscles, there are always more ripe bananas than can be used.

Sixaola: The **Sixaola River** forms the border between Panamá and Costa Rica; and on both sides of its banks, connected by an ancient bridge with railroad tracks, border towns have grown up. Panamanians walk across the narrow bridge with their dollars to take advantage of the favorable foreign exchange and purchase groceries, cheap by their standards. One sees them struggling back under the weight of large, white woven plastic bags filled with rice, beans, flour and other staples. Costa Ricans cross to do another type of shopping: they are interested in imported clothes, perfumes, cosmetics and especially *electrodomésticos*, televisions, radios, small home appliances, which can be purchased without the hefty taxes imposed on them by the Costa Rican government.

Both sides of the river are dirty, graceless places, built only to serve the short-term economic needs of those who use them, muddy in the rain, dusty when its not wet, but like many border towns, there's a gutsy vitality to them, and the 4-hour round-trip by car from Puerto Viejo can provide an interesting outing when life on perfect Caribbean beaches calls for a change of scene.

Banana plantations near the Panamanian border.

SEA TURTLES

People like turtles. They are not particularly lovable or attractive, though some turtle conservationists would argue otherwise. In contrast to the modern-day way of life, the turtle's ponderous pace, non-violent nature, and steady perseverance in getting from here to there, seems a more reasonable way to conduct affairs.

Turtles have a prominent place in the religious and folk histories of many cultures. Some Hindu sects venerate the turtle as a living god, the reincarnation of Shiva, creator and destroyer of all life. Myth states that a turtle brought the Buddhist world from the sea on its back.

Unfortunately, sea turtles happen to be considered delicious by many, and are covered with beautiful tortoise shell, characteristics which have driven 6 of the 7 species to the brink of extinction. To early explorers, fresh turtle meat was a welcome change from salt beef and sea biscuits.

Tropical peoples still relish meat from the sea turtle. But sadly, the species is being endangered more from frivolous use than for subsistence purposes. In bars from the Caribbean to Sri Lanka, sea turtle eggs are sucked from the shells as aphrodisiacs. Tortoise shell has a high value when carved, polished, and made into jewelry, combs and spectacle frames. Turtle skin is even being used as a substitute for alligator skin in shoes and purses.

Sea turtles look more like their close but extinct relatives, the dinosaurs, than modern animals. Remarkable adaptations to life in the sea have enabled them to survive, largely unchanged, for over 150 million years. They "fly" like birds through the water using front flippers as wings. Yet they retain terrestrial traits and must surface to breathe air and crawl ashore to nest and lay their eggs.

Costa Rica is home to 5 species of sea turtles: Green, Hawksbill, Olive Ridley, Leatherback, and Loggerhead. They are more easily viewed here than any other place else in the world. They nest at several well-known beaches on both Atlantic and Pacific shores, and during the nesting season, if you happen to be in the right place at the right time, you may see one of the most amazing spectacles in the animal kingdom: 100,000 or more Olive Ridley turtles coming ashore to nest. Or, equally spectacular, the sight of a 1,500-pound Leatherback hauling her massive body out of the water and up the beach to bury her clutch of eggs in the sand. Tortuguero Beach, a 22-mile stretch of beach on the Atlantic side of Costa Rica is the most important nesting area for Green Turtles in the Western Caribbean. On any night, you might see Green Turtles, Hawksbill Turtles and Ridleys nesting.

The Green Turtle colony at Tortuguero has the distinction of being the most thoroughly-studied population of sea turtles in the world. The late Archie Carr, a charter member of the Brotherhood of the Green Turtle, founded the Caribbean Conservation Corps at Tortuguero in 1954.

Green Turtles mate and nest several times from September through November. With the sharp hook on his front flippers, the male holds and mounts the female. If the sexually-aggressive male doesn't locate a mate, he will eagerly clamber on top of anything that floats. Chunks of wood, other male turtles, even skin divers are not safe from a male's passion.

An impregnated female waits offshore until

The timeless act of coming ashore to lay and bury her eggs.

dark before beginning her long struggle up the beach to the nesting site. During her crawl up the beach, disturbances such as noise and light will cause the female to abort the nesting procedure, and to return to the safety of the sea. But once she has begun digging the nest, nothing will distract her. Using her rear flippers, she scoops out a vase-shaped urn, approximately two-feet deep. One hundred or more leathery, golf-ball-sized eggs covered with a mucus "fungicide" drop into the nest one or two at a time until the entire clutch is deposited. She covers the nest, tamps down the sand and begins her crawl back to the sea, leaving her progeny at the mercy of coatimundis, dogs, raccoons, human *hueveros* and other assorted scavengers who steal the eggs and sell them to local bars.

In undisturbed nests, baby Green Turtles hatch in a couple of months. Using a temporary egg tooth, they tear open their shells. Soon the entire clutch is ready to rise to the surface. A critical mass of about 100 cooperating turtles is needed to excavate the 2 feet of sand covering them. Usually before dawn, they erupt onto the beach, look for the brightest part of the horizon over the sea, and scramble for the water through a gauntlet of ghost crabs and birds, perhaps then only to be met by sharks and predatory fish once they do reach the water. Hundreds of thousands race for the sea and only a few, probably less than 3 percent, survive. Those that do make it go offshore to floating rafts of Sargassum weed where they are able to find shelter and food for their first and most difficult months at sea.

For the next several decades, they live nomadic lives, migrating over vast distances of the open ocean to feed on turtle grass in the remote Miskito Keys off Nicaragua or at Cahuita on the Talamanca Coast. Some navigate several thousand miles to the Windward Islands, using no apparent landmarks or visual cues. It is thought that crystals of magnetic iron located in the turtles' brains perhaps serve as an internal compasses, guiding them across the seas.

In about 50 years they reach sexual maturity and reconvene on the beaches where they were born, to mate, nest and complete their incredible reproduction cycle.

Sea turtles remain on the endangered species list although worldwide conservation programs are underway. Importation of turtle products into the United States, as an example, is illegal and carries stiff penalties. Nonetheless, turtle eggs are still plundered by *hueveros*; adult turtles are accidently caught in shrimp trawls; and fishermen continue to hunt them, sometimes legally—the Costa Rican government grants permits to the people of Limón province to take 1,800 turtles per year.

Despite their dwindling numbers, to many local people it seems that the sea turtle will never be extinct. The late Archie Carr's son, David, now director of the Caribbean Conservation Corps, once asked the cook at the Tortuguero Research Station how long people would continue to kill turtles for food. "The tel-tel never finish," she replied. Because they have the whole sea to come from."

Silt from illegally deforested land near Tortugero washes onto the beaches, bringing weeds which grow and take valuable nesting space from the turtles. Floodlights from beachside hotels and developments frighten off females ready to nest, and disorient hatchlings trying to find the sea. Perhaps their greatest hope for survival lies in the notion that people like turtles, and will travel great distances just to observe them. ∎

Against all odds, a baby turtle makes it to ocean's edge.

THE NORTH

The landscape to the north of San José rolls dream-like, lush and impossibly green along the **Central Mountain Range**, the farms punctuated by black and white cows that are, surely, contented. This is dairy country. These Holsteins, so familiar to North Americans, seem worlds apart from the exotic Brahma cattle of the lowlands.

Daytrip to Sarchí and Zarcero: For a 3 or 4 hour excursion from San José, go through Alajuela to Sarchí and Zarcero. Along the road, stop at a roadside stand for some *natilla*, the rich, smooth sour cream, and perhaps some local honey or marmalade and continue through the pastoral villages of these highlands.

Grecia, the pineapple capital of Costa Rica, is definitely worth a stroll and a visit to the dark red, all-metal church.

The approach to the mountain town of **Sarchí** is unmistakable. Distinctive and colorful Sarchí decorative designs can be seen on bus stops, bars and bakeries, restaurants and houses.

Sarchí is a heavily touristed crafts center where one can view artisans painting traditional ox-cart designs and creating household furnishings out of tropical hardwoods. Around the year 1910, as legend has it, a *campesino* was crossing the Beneficio la Luisa when it occurred to him to decorate his ox-cart wheels with colorful mandala-like designs derived from ancient Moorish influences. The art form caught on. Originally each district in Costa Rica had its own special design and one could tell by looking at the cart where the driver lived. Each cart also had its own *"chirrico"*, or song of the wheels. By listening, one could simply easily identify which of his neighbors was passing by.

As late as 1960, the most typical mode of transportation was the ox-cart. It was the only vehicle which could transport agricultural products through the rugged Costa Rican terrain. The father of former president Oscar Arias Sánchez made his original fortune hauling coffee by ox-cart to Puntarenas. The painted carts, pulled by oxen, are still in use today in villages such as San Antonio de Escazú.

In addition to the hardwood furniture and brightly painted replicas of oxcarts for sale in the stores along the highway, one can find in Sarchí such unusual items as canes made from several species of hardwood, with brightly-painted, carved parrot-head handles, and complete croquet sets made of 5 different hardwoods.

There are pleasant little roadside stalls on the outskirts of Sarchí, selling homemade candied fruits and honey and fudge. Here, one will find the proprietors to be unusually kind, and talkative. In comparison to the large touristic furniture shops of Sarchí, a visit to these small stands is a highly personal one, as though stepping into a Costa Rican home.

About 9 miles (15 km) up the road is the town of **Zarcero**. Should you arrive on a day when the highland clouds are swirling through the town or when a

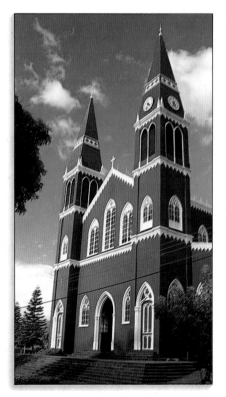

drizzling fog is bathing everything in soft, diffused light, you might feel as though you've just intruded into someone's dream.

Unique in Costa Rica, and possibly the world is the **Central Park** in Zarcero where, for over 2 decades, Evangelisto Blanco, the park gardener, has been clipping and pruning cypress bushes and hedges into a whimsical garden of amazing creatures: bulbous elephants with lightbulbs for eyes, a bull ring complete with spectators, matador and charging bull, Christ bearing His cross and a cat with tail flying, riding a motorcycle along the top of a hedge. Evangelisto has been sculpting the hedges alone for 25 years, 7 days a week, including holidays. The energetic compulsion of his work is reminiscent of Antonio Gaudí, in Spain, and of Simón Rodia, who created the Watts Towers in Los Angeles. Unable to afford marble, Evangelisto works with the plants as his medium of self-expression.

Though he has been offered jobs sculpting gardens in San José and the States, he prefers the small town of Zarcero, where he can leave his clippers out overnight and know that they'll be there in the morning. In the park in front of the church, he is sure to be found gardening, or taking a short break by a wooden shack under a blazing purple bougainvillea.

After the highway turnoff to Zarcero is the 200-year old colonial town of **Palmares**. This lovely area used to be the tobacco-growing center. Perhaps because there is so little tourism in Palmares it is a model town through which to stroll and view Tico life.

Extended trip to Arenal Volcano and Arenal Lake: After perusing gentle Zarcero, instead of returning to San José, consider continuing on the road for another couple of hours, on the highway from Zarcero towards **Arenal Volcano**, the most active volcano on Earth.

After Ciudad Quesada (also called San Carlos) is **Fortuna de San Carlos**. For a night or two in this village, which lies near the base of Arenal Volcano,

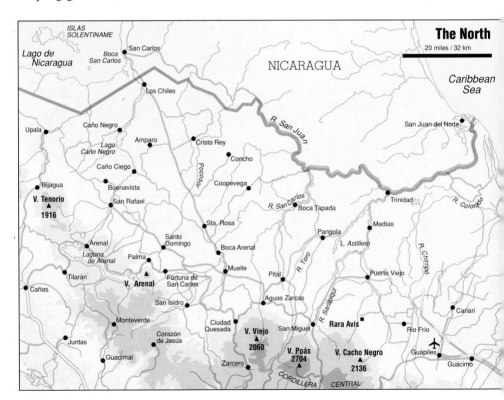

The North

20 miles / 32 km

one might stay at the inexpensive **Albergue Burío**, belonging to world famous fishing guide Peter Gorinsky, or at **Hotel Las Colinas**. More basic and more Tico is the **Hotel Central** in the middle of town, facing the soccer field and church. Avoid rooms facing the main road, unless you wish to be governed by the sounds and rhythms of rural Costa Rica, including the church bell which is rung loudly at 4:00 a.m. by the village crier.

Arenal rises up out of the nearby countryside and looks down upon this simple village and its inhabitants. And, should you be staying there at that time, full moon over Arenal is worth the trip to Costa Rica in itself.

Closer to the volcano, between the town and Lake Arenal, are the **Tabacón Thermal Baths**. From here one can look directly up the small valley to the side of the volcano, at cascades of glowing hot boulders. It appears dangerously close. Arenal heats Tabacon's therapeutic waters to a perfect temperature. Tiled slides and pools are surrounded by tumbling warm water creeks. Take a slide down the mossy aqueduct. At night, one of the natural pools in the meadow beyond the waterworks is a quiet place from which to watch the erupting volcano.

Down the highway past the Thermal Baths is a dirt road going to the left and the **Smithsonian's Observatory**. Arenal is only a mile and a half away. From this point the night air is rich with the sounds of monkeys howling in the distance, of fireflies and a moon rising over Arenal.

Until early July 1968, Arenal was a heavily wooded low hill, similar to others in the area, near the village of La Fortuna. Then one morning the people there began feeling a few earth tremors. Suddenly, the forest started smoking and steaming. Women washing their clothes marvelled at the suddenly warm water which flowed in the creeks. On July 29, it all broke loose and Arenal exploded. Rolling clouds of gas and fountains of red hot boulders and molten lava hit the countryside like a bomb.

Official estimates put the death toll at 62, but local people claim that many more were killed. Over 5 square kilometers of land near the volcano was abruptly changed from pastoral farmland to a landscape out of the Inferno.

Since then, Arenal has been continuously active. It is everyone's preconception of a volcano: conical, rising abruptly out of flatland vegetation. Its volcano-ness is seductive. But do not attempt to climb Arenal Volcano. In 1988, an ex-Peace Corps volunteer ignored warnings, attempted to climb Arenal and was abruptly incinerated.

From the porch of the **Arenal Lodge**, you can sit and watch the volcano showing off in the distance, throwing massive plumes of magenta fire thousands of meters into the sky. The Arenal Lodge is a cozy, elegant place, at the end of a long, tortuous dirt road, with signs warning of Africanized Killer Bees, and chuckholes which discourage casual visits. The surroundings are quiet and intimate, and evenings are conducive to conversation and watching Arenal.

Lake Arenal offers some of Costa Rica's most challenging fresh water fishing. The *guapote* , or rainbow bass, is the favorite of fishermen there. Whether you choose to fish or not, charter a boat and guide to take you sightseeing on the lake. It is preferable to go in the early morning, when, for much of the year, the lake's surface is like glass and the volcano can be viewed as a crystaline reflection. The birding is excellent, the scenery stunning. A few local fishermen will probably be out in the middle of the lake, sitting on chairs perched on a pair of floating balsa logs, fishing for *guapote* with simple handlines.

From December through March, usually in the afternoons, northeasterly winds blow almost daily, and the lake is definitely not calm and glassy. Forty to 50 knots of sustained breeze is not uncommon and whip Arenal into a sea of whitecaps and a destination for windsurfers. There are still only a handful of windsurfers in Costa Rica and little equipment is available. But the

Naturalists or a Sarapiquí bridge near Selva Verde.

wind and waves are there and several windsurfing resorts are in various stages of planning or construction near Tilarán, the best end of the lake for short-board sailing. Some of the places catering to windsurfers are **Rock River Lodge**, **Cabinas Xilde**, and **Aventuras Tilarán**.

Travelers going from Guanacaste to Lake Arenal, whether by bus or car, will pass over some very bad roads to the small town of **Tilarán**. It is a good place to spend the night as it is situated in the hills above the Guanacaste lowlands and is much cooler than Cañas. The countryside around the town is pastoral, the upland meadows spotted with dairy cattle. Villagers will arrange for boats and fishing guides on Lake Arenal. Several small hotels are as clean and friendly as the town.

It is perhaps predictable that such a mythical-appearing lake as Arenal would have a resident monster. A few years ago, some local men were fishing on their balsa raft early one evening and felt a strange vibration, a rumbling in the water. Suddenly, right in front of their frail craft, an enormous black, hairy serpent with horns broke through the surface with a belching roar and a stench. Moments later it slid back into the depths, trailing a tail over 6 feet long. The fishermen scurried back to town and told the story over and over. The story went around and, amplified by time and accounts of half-eaten horse carcasses found floating on the lake, the Monster of Lake Arenal is securely entrenched in local folklore.

A footnote to the local narrative regards a recent high altitude photographic survey of the fault zones around Arenal conducted by NASA. One photo revealed a huge disc of material similar in appearance to polished aluminum hovering over the lake. From NASA's calculations, it seems to have emerged from the water in the northern sector of the lake. At about the same time the photo was taken, local residents reported a strange glow in the lake at the same location as the UFO sighting.

North of Arenal, toward the Nicaraguan border, is the magnificent and still seldom-visited **Caño Negro Wildlife Reserve**. In the heart of this vast area is 2,000 acre (800 hectares) **Lake Caño Negro**. Access to this refuge are from Los Chiles or Upala, on good roads northwest of Cañas.

The Sarapiquí Region: The lush, tropical jungles along the **Sarapiquí River region**, on the Atlantic side of the Cordillera Central, are less than 62 miles (100 km) east of San José. It seems as another continent. La Selva Biological Station, Selva Verde Lodge, and Rara Avis, private reserves with lodging, are all accessible via a paved circuitous highway which begins and ends in San José. The entire circuit, departing via Heredia and returning on the highway through Braulio Carrillo Park, requires approximately 5 hours of driving. A recommended stop along the route is **Rancho Leona**, in La Virgin. Good food, right there in the jungle.

From Heredia, the highway winds up the slope of Poás Volcano to Varablanca, where the short entry road to Poás intersects the main highway. With an early morning departure, there would be ad-

Having fun on the Sarapiquí.

equate time for a visit to the volcano, before crossing the ridge and heading down through heavily forested mountain slopes, past a spectacular waterfall, to the lowland rain forest of the Atlantic seaboard.

Selva Verde Lodge is located on the highway approximately 4 miles (6 km) before reaching **Puerto Viejo de Sarapiquí**, a small port town from which river boats depart for otherwise inaccessible settlements along these jungle waterways. Motor-driven dugout canoes laden with passengers and cargo depart regularly for the full-day trip up the Sarapiquí to the **San Juan River**, on the Nicaraguan border, and then east to Barra del Colorado and the Atlantic.

Several kilometers past Puerto Viejo, it will be necessary to ask a local residents for directions to "OTS" and then locate the unmarked gravel road to La Selva Biological Reserve and Research Station.

Rara Avis' main office and departure point in Las Horquetas is about 10 miles (17 km), a half hour drive, south

of Puerto Viejo. To return to San José, continue past Las Horquetas for another 30 minutes to the intersection with the highway, through Braulio Carrillo park, and then turn right for San José.

Rain forests cover less than 7 percent of the world's surface, yet they contain well over one half of the world's biota. The diversity and abundance of life in the lowland tropical forest of the Sarapiquí River region first attracted the attention of tropical biologists, who founded the **Organization for Tropical Studies (OTS)** and established **La Selva Biological Reserve and Research Station** over 25 years ago.

In 1986, the Costa Rican government made a major commitment to rainforest conservation by extending the boundaries of Braulio Carrillo National Park to meet the 1,500 acre (607 hectares) La Selva Reserve. A total of 52,000 acres (2,104 hectares) of virgin forest extending from sea level to more than 9,800 feet (3,000 meters) in elevation now preserves the migratory pathways and large territories required for the survival of rare and endangered birds and mammals.

Virtually all of the world's tropical biologists have spent time at La Selva as students, teachers or scientists, or they have been strongly influenced by the vast amount of scientific research which has been accomplished there over the past quarter of a century. Dan Janzen, of Guanacaste, one of Costa Rica's most renowned ecologists, first studied at La Selva. He ultimately redesigned and taught the important course in tropical biology which has been taken by hundreds of students.

Many Sarapiquí residents who work at ecotourist lodges were trained as naturalist guides at La Selva, in an innovative program taught by OTS scientists. As a result of this, 2 generations of local people have become interested in and have learned the ways of rain forest conservation. On hikes into the jungle, one can often see young *campesinos* with binoculars who have taken up bird watching, or who are studying to become guides at the burgeoning number of ecotourism centers in the Sarapiquí re-

Enroute to Rara Avis.

gion.

La Selva is primarily a research and educational facility, but tours of the facilities and reserve trails can be arranged by calling La Selva in advance. Tourists are encouraged to seek accommodations at Selva Verde or Rara Avis.

The most spectacular birds can be viewed from the porch of the beautifully designed and constructed **River Lodge**, at Selva Verde, located in the lowland jungle bordering the **Sarapiquí River**. In order to take full advantage of Selva Verde's attractions, have binoculars available at all times. Keel-billed and chestnut-mandibled toucans are two of the most common species to be seen feeding on the fruit of the nutmeg trees, near the front porch of the lodge. Toucans crack open the fruits and swallow the nutmeg.

A stroll along the path to the main lodge building is likely to be rewarded with the iridescent colors of several species of hummingbirds. Nearby, Montezuma Oropendulas utter gurgling mating calls, which harmonize with the songs of other birds and countless frogs and insects in a continual symphony. There are nearly 100 species of birds to be seen at Selva Verde.

In 1986, Giovanna and Juan Holbrook, conservationists from Florida, bought Selva Verde, which consists of 500 acres of primary and secondary tropical lowland forest, along the banks of the Sarapiquí River, in order to save the land from deforestation.

They designed the river lodge to have a minimal impact on the environment. It rests lightly on posts above the forest floor, resembling the jungle spiders which inspired its construction. Guests reside in tropical hardwood rooms at the end of covered corridors, which radiate from a central conference room into the forest. The jungle and its denizens are never more than a few feet away. An extraordinary feeling engendered by this immersion in the lowland forest is one which encourages people to whisper as they speak.

Selva Verde is an exemplary ecotourist center, with a courteous and

Road to Arenal Lodge.

professional staff. Guests are provided with accommodations so comfortable that even the ubiquitous mud and drizzle which characterize the lowland jungle are rarely considered an inconvenience.

Informative tours of Selva Verde's extensive and well-marked trails are guided by local naturalists with decades of experience in the lowland forest. During your visit, plan to take a half day voyage on the Sarapiquí River, where crocodiles, howler monkeys, and exotic birds are to be seen.

One of Selva Verde's main attractions, the incredibly slow-moving arboreal sloth, has a metabolic rate of half of what it should be for an animal of its size. The sloths only descend to the forest floor once a week to defecate, a peculiar and potentially life-threatening behavior which puzzles scientists.

From Selva Verde, drive through Puerto Viejo, and on to El Tigre, several kilometers up the road. Stop for a visit, a cup of herbal tea and possibly a supply of medicinal herbs at the **MUSA**, a co-operative of Sarapiquí women.

Ecologically sensible alternatives to destructive monoculture banana farming, slash and burn agriculture, and cattle ranching, are becoming increasingly recognized by *campesinos* in this area who have come to realize, through their contact with these reserves, that their future depends on the surrounding forest. For them, killing the forest is akin to killing both the chickens and their eggs, leaving nothing for tomorrow.

Whether going by horseback or tractor-drawn cart, travel to **Rara Avis** is difficult and can only be recommended for those who are both physically and mentally fit. The grueling 4 hour journey, over ruts, bogs and rivers, is all part of the commitment to the adventure of Rara Avis, Amos Bien's pristine 1,500-acre rainforest reserve in the mountains above Los Horquetas.

On the road, the transition from cattle ranches to deep jungle illustrates the devastating effects of deforestation more dramatically than any book or film. The tractor and cart lurch along an eroded

Selva Verde's serene walkway.

path, through cattle ranches littered with fallen and unused timber. Even cattle are few and far between. The open land is hot, dry, dusty and inhospitable. Soil is baked crisp by the tropical sun. As a resident along the Sarapiquí for 45 years, phrased it, "The first 35 years here were the best: *Pura bosque, pura vida.* (Pure forest, pure life.)"

Deforested land ends at **El Plástico Lodge**, the last stop before the final 4 mile trip to Waterfall Lodge, high in the forest. This former prison colony gets its incongruous name from the plastic sheets under which the inmates slept. From El Plástico, the road plunges into a dark, cool cathedral-like forest, which teems with life. Less than 2 percent of the tropical sun reaches the forest floor here. The earth is a dense tangle of roots, tree trunks and leaves, soaked in water and bathed in mud.

Amos Bien sells shares in the rainforest. With Rara Avis, he is demonstrating that ecotourism and rainforest conservation for profit are viable economic alternatives to destructive and ineffi-

cient cattle ranching. In Costa Rica, for example, one cow requires nearly one hectare of grassland to produce between 90 and 130 kilograms of meat per year.

Vines used to make furniture, nuts, fruits, medicinal and ornamental plants are renewable forest resources available for harvest and marketing. Bien hopes to show a profit from the horticulture and sale of a rare species of ornamental palm which he recently discovered growing wild at Rara Avis.

The profit that Rara Avis revenue generates for investors and paying guests is shown on the receipt for accommodations. An example would be: .00005 jaguars, .00085 bird species, .01 white lipped peccaries, .1 agoutis, 10,000 mushrooms, one million ants, etc.

The **Waterfall Lodge** at Rara Avis accommodates guests in comfortable rooms with private baths. Hot water showers are welcome when the evening chill arrives. One of Rara Avis' main attractions is the swimming hole and 180-foot waterfall, draped with vines, ferns and tropical flowers. And amidst this idyllic tropical paradise can be heard the incongruous creaking of a cable car passing overhead.

Donald Perry, a "free lance biologist" with a love of tropical rainforests and a flair for the dramatic has provided scientists with a direct look at a previously inaccessible habitat. His book, *Life Above the Jungle Floor,* is excellent. Many feel that the elevated canopy habitat contains nearly 50 percent of earth's plants and animal species. On his bizarre-looking **AWCE,** or **Automated Web for Canopy Exploration**, a cable car travels on wires over the river gorge above the waterfall, and through the forest canopy. After signing a liability release, travelers may accompany one of the guides on a 15- minute excursion through one of earth's last truly unexplored frontiers.

Because it is such a rarified and isolated place, one should always arrange transportation in advance by calling Rara Avis. Access is difficult, but most feel that the mud and almost non-existent roads into the area are just part of the experience.

White Ibises at treetop.

The South

20 miles / 32 km

V. Barva
2906

Guápiles

Guácimo

R. Pacuare

Siquerres

Matina

Bahía
Moin

Puerto
Limón

UVITA

Caribbean

Sea

V. Turrialba
3328

Heredia

V. Irazú
3432

San José

Turrialba

Asunción

Bomba

Penshurst

Cartago

Presa
de Cachi

La Suiza

C. Matama
2251

Frailes

Cristóbal

Chirripó Abajo

Pandora

Pto. Viejo

San
Isidro

San
Pablo

R. Pacuare

Chirripó
Arriba

R. Telire

Shíroles

Bribrí

Copey da Dota

San
Marcos

San
Rafael

C. Vueltas

3156

Teliré

R. Chirripó Atlántico

Kichuguecha

CORDILLERA TALAMANCA

C. La Muerte

3491

Naranjito

R. División

Cerro Chirripó

3820

R. Chirripó Pacific

C. Stútuk
2416

Alto Lari

R. Teribé

Savegre

C. Dúrika

3280

C. Utyúm

3078

Hatillo

PL. BARÚ
Dominical

PL. DOMINICALITO

Plátanillo

San Isidro

Esperanza

Cajón

C. Kámuk

3549

PANAMA

San Rafael

VALLE DE EL GENERAL

Volcán

R. Siní

Uvita

Buenos Aires

Cabagra

R. General

C. Echandi
3167

Boca Coronado

Coronado

Potrero
Grande

C. Pittier
2869

Palmar
Norte

Boruca

Cortés

Boca Brava

Palmar
Sur

R. Grande de Térraba

Coto Brus

C. Pando
2468

Bahía de

Coronado

R. Sierpe

Pilón

Piedras
Blancas

San Vito

Wilson
Botanical Gardens

ISLA
DEL CAÑO

Bahía Drake

PL. COLORADA

Rincón

PL.
CATIVO

Golfito

Agua Buena

Río Claro

Neily

R. Chiriquí Viejo

San
Andrés

Marenco
Biological Station

PENÍNSULA

San Pedrillo

PL. LLORANA

Los Patos

DE

PL. CACAO

Golfo
Dulce

Zancudo

Canoas

Sirena

OSA

Port
Jiménez

Pueblo
Nuevo

La Cuesta

PL. PAVONES

Carate

Río Claro

Pacific

Cabo
Matapalo

Tiskita

Pto. Armuelles

Ocean

PENÍNSULA
DE BURICA

Bahía de
Charco Azul
o de David

Pta. Burica

THE SOUTH

For more than 31 miles (50 km), the **Osa Peninsula** juts into the Pacific, sheltering **Golfo Dulce** from ocean swells and creating a magnificent natural harbor. It is sculpted with picturesque beaches, rocky headlands and is dissected by streams and rivers which cascade over volcanic cliffs on their way to the sea. Parts of the coastline resemble California's Big Sur Coast, but as yet there have been no poets, photographers or painters to celebrate it. The most majestic forests in this country cover the hills and line the valleys of this peninsula and, in many cases, represent the last stronghold of nature and endangered animals and plants which are endemic to Southern Pacific Costa Rica. It is an imposing, impressive and wild place.

Corcovado National Park, a 100,000 acre (40,470 hectare) sanctuary of biological diversity and endangered wildlife, dominates the rugged **Osa Peninsula**. It is the site of many of Costa Rica's most significant environmental conflicts. The park is one of wild animals living among tall trees that are draped with vines and lianas, supported by massive buttress roots, on a forest floor teeming with life.

The Indians of the Diquis region were the first inhabitants of the Peninsula, named Osa for one of their chiefs. The Indians were accomplished goldsmiths and fashioned religious and ceremonial pieces from gold they found in the Tigre and Claro Rivers. Throughout the Conquest, the Spanish made repeated explorations into Osa, killing the Indians, plundering their gold and searching for the legendary mines of Veragua.

Gold continues to cause problems for Corcovado and the people of the Osa Peninsula. In the 1980s, Corcovado's rivers produced gold in quantities large enough to create a gold rush. The discovery of a 25-pound gold nugget was enought to inspire farmers to become prospectors and invade the park, where they tore up creeks and rivers for flakes of placer gold, hunted wild life, and burned the forest to plant crops. Gold fever destroyed many thousands of acres of park land. Alcoholism, prostitution, and the socio-economic ills accompanying a gold rush boom town plagued Corcovado. Government officials closed the park for years while they attempted to evict the trespassers. After a minor civil war, officials reluctantly agreed to pay the miners a stipend to leave the park. The payoff was moderately successful, but 100 or more miners continue to live and mine gold inside Corcovado. Their impact on the El Tigre River continues, yet the government has chosen to ignore them, rather than risk more civil strife.

Because Corcovado Park is innundated with nearly 20 feet of rain a year, it is technically known as a "tropical wet forest." The simplicity of that classification belies the ecological complexity of the park. Thirteen distinct habitats here are each characterized by unique assemblages of plants, animals and topography. Five hundred species of trees—one fourth of all the species in

Costa Rica, 10,000 insects, hundreds of species of birds, frogs, lizards, and turtles, and many of the world's most endangered and spectacular mammals live here.

With the support of hundreds of scientists worldwide, in 1975 President Daniel Oduber acknowledged the inestimable scientific value of Corcovado's diverse biological resources by establishing Corcovado National Park. The presidential decree went into effect just in time. A gigantic logging operation was about to begin and squatters, hunters and gold miners settling in the Osa Peninsula in increasing numbers were rapidly destroying the forest.

One of Corcovado's blessings is its inaccessibility. It is a park for naturalists prepared to make a considerable commitment in time and energy to experience it in its entirety.

There are some simple, but fairly expensive, ways to sample Corcovado's wealth without spending a week or two on grueling hikes, fording rivers and battling insects.

From San José, one-hour charter flights depart for the **Marenco-Drake Bay** airstrip adjacent to Corcovado Park. The flights pass over Manuel Antonio Park and provide aerial perspectives of the south Pacific coast enroute to Corcovado. After landing on the grass airstrip, scarlet macaws may be seen flying from their roosts in the trees near the airstrip. Boats from Marenco or Drake Bay meet guests on the beach in front of the airstrip.

Marenco Biological Station is situated adjacent to Corcovado on its own 1,200-acre (486 hectare) reserve above the beach. Guests reside in rustic, thatched-roof lodgings with views of the Pacific and Caño Island Biological Reserve. Three-day package tours include naturalist-led hikes through Marenco's rainforest, a day on the fringes of Corcovado hiking the trails to Llorona waterfalls and swimming in the fresh water pools of the Río Claro, followed by a day exploring Caño Island. **Drake Bay Wilderness Camp** just north of Marenco offers similar programs in

Marenco's airstrip in the rainforest.

addition to boat trips up the Sierpe River, and leisurely canoeing in the jungle river next to the lodge.

If you decide to spend a week or more hiking and camping in Corcovado, make advance arrangements with the park headquarters in Puerto Jiménez, on the east coast of the Osa Peninsula, or telephone from San José. An ideal 8 day itinerary might include 2 nights at each of 3 park stations in Corcovado, with days spent hiking from one station to the next. Stations are joined by trails each of which require from 3 to 10 hours of hiking time.

The park stations can be reached by charter plane, by hiking or by vehicle during the dry season, December through April. Of the two charter aircraft companies, Aeronaves has a poor record of meeting pre-arranged schedules. Passengers with confirmed reservations have been left marooned in the park, or charged exorbitant fees for their return trips. Saeta Airlines, on the other hand, has an excellent record of meeting pre-arranged schedules. **Sirena Station**, near the beach, is a pleasant place to spend at least 2 days. Accommodations and meals cost about $15 per night. There are several well-marked and well-maintained trails into the forest and along the beach. Swimming in nearby **Río Claro** is refreshing, but sharks are said to frequent the ocean near the river mouth.

Los Patos station is a 7- mile hike from **Sirena** on a wide trail paralleling the **El Tigre River**. The heavy siltation in the river is the result of illegal gold panning activity which is still done in this area. The wide trail allows relatively easy wildlife viewing. Even though it passes through thick forest, you stand a reasonably good chance of seeing at least tracks of jaguar, ocelot and tapir, if not the animals themselves. At **Los Patos**, there are simple accommodations available. A 4–wheel drive road to the station is open during the dry season.

The trek to or from **San Pedrillo Station** and nearby **Llorona Waterfalls** requires careful advance planning. Two rivers must be crossed at low tide during the 7 to 10 hour hike. Rangers at Sirena can provide unreliable estimates of transit times and tidal heights. Plan to take a tide table, food, water, and camping gear; you may need to use them enroute to San Pedrillo. San Pedrillo is also accessible by a 2 hour trail from the Marenco-Drake Bay airstrip.

In Corcovado, be advised that you are mostly on your own, surrounded by a remote, overwhelming and magnificent environment which is potentially dangerous. Though rare, coral snakes and vipers such as the fer-de-lance do live in the forest and their bites can be life threatening. Bring and know how to use antivenin kits for both varieties of snakes.

Don Rómulo, a resident of the Osa Peninsula forest for over 35 five years, has been bitten 4 times by the fer-de-lance, or *terciopelo*. These brown vipers grow to more than 6 feet long and are characterized by their triangular head. Fortunately they are rare, but they deserve their fearsome reputation. They attack readily and inject large quantities of virulent neurotoxin. People familiar with the forest pour a concoction of hot cooking oil and garlic directly on the

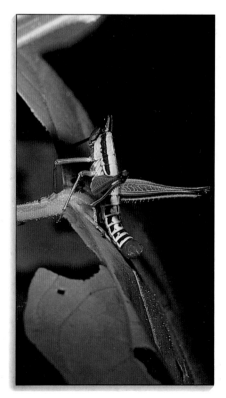

Colorful grasshopper.

wound to denature the protein in the venom. The fact than Don Rómulo is still alive attests to the efficacy of local folk medicine.

Of the estimated 250 jaguars remaining in the country, most are found in the forests of Corcovado, Tortuguero, and the Talamanca Cordillera on the southern Atlantic Coast. An adult jaguar needs an enormous amount of land with abundant prey animals such as peccaries, deer and agouti to meet its food requirements. Since Corcovado Park was established, its jaguar population has more than tripled. Tracks are commonly seen on many of the trails, and are relatively easy to identify. The prints are wider than they are long, have 3 rear pads, and 4 unequal toes showing no claw marks. A large male jaguar has been seen regularly in the forest just behind the Marenco-Drake Bay airstrip.

Herds of white-lipped peccaries roam the forest and root in the leaf litter for food. Evidence of their passing is easily seen. It will look much like a bulldozer has gone through the forest. Stories of

hunters being eaten ("There was nothing left but his boots.") by herds of peccaries with the frightening habit of gnashing their teeth before they attack, are unnerving. Though their reputation as the forest's most ferocious animals are exaggerated, do not hesitate to climb the nearest tree if you find yourself in the unenviable position of being surrounded by them.

Nearly 300 species of birds live in Corcovado, of which scarlet macaws are the most spectacular. They loudly announce their arrival with gravelly shrieks. If you hear a cry like a puppy, look for a toucan hopping through the trees, with its outlandish yellow bill. Seeds or husks dropping through the forest will often reveal the presence of a flock of yellow-cheeked parrots, or possibly troops of squirrel monkeys or spider monkeys foraging in the canopy overhead. To enhance your chances of seeing these animals, be on the trail very early, preferably before dawn.

Orchids, bromeliads, philodendrons and ferns grow attached to trees high in the forest where they find abundant light, airborne nutrients and water. Rich compost created by the epiphyte gardens is often exploited by the host tree which sprouts roots from its branches, and taps into the aerial soil.

The dense growth of epiphytes in the trees creates a fantastic home for tiny red and blue poison dart frogs, who live in pools of water caught by bromeliad leaves. Females lay their eggs on land, and later carry the developing tadpoles on their backs 100 feet or more up the trees to these pools, where they lay unfertilized eggs to feed their offspring.

Mushrooms and bracket fungi with strange shapes and astounding colors stud the rotting trunks of fallen trees. Fingernail-sized frogs, and tiny salamanders live in the damp hollows of logs or under moist leaf litter. They are difficult to see, but the sudden movement of a leaf might reveal their whereabouts. More obvious are the basilisk or Jesus Christ lizards, so named because they appear to walk on water as they move over the surfaces of ponds on their hind legs.

The lodge at Marenco.

ANTS IN YOUR PLANTS

Should someone point out a "bull's horn acacia" to you, stop and have a close look at this thorny shrub. Between 4 and 10 feet tall, this acacia has branches along which are pairs of reddish spines that look like miniature replicas of a Texas steer's horns. Hence its name.

Of the many relationships which have evolved between tropical ants and plants, that of the bull's horn acacia and its stinging ants is one of the most curious. It is also one of the most dramatic examples of tropical co-evolution between species.

With some caution, shake the end of a branch. Ants burrow into the end of the spines (notice the tiny hole), excavate the inside of the branch, and set up a colony where they rear their young and go about the business of being ants. When the plant is disturbed, as in the case of your shaking the branch, the pugnacious ants charge aggressively from the spines, stingers armed and ready to defend their acacia host. It would only take one nasty sting to convince you that this defense system works.

In addition to repelling would-be grazers, ranging in size from caterpillars to cattle, the ants manicure the ground around the acacia, keeping it clear of sprouts from other plants which might deprive their host for living space in a tropical forest containing 1,200 species of trees and countless other plants.

And the acacia is appreciative. Not only does it shelter its guardian ants, it also feeds them. Tiny, sausage-shaped bodies hang from the ends of the leaflets. Loaded with sugar and protein, they are harvested by the ants.

On the forest floor you're almost sure to spot trails carved by leaf cutter ants as they march through the jungle in search of tender leaves to attack. Their trails are veritable highways of activity. Imagine thousands of people walking home on the highway, each rushing along, carrying a 4 foot by 8 foot sheet of green plywood overhead, and you have the concept of these ants. Leafcutters are amazingly industrious insects. They can completely denude a full-grown mango tree overnight, carving circular slabs of leaf about half an inch in diameter, hoisting them overhead and marching down the tree trunk back to the hive, perhaps a half mile away or more.

Several highways lead to their hive—often around the buttress roots of a large tree. Hives of over 100 square meters, 2 meters deep in the forest floor are not uncommon.

In these hives, millions, perhaps billions, of ants chew the leaf fragments, mixing them with nutrient-rich saliva, into a gruel. From this gruel the ants grow and harvest mushrooms which provide their food source.

Large ant colonies can cut and process nearly a hundred pounds of leaves a day. During the decades long life span of an ant colony, tons of vegetation decompose and are worked back into the forest floor. Constant rain and heat rapidly degrade tropical soils, and so the vast storehouse of nutrients and compost from the ant mounds create a rich oasis in the soil, which, without the ants would be nearly sterile. These underground grottoes of fungi must be one of the planet's strangest places to live. The mushrooms grow nowhere else. When a colony divides, the pregnant, dethroned queen carries a bit of fungus and compost with her, to set up a garden and feed her new brood.

Watch the forest floor and note the intense activity going on, just beside your feet. ∎

Leafcutters in action.

Caño Island sits low on the horizon, 9 miles (15 km) seaward of the Corcovado coastline, and a pleasant one-hour boat ride from either Marenco or Drake Bay. Caño, according to prominent archaeologists, was both a cemetery for indigenous people and a refuge for pirates.

Spotted dolphins riding the boat's bow wave, and flying fish sailing off the top of ocean swells sometimes escort the traveler to the island. Between December and April, 40-ton humpback whales come from their feeding grounds in Alaska. Males sing haunting songs to attract females, and often leap clear of the water in impressive breaches during their procreative sojourn through Costa Rican waters.

In 1978, Caño Island was declared a biological reserve. But a more important event in Caño's history took place in 1973. At that time the island was rented to a foreign conglomerate, to be developed as a major tourist resort, which threatened to do serious environmental damage to the island. Extraordinary coral and reef fish communities would be destroyed by contaminated water and waste; a pre-Columbian cemetery would be desecrated by bulldozers; and the surrounding forest devastated. In what is today known as Costa Rica's first "ecological feat," a protest movement of students, citizens, and the Association of Biologists permanently stopped construction of the resort and saved Caño Island.

The island is ringed with turquoise water, tiny beaches, and acres of coral-covered rock reefs. Brilliantly colored tropical fish are easily seen by skin divers within 50 feet (15 meters) of the shore at the park headquarters.

Well-manicured trails lead through a rich forest drooping with epiphytes. There are philodendrons here so large that any of them would easily fill a living room. Ask a guide to identify sour cane. Peel the hairy skin off of a piece of stem and chew on the pulp for a taste of the juice.

At the highest point on Caño, the forest thickens and becomes silent. Dried

The isolated beaches of Caño.

leaves crackle underfoot as one approaches the **pre-Columbian cemetery of the Bruncas Indians**. Two stone spheres sit among the trees. Green with moss and lighted with shafts of sun from the forest canopy, the enigmatic spheres seem impossibly symmetrical in this forest of twisted plants. Though their exact origin and significance have defied explanation, it is speculated that they were made in villages on the Osa Peninsula near Palma Norte and Indians brought them to Caño in canoes, and possibly rolled them to the highest point on the island, the cemetery. Though stone spheres the size of oranges were possibly toys, larger ones, up to 2 meters in diameter, may have indicated the political or social standing of the deceased. Graves with spheres as headstones, oriented to the east, had secret chambers for precious ornaments and were covered with layers of sand, coral and pebbles.

To leave the Osa Peninsula, charter a boat from Marenco Station or Drake Bay Wilderness camp, or hire a local dugout canoe, and travel up the wide, muddy **Sierpe River** to the town of **Sierpe**.

The shores of the river are lined with mangrove trees. The maze of roots of these trees is inhabited by many species of small fish. On the way upriver, look for crocodiles and their smaller relatives, the caimans, lurking around the fringes of tangled roots. Blue herons and flocks of snowy egrets may fly from the trees as the boat passes.

These maritime mangrove forests are not immune to deforestation. Mangroves are cut and used to make charcoal. The bark is stripped and tannin, used to cure leather, is extracted. Fortunately, damage has been minimal so far, and the Sierpe mangroves continue to provide refuge for many animals living on the boundary between land and sea.

The voyage may give you the feeling that you have just stepped aboard the *African Queen*. A wide variety of boats ply their trade on the Sierpe. Weatherbeaten dugout canoes loaded down with bananas, and smoking cargo boats share the river with vacationers'

speedboats and naturalist tour vessels from nearby lodges. About 2 hours upriver is the **Las Vegas Bar** in the dusty town of Sierpe where a bus can be caught to take the traveler south to Golfito.

Golfito, situated on the eastern shore of the Golfo Dulce, is sheltered from the open sea by islands and peninsulas which form a perfect harbor within the gulf. In 1938, United Fruit Company realized Golfito's potential, and built a major shipping port here. By 1955 over 90 percent of the bananas shipped from Costa Rica departed on the Great White Fleet of banana boats from Golfito. Boatloads of crewmen and 15,000 *Guanacasteco* immigrants came to work the plantations. They turned Golfito into a boom town of brothels, smugglers and drunks. United Fruit or "Mamita Yunai," not the most benevolent of companies, was seen to be funneling profits out of Costa Rica and into the pockets of rich North American stockholders and became the symbol for hated Yankee imperialism.

Oropendula nests.

Following crippling strikes and conflicts with labor, United Fruit decided to close down and leave Golfito in 1985. Depression set in and former employees of the company found themselves leaving town or searching for work as fishermen or farmers. Recently Golfito has begun to make a slow comeback and the old town, referred to as the **Pueblo Civil**, is regaining a touch of its boom town atmosphere. Bars and prostitutes do business on the side streets; lively outdoor cafes overlooking the pier have taken over the main street.

In the recently classified "**duty free zone**" on the waterfront, TVs, refrigerators, bedroom sets and other consumer dreams sell at about 40 percent off the San José price. Shoppers must be Costa Rican and are limited to spending US$400, once every 6 months. Additionally, they must stay in the zone for at least 24 hours, spending much of the money they might have saved on expensive hotel rooms.

The **American Zone of Golfito** has a sleepy, suburban atmosphere. This former United Fruit Company neighborhood is one of large wooden plantation style homes on stilts, with screened porches and hip roofs.

Before leaving Golfito, drive to the top of **Golfito Forest Reserve**. A sign marks the road in Barrio Invu across from the Plaza Deportes soccer stadium. During the drive, watch for toucans and sloths in the trees beside the steep, winding, gravel road. At the top, the panoramic views of beautiful **Golfo Dulce** are spectacular.

South of Golfito from the mouth of the Río Coto to Punta Banco some of Costa Rica's most inaccessible and remote beaches line the eastern shore of Golfo Dulce. In the forest above Punta Banco is the Tiskita Jungle Lodge. To make the trip to Tiskita, a 4 wheel drive vehicle is essential. This will become immediately obvious as one approachs the loading ramp to the aging 2 car ferry across the **Río Coto**. While waiting for the ferry, which runs until 10 p.m., but only on a high tide, enjoy a meal of perhaps the best shrimp in salsa in Costa

A naturalist gathers butterflies in the Golfito reserve.

Rica at the riverside restaurant next to the ferry.

In **Pueblo Nuevo**, the first town after the ferry, turn right for **Zancudo Beach**, along sand crescent, in which developers are just beginning to take interest. Continue on the road paralleling the coast to **Pavones**, a surf spot just before Río Claro. After the seemingly endless pot holes, bogs and washboard bumps in the road, continue on for another 30 minutes to **Punta Banco**, the last major point of land before the Panamanian border. Wide intertidal flats of volcanic and sedimentary rock, riddled with tidepools full of marine life and battered by continual surf characterize Punta Banco.

At the end of the point, a pasture and gate on the left mark the entry to **Tiskita Jungle Lodge**, Peter Aspindall's private rainforest reserve, experimental tropical fruit farm, and eco-lodge. Far removed from civilization, here there are contemplative encounters with forest, waterfalls, monkeys, birds and tidepools.

The tortuous drive can be avoided by using a package tour, including a private airplane charter which sets down on a grass airstrip near the lodge. Isolated cabins with ocean views are less than a 10 minute walk from the main lodge. Well-designed and manicured trails lead to waterfalls, idyllic swimming holes, and points of natural history interest in Tiskita's 400-acre (162 hectare) forest.

Over 100 species of fruit trees from around the tropical world are under cultivation here. A fruit-tasting trip through the farm makes one wonder why vendors in San José do so well selling Washington State apples and California table grapes.

For a more academic experience in tropical botany, visit **Wilson Botanical Gardens** in **Las Cruces,** almost 4 miles (6 km) from the Italian colony of San Vito on Highway 16. The gardens are operated by the Organization for Tropical Studies (OTS) as a center for research, scientific training and public education in tropical botany. Designed

Little "Mirror" butterflies mating.

by an Italian landscape architect, trails through extensive collections of "lobster claw" heliconias, bromeliads, tree ferns, orchids and palms ultimately lead into the wild forest reserve behind the gardens.

The gardens offer simple, dormitory-style accommodations and the opportunity to talk with visiting scientists in residence, or attend seminars by horticultural societies from around the world.

Villa Neilly-San Vito Road, like the Inter-American Highway, was built in 1945 by the USA as a strategic protection point, being situated due west of the Panamá Canal. The gravel road rises sharply into the cool mountains that lead to **San Vito** at 3,150 feet (960 meters) above sea level. San Vito was founded by immigrants from post-war Italy, who were encouraged by the Costa Rican government to settle there. It's a clean, modern town of 10,000, located high in a moutain valley, where one can get a good Italian meal and hear Italian spoken on the streets. One place to stay in San Vito is **Cabinas Las Mirlas**—or

one could spend the night at Wilson Botanical Gardens, 3 miles (less than 5 km) away.

El Valle de El General (The Valley of the General):People had attempted to find a pass through the Talamanca Mountains to join the Central Valley with the unknown lands on the other side of the Dota Mountains since Colonial times, but it was not until the end of the 1860s that Don Pedro Calderón, responding to a prize offered by the government, found the way. The opening of the road led to the colonization of the **Valle de El General,** and later, to the building of the Inter-American Highway, which connects San José and the Central Valley with the southern Pacific section of Costa Rica. To travel to the Valle de El General and destinations to the south, get an early start, hopefully to avoid the fog and rain which often appear later in the day, and take the Inter-American Highway through Cartago. Once on the other side of Cartago, take the road to San Isidro.

The route to the Valle de El General passes over the spectacular **Cerro de la Muerte** (Mountain of Death), which rises to 11,000 feet (3,353 meters). Named for early foot travelers who died crossing the mountain, presumably from the storms and frigid temperatures, Cerro de la Muerte is not as inhospitable as its name suggests. Rain, cold and fog can make the first half of the drive miserable, but quickly the road is above the clouds in cool, crisp sunshine, surrounded by fields of flowers and hillside farms. Purple foxglove, azaeleas and white cala lilies grow wild. Clouds swirl through the valleys and over peaks. Views are unsurpassable.

As you are ascending Cerro de la Muerte, **Empalme,** a crossroads store and *soda,* is on the right. It's a good opportunity to stretch your legs, breathe some brisk mountain air, and warm yourself with a hot cup of coffee. The store sells a variety of locally produced items, from fresh peaches and apples to delicious coconut cookies and milk fudge.

La Lucha Sin Fin (The Endless Struggle), the finca of former president

Misty Cerro de la Muerte contains several life zones.

A TROPICAL FOREST WATCHER'S GUIDE

Do not be disappointed if, on your first few visits to tropical rain forest you fail to see the hundreds of birds species and spectacular large cats, monkeys and sloths that are listed as living there. In fact, your first impression of the rain forest will be of green wall of vegetation, not the spectacular variety of colorful animals you had come to expect. A great diversity of organisms inhabit the tropical forest because, for millenia, they have succeeded in avoiding the attention of predators.

Before setting off into the forest: Familiarize yourself with guidebooks which describe animals living in the area. Note characteristics which are used to identify them, such as color, shape and behavior.

Determine the time of day or night when they are most active. A good pair of binoculars is essential. They can also be used backwards as a powerful magnifying glass.

Take every opportunity to charter a boat for lake or river trips. They are always worth the investment.

Observe safety tips before proceeding. Remember that even though it may look like Disneyland, it isn't.

Notify someone of your intentions: where you are going, when you plan to arrive. Bring water, insect repellent, flashlight, sunscreen, umbrella or rain poncho, and hat.

Look before you touch, step, sit or lean. Scan the trail for slippery rocks, mud, downed trees, ants and snakes. Then move ahead while you search the canopy for animals. Continually shift your gaze. Do not wander off into the woods following a bird without carefully looking where you step. Snakes are rare but potentially lethal.

General guideline: Forest wildlife viewing is easiest and most productive along habitat "edges" next to rivers, beaches, open fields, roads and trail heads.

Look for shapes, colors and behaviors which stand out and do not appear to "fit" the design of the forest vegetation.

In the dry season: deciduous forests lose their leaves, opening the canopy for viewing; water sources are frequented by thirsty animals.

Wildlife observation tips: Seasoned forest watchers, like legendary animal trackers, are alert to certain small and easily overlooked clues which indicate the presence of animals or birds in the forest. Things rustling, or dropping from the forest canopy, especially on a windless day, and unexplained noises, often indicate the presence of a nearby animal. Seeds or leaves dropping from above are probably caused by parrots, monkeys or sloths in the canopy. Fruits, nuts, seed husks or leaf fragments in the trail mean a food tree is nearby and perhaps feeding animals or birds.

Large, dark shapes and tree crotches might be sleeping sloths, anteaters or monkeys. Logs on river banks could be crocodiles. Rotten tree sections are often home to amphibians, insects, fungi and mosses. Holes in trees might contain bird's nests.

When you have developed some skills in seeing and identifying some of the plants and animals, think about why they live where they do; what they eat; what other animals they are living with. Soon you will begin to understand the complexity which makes the tropical forest so mesmerizing. ■

Capuchin monkey.

Don Pepe (José) Figueres and the site of the beginnings of the 1948 War of National Liberation, as he called it, is nearby, off the highway. Down the road to the right from Empalme, is **Santa María de Dota**, a small town with a beautiful little park and a monument commemorating those who lost their lives in that conflict. The road continuing towards San Marcos de Tarrazú, San Pablo de Léon Cortes and San Cristóbal Sur, called **La Ruta de Los Santos** (The Route of the Saints), is best driven in a 4 wheel drive vehicle.

In **Copey**, a village in the mountains above Santa Maria, one can rest at a waterfall and lake, visit rose nurseries or Don Fernando Elizando's trout farm, rent horses and have a trout lunch at William Rodríquez' *soda*.

Continuing on the Inter-American Highway, about half an hour from Empalme, is a sign which says "San Gerardo." This is the turn-off for **San Gerardo de Dota**, 5.6 miles (9 km) down a good but unpaved road which parallels the Río Savegre. It's a beautiful drive in the fresh mountain air, the sound of the river rushing over rocks and through the green valley. In the midst of the valley, Don Efráin Chacón, his daughter, sons and daughters-in-law offer simple cabinas, delicious homemade meals and a taste of Costa Rican hospitality at its most hospitable. Look for a bridge and some clean white buildings painted with bright red apples on the left just above the river. Here is where the Chacón family live and work. They raise prize-winning dairy cattle, peaches and tangy apples called Manzanas Ana.

San Gerardo de Dota is known for its cloud forests and offers perhaps one of the best opportunities in the country to see the Resplendent Quetzal. The quetzals feed in trees almost in Don Efráin's backyard. Don Efráin's guest book is full of enthusiastic comments such as: "Eight quetzals today!" "No trout but saw a quetzal!"

The trout are definitely another attraction of San Gerardo de Dota. Even if you don't catch one, you can have trout for dinner, fresh from Don Efráin's trout farm and skillfully prepared in the kitchen.

Taking a walk into the hillsides above the cabinas or along the road, next to streams whose banks are choked with watercress and lined with wildflowers, it is easy to forget that one is in an equatorial country which is the second largest exporter of bananas in the world. Bring plenty of warm clothing and dress in layers. It becomes surprisingly, refreshingly, chilly and the three heavy blankets on the bed are welcome at the end of the day.

San Gerardo de Dota, like most places in Costa Rica, is accessible by bus. Call ahead for reservations and arrange to have Don Efráin pick you up on the Inter-American Highway at the San Gerardo turnoff.

The drive to **San Isidro de El General** is beautiful once the fog clears from Cerro de la Muerte. San Isidro is the commercial center for this agricultural area, a busy town with a large central park and lots of noisy traffic. On the road you are likely to see trucks

Young puma (cougar) near La Pacifica reserve.

piled high with pineapples grown in the valley—or logs cut from the nearby forests. Stop at **Hotel Chirripó** and talk with Luis Quesada, who can help you arrange a trip to Chirripó. There are several places to stay in San Isidro, including the **Hotel Amaneli**. Ask for a room which does not face the highway. Just outside of town is the **Hotel del Sur**, with a pool and tennis courts.

Naturalist author Alexander Skutch, has lived in the area since before the opening of the Inter-American Highway, when San Isidro was "a small village, with a few stores that sold cheap clothing and household necessities to customers who mostly came with bare feet." He has a farm and reserve, **Los Cusingos**, a few miles from San Isidro, which he opens to nature tour groups, but unfortunately, not to individual travelers. Mr. Skutch is the author of the well-illustrated and annotated book, *The Birds of Costa Rica*, a must for traveling birders and *A Naturalist on a Tropical Farm*, a luminous, sensitive account of his early days as Los Cusingos.

Chirripó National Park: **Chirripó National Park**, 94 miles (151 km) south of San José is of interest for its great diversity of landscapes, including páramos, Andean-like flatlands with stunted growth; oak forests; fern groves; cloud forests; swamps; crystal-clear glacial lakes and the tallest mountain 12,529 feet (3,819 meters) in southern Central America. Chirripó was made a national park in August of 1975 and covers 108,000 acres (43,700 hectares). The names of places within the park give clues as to what one will find there: Savanna of the Lions, where cougars are frequently seen, Rabbit Valley, a beautiful valley surrounded by rocky peaks which was recently badly damaged by a forest fire, and Lake Valley, where tapirs wade into the lake to bathe in the cold, clear water.

Three mountain cabins for hikers and several trails which are regularly maintained make the ascent to **Chirripó Peak**, if not easy, one that can be accomplished by steadfast hikers willing to brave long days of hiking, the cold

A hesitant tapir.

and quite possibly, the rain. Maximum daytime temperatures in the 80s F are possible, with sudden nighttime drops into the 30s and 40s F. The best months to attempt Chirripó are February and March, the driest time of year, but hikers who have gone during the rainy months say the flora is wondrous.

Before entering the park, check in at park headquarters in **San Gerardo** and pay the nominal entrance and overnight fees. Park maps are available there, but they are basic and abbreviated, and rangers often do not have the information hikers request. Some people purchase good, large scale topographical maps in San José before coming. Rangers can put you in touch with local *campesinos* with horses who will haul your pack to the hut ahead of you.

Spend the first night in Chirripó on the lawn of the park service building, where rangers sometimes permit campers to sleep, or at the **Salón Comunal** or **Cabinas Chirripó** in San Gerardo. The next day's hike is a long and grueling 9 mile (14 km) walk straight uphill to the huts, which are 2 miles (4 km) below the summit. It takes most people 10 to 14 hours to reach them. Carry water with you, as the first opportunity to get water is 4 or 5 hours into the hike. The trail is well-marked. Frequent signs state the altitude and distance to the summit. A large cave which can accommodate 10 people if it doesn't rain (5 if it does) is located an hour and a half below the huts.

Make the ascent to the summit the next morning. It is usually clear until 9 a.m. or so when the valley fills up with fog and dense clouds. Leaves and grasses are often frost-covered in the early morning.

Below Chirripó is **Lago San Juan**, a good place for a midday swim.

Be sure to bring sufficient warm clothing, rain gear, a warm sleeping bag, enough food and water. Fires are not permitted in the park.

Playa Dominical and the beaches of the South: Playa Dominical is a long stretch of brown, silty beach offering good

Jungle quietude.

waves for surfing and pleasant, shady places on the sand for camping (but no facilities). "Town" is a small, somewhat funky settlement, not yet big enough to qualify as a village, with a few basic vacation homes, cabinas and *sodas*. During the dry season it can be impossibly hot, breezeless and the landscape barren.

Dominical is 22 miles (35 km) via mostly paved road from San Isidro, a beautiful drive through the southern section of El Valle de El General. (The trip from San José to Domincal via San Isidro, takes about 4 hours, including rest stops.) Dominical can also be reached bye 2 hour drive along the coast from Quepos. The road from Quepos is not good, but the scenery is—and a stay at the pretty and well-kept **Cabinas Punta Dominical**, just outside of Dominical on a point overlooking the ocean, makes the trip worthwhile. Call ahead to make sure they have a room, as the cabinas fill up quickly, especially on weekends and during vacations.

Naturística, S.A. is a private nature reserve offering a variety of day tours and one special "overnight in the jungle" with equipment provided. They are located just north of Dominical on the road to Quepos.

South of Dominical, along the unfinished **Costanera Sur Highway**, are the beaches of the Pacific: **Matapalo, Barú, Playa Hermosa** and **Uvita**. With a 4 wheel drive vehicle, you can cross the **Uvita River**, which has no bridge, and continue on to **Cortés**, where the road connects with the Inter-American Highway once again.

Boruca is a small indigenous village located in a valley near Buenos Aires, where life moves at a leisurely pace. Local people make carved balsa wood masks, woven belts, purses and tablecloths from naturally dyed cotton yarn. On the 30th of December each year the Boruca Indians celebrate the Fiesta de los Diablitos (Celebration of the Devils), a re-enactment of the war between the Spanish and Indians—but in this one, the Indians win.

La Amistad Biosphere Reserve: La

Heading up river.

Amistad (Friendship) **Biosphere Reserve** is an enormous complex of protected areas that cover approximately 1.5 million acres, or 12 percent of Costa Rica's territory. Within the biosphere reserve's boundaries are 10 national parks, reserves and protected areas, including La Amistad National Park, Chirripó National Park, Hitoy Cerere Biological Reserve, Tapantí Wildlife Refuge, 8 indigenous reserves and the Wilson Botanical Gardens.

One doesn't "visit" La Amistad in the same sense that one visits Manuel Antonio or Poás National Parks, but certainly one can visit parts of it. Tapantí Wildlife Reserve, for instance, one of the 6 wettest regions of the world, with gorgeous, wet, cloudy forests, is a short drive from San José. Wilson Botanical Gardens, which combines beautiful horticultural areas with a 150-acre piece of stunning forest, is an island surrounded by agriculture. Hitoy Cerere Biological Reserve, composed of lowland, wet forests and surrounded by Indian reserves, is about 1.5 hours from Cahuita along a scenic, bumpy road.

Seventy percent of the wildlife species found in Costa Rica, with 6 species of wild felines, 90 per cent of Costa Rica's flora, including more than 10,000 species of flowering plants, and nearly 70 per cent of Costa Rica's bird species, including the quetzal, can all be found within the biosphere reserve.

The unique characteristics of Amistad led UNESCO to declare the region a Biosphere Reserve in 1982. The following year, it was declared a World Heritage Site.

The problems of maintaining the biosphere reserve in the face of demands for its Indian Reserve lands, its oil and mineral wealth, its transportation and logistical importance, and its other natural resources, are very great indeed. Governmental ministers, international conservationists, officials from the Organization of American States and Conservation International are all important players in the drama of La Amistad, working to develop a strategy for harmonizing the varying interests of the reserve and the surrounding areas.

La Amistad International Park remains a plan and a promise to create a bi-national conservation area, a joint management project between Costa Rica and Panamá, which will eventually create a reserve nearly 2.7 million acres in size spanning both of the countries.

La Amistad National Park, adjacent to Chirripó, and on the interior of La Amistad Biosphere Reserve is, for the most part, inaccessible. There are few facilities to accommodate visitors, and much of the park has yet to be explored and mapped. Trails are limited and unmarked. Camping is permitted near the park entrances at **Las Mellizas** (the most accessible area—and the best for hiking), **Aguas Calientes** and **Helechales**. Hiking more deeply into the park should be undertaken only by those with extensive experience. There are wild animals, abrupt topography and great fluctuations in temperature. Contact the Parks Service before visiting and inquire about guides and horse rental. Or plan a day trip to Amistad from a base in San Isidro or San Vito.

Left: the Bejuquillo, a vine snake often seen in Amistad. **Right:** the Kissing Plant bids the traveler a fond "adios".

INSIGHT GUIDES
Travel Tips

FOR THOSE
WITH MORE THAN
A PASSING INTEREST
IN TIME...

Before you put your name down for a Patek Philippe watch *fig. 1*, there are a few basic things you might like to know, without knowing exactly whom to ask. In addressing such issues as accuracy, reliability and value for money, we would like to demonstrate why the watch we will make for you will be quite unlike any other watch currently produced.

"Punctuality", Louis XVIII was fond of saying, "is the politeness of kings."

We believe that in the matter of punctuality, we can rise to the occasion by making you a mechanical timepiece that will keep its rendezvous with the Gregorian calendar at the end of every century, omitting the leap-years in 2100, 2200 and 2300 and recording them in 2000 and 2400 *fig. 2*. Nevertheless, such a watch does need the occasional adjustment. Every 3333 years and 122 days you should remember to set it forward one day to the true time of the celestial clock. We suspect, however, that you are simply content to observe the politeness of kings. Be assured, therefore, that when you order your watch, we will be exploring for you the physical—if not the metaphysical—limits of precision.

Does everything have to depend on how much?

Consider, if you will, the motives of collectors who set record prices at auction to acquire a Patek Philippe. They may be paying for rarity, for looks or for micromechanical ingenuity. But we believe that behind each $500,000-plus

bid is the conviction that a Patek Philippe, even if 50 years old or older, can be expected to work perfectly for future generations.
In case your ambitions to own a Patek Philippe are somewhat discouraged by the scale of the sacrifice involved, may we hasten to point out that the watch we will make for you today will certainly be a technical improvement on the Pateks bought at auction? In keeping with our tradition of inventing new mechanical solutions for greater reliability and better time-keeping, we will bring to your watch innovations *fig. 3* inconceivable to our watchmakers who created the supreme wristwatches of 50 years ago *fig. 4*. At the same time, we will of course do our utmost to avoid placing undue strain on your financial resources.

Can it really be mine?

May we turn your thoughts to the day you take delivery of your watch? Sealed within its case is your watchmaker's tribute to the mysterious process of time. He has decorated each wheel with a chamfer carved into its hub and polished into a shining circle. Delicate ribbing flows over the plates and bridges of gold and rare alloys. Millimetric surfaces are bevelled and burnished to exactitudes measured in microns. Rubies are transformed into jewels that triumph over friction. And after many months—or even years—of work, your watchmaker stamps a small badge into the mainbridge of your watch. The Geneva Seal—the highest possible attestation of fine watchmaking *fig. 5*.

Looks that speak of inner grace *fig. 6*.

When you order your watch, you will no doubt like its outward appearance to reflect the harmony and elegance of the movement within. You may therefore find it helpful to know that we are uniquely able to cater for any special decorative needs you might like to express. For example, our engravers will delight in conjuring a subtle play of light and shadow on the gold case-back of one of our rare pocket-watches *fig. 7*. If you bring us your favourite picture, our enamellers will reproduce it in a brilliant miniature of hair-breadth detail *fig. 8*. The perfect execution of a double hobnail pattern on the bezel of a wristwatch is the pride of our casemakers and the satisfaction of our designers, while our chainsmiths will weave for you a rich brocade in gold *figs. 9 & 10*. May we also recommend the artistry of our goldsmiths and the experience of our lapidaries in the selection and setting of the finest gemstones? *figs. 11 & 12*.

How to enjoy your watch before you own it.

As you will appreciate, the very nature of our watches imposes a limit on the number we can make available. (The four Calibre 89 time-pieces we are now making will take up to nine years to complete). We cannot therefore promise instant gratification, but while you look forward to the day on which you take delivery of your Patek Philippe *fig. 13*, you will have the pleasure of reflecting that time is a universal and everlasting commodity freely available to be enjoyed by all.

Should you require information on any particular Patek Philippe watch, or even on watchmaking in general, we would be delighted to reply to your letter of enquiry. And if you send

fig. 1: The classic face of Patek Philippe.

fig. 4: Complicated wristwatches circa 1930 (left) and 1990. The golden age of watchmaking will always be with us.

fig. 9: Harmony of design is executed in a work of simplicity and perfection in a lady's Calatrava wristwatch.

fig. 6: Your pleasure in owning a Patek Philippe is the purpose of those who made it for you.

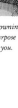

fig. 10: The chainsmith's hands impart strength and delicacy to a tracery of gold.

fig. 5: The Geneva Seal is awarded only to watches which achieve the standards of horological purity laid down in the laws of Geneva. These rules define the supreme quality of watchmaking.

fig. 7: Arabesques come to life on a gold case-back.

fig. 2: One of the 33 complications of the Calibre 89 astronomical clock-watch is a satellite wheel that completes one revolution every 400 years.

fig. 11: Circles in gold: symbols of perfection in the making.

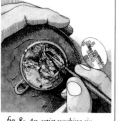

fig. 3: Recognized as the most advanced mechanical regulating device to date, Patek Philippe's Gyromax balance wheel demonstrates the equivalence of simplicity and precision.

fig. 8: An artist working six hours a day takes about four months to complete a miniature in enamel on the case of a pocket-watch.

fig. 12: The test of a master lapidary is his ability to express the splendour of precious gemstones.

PATEK PHILIPPE
GENEVE

fig. 13: The discreet sign of those who value their time.

your card marked "book catalogue" we shall post you a catalogue of our publications. Patek Philippe, 41 rue du Rhône, 1204 Geneva, Switzerland, Tel. +41 22/310 03 66.

So, you're getting away from it all.

Just make sure you can get back.

AT&T Access Numbers
Dial the number of the country you're in to reach AT&T.

ANGUILLA	1-800-872-2881	**CHILE**	**00◇-0312**	HONDURAS[†]	123
ANTIGUA (Public Card Phones)	#1	**COLOMBIA**	**980-11-0010**	JAMAICA[††]	0-800-872-2881
ARGENTINA◆	001-800-200-1111	*COSTA RICA	114	MEXICO◇◇◇	95-800-462-4240
BAHAMAS	**1-800-872-2881**	**CURACAO**	**001-800-872-2881**	MONTSERRAT[†]	1-800-872-2881
BARBADOS[†]	1-800-872-2881	DOMINICA	1-800-872-2881	**NICARAGUA**	**174**
BELIZE◆	555	DOMINICAN REP.[††]	11-22	PANAMA	109
BERMUDA[†]	1-800-872-2881	ECUADOR[†]	119	PARAGUAY[†]	0081-800
*BOLIVIA	0-800-1112	*EL SALVADOR	190	ST. KITTS/NEVIS	1-800-872-2881
BONAIRE	**001-800-872-2881**	GRENADA[†]	1-800-872-2881	**ST. MAARTEN**	**001-800-872-2881**
BRAZIL	**000-8010**	*GUATEMALA	190	**SURINAME**	**156**
BRITISH V. I.	1-800-872-2881	*GUYANA[††]	165	URUGUAY	00-0410
CAYMAN ISLANDS	1-800-872-2881	HAITI[†]	001-800-972-2883	*VENEZUELA	80-011-120

Countries in bold face permit country-to-country calling in addition to calls to the U.S. **World Connect**™ prices consist of **USADirect**® rates plus an additional charge based on the country you are calling. Collect calling available to the U.S. only. *Public phones require deposit of coin or phone card. ◇Await second dial tone. [†]May not be available from every phone. [††]Collect calling only. ◆ Not available from public phones. ◇◇◇When calling from public phones. use phones marked "Ladatel" ©1994 AT&T

Here's a travel tip that will make it easy to call back to the States. Dial the access number for the country you're in to get English-speaking AT&T operators or voice prompts. Minimize hotel telephone surcharges too.

If all the countries you're visiting aren't listed above, call **1 800 241-5555** for a free wallet card with all AT&T access numbers. Easy international calling from AT&T. **TrueWorld Connections.**

AT&T

TRAVEL TIPS

GETTING THERE

BY AIR

International flights arrive in Costa Rica at Juan Santamaría Airport, located in the Central Valley about 10 miles from San José, the capital city. Get reservations (ask for your confirmation or tracking number) as far ahead as possible, especially during December to February, as these flights are usually booked well in advance. Confirm 72 hours before departure. Reserve a specific seat. (Nonsmoking window seats from the third row back are best; the first two rows have underseat storage problems.) For the budget traveler, or those making last minute reservations, a number of discount "bucket shops" should be considered. Check the Sunday travel and classified sections of the New York Times and Los Angeles Times. To avoid getting "bumped" by overbooking, arrive 3 to 4 hours before your flight. You may be able to fly free if you let the counter agent know you are willing to wait until the next flight. If you do get "bumped" insist on seeing the supervisor, and ask for hotel and food vouchers.

AIRLINES

American	Tel: 255 1911
Aeronica	Tel: 223 0226
Copa	Tel: 211 5596
Iberia	Tel: 221 3311
LACSA (national airline)	Tel: 231 0033
KLM	Tel: 221 0922
Mexicana	Tel: 222 1711
SASHA	Tel: 221 5774
SAM	Tel: 233 3066
TACA	Tel: 222 1744
Varig	Tel: 221 3087

If you are bringing a lot of baggage, determine what the weight limits of your airlines are (usually 66 lbs.) and, if needed, determine how they handle surfboards, bicycles, etc. Be prepared in case your luggage is lost. There is a $6 airport exit tax when departing Costa Rica.

It's a 20-minute ride (about $10 by taxi) from San José to the airport. If there is no meter in the cab agree on the fare before committing yourself. A bus (¢20) is also usually available.

BY BUS

Bus travel to Costa Rica may be effected from Panamá or Nicaragua. Be prepared for long waits at the border which may be closed for lunch or holidays.

BY CAR

The Inter-American Highway allows fairly rapid transit into Costa Rica by way of Panamá or Nicaragua. Avoid traveling at night. Bringing a vehicle into the country will be duly noted in one's passport; there is no exiting the country without it.

BY SEA

Cruise ships come into Puerto Limón on the Atlantic Coast and Puerto Caldera on the Pacific. The following companies sail to Costa Rica: Carnival, Costa Cruises, Cunard, Holland America, Ocean, Royal Viking, Sitmar. Ask a travel agent.

Private yachts are increasingly popular as a means to visit. Check in to a port of entry with four copies of the crew list, ship's papers and a notarized statement from the owner if not on board. Fly a yellow "Q" (quarantine) flag upon arrival and wait until boarded and cleared before going ashore.

BY RIVER

The truly adventurous can come through Nicaragua down the Río San Juan, which is the border between Nicaragua and Costa Rica. Consider bringing official-looking papers with stamps and seals to show that you are on a scientific expedition.

Engineers have been unsuccessfully lobbying to develop the Río San Juan as an alternate Panamá Canal route for over 100 years, yet it remains one of the least inhabited and most beautiful waterways in the Americas. Along the San Juan, there is an abundance of wildlife, and the river is full of fish including 100 pound tarpon, and the very rare fresh-water shark.

Take a bus from Managua to the beautiful town of Granada on Lake Nicaragua. The boat to the village of San Carlos, where the Río San Juan begins, leaves from the pier. Use a hammock for the overnight trip, which arrives at dawn. Negotiate in San Carlos for a dugout canoe that will be large enough to be comfortable, but not so heavy as to be unmanageable; or get passage on the river boat to the town of El Castillo and buy a dugout there. Ensure that the paddles are well seasoned, otherwise they will be heavy and tiring to handle. If the river is raging because of recent rains, wait until it is manageable. Small amounts of cash can be exchanged for food and a covered place for your hammock at the many small farms along the river. Be prepared

THOMAS COOK MASTERCARD TRAVELLERS CHEQUES...

...HOLIDAY ESSENTIALS

Travel money from the travel experts

THOMAS COOK MASTERCARD TRAVELLERS CHEQUES ARE
WIDELY AVAILABLE THROUGHOUT THE WORLD.

INSIGHT GUIDES

COLORSET NUMBERS

North America
160	Alaska
173	American Southwest
184I	Atlanta
227	Boston
275	California
180	California, Northern
161	California, Southern
237	Canada
184C	Chicago
184	Crossing America
243	Florida
240	Hawaii
275A	Los Angeles
243A	Miami
237B	Montreal
184G	National Parks of America: East
184H	National Parks of America: West
269	Native America
100	New England
184E	New Orleans
184F	New York City
133	New York State
147	Pacific Northwest
184B	Philadelphia
172	Rockies
275B	San Francisco
184D	Seattle
	Southern States of America
186	Texas
237A	Vancouver
184C	Washington DC

Latin America and The Caribbean
150	Amazon Wildlife
260	Argentina
188	Bahamas
292	Barbados
251	Belize
217	Bermuda
127	Brazil
260A	Buenos Aires
162	Caribbean
151	Chile
281	Costa Rica
282	Cuba
118	Ecuador
213	Jamaica
285	Mexico
285A	Mexico City
249	Peru
156	Puerto Rico
127A	Rio de Janeiro
116	South America
139	Trinidad & Tobago
198	Venezuela

Europe
155	Alsace
158A	Amsterdam
167A	Athens
263	Austria
107	Baltic States
219B	Barcelona
1187	Bay of Naples
109	Belgium
135A	Berlin
178	Brittany
109A	Brussels
144A	Budapest
213	Burgundy
122	Catalonia
141	Channel Islands
135E	Cologne
119	Continental Europe
189	Corsica
291	Côte d'Azur
165	Crete
226	Cyprus
114	Czech/Slovak Reps
238	Denmark
135B	Dresden
142B	Dublin
135F	Düsseldorf
149	Eastern Europe
148A	Edinburgh
123	Finland
209B	Florence
154	France
135C	Frankfurt
135	Germany
148B	Glasgow
279	Gran Canaria
124	Great Britain
167	Greece
166	Greek Islands
135G	Hamburg
144	Hungary
256	Iceland
142	Ireland
209	Italy
202A	Lisbon
258	Loire Valley
124A	London
201	Madeira
219A	Madrid
157	Mallorca & Ibiza
117	Malta
101A	Moscow
135D	Munich
158	Netherlands
111	Normandy
120	Norway
124B	Oxford
154A	Paris
115	Poland
202	Portugal
114A	Prague
153	Provence
177	Rhine
209A	Rome
101	Russia
130	Sardinia
148	Scotland
261	Sicily
264	South Tyrol
219	Spain
220	Spain, Southern
101B	St. Petersburg
170	Sweden
232	Switzerland
112	Tenerife
210	Tuscany
174	Umbria
209C	Venice
263A	Vienna
267	Wales
183	Waterways of Europe

Middle East and Africa
268A	Cairo
204	East African Wildlife
268	Egypt
208	Gambia & Senegal
252	Israel
236A	Istanbul
252A	Jerusalem-Tel Aviv
214	Jordan
270	Kenya
235	Morocco
259	Namibia
265	Nile, The
257	South Africa
113	Tunisia
236	Turkey
171	Turkish Coast
215	Yemen

Asia/Pacific
287	Asia, East
207	Asia, South
262	Asia, South East
194	Asian Wildlife, Southeast
272	Australia
206	Bali Baru
246A	Bangkok
234A	Beijing
247B	Calcutta
234	China
247A	Delhi, Jaipur, Agra
169	Great Barrier Reef
196	Hong Kong
247	India
212	India, South
128	Indian Wildlife
143	Indonesia
278	Japan
266	Java
203A	Kathmandu
300	Korea
145	Malaysia
218	Marine Life in the South China Sea
272B	Melbourne
211	Myanmar
203	Nepal
293	New Zealand
205	Pakistan
222	Philippines
250	Rajasthan
159	Singapore
105	Sri Lanka
272	Sydney
175	Taiwan
246	Thailand
278A	Tokyo
255	Vietnam
193	Western Himalaya

to camp. Don't drink any untreated water or eat uncooked food or unpeeled fruit. About half way on this trip you will enter Costa Rica. Get your passport stamped (or signed if the official can't find his inkpad) at the *aduana* shack. It's less than a 2-week trip from Lake Nicaragua to the Atlantic Coast where you can take the very protected and fairly well traveled coastal canal. Or descend on a coconut barge or other river traffic to Limón. *Buen Viaje!*

TRAVEL ESSENTIALS

TRAVEL ADVISORIES

To enter Costa Rica, citizens of the United States and Canada need a valid passport or tourist card which is available by presenting a birth certificate and driver's license with a recent picture at a Costa Rican consulate, port of entry, some travel agencies or the ticket office of your airline along with $2.00. Always carry identification (or at least a photocopy of it) in case of immigration authorities' spot checks. Report lost identification immediately. You may usually remain for 90 days without an extension or exit visa. Cross any border and re-enter to get a 90 day extension. Travelers from other nations can contact the Costa Rica Tourist Institute or the nearest Costa Rican consulate or embassy. For more information contact:
Embassy of Costa Rica, Washington DC 20009
Instituto Costarricense de Turismo, Apdo 777-1000, San José, Costa Rica. Tel: 506 22 1090

A US citizen traveling from other countries may be required to have a valid passport and a visa.

To extend the time limit that one can legally stay in the country, wait in line at the *Imigración* (Immigration) office, *Departamento de Extranjeros*, east side of the Corte building, c 21, av 4-6. An exit visa is required for overstaying the limit, obtained at the airport for $12 plus $4 per month. Anyone who resides in Costa Rica as a resident, retiree, or a tourist with a stay of longer than ninety days must obtain a document in order to leave the country. This document states that the traveler is not leaving behind any family members who might become destitute during the traveler's absence. This may be obtained from the *Alcaldia de Pensiones Alimenticias* at the Supreme Court building.

Costa Rica, like many other Latin American countries, does not permit minor children (up to and including 17 years of age) to leave the country unaccompanied by both parents without the permission of the child welfare organization, *Patronato Nacional de la Infancia* (Tel: 223 8355). If one parent wishes to take the child out of the country, or the parents wish to send the child with a designated guardian, both parents must go to the *Patronato* offices, c 19, av 6, with the child's passport and request permission. Because of the above restrictions, a child visiting Costa Rica may fall under the jurisdiction of the *Patronato*. Should the child be traveling in the company of a guardian or of only one parent, written permission to travel (notarized by the Costa Rican consul abroad) must be presented to the *Patronato* to permit the child to leave the county. Travel agents, for a fee, can handle some of the steps involved.

Citizens of the following countries are given 90-day visas:

Argentina, Austria, Canada, Columbia, Denmark, Finland, France, Great Britain, Holland, Italy, Israel, Japan, Luxembourg, Northern Ireland, Norway, Rumania, South Korea, Spain, United States of America

Citizens of other countries are usually given 30-day visas.

CONSULATES

Austria	Tel: 223 2822
Belgium	Tel: 225 6633
Canada	Tel: 223 0446
England	Tel: 221 5566
France	Tel: 225 0733
Germany	Tel: 232 5533
Italy	Tel: 224 6574
Japan	Tel: 232 1255
Spain	Tel: 221 7005
Sweden	Tel: 232 8549
Switzerland	Tel: 221 4829
USA	Tel: 220 3939

Personal effects may be brought into the country and up to 6 rolls of film, 500 grams of tobacco, 2 kilos of candy, 3 liters of wine or liquor (if over 21). Carry prescription drugs in original containers. Costa Rica is serious about illegal drug laws: 8 to 20 years in jail and no bail. The airport has recently acquired drug-sniffing dogs to deal with illegal substances.

You must have $400 and a ticket to another country to enter Costa Rica. An international bus ticket may suffice.

PETS

To bring in pets, an import permit is required, and obtaining this permit can take three or four months:

Jefe del Dept. de Zoonosis, Ministerio de Salud, Aptdo 10123, San José, Costa Rica, Tel: 223 0333 ext 331

CURRENCY & EXCHANGE

The currency unit is the *colón*. The current rate of exchange can be found in the daily newspaper. The exchange rate is about 150-160 *colones* per US dollar. Call Tel: 800 327 7933 or Tel: 305 358 2150 for the current rate. Exchange money at the airport before departure. Upon arrival money can be changed at the airport until 5pm. The Gran Hotel Costa Rica, by the *Téatro Nacional*, will often change money even for non-guests. It is common, although illegal, to change money on the streets. Banking hours are weekdays, 9 am - 3pm. Some banks will allow you to draw *colones* using your Visa, Mastercard or American Express credit cards. TAM Travel Agency Tel: 223 5111, c 1, av ctl-l, or Credomatic Tel: 224 2155, av ctl, c 29-31, will provide cash charged against VISA or MASTERCARD. It is advisable to have some traveler's checks in small denominations. Carry change and small denomination notes; you may not be able to break larger bills. When asking prices you may be told the amount by the color of the bill (as in "*dos rojos*" or two red ones, referring to the red color of the one thousand *colón* note.) The airport bank will cash only $50 of *colones* back into dollars for departing travelers.

Theft is common in Costa Rica, especially in the city of San José. You are encouraged to take precautions to protect personal belongings. Don't leave valuables unattended on the beach; do not needlessly display money or jewlery. Keep cameras and pocketbooks close to the body and carefully watched. Pickpockets work crowded areas. Cars are vulnerable, especially at night. Don't leave valuables in sight; park in guarded areas. Don't wear gold chains and earrings on the streets of San José.

HEALTH

Costa Rica ranks near the United States, Canada and other Western nations in health care. Water in San José and Central Valley is treated. It is, with some few exceptions, potable throughout the country. If you have persistent intestinal problems, take a stool sample to a hospital (see Emergencies) to be analyzed (about $3.50, results in 24 hrs).

Be aware that there are several types of poisonous snakes in Costa Rica. Go to one of the museums specializing in snakes to get acquainted. Africanized bees, through not common, have been a problem. On the beach, avoid the manzanillo tree, a small evergreen with many branches that provide shade.

The leaves, bark, and small yellowish fruit produce a white latex which stings and causes blisters. Sometimes fatal if ingested, one antidote is large quantities of bitter lemon juice.

It's a good idea to bring insect repellent and sun screen with you. They are often expensive and difficult to find, especially outside of San José.

GETTING ACQUAINTED

Did you know that Costa Rica has:

130 species of freshwater fish
160 species of amphibians
208 species of mammals
220 species of reptiles
850 species of birds
1,000 species of butterflies
1,200 varieties of orchids
9,000 species of plants
34,000 species of insects
Canal networks through jungles
Cloud forests
Coral reefs
Deciduous forests
Elevations from sea level to 12,529 feet (3,820m)
Mangrove swamps
Rain forests
Tropical dry forests
Volcanoes (112 craters)
White, black, and pink shell beaches on Atlantic and Pacific coasts
Extensive networks of rivers

CLIMATE

Essentially, Costa Rica has two seasons: the rainy season, which Costa Ricans call "winter," from May to November; the dry season, or "summer," from December to April. In the Central Valley, the climate is referred to as one of perpetual spring. And, as in spring, the weather can be unpredictable. The average temperature in the highlands is 72°F (22°C), and the coast varies from the high 70s (25+°C) to the low 90s (30+°C). San José has an average temperature of 75°F (24°C). Ticos use the word *temporal* for "storm;" it has the double meaning of "temporary." Rain can fall at any time on the Caribbean coast. It is, generally, more humid on the Atlantic side than on the Pacific. Even during the rainy season, most mornings are bright and

American Express offers Travelers Cheques built for two.

Cheques *for Two*^{SM} from American Express are the Travelers Cheques that allow either of you to use them because both of you have signed them. And only one of you needs to be present to purchase them.

Cheques *for Two* are accepted anywhere regular American Express Travelers Cheques are, which is just about everywhere. So stop by your bank, AAA* or any American Express Travel Service Office and ask for Cheques *for Two*.

A Wise Man Never Thinks How Far He's Come. He Thinks How Far He Can Still Travel.

REMY XO BECAUSE LIFE IS WHAT YOU MAKE IT

sunny. In the highlands above Heredia temperatures will drop 10 degrees with a climb of 500 feet (150 meters).

CLOTHING

Plan to dress in layers. Sweaters and jackets are needed for activities in the mountains and cool evenings. Shorts are worn for athletic activities or at the beaches, never in the cities. Bring raingear and boots if you plan to do much hiking. A folding umbrella will often be welcome. Have a comfortable pair of walking shoes that are already broken in. Sidewalks are nonexistent in many areas, and uneven at best. Costa Ricans dress more formally than people in other countries and are always well-groomed. Bring dressy clothes for San José restaurants and nightlife.

GEOGRAPHY

With a land area of only 19,700 square miles (51,000 square km), Costa Rica comprises an area only slightly smaller than West Virginia. It is the second smallest country in the Americas; El Salvador is the smallest. Mountains dominate the country, the northern ones made up of active and dormant volcanoes. The southern Talamanca range has the tallest peaks in the country. From the mountains 32 major rivers flow to the seas. The Pacific Coast is more than 630 miles (1000 kms) in length and the Atlantic 125 miles (200 kms).

TAXES & TIPS

Hotels and restaurants include a 13 percent tax to the bill. Hotels also charge a 3 percent tourism tax on room charges. Hotel bellboys should be tipped.

Restaurants add 10 percent gratuity to your check, but it's customary to additionally leave small change on the table if the service warrants it.

TIME

Costa Rica's time is the same as US Central Standard Time. When people refer to "Costa Rican time," however, they mean between thirty minutes to three hours late...no kidding.

ELECTRICITY

Costa Rica uses 120 volts, 60 cycle current. Most wall sockets are two prong, able to accommodate both flat and round plugs. Bring an adapter for three prong appliances.

COURTESIES & CUSTOMS

People in Latin America shake hands with each other when first introduced. In Costa Rica this may be an even more friendly "wrist or forearm" shake, where the hand is purposely missed and the wrist or forearm is lightly held instead. Women usually greet each other with a kiss on the cheek and say goodbye in the same fashion. When a friendly relationship exists, men and women often greet in the same way. Children are very affectionate and greet their elders with a kiss. Excessive demonstrations of affection in public are not well received. As an indication of the formality of the country, note that in Spanish the "usted," or formal pronoun for "you" is used even between parents and their children.

Nude bathing on beaches is not acceptable to Costa Ricans, nor is wearing bathing suits on the streets.

Prostitution is legal in Costa Rica and prostitutes are supposed to be certified by the health department. Some apparently-beautiful women are male cross-dressers.

LIVING IN COSTA RICA

There is a weekly Newcomers' Seminar offered free. Answers to your questions by lawyers, doctors, CPAs and longtime residents. See the back cover of the *Tico Times* newspaper for information as to time and place.

For information on *pensionado* (retiree) status which provides special tax breaks for foreigners living in Costa Rica, contact:

Asociacion de Pensionados y Rentistas de Costa Rica Apartado 700-11011, San José, Costa Rica.

The APR works in cooperation with the Costa Rica National Tourist Institute *pensionado* section. Membership costs $35 per year. The association will help process members' documents for *pensionado* or *rentista* status. They also help keep members up to date at the tourist bureau, help obtain or renew contacts, and give general information. The US Embassy encourages all US citizens living abroad to complete a registration card in the consular section. This facilitates identification and speeds up issuing of replacement documents in case of lost passports. Citizens of other countries should check with their embassies for advice.

Buying land should be approached with caution. Unscrupulous persons (including North American lawyers) have caused much grief to unwitting land buyers. Investigate thoroughly any "deals". Using a licensed agent may help.

Theft is a big problem. Most homes in San José have iron bars over their windows for security.

There exist many opportunities for starting businesses, but you won't be welcome if you compete for jobs. Hiring anyone (including housekeepers) involves complex and binding laws.

Shipping a car costs about $850 from Miami. Be informed that there are high import taxes that must be applied to a vehicle after it is in the country for between 3 and 6 months. Removing the air-conditioning unit could save you over $1,000 in import taxes. Despite rumors, it's often simpler to buy a vehicle here.

Videos for armchair tourism:
Costa Rica Making the Most of Your Vacation, (1 hr 36 min). Marshall Productions, POB 534, Carlsbad, NM 88221

Costa Rica Today, (1 hr). Thomas, Carlos, POB 5042, Dept TT, New York, NY 10185

GETTING AROUND

San José uses a grid system for its streets. North-south running streets are *calles*, east-west running streets are *avenidas*. Avenida Central, (av ctl), divides the city north and south; it becomes Paseo Colón west of Hospital San Juan de Dios. Calle Central, (c ctl), divides San José east and west. The southern and eastern streets are numbered evenly. The northern and western streets are numbered using odd numbers. Abbreviations used for addresses: c = calle, av = avenida, m = meters, ctl = central, apto or apdo = apartado (post office box, for mailing addresses). When a direction is given using the street and avenues, the first part is the street or avenue on which the building is located, and the second part of the address indicates the streets or avenues the building is between. For example: The location of the Metropolitan Cathedral is: c ctl, av 2-4. That is, the Cathedral is on Calle Central between Avenidas 2 and 4. (*See* the San José city map.)

Directions given in Costa Rica are unique, and locating a destination will result in requiring that one speak to quite a few people. Although downtown San José has numbered avenues and streets, Costa Ricans do not refer to them. Homes and buildings are not numbered. Usually an address is given as the distance in meters (metros) north, east, south, or west from a known landmark, an example of which is: "150 meters south of Matute Gómez's house, 100 meters east of the Banco Anglo, adjacent to the red painted fence, and 25 meters north of the papaya vendor stand." This is true. Consult the *Landmarks* section at the end of this chapter.

BY AIR

Domestic Flights (*vuelos locales*) are quite inexpensive and can provide a comfortable alternative to many hours on bad roads.

SAHSA. av C, c 1-3. Tel: 221 5774, Airport Tel: 441 1064
SAM. av 5, c 1-3. Tel: 233 3066, Airport Tel: 441 2954
TACA. c 1, av 3. Tel: 222 1790, Airport Tel: 441 5090
SAETA. Tel: 232 9514. Offers a ten-minute flight, touring over San José, leaving from Tobias Bolaños Airport. Also offers an air taxi service to Flamingo, Jaco, and Puntarenas.
SANSA. av ctl, c 224. Tel: 233 0397. Offers regular DC 6 service to Coto, Golfito, Palmares, Barra del Colorado, Playa Sámara, Tamarindo, and Quepos airports. If you have not paid for your flight (even if you have confirmed reservations), your seat will be sold if the flight fills up. Pay now or fly later. Surfers: SANSA no longer handles surfboards.

Airports
Juan Santamaria (international). Tel: 441 0744
Tobas Bolanos (PAVAS) (domestic). Tel: 232 2820

BY BUS

You can go virtually anywhere by bus in Costa Rica; it's the way the Ticos travel. The general destinations of buses can often be identified by their colors, as they are usually painted with the colors of the soccer team of the town they go to (yellow and red for Heredia). Drivers take great pride in their vehicles; they are usually clean and well maintained, sometimes with expensive stereo systems and many have names with corresponding graphics emblazoned upon the sides: Superman, Rey de la Montaña (King of the Mountain), etc.

The main bus stop in the center of San José is the "Coca Cola" terminal, located near the place where a bottling plant used to be at c 16, av 1-3. Departure places and times may change. The ICT Office located below the Plaza de la Cultura has a list of the bus companies names and telephone numbers. Tel: 222 1090.

CENTRAL VALLEY

Following is a bus schedule which includes frequency and journey times:

Alajuela, av 2, c 12-14, every 15 min, 30-min ride.
Arenal Volcano, av 1, to Ciudad Quesada every 45 min, 3-hr ride. Then take hourly bus to La Fortuna, then a cab to Tabacón Hot Springs on northeast side of volcano.
Cartago, av ctl, c 13-15, every 15 min, 45-min ride.

Heredia, c 1, av 7-9 (through Tibás), c 12, av 2 (through Uruca).

International Airport, take Alajuela bus Orosi Valley; go to Cartago where hourly bus leaves from one block south of Las Ruinas park.

Póas Volcano, c 12, av 2-4, Sundays only at 8.30am, 1½-hr ride.

Sarchí, take bus for Alajuela, get off at last stop, buses leave every 30 minutes.

Turrialba, c 13, av 6, leaves hourly 5am-9pm, 2-hour ride.

ATLANTIC COAST

Limón, av 3, c 17-19, 5am-8pm every half hour. 2-hr ride.

Cahuita, av 11, c ctl at 6am, 2.30 & 4.30pm, 4-hr ride.

Puerto Viejo. Same bus as Cahuita.

Sixaola. Same bus as Cahuita.

SOUTH PACIFIC COAST

Golfito, c 2, av 18, 6.30am & 11am, 8-hr ride.

CENTRAL PACIFIC COAST

Puntarenas, c 12, av 7-9, 6am-6pm, 2-hr ride.

Jaco Beach, c 15, av 1-3, 7.15am & 3.30pm, 2½-hr ride.

Quepos, c 16, av 1-3 (Coca Cola), 6am, noon & 6pm, 3½-hr ride.

Manuel Antonio, same bus as Quepos.

NORTHWEST

Liberia Coca Cola, 7, 9, 11am; 1, 4, 6pm, 4-hr ride.

Santa Cruz Coca Cola, 7.30am & 2, 4, 5.30pm, 4.5-hr ride.

Potrero, Flamingo, Brasilito beaches. Take the bus from the park in Santa Cruz at 4, 10.30am & 2.30 & 6pm.

Flamingo, Brasilito beach express, c 20, av 3, 10.30am, 6-hr ride.

Monteverde, c 12, av 5-7, 6.30am Friday-Saturday, 2.30pm Sunday-Wednesday, 4 hrs.

Nicoya, c 12, av 5, 6, 8, 10am & 1.30, 3pm, 5-hr ride.

Samara, Carrillo beaches. Take bus from Nicoya at 8am, 2 & 3pm, 3 hrs.

Nosara, Garza beaches. Take bus from Nicoya at 1pm, 3-hr ride.

Playas del Coco, c 15, av 1-3, 10am, 5-hr ride.

Tamarindo, c 14, av 5, 3:30pm, 5-hr ride.

INTERNATIONAL BUSES

Call ICT Office (Tel: 222 1090) to get latest information. Buy tickets and reserve a window seat in advance; keep an eye on your stuff.

Panamá City, av 4, c 9-11, 10pm, 20 hrs ¢1,512 RT.

Managua, av 4, c 9 at 7am, 11 hrs ¢540 OW.

BY TAXI

Widely used and inexpensive, taxis are a good way to get around. Fares within San José are often around one dollar. All taxis should have operational meters (*marias*); be sure the drivers use them. Otherwise, negotiate before getting in to avoid unpleasant scenes. If you are being greatly overcharged, write down the driver's name and license number, and call the taxi company number marked on the outside of the cab, or tell the driver to find a policeman or get out of the cab and hand the driver the proper fare. Overcharges are serious matters and can be taken to the Transportation Department. Arrangements can be made to take trips by taxi to places outside San José; speak to the taxi drivers parked outside the main hotels and at the airport. Taxis are red and have a Taxi sign on the roof of the car. If they are not red, then they are pirate taxis, or *piratas,* and are unlicensed.

Taxi companies:
Tel: 221 6865
Tel: 235 9966
Tel: 221 2552
Tel: 254 3211
Tel: 226 1366

BY FERRY

NICOYA PENINSULA

Puntarenas–Playa Naranjo. Departs 7am, 4pm plus 11am Thursday and weekends.

Playa Naranjo–Puntarenas. Departs 9am and 6pm plus 1pm Thursday and weekends.

Puntarenas–Paquera launch. Departs 6am and 3pm daily.

Paquera–Puntarenas. Departs 8am and 5pm daily.

Tempisque River. On the hour 7am to 6pm.

BY TRAIN

The ICT Office (Tel: 222 1090) has information on train schedules.

Puerto Limón Ferrocarril del Atlantico station, c 19, av 3.

Puntarenas Ferrocarril del Pacifico station, c 2, av 20.

BY BICYCLE

Increasingly popular, mountain bikes are a good way to get around, especially on the lightly traveled dirt roads which crisscross the rural areas. Bicycle riding can be dangerous on the roads as they have no shoulders. Check with the consulate about import taxes, and consider installing kevlar inner tube protectors (e.g. Mr. Tuffy). Bring a good lock. Check with your airline about shipping.

BY CAR

Car rental: While not recommended for getting around San José, renting a car makes sense for trips outside of the city. Reserve well in advance and get written confirmation. Prepayment is advised, especially during high season. Rates are generally around $50 per day, including insurance. Renting without a credit card usually involves a large deposit. When reserving four-wheel drive (more expensive) find out what kind of vehicle you are getting. All of the following agencies accept American Express, Master Card and Visa.

Ada	Tel: 233 7733, c 11-13, av 18
Amiga	Tel: 255 4141, c 3, av 13; S. José
Ancla	Tel: 233 7733, c 11-13, av 18; S. José
Avis	Tel: 232 9922, 1 block E. Datsun, Sabana
Economy	Tel: 232 9130, north side of Sabana
Elegante	Tel: 221 0136, c 10, av 13-15; S. José
Fantasy	Tel: 232 4811, Irazú & Jaco Beach Hotels
Global	Tel: 223 4056, c 7-9, av 7; S. José
Happy	Tel: 233 3435, av 7, 1 block north of Aurola
Hertz	Tel: 221 1818, Paseo Colón and c 38
National	Tel: 233 404, 4 blocks north Purdy Motors, av 3
Pilot	Tel: 222 8724, c 30, av 1, Paseo Colón
Santos	Tel: 221 7793, c 26-28, av 3
Tico	Tel: 222 1765, c 24-26, Paseo Colón
Toyota	Tel: 223 2250, c 30-32, Paseo Colón
Tropical	Tel: 223 4211, av central, Dent Blvd.

DRIVING

Four-wheel drive (*doble tración*) is recommended for many areas as the roads outside of the Central Valley, especially during the rainy season, are muddy, rutted and often impassable for a vehicle with low ground clearance. Chains work well in the mud; try letting some air out of your tires to increase traction, if the car is stuck.

Operating a motor vehicle without a license is a serious violation of Costa Rican law and invalidates any insurance carried on the vehicle. A valid driver's license from another country can be used for three months. Always carry your passport or tourist card (photocopies may sufffice). Foreign vehicles brought into Costa Rica for a period over 90 days must pay a large import tax. If you enter with a vehicle, you cannot leave without it.

Drivers weave all over to avoid the many ruts; after dropping into a few large holes, you will too. Two headlight blinks usually indicate the other driver is giving you the right of way (especially when you are making a left); on the highway two headlight blinks may mean that the police are ahead. Radar is often used. If waved over by the police, don't try to get away. They will radio ahead to have you stopped.

Costa Rica has a high accident and death rate for drivers. Always drive defensively. Don't drive an uninsured vehicle. Costa Rican law requires that all motorists carry a set of reflecting triangles in case of breakdown or accident. If you are in an accident, do not move your car until the police arrive. Give no statements, but take the names of any witnesses.

Be careful not to park illegally. The yellow curb means no stopping. Even if you are in the car, police may prevent you from leaving and call a tow truck (*grúa*). You can ride in the car to the yard. Be prepared to pay approximately $30. You can save yourself worries by parking in one of the many inexpensive parking lots (*parqueos*) around town. This will inhibit theft, as well.

Unfortunately there are corrupt police who may target foreign drivers for the purpose of extracting some *colones*. One can be stopped for not wearing a seat belt, speeding, turning the wrong way on one of the many unmarked one-way roads, or for no apparent reason at all. Be sure to have all necessary automobile documents in the car. Be polite. Sometimes pretending not to speak Spanish will be the best tactic. Often the officer won't actually write a ticket, but will go through all the motions. Regardless, it is illegal for the police to require that you pay on the spot. If you are badly treated, ask for the officer's identification, write it down, and report to the *Dirección de Tránsito*.

LANDMARKS

The following are points of references commonly used when giving or asking for directions. These points of reference are used instead of street numbers, which do not exist:

SAN JOSÉ AND LOS YOSES
Auto Mercado Centro, c 3, av 3.
Auto Mercado del Este, Plaza del Sol, Curridabat.
Autos La Castellana, c 8, av 10
Banco Anglo, San Pedro.
Banco de Costa Rica, c 4-6, av ctl 2.
Banco Nacional, av ctl 1, c 2-4.
Botica Mariano Jimenez, c ctl, av 10.
Casa de Matute Gómez, av 10, c 19-21.
Catédral Metropolitana, c ctl 1, av 2-4.
Centro Colón, Paseo Colón, av 1, c 38-40.
Centro Comercial Coconut, c 30, av 1.
Centro Comercial del Este (Plaza del Sol).
Centro Comercial Guadalupe, Guadalupe.
Centro Comercial Omni, av 1, c 3-5.
Centro Comercial Yaohan, airport highway.
Clínica Blblica, c 1, av 14.
Clínica Católica, Guadalupe.
Clínica Santa Rita, av 8, c 15-17.
"Coca Cola" bus terminal, av 3, c 16-18
Correos (main post office), c 2, av 1-3.
Cortes/Tribunales, c 19, av 6-8.
Cruz Roja (Red Cross), c 14, av 6-8.
Chelles Bar, av ctl, c 9.
Edificio Las Arcadas, c 1, av ctl 2.

El Pueblo (shopping center), Urb. Tournón.
Farmacia Fischel, c 2, av 3.
Ferrocarril Atlantico, av 3, c 15-17.
Ferrocarril Pacífico, av 20, c 2.
Gran Centro Comercial del Sur, 500 m south of Plaza Víquez.
Hospital Calderón Guardia, c 17, av 9.
Hospital Nacional de Niños, c 20, av ctl 4.
Hospital San Juan de Dios, av ctl, c 14.
I.C.E. building, San Pedro, just east of Los Yoses at fountain circle.
I.C.E. building, Sabana Norte, faces La Sabana park.
ICT building, av 4, c 5-7.
Iglesia La Merced, c 12, av 2-4.
Iglesia La Soledad, c 9, av 2-6.
I.N.S. building, av 7, c 9-9B.
Kentucky Fried Chicken, Los Yoses, av ct 1, c 31.
Kentucky Fried Chicken, Paseo Colón, c 32-34.
La Sabana, a park west of Paseo Colón.
Mas x Menos, Paseo Colón.
McDonald's Centro, c 4, av ctl 1.
McDonald's Sabana Sur, southeast corner of La Sabana.
Parque Bolivar (zoo), c 7, av 11.
Parque Central, c ctl 2, av 2-4.
Parque Morazán, av 3, c 5-9.
Parque Nacional, av 1-3, c 15-19.
Paseo de los Estudiantes, c 9, av 8-14.
Pizza Hut, Barrio La California.
Pizza Hut, Paseo Colón, c 28.
Plaza de la Cultura, av ctl, c 3-5.
Plaza del Sol shopping center, Curridabat.
Plaza Gonzalez Vlquez, av 18-22, c 11-13.
Soda Tapia, Sabana Este, av 2, c 42.
University of Costa Rica, San Pedro.

ESCAZÚ AND ROHRMOSER
Autopista Escazú-Villa Colón (highway) goes west from Gimnasio Nacional, La Sabana park. Also exit at Santa Ana.
Bello Horizonte (residential area); first entrance (*primera entrada*) is west and south of Puente Los Anonos.
Casa de la Alabanza/Antiguo Intex, in Escazú: from Cruce Santa Ana continue southward toward San Miguel de Escazú to intersection with obligatory right turn; building is on left corner.
Centro Comercial del Oeste, Pavas Road Centro Comercial, Los Anonos (shopping center including Pizza Hut), Escazú.
Colegio Humboldt, adjacent to US Embassy, Rohrmoser.
Costa Rica Country Club, Escazú.
Cruce Santa Ana, divides old road to Santa Ana from first entrance Escazú.
I.C.E. building, Pavas, road to Pavas.
I.C.E. building, Sabana Norte.
La Sabana, a park west of Paseo Colón.
Lamm's (meat market), old road to Santa Ana in San Rafael de Escazú.

Los Laureles (residential development), north side of old road to Santa Ana.
Mas x Menos (supermarket), San Rafael de Escazú.
Paco (factory), Escazú, south side of old road to Santa Ana.
Parque La Amistad, Rohrmoser Boulevard.
Pizza Hut, Escazú, Los Anonos Shopping Center.
Puente Los Anonos ("suicide" bridge).
Tega (meat market), San Rafael de Escazú.
Valle del Sol (residential area), old road to Santa Ana, west of Escazú.

WHERE TO STAY

Check with the Instituto Costarricense de Turismo (ICT) office in San José for a list of approved hotels. Tel: 222 1090, for the latest rates and services. Rates and facilities are subject to change.

The airport ICT desk, tel: 42 1820, can help if you arrive without advance hotel reservations. Avoid, if you can, staying in downtown San José, which is a large city choked with diesel fumes. Alajuela, Heredia, Escazú and other central valley towns are less expensive and more enjoyable, with easy bus access to San José. *See also* Homestays.

When arriving during high season, be forewarned that any reservation not paid for may not be held, especially near the beaches and Monteverde.

HOTELS

A partial listing. Rated double occupancy per night, some discount for longer stays. Rates subject to change without notice.

Luxury: $80 and up
Expensive: $50–$80
Moderate: $30–$50
Budget: $15–$30
Inexpensive: under $15

DOWNTOWN SAN JOSE

Aparotel Napolean. Tel: 223 3252. Nice. Moderate.
Hotel Alameda. Tel: 221 3045. Friendly. Budget.
Hotel Amstel. Tel: 224 4622. Good restaurant. Moderate.
Apartotel El Conquistador. Tel: 224 2455. Moderate.
Hotel Astoria. Tel: 221 2174. Inexpensive.
Hotel Balmoral. Tel: 222 5022. Moderate.

Hotel Bellavista. Tel: 223 0095. Inexpensive.
Hotel Bougainvillea. Tel: 233 6622. Expensive.
Hotel Boruca. Tel: 223 0016. Very Inexpensive.
Hotel Cacts. Tel: 221 8616. Includes Breakfast. Budget.
Hotel Corobicí. Tel: 232 8122. Health Club. Wheelchair access. Luxury.
Pensión Costa Rica Inn. Tel: 222 5203. Budget.
Hotel Diplomat. Tel: 221 8133. Budget.
Hotel Europa. Tel: 222 1222. Older hotel. Expensive.
Friends Peace Center. Tel: 233 6168. Pensión with Kitchen. Inexpensive.
Hotel Galilea. Tel: 233 6925. Nice rooms. Budget.
Gran Hotel Costa Rica. Tel: 221 4000. Older landmark hotel; overlooks Plaza de la Cultura. Dining room on top floor, casino, street level café. Expensive.
Gran Hotel Centroamerica. Tel: 221 3362. Wheelchair access. Moderate.
Hotel La Gran Vía. Tel: 222 7737. Balconies. Moderate.
Holiday Inn Aurora. Tel: 233 7233. Wheelchair access. Casino. Luxury.
Hotel L'Ambiance. Tel: 222 6702. Small Euro-style. Good restaurant. Luxury.
Apartotel Lamm. Tel: 221 4920. Kitchens. Expensive.
Hotel Musoc. Tel: 222 9437. Budget.
Hotel Presidente. Tel: 222 3022. Luxury.
Hotel Principe. Tel: 222 7983. Group kitchen. Private baths. Inexpensive.
Hotel Ritz. Tel: 222 4103 (US Tel: 305 271 7829). Includes Breakfast. Budget.
Hotel Roma. Tel: 223 2179. Inexpensive.
Royal Gardens. Tel: 257 0022. Casino. Moderate.
San José Palacio. Tel: 220 2039. Expensive
Hotel Santo Tómas. Tel: 255 0488. Renovated mansion. Expensive.
Hotel Talamanca. Tel: 233 5033. Casino. Budget.
Albergue Toruma. Tel: 224 4085. Hostel. Kitchen. Very inexpensive.

NEAR THE AIRPORT

Hotel Cariari. Tel: 239 0022. Access to Country Club. Luxury.
Sheraton Heradura. Tel: 239 0033. Access to Country Club. Luxury.
Hotel Irazú. Tel: 232 4549. Luxury.
Irazú Apartments. Tel: 232 4811. Expensive.
Hotel Torremolinos. Tel: 222 9129. Expensive.
Villas de Cariari. Tel: 239 1003. Access to Country Club. Luxury.

CENTRAL VALLEY

Hotel Alajuela. Tel: 441 1241. Budget.
Albergue Volcán Póas. Tel 255 3486. Moderate
Apartotel Maria Alexandria. Tel: 228 1507. San Rafael de Escazú. Moderate.
Cabañas las Ardillas. Tel: 222 8134. Heredia. Budget.

Casa Maria. Tel: 228 2270. Escazú. B&B. Airport and city pickup. Moderate.
El Pórtico. Tel: 237 6022. San José de la Montana. Expensive.
Finca Rosa Blanca Inn. Tel: 239 9392. Above Heredia. Lovely. Luxury.
Gestoria Irazú. Tel: 253 0827. Irazú. Inexpensive.
Hotel Interamericano. Tel 556 1566. Turrialba. Inexpensive.
La Calzada. Tel: 551 3677. Guayabo National Monument. Inexpensive.
Mirador Pico Blanco. Tel: 228 1908. San Antonio de Escazú. Budget.
Motel Río. Tel: 237 4466. Barva de Heredia. Inexpensive.
Pochotel. Tel: 556 0111. Turriabla. Budget.
Posada Pegasus. Tel: 228 4196. San Antonio de Escazú. Small pensión. Moderate.
Casa Verde Escazú. Tel: 228 4080. Moderate.
Tara. San Antonio de Escazú. Beautiful views. Expensive.
Tirol. Tel: 239 7070. San Rafael de Heredia. Swiss cabins in lovely alpine setting. Expensive.
Turrialtico. Tel: 556 1111. Turrialba. Budget.
Verano. Tel: 237 1616. Heredia. Inexpensive.
Wagelia. Tel: 556 1566. Turrialba. Budget.

CENTRAL PACIFIC

JACO BEACH AREA

Cabinas Antonio. Tel: 643 3043. Inexpensive.
Cabinas Las Palmas. Tel: 634 3005. Budget.
El Jardín. Tel: 643 3050. Budget.
Hotel El Delfín. Tel: 17 1640. Esterillos Este. Expensive.
Jaco Beach. Tel: 643 3032. Moderate.
Jacofiesta. Tel: 643 3148.
Tangieri. Tel: 442 0977. Expensive.
Villas Miramar. Tel: 643 3003. Moderate.

QUEPOS AND MANUEL ANTONIO

Albergue de Playa Vela Bar. Tel: 777 0413. Budget.
Cabinas Los Almendros. Tel: 777 0225. Budget.
Divisamar. Tel: 777 0371. Moderate.
El Salto. Tel: 777 0130. Nature reserve high on a hilltop. Pool. Expensive.
Hotel Ceciliano. Tel: 777 0192. Inexpensive.
Hotel Costa Verde. Tel: 777 0584. Complete units. Recommended. Expensive.
Hotel Malinche. Tel: 777 0093. Quepos. Inexpensive.
Karché. Tel: 777 0170. On a hill, above beach. Pool. Expensive.
La Mariposa. Tel: 777 0355. (US Tel: 1 800 233 6510). Adults only. Luxury.
Cabinas La Quinta. Tel: 777 0434. Budget.
Plinio. Tel: 777 0555. Small, above beach. Budget.
Naturalists Beach Front Apartments. Tel: 777 1473. Right on the beach. Expensive.

PUNTARENAS

De Paso. Tel: 661 2610. Moderate.
Hotel Fiesta Beach. Tel: 239 4266. All the amenities. Huge. Luxury.
Hotel Cayuga. Tel: 661 0344. Budget.
Hotel Las Brisas. Tel: 661 2120. Budget.
Hotel Tioga. Tel: 661 0271. Budget.
Porto Bello. Tel: 661 1322. Expensive.
Punta Leona Club and Hotel. Activities. Outside of town. Expensive.
Villas Palma Del Mar. Tel: 663 1736. Family style villas. Moderate.
Yacht Club. Tel: 661 0874. Moderate
Yadran. Tel: 661 2662. On the point by the municipal pool. Luxury.

ON THE WAY TO MONTEZUMA

Hacienda Tambor. Tel: 661 2980. Tambor. Good private beach. Recommended. Moderate.
Hotel Dos Lagartos. Tel: 661 1122 ext. 236. Tambor. Inexpensive.
Hotel Bahía Gigante. Tel: 661 2442. Bahía Gigante. Budget.
Hotel Oasis del Pacífico. Tel: 661 1555. Playa Naranjo. Budget
Tango Mar Surf and Saddle Club. Tel: 223 1864. Luxury.

MONTEZUMA

Phone communication with Montezuma is difficult, as most places do not have phones. Try leaving a message at Chico's Bar/Cabinas Mary Cielo (Tel: 661 2472) and hopefully you will receive a return call confirming your reservation. Reservations are a must during Christmas and Easter. Best chance of finding vacancies during high season is on weekdays. Good luck.

Cabinas Iaconna. Tel: 661 1122. Houses on the beach. Recommended. Moderate.
Cabinas Karen. No phone. Inexpensive.
Cabinas Las Arenas. No phone. Inexpensive.
Cabinas Mar y Cielo. Tel: 661 2472. Inexpensive.
Casa de Huéspedes Alfaro. No phone. Inexpensive.
Hotel Lucy. No phone. Inexpensive.
Hotel Montezuma. No phone. Inexpensive.

MONTEVERDE

El Sapo Dorado Hotel. Tel: 661 2952. Recommended. Moderate.
Belmar. Tel: 661 1001. Moderate.
Hotel de la Montaña Monteverde. Tel: 661 1846. Expensive.
Pensión Heliconia. Tel: 661 1009. Budget.
Pensión Monteverde Inn. Tel: 661 2756. Inexpensive.
Pensión Quetzál. Tel: 661 0955. Moderate. Includes all meals.
Pensión Santa Elena. Tel: 661 1151. Inexpensive.

GUANACASTE

LIBERIA & VICINITY

Albergue Rincón de la Vieja. Tel: 666 0473. Budget.
La Siesta. Tel: 666 0678. Downtown Liberia. Moderate.
Hotel El Sitio. Tel: 257 0744. Liberia. Budget.
Hotel Hacienda Los Inocentes. Tel: 239 5484. Horse trips. Expensive.
Hotel Las Espuelas. Tel: 666 0144. Near Liberia. Moderate
Hotel Nuevo Boyeros. Tel: 666 0722. Liberia. Moderate.
La Pacífica Ecological Center. Tel: 669 0050. Near Cañas. Pool. Moderate.

BEACHES OF GUNACASTE

Cabinas Playa Hermosa. Tel: 670 0136. On Playa Hermosa. Budget.
Cabinas Pozo Azul. Tel: 680 0147. Playa Tamarindo. Budget.
Cabinas Zuly Mar. Tel: 224 4732. Playa Tamarindo. Inexpensive.
Condor Club. Tel: 680 0920. On hill above beach. Moderate.
Hotel Antumal. Tel: 680 0506. Playa Junquillal. Moderate.
Hotel Condovac La Costa. Tel: 670 0267. Playa Hermosa. Luxury.
Hotel Sugar Beach. Tel: 680 0959. Sugar Beach. Moderate.
Hotel Tamarindo Diriá. Tel: 680 0652. Tamarindo. Luxury.
Guanamar. Tel: 239 4544. Marina, water sports. Luxury.
Hotel Villa Serena. Tel: 680 0737. Playa Junquillal. Luxury.
El Ocotal. Tel: 670 0231; 670 0083. Deluxe beach resort. Expensive.
Flor De Itabo. Tel: 670 0011. Inland near Coco Beach. Pool. Amenities. Moderate.
Hotel La Costa. Tel: 221 8949. Luxury.
Club Flamingo. Tel: 680 0996. Luxury.
Flamingo Marina Resort. Tel: 221 8903. Marina. Apartments. Luxury.
Hotel Las Brisas del Pacífico. Tel: 255 2380. Playa Sámara. Moderate.
Hotel Playa Nosara. Tel: 680 0495. Above Nosara Beach. Budget.
Hotel Villagio La Guaria Morada. Tel: 680 0784. South of Nosara. Expensive.

SANTA CRUZ, NICOYA

Sharatoga. Tel: 669 0011. Budget
Hotel Curime. Tel: 685 5238. Near Nicoya. Pool. Moderate.

ATLANTIC COAST

LIMON

Hotel Acón. Tel: 758 1010. Limón. Budget
International. Tel: 758 0434. Limón. Budget.
Hotel Las Olas. Tel: 758 1414. Outside Limón. Luxury.
Hotel Maribu Caribe. Tel: 758 4543. Best in Limón area. Expensive.
Hotel Matama. Tel: 758 1123. Outside Limón. Expensive.

CAHUITA

Cabinas Black Beach. Tel: 758 1515 ext 251. Cahuita. Inexpensive.
Cahuita Country Club and Camping. Tel: 758 2861. Budget.
Hotel Cahuita. Tel: 758 1515 ext 201. Inexpensive.
Cabinas Palmer. Tel: 758 1515 ext 243. Inexpensive.

PUERTO VIEJO

Phone communication with Puerto Viejo is difficult as many places do not have phones. Try leaving a message at Manuel Leon's grocery store (Tel: 758 0854) or the Hotel Maritza (Tel: 758 3844) and hopefully you will receive a return call confirming your reservation. Reservations are a must during Christmas and Easter. Best chance of finding vacancies during high season is on weekdays.
Cabinas Chimuri. No phone. Address: Mauricio Salazar, Puerto Viejo de Talamanca, Limón. Horseback tours. Inexpensive.
El Pizote Surf Lodge. Tel: 229 1428. Expensive.
Kiskadee. No phone. Nature lodge. Budget.
Hotel Maritza. Tel: 758 3844. Inexpensive.
Miraflores Lodge. Tel: 255 8974. Inexpensive.
Villas Del Caribe. Tel: 233 2200; fax: 221 2801

TORTUGUERO AND BARRA DEL COLORADO

Tatané. Tel: 710 6716 & leave message with Marco Zamora. On the canal to Barra del Colorado. Basic. Inexpensive.
Casa Mar. Tel: 433 8834. Barra del Colorado. Inexpensive.
Jungle Lodge. Tel: 233 0155. Tortuguero. Includes transportation and meals. Luxury.
Mawamba. Tel: 233 9964. Tortuguero. Includes transportation and meals. Luxury.
Hotel Ilan Ilan. Tel: 255 2031. Tortuguero. Includes transportation. Expensive.
Parismina. Tel: 222 6633. Parismina. Budget.
Río Colorado Lodge. Tel: 232 4063. Tortuguero. Deluxe fishing lodge with mini zoo. Includes meals and transportation. Luxury.
Cabinas Tarponland. Tel: 710 6917. Barra del Colorado. Inexpensive.

Tortuga Lodge. Tel: 222 0333. Opposite the turtle stations in Tortuguero. Includes transportation and meals. Luxury.

THE NORTH

LAKE ARENAL AREA

Albergue Arenal. Tel: 224 4085. Youth hostel. Inexpensive.
Arenal Lodge. Tel: 460 1881. Elegant retreat. Views of volcano. Expensive
Cabinas Xiloe. No phone. Tilarán. Cabins. Windsurfing rentals. Moderate.
Hotel Central. Tel: 688 9004. Downtown La Fortuna. Inexpensive.
Hotel Las Colinas. No phone. La Fortuna. Great views. Moderate.
Tucano Hotel and Country Club. Tel: 460 1822 Aguas Zarcas. Thermal baths. Moderate.

SARAPIQUI REGION

El Gavilán. Tel 253 6540. Former cattle ranch east of Puerto Viejo. Includes meals. Expensive.
El Plástico Lodge. Tel: 253 0844. Rara Avis. Includes meals. Moderate.
La Selva Biological Station. Tel: 236 6696. Includes meals. Expensive.
Selva Verde Lodge (creek/river lodge). Tel: 710 6459. Includes meals. Moderate-expensive.
Waterfall Lodge. Tel: 253 0844. Rara Avis. Includes meals. Expensive.

THE SOUTH

CORCOVADO

Drake Bay Wilderness Camp. Tel: 771 2436. Includes meals. Luxury.
Marenco Biological Station. Tel: 221 1594. Includes food, guide and transport from San Jose. Luxury.
Lapa Rios. Tel: 735 5130. Private 200-acre rainforest. Luxury.

GOLFITO-SAN VITO

Cabinas Las Gaviotas. Tel: 775 0062. Golfito. Pleasant. Budget.
Hotel Delfína. Tel: 775 0043. Golfito. Clean, basic. Inexpensive.
Tiskita Jungle Lodge. Tel: 255 3518. Includes meals. Luxury.
Captain Tom's Place. Converted 62-foot trawler/hotel outside of Golfito.
El Puente. Tel: 775 0034. Golfito. Inexpensive.
Wilson Botanical Gardens. Tel: 236 6696. Includes meals. Expensive.
Cabinas Las Mirlas. Tel: 773 3054. San Vito. Inexpensive.

SAN GERARDO DE DOTA-SAN ISIDRO-SAN GERADO-DOMINICAL

Cabinas Chacón (Albergue de Montaña Savegre). Tel: 771 1732. San Gerardo de Dota. Includes meals. Recommended. Moderate.
Cabinas Chirripó. No phone. San Gerardo. Inexpensive.
Cabinas Punta Dominical. Tel 225 5328. Just outside Dominical. Budget.
Hotel Amaneli. Tel: 771 0252. San Isidro. Inexpensive.
Hotel Chirripó. Tel: 771 0529. San Isidro. Inexpensive.
Hotel del Sur. Tel: 771 0233. Near San Isidro. Pool. Budget.
Salón Comunal. No phone. San Gerardo. Inexpensive.

HOME STAYS

For those wishing to understand the people and culture of Costa Rica, a unique opportunity is available in the recently developed **Home Stay Service**. It is designed to offer a cross-cultural experience to both visitors and Costa Ricans. Visitors are lodged in the guest room of a host family and participate in the family activities to the extent that they wish. The home may be a base from which the visitor goes out to see the sights and attractions of Costa Rica. The host family will help to orient the guest, giving advice on places not to miss and places to avoid, answering the inevitable questions that arise. The Home Stay hosts provide their guests with breakfast, often eaten with the family. Other meals with the family can be arranged.

Costa Rican families have been chosen on the basis of the quality of their homes and their hospitality, and some speak English. A brochure sent to prospective visitors profiles the host families so visitors can select hosts with similar interests. Often long-lasting friendships are formed. Most are in the San José area, close to public transportation and quite inexpensive.

Visitors receive an information pack with their reservation, including data on Costa Rica, a map with directions to the host residence and an introduction to the host family. Airport and hotel pick-up service available.

Bells' Home Hospitality
PO Box 185-1000, San José, Costa Rica. Tel: 225 4752. Fax: 224 5884. Or in the US, PO Box 25216, Miami, Florida 33102-5216.

Local families sometimes rent rooms for about $450 per month including meals and laundry. Try checking around the university, and see ads in the local papers, or call the language schools.

ACCOMMODATION

NATURE LODGES AND RESERVES

Throughout the more remote areas of Costa Rica are nature lodges and privately owned reserves. They are there for the naturalists, the eco-traveler, the ever-expanding numbers of visitors who come to Costa Rica for the natural wonders of the country. Not for everyone, such places are often difficult to get to, sometimes requiring transportation by four-wheel drive vehicle, chartered plane or boat, but those travelers who do seek out and stay at these private and personal places almost inevitably chorus that the experience is unforgettable and often a profound one.

THE NORTH

Rara Avis, a private 3,337-acre (1,335 hectare) rainforest reserve near Las Horquetas, borders Braulio Carrillo National park and the Selva Protected Zone. Here narrow trails wind under ancient towering trees with limbs containing colonies of orchids and bromeliads. Over 330 species of birds, including toucans, parrots and macaws have been identified in the reserve. English-speaking guides are available. Hikers refresh themselves in the natural pools formed by an 180-foot, three-tiered waterfall.

The ten miles (16 km) to Rara Avis on non-existent roads from Las Horquetas can mean hours of being pulled by a tractor in a cart, when the tractor is working.

The Waterfall Lodge has spacious rooms, private bath, and a spectacular view. Lodging in the dormintory-style El Plástico Lodge is available for substantially less. Discounts are available for students, scientists and those wishing a longer stay. Tel: 253 0844.

La Selva, a 3,500-acre (1,400 hectares) biological reserve run by the Organization for Tropical Studies (OTS), is a research station where international scientists meet to study the wealth of tropical plants and animals. Some 81 species of reptiles, 48 species of amphibians, 113 species of mammals and 400 species of birds as well as 450 species of trees have been identified here. In one day over 300 species of birds were observed by Audubon Society members in the annual Birdathon. Prices are high at La Selva in order to finance the research done here. Reservations through OTS in San José. Tel: 236 6696.

Selva Verde is in Chilamate, near La Selva. A 480-acre (194 hectare) private reserve with excellent trails into tropical lowland forest. A thoughtfully done, beautiful place, the lodge offers attention to detail and service that is rare. Boat trips down the San Juan river, and rafting or kayaking on other rivers can be arranged. Tel: 710 6459.

El Gavilán Lodge and Oro Verde Station are located between the Sarapiquí and Sucio rivers on a 432-acre (173 hectare) private reserve 60 miles (96 km) from San José. They offer "Sarapiquí Jungle Adventure" packages, tours lasting between a day and a week which include boat rides and horseback riding. Visitors can view monkeys, birds, otters, sloths, crocodiles and wild cats. All-inclusive tours available. Tel: 253 6540.

Arenal Observatory, a research facility for vulcanologists, offers a place for tourists to view the spectacular eruptions of Arenal volcano. Guests are accommodated in rustic cabins with hot water and bath. The observatory grounds constitute 300 acres (750 hectares) of primary forest reserve. There are scenic walks and fishing is good in nearby Lake Arenal. There are scenic walks and fishing is good in nearby Lake Arenal. Reservations can be made through Costa Rica Sun Tours. Tel: 255 3418.

Arenal Lodge is an elegant place, located in a converted home up a purposefully difficult access road above Lake Arenal, with a billiard table and a good library as well as spectacular views of the eruptions of Arenal. The master suite at Arenal Lodge is definitely not roughing it. Fishing trips with equipment, guide and a snack are available, as is horseback riding. Tel: 228 2588.

GUANACASTE

La Pacífica Ecological Center in Guanacaste is home to over 225 species of birds. Guests are housed in attractive cabins near a swimming pool. The property is adjacent to a private zoo with endangered species of Costa Rica's big cats. Tel: 669 0050.

Los Inocentes, also in Guanacaste, near La Cruz, is a 2,000-acre (5,000 hectare) cattle ranch where guests stay in a remodeled two-story hacienda. Facilities include a sometimes-available swimming pool and horseback riding trips to a nearby forest and Orosi volcano. Tel: 239 5484.

Las Imágenes, north of Liberia, is a working cattle ranch with a biological station for scientific study. Guest stay in basic cabins with shared baths. A nearby ranch offers barbecues and the area may be explored by horseback. Butterflies and parrots abound. Day tours to Rincón de la Vieja National Park. Tel: 666 0473.

Rincón de la Vieja Mountain Lodge is a 660-acre (260 hectares) farm located on the slopes of Rincón de la Vieja Volcano. The farmhouse offers dormitory-style rooms, shared baths and home cooking. Visitors are taken by horseback to see hot springs, geysers, and the summit of the volcano. Tel: 666 0473.

The Ecoadventure Camp is located in the Guanacaste Mountain Range, next to Cote Lagoon. The base camp has extensive amenities and offers activities which include hiking, horseback riding, mountains and the Venado caves. Ecoadventure Camp is unique in that it provides a complete educational experience, with trained guides and lectures, as part of each nature adventure. Tel: 223 2811.

CENTRAL VALLEY

Rancho Naturalista near Turrialba, only a couple of hours from San José, offers a tranquil environment and an extensive network of trails through 125 acres (50 hectares) of tropical rainforest. This very personal place offers amenities such as benches and covered observation points to aid birders. Guided horseback and birdwatching tours are available. Thousands of species of moths, hundreds of species of birds. Rooms must be reserved for a minimum of three days. Rates include transportation to and from San José, local tours, horseback riding, maid service and full board. Tel: 239 7138.

CENTRAL PACIFIC

Monteverde Cloud Forest. Monteverde offers extensive lodging facilities for those interested in exploring the cloud forest. Generally, visitors are on their own, although trained naturalists are available in the area to serve as guides. Monteverde is now heavily trafficked and has become an obligatory destination for most ecotourists, as well as the casual visitor of Costa Rica, thus it is essential to make reservations well in advance. Some of the lodges and hotels in the area include:
The Sapo Dorado. Tel: 661 2952
Albergue de Montaña Heliconia. Tel: 661 1009
Alberge de Monteverde. Tel: 222 6241
Hotel de Montaña Monteverde. Tel: 661 1846
Pension Flor Mar. Tel: 661 0999
Fonda Vela Lodge. Tel: 661 2551
Pensión Quetzal. Tel: 661 0955
Belmar. Tel: 661 1001

THE SOUTH & OSA PENINSULA

The Marenco Biological Station has cabinas with shared baths and hearty meals. Access to Corcovado National Park and tours to Caño Island and Rio Claro. Very lengthy hikes through the jungle and under huge waterfalls. Getting there is best by air or boat. Tel: 221 1594.

Drake Bay Wilderness Lodge offers land and sea tours similar to those of Marenco. Located just north of Marenco, this attractive place also has boat trips up the Sierpe River, and leisurely canoeing in the jungle river next to the lodge. Tel: 771 2436.

La Paloma Lodge has spectacular ocean views from each the thatched-roof cabins that house visitors. Cabins have private baths and porches. Visitors eat in the Jungle Club House. Hiking tours go to nearby Corcovado National Park and boat tours to Caño Island. Tel: 239 0954.

Casa Corcovado Jungle Lodge, a new 300-acre (120 hectare) preserve adjacent to Corcovado National Park, is open from December 1 to the end of July and can accommodate ten guests. Available is a 5-day tour which includes overnight camping in the park and a snorkeling trip to Isla del Caño. The charter flight from San José is an additional fee to those quoted for tours.

Tiskita Lodge is two hours south of Golfito on rough roads at Bahía Pavones and has cabins with private baths and great views. Birds and monkeys are attracted here by the 80 varieties of tropical fruits on the property. Reservations through Sun Tours at 255 3418.

Wilson Botanical Garden is 205 miles (330 km) from San José near the Panamá border, Amistad National Park, and the Italian settlement of San Vito. With 25 acres (10 hectares) of groomed planted gardens and trails, adjoining OTS's 358-acre (145 hectares) natural forest reserve. Two thousand species of plants, 220 species of birds, 80 species of mammals. Basic rooms and family-style dining. Tel: 773 3278.

Albergue de Montaña Savegre is located high in the beautiful mountains near Cerro de la Muerte by the small village of San Gerardo de Dota. This is a family-run lodge set in a narrow mountain valley, six miles (9 km) from the Inter-American highway. Ideal for hikers and birders, the Albergue is perhaps the best place in all of Costa Rica to spot the near-mythical quetzal. Home-cooked meals often include fresh trout from the river nearby, cheese made in the family dairy and fruit from the farm orchard. Transportation from the Inter-American highway can be provided. Call in advance to be picked up for the final rugged 6 miles. Tel: 771 1732.

ATLANTIC COAST

The Pizote Lodge, just before the town of Puerto Viejo off of a black sand beach, has well-designed cabins, bungalows and a good restaurant. The grounds are exceptional. Not strictly a nature lodge, but tours into the neighboring jungle are available. Tel: 225 2813.

Cabinas Chimuri, also outside of Puerto Viejo, is a 35-acre (14 hectare) reserve run by Mauricio Salazar, a Bribri Indian and his European wife, Colocha. Guests stay in traditional Bribri houses of bamboo, on stilts. Highly personalized horseback

tours and three-day trips into the Talamanca Indian Reserve are offered. Inexpensive. Tel: 758 3844 and leave a message for Mauricio.

Aviarios Rio Estrella is a wildlife sanctuary located about 20 miles (30 km) from Limón on the coastal highway. In an exceptionally handsome setting are miles of fresh water canals and lagoons, through which you can take guided tours on the Arroyo family's power launch or canoes. Also available are trails into the rain forest and virtually untouched Caribbean beaches. Tel: 224 7822.

Tortuguero Lodges. These lodges, located along the magnificent canals of Tortuguero, with access by river boat from the town of Moín, originally were designed exclusively as destinations to serve the turtle naturalist and fisherman. Over the years they have become more broad-based, more commercial, in attempting to provide amenities for the appetites of a much wider variety of tourist. The turtles are still there, as are the snook and tarpon, and those that love them. So, too, are canal tours, party boats, canal barges, dugout canoes, crocodiles, monkeys and birds, a wide variation in the quality of the lodges and their services, and some serious deforestation in the surrounding areas. Inquire beforehand as to the inclination of the lodge and the training of its guides. Some naturalists have been surprised by untrained guides shouting into loudspeakers promoting a party. Some of the lodges there are:

The Jungle Lodge	Tel: 233 0155
Mawamba	Tel: 233 9964
Tortuga Lodge	Tel: 222 0333
Hotel Ilan Ilan	Tel: 255 2031
Rio Colorado Lodge	Tel: 710 6879

COMMUNICATIONS

TELEPHONES

Costa Rica has the best telecommunications systems in Latin America. Fax machines are increasingly popular; many hotels and businesses use them to avoid the post office system, which is known for long delays.

COIN-OPERATED PHONES

Use a two-, five- or ten-*colón* coin (the larger old two-*colón* coin will not work). Set the coins in the slot on top of the phone, then dial the number; the coin will drop down when the connection has been made. Extra coins set in the slot will be used only as needed.

Local collect calls	Tel: 110
Information	Tel: 113
International calls, direct	Tel:124
International calls, AT&T	Tel:114 (collect & credit card only)
International calls, operator assisted	Tel: 116
Airport information	Tel: 441 0744
Rate of exchange	Tel: 255 4455
Time	Tel: 112
Tourist information	Tel: 222 1090
VISA / Mastercard	Tel: 224 2155
American Express	Tel: 233 0044

(*see* Emergencies *for additional telephone numbers*).

Direct Dialing: Lift the receiver and wait for the dial tone. Dial the international address code for the country you are calling, listed in the telephone directory under *Lista Alfabetica de Códigos MIDA*. Dial area code, then dial phone number desired. For example, should you wish to dial 123 4567 in Washington, DC; dial as follows:
001 - international access USA; **202** - Washington DC area code; **123 4567** - individual phone.
If you have a problem, hang up and call, Tel: 124.
Direct dial international, information: Tel: 124.
For written telecommunications contact:
Radiografica Costarricense, S.A. (RACSA), av 5, c
I. Tel: 233 5555. Services include telegraph, telex, facsimiles, leased channels, and data transmission.

Telegrams	Tel: 123
Public FAX	Tel: 87 0087

POSTAL SERVICES

Air mail between the United States or Europe and Costa Rica should take about five days, but a wait of two weeks is not uncommon. The central Post Office is located at c 2, av 1-3. Tel: 223 9766. Mail can be received there in the general delivery section (*Lista de Correos*). Outgoing mail should be posted at either a hotel desk or a post office. It is usually difficult, time consuming, and expensive to receive packages in the mail, including, for example, blank checkbooks, books, recorded cassette tapes, film and auto parts. Outrageous duties are sometimes applied and you can spend days trying to deal with numerous officials. A receipt showing a low value may help if included with the package. There are agents, (*agencias de aduana*) listed in the phone book, who will handle the hassles of customs clearances for you.

There are many international mail courier services. Some of the most popular include: DHL, UPS, TNT Skypack, and Lacsa Flash.

Aero Casillas, tel: 255 4567. Centro Comercial Yaohan across from Hotel Corobicí. Above Yaohan supermarket is a mailing service that uses a Miami address to send and receive mail for about $30 per month. You are billed for US postage, and have the benefit of reliable and timely service. Well worthwhile if you need reliable mail service.

TELEVISION

Many programs received in English via satellite and cable.

NEWSPAPERS & MAGAZINES

Available in English, Spanish, and other languages at bookstores, supermarkets, newsstands, and other outlets. A large selection of magazines available at:
La Casa de las Revistas, c ctl, av ctl 1. Tel: 221 6680.

The Bookshop, av 1, c 2-4. An excellent English language bookstore carrying maps, magazines and books.

Tico Times, published on Friday. Widely available. Tel: 222 0040.

For up-to-date listings of what's happening, and where. Look in the classified section which has valuable information, and places for rent. An excellent special Tourist Edition contains an overview of the country.

Spanish language newspapers include: *La Nación*, *La Prensa Libre* and *La República*.

Don't be overcharged for overseas calls.

Save up to 70% on calls back to the U.S. with WorldPhone.®*

While traveling abroad, the last thing you need to worry about is being overcharged for international phone calls. Plan ahead and look into WorldPhone – the easy and affordable way for you to call the U.S. and country to country from a growing list of international locations.

Just dial 1-800-955-0925 to receive your free, handy, wallet-size WorldPhone Access Guide – your guide to saving as much as 70% on phone calls home.

When calling internationally, your WorldPhone Access Guide will allow you to:
- Avoid hotel surcharges and currency confusion
- Choose from four convenient billing options
- Talk with operators who speak your language
- Call from more than 90 countries
- Just dial and save – regardless of your long distance carrier back home

WorldPhone is easy. And there's nothing to join. So avoid overcharges when you're traveling overseas. Call for your free WorldPhone Access Guide today – before you travel.

Call 1-800-955-0925.

THE TOP 25 WORLDPHONE COUNTRY CODES.			
COUNTRY	**WORLDPHONE TOLL-FREE ACCESS #**	**COUNTRY**	**WORLDPHONE TOLL-FREE ACCESS #**
Australia (CC)◆		**Japan (cont'd.)**	
To call using		To call anywhere other	
OPTUS ■	008-5511-11	than the U.S.	0055
To call using		**Korea** (CC)	
TELSTRA ■	1-800-881-100	To call using KT ■	009-14
Belgium (CC)◆	0800-10012	To call using DACOM ■	0039-12
(Available from most major cities)		Phone Booths +	Red button 03,
China (CC)	108-12		then press*
For a Mandarin-speaking		Military Bases	550-2255
Operator	108-17	**Mexico** ▲	95-800-674-7000
Dominican Republic	1-800-	**Netherlands** (CC)◆	06-022-
	751-6624		91-22
El Salvador ◆	195	**Panama**	108
France (CC)◆	19▼-00-19	Military Bases	2810-108
Germany (CC)	0130-0012	**Philippines** (CC)◆	
(Limited availability in eastern		To call using PLDT ■	105-14
Germany.)		To call PHILCOM ■	1026-12
Greece (CC)◆	00-800-1211	For a Tagalog-speaking	
Guatemala ◆	189	Operator	108-15
Haiti (CC)+	001-800-444-1234	**Saudi Arabia** (CC)+	1-800-11
Hong Kong (CC)	800-1121	**Singapore**	8000-112-112
India (CC)	000-127	**Spain** (CC)	900-99-0014
(Available from most major cities)		**Switzerland** (CC)◆	155-0222
Israel (CC)	177-150-2727	**United Kingdom** (CC)	
Italy (CC)◆	172-1022	To call using BT ■	0800-89-0222
Japan ◆		To call using	
To call to the U.S.		MERCURY ■	0500-89-0222
using KDD ■	0039-121		
To call to the U.S.			
using IDC ■	0066-55-121		

(CC) Country-to-country calling available. May not be available to/from all international locations. Certain restrictions apply.

+ Limited availability.

▼ Wait for second dial tone.

▲ Rate depends on call origin in Mexico.

■ International communications carrier.

◆ Public phones may require deposit of coin or phone card for dial tone.

WORLDPHONE SM
From MCI
Let it take you around the world.

Swatch. The others just watch.

seahorse/fall winter 94-95

shockproof
splashproof
priceproof
boreproof
swiss made

swatch✚
SCUBA 200

EMERGENCIES

Costa Rica has an excellent health care system, much less expensive than the USA.

Office visits are under $20. Many doctors have been trained in the USA or Europe and speak English, especially at the private clinics.

Public Medical Centres

San Juan de Díos Hospital	Tel: 222 0166
México Hospital	Tel: 232 6122
Dr. Calderón Guardia Hospital	Tel: 222 4133
National Children's Hospital	Tel: 222 0122

Private Medical Centres

American Clinic	Tel: 222 1010
Biblical Clinic	Tel: 223 6422
Catholic Clinic	Tel: 225 5055
Santa Rita Clinic *	Tel: 221 6433

*maternity & gynecology

Plastic surgery is a big business here with people coming from the USA and Europe for reconstructive and cosmetic procedures. The Clínica de Cirugia Plastica in Pavas does abdominal liposuction ($2000), facelifts ($3000) and eyelids ($700). Dr. Fournier, tel: 222 1743, is highly respected.

Emergency Numbers

Detective dept.	Tel: 222 1365
Fire dept.	Tel: 118
Highway police	Tel: 227 7150
Police	Tel: 117
Rural Guard	Tel: 127
Traffic dept.	Tel: 227 8030
Computer help	Tel: 223 1022
Drugstore delivery	Tel: 223 0909

FOOD DIGEST

RESTAURANTS

It is highly recommended that you call and check hours of operation before going to restaurants in Costa Rica. Many are closed on Mondays. Smaller, informal restaurants with limited menus are called *sodas*.

SAN JOSÉ & SURROUNDING AREA

Abacus: San Rafael de Escazú, next to Tega meat market. Tel: 228 9616. Good crepes.

Altamira: (Italian) across from Balmoral Hotel.

Antojitos: (Mexican) Paséo Colón near Pizza Hut, and in Los Yoses.

Ambrosia: Centro Comercial de la Calle Real, San Pedro. Sandwiches to complete meals, many vegetarian. Pleasant ambience.

Amstel: c 7, av 1-3. Tel: 222 4622. Excellent reputation.

Arirang: (Korean) Edificio Colón. Tel: 223 2838.

Azfran: (coffee shop) Los Yoses, 25m east of Panadería Pancel.

Ave Fenix: (Chinese) San Pedro, 200m west of church. Tel: 225 3362.

Balcon de Europa: (Italian) Across av Central from Hotel Balmoral, up from Plaza de la Cultura. Tel: 221 4841.

Banco de Mariscos: (seafood) Santa Barbara de Heredia off town square, owns their own fishing boats. Very busy.

Barbecue Los Anonos: West of Anonos Bridge, San Rafael de Escazú. Tel: 228 0180. Grilled meat specialties. A favorite with Tico families.

Beirut: (Middle Eastern) c 32, av 1, 100 m north of Kentucky Fried Chicken. Tel: 257 1808.

Bougainvilla: Near Centro Comercial El Pueblo, Barrio Tournón in downtown San José. Tel: 233 6622. Great sea bass (*corvina*). Guitar music at night.

Casa España: (Spanish) c 11 av 3-5 in Bank of America/Banco de San José building, sixth floor, across from the Hotel Europa. Tel: 233 0301. Inexpensive, and good; paella and seafood.

Casino Español: c 7, av ctl. Tel: 222 9440. Huge menu of meat and seafood.

Chalet Suizo: av 1, c 5-7. Tel: 222 3118. Specialty is fondue.

Don Sol: (vegetarian) av 7, c 15 northeast of Casa Amarilla.

El Che: (Argentine Parrillada) 100 m south of traffic light on old road to Santa Ana in Escazú. Tel: 228 1598. Beef specialties.

El Chicote: (steak) Tel: 232 0936. Sabana Norte, near I.C.E. building, in Barrio Las Americas.

El Churrasco: Tel: 228 9332. 75 m south of Blvd de la Rosa, Escazú.

El Cuartel de La Boca: (typical Costa Rican) av 1, c 21-23, 150 m east of Parque Nacional. Tel: 221 0327. Art gallery, bar and restaurant.

El Escorial: av 1, c 5-7, Inexpensive and tasty, buffet.

El Rodeo: (steak) San Antonio de Belén, 4 km west of Cariari Hotel. Tel: 239 0677.

El Tapatío: (Mexican) Tel: 231 5132. Lower level at San José 2000. Shopping center.

El Tirol: (French) Part of the Hotel Chalet Tirol in an alpine setting near San Rafael de Heredia. Tel: 239 7070. French chef. Reservations recommended.

Fiesta de Maíz: La Garita de Alajuela on road to Atenas west of autopista. Tel: 487 7588. Small countryside eatery. All dishes are made of corn base. Take out service. Weekends only.

Finisterre: av ctl, across from the Balmoral Hotel and next to its sister restaurant, El Balcón de Europa. Tel: 222 0023. Great sandwiches.

Flor de Loto: (Chinese) Sabana Norte across from Los Angeles high school. Tel: 232 4652. Take out service.

Friday's: (North American) North of San Pedro Fountain. Tel: 224 5934. Unique menu, potato skins, steak on a stick, etc. Take out service.

Fulusu's: (Chinese) Across from L'Ille de France. Reputed to be one of the better Chinese restaurants.

Giacomín: Next to Los Yoses Auto Mercado. Tearoom with great pastries.

Gopal: (vegetarian) c 1, av 6. Run by the Hare Krishna community.

Gran Hotel Costa Rica: c 3, av ctl 2 facing Teatro Nacional. Tel: 221 4000.
•Le Jardin Room; top floor, good view of San José. Good lunch buffet.
•Café Parisien has buffet on terrace. Open 24 hours.

Greta's: (fine French and Belgian) Lourdes Montes de Oca. Tel: 225 2153. Piano bar starts at 8pm.

La Cascada: Los Anonos, across from Saretto supermarket on road to Escazú. Tel: 228 0906. Good steaks and shrimp; nice place to take the family.

La Fuente de los Mariscos
•Plaza del Sol, (lower floor). Tel: 234 1931.
•San José 2000 shopping center. Tel: 231 0631.

La Galería: (German) Los Yoses behind Apartotel Los Yoses 125 m west of I.C.E. building. Tel: 234 0850. Reservations required.

Le Tulá: (Italian) San Rafael de Escazú. Considered to be one of the best in the area. Tel: 228 0053.

L'Ile de France: (French) c 7, av ctl 2, 75 m south of Balmoral Hotel. Tel: 222 4241.

La Masia de Triquell: (Spanish/Catalán) av 2, c 40,

100 m east of the Soda Tapia de La Sabana. Tel: 221 5073.

La Mazorca: (Vegetarian) Tel: 224 8069. From Banco Anglo in San Pedro, 100 m north and 25 m west. Freshly baked natural breads, pastries. Take-out service.

La Nutrisoda: (Vegetarian) Next to Gran Hotel Costa Rica.

Las Chorreadas: (typical Costa Rican). Monrovia.

Lamm's Barbeque: San Rafael de Escazú on old road to Santa Ana. Tel: 228 2539. Good sandwiches and Salvadorean tortillas (*pupusas*).

Lancer's Steak House: Centro Comercial El Pueblo, Barrio Tournón in downtown San José. Tel: 222 5938.

La Galería: (Continental) Reservations necessary. Tel: 234 0850. Exceptional.

La Petite Provence: (French) av ctl, c 27, next to Pizza Hut. Tel: 39 1640. Excellent cuisine. Piano player and vocalists at dinner. Coat and tie.

La Piazetta: (Italian) Paseo Colón across from Centro Colón. Tel: 221 8451.

La Subasta: Pozos de Santa Ana. Tel: 228 6095. Specialty is steak. Cattle auctions on Tues, Weds and Thur, 10am–noon. Reservations.

Le Bastille: (French) Paseo Colón, c 22. Tel: 222 0243.

Le Bistrot: (French) San Pedro, 100 m east, 20 m north of San Pedro Church. Tel: 253 8062. Small, friendly; cuisine from the Dijon region.

Le Chandelier: (French) Paseo Colón, c 30-32. Tel: 221 7947. Coat and tie required; call for reservations.

Los Antojitos: (Mexican)
•Centro Comercial del Sur. Tel: 227 4160.
•Carratera to Tibas. Tel: 235 3961.
•Los Yoses. Tel: 225 9525.
•Paseo Colón, c 26. Tel: 228 9086.
•Pavas, 600 m west of La Sabana. Tel: 231 5564.
Not the best Mexican food in the world, but reasonably priced; enjoyable atmosphere.

Louisana: (Cajun) Old Escazú road, E. side of Sabana. Crawfish etouffé.

Los Lechones: c 11 , av 4-6. Tel: 223 2957. Pork, *chicharrón*. Calypso and reggae music Friday and Saturday evenings.

Machu Pichu: (Peruvian) c 32 , av 1-3, 150 m north of Paseo Colón Kentucky Fried Chicken. Tel: 222 7384. Recommended by many.

Maybo: (Italian) San Pedro east of Mas x Menos supermarket. Tel: 224 1014. Antipasto table. Piano bar.

Medio Oriente: (Middle Eastern) Downstairs at San José 2000 shopping center. Tel: 231 5376. Pleasant atmosphere.

Mordiscos: Paseo Colón. Exceptional, gourmet natural cuisine.

Paprika: Los Yoses, 50 m east of Kentucky Fried Chicken at av ctl, c 29-33. Tel: 225 8981. Pleasant atmosphere. Homemade soups and sandwiches.

Piccola: (Italian) c 24, av 2 near Paseo Colón. Tel: 223 1073.

Rias Bajas: (seafood) Centro Comercial El Pueblo, Barrio Tournón in downtown San José. Tel: 221 7123. Call for reservations.

Rosti Pollo: (Nicaraguan) Small, chicken roasted over coffee tree wood. Take out service.
- San Rarael de Escazú, near Tega. Tel: 228 2488.
- Centro Comercial de la Calle Real, San Pedro.

Sakura: (Japanese) Sheraton Hotel. Tel: 239 0033. Sushi, expensive.

Shakti: (Vegetarian) c 13, av 8.

Soda La Casita: av 1, c ctl. For a quick downtown meal on weekdays.

Soda Central: av 1, c 3-5. Good chicken empanadas.

Soda Tapia: La Sabana Gimnasio. One of the best sodas in San José.

Spoon: Good pastries and *bocas*, very good chicken lasagna.
- Downtown Tel: 221 6702. av ctl, c 5-7.
- Los Yoses Tel: 224 0328.
- Pavas, across from US Embassy. Tel: 231 635.

The Lobster Inn: (seafood) Paseo Colón, c 24 across from the Mercedes-Benz dealership. Tel: 223 8594. Call for reservations.

Tiquicia: (typical Costa Rican) El Naranjo, San Antonio de Escazú. Tel: 222 0468. Rustic farmhouse setting with view of the Central Valley. Marimba music daily; folkloric ballet Friday at 7:30pm. Always call first.

Valerio's: (Italian) Los Yoses west of overpass on road to San Pedro. Tel: 225 0838. Known for their pizza.

Vía Veneto: (Italian) Across from Plaza del Sol, Curribat. Tel: 234 2898. Excellent pasta; good pastries and chocolate. Take-out pastry shop branch in San Rafael de Escazú.

Villa Bonita: (Chinese) From Centro Comercial del Oeste (Pavas) 25 m west. Tel: 232 9855.

Villa Franken: (German) San Pedro, 100 m east and 75 m south of Banco Popular. Tel: 224 1850. Gourmet cuisine from the Franken region.

Zermatt: (Swiss) San Pedro 100 m north and 25 m east of Santa Teresita Church. Tel: 222 0604.

THINGS TO DO

SIGHTSEEING

SAN JOSÉ AREA

Central Park: (*Parque Central*) In front of Metropolitan Cathedral, c ctl, av 2. Artisan stalls and music on Sundays.

La Merced Church: Beautiful example of colonial church, the oldest in Costa Rica. c 10-12, av 2-4

La Sabana: Family park west of San José with Olympic-sized swimming pool, tennis courts, basketball and handball courts, baseball and soccer fields, and a manmade lake.

Metropolitan Cathedral: c ctl, av 2-4.

Moravia: Small town just northeast of San José with many souvenir shops selling wood and leather items.

National Theater: (*Teatro Nacional*) c 3, av 2. Constructed in the Renaissance style, an architectural jewel. A wonderful café; often has local artists' works on exhibit.

Ojo de Agua: (Eye of Water) A popular recreational complex near San Antonio de Belén with swimming pools, lake with rowboats, restaurant. Take bus from av 1, c 18-20.

Parque de Diversiones: 2km west of Hospital Mexico. Tel: 231 2001. Children's amusement park. Hours vary, call to confirm.

Plaza de la Cultura: Adjacent to the *Teatro Nacional*. Artists fair each weekend, often music and events. A stairway leads down to the Gold Museum and information office of the Tourist Institute (ICT).

San Pedro: Just east of San José, includes residential area of Los Yoses and the University of Costa Rica.

CENTRAL VALLEY
MESETA CENTRAL

Club Campestre El Castillo
A private country club, 30 minutes north of San José, passing through the National University in San Rafael de Heredia. Tel: 239 7111. Open to public for a small fee. Among other amenities, has only ice skating rink in Latin America.

Calypso Boat Tour
Tel: 233 3617. The Calypso is a 50-ft yacht which sails from Puntarenas to either Tortuga Island or Punta Cuchillo in the Gulf of Nicoya. Bus pick up in San Jose. The boat trip takes 2 hours to a beautiful

white beach for swimming, sunning, and and a gourmet lunch, returning to San José about 7pm.

Cartago
One of Costa Rica's oldest cities and the country's first capital, until 1823. The image of the patroness of the country, Nuestra Señora de Los Angeles, the Black Virgin, whose feast day is on August 2, is housed within the Basilica, a magnificent example of Byzantine architecture.

Escazú, Santa Ana, Puriscal
A scenic drive going west from San José. In Escazú go all the way up the mountain to San Antonio de Escazú; see 100-year-old adobe houses with tile roofs, whitewashed homes with blue-painted borders. Several sugar mills (*trapiches*) are in operation. Continuing on the old road to Santa Ana, stop at the roadside stands selling items of pottery. Take the Escazú-Villa Colón highway to Puriscal; at points along the way colorful woven baskets and straw mats are displayed for sale by the only Indian tribe remaining in the Central Valley, the Quitirrsi.

Grecia, Sarchí, Zachero
Take the airport highway northwest out of San José to Grecia, a center of pineapple, sugar cane, and coffee production. Visit the church of Grecia, completely covered with red-painted metal. Ask directions to Sarchí, home of the famous hand-painted oxcarts and the principal center of furniture-making and wooden souvenir production in Costa Rica. Continue to the town of Zarcero, known for its cypress hedges shaped into animals and other figures, which can be seen in front of the church.

Guayabo National Park
12 miles (19 km) north of Turrialba on a dirt road; considered the most important archaeological site in Costa Rica. A pre-Columbian site still under excavation.

Irazú Volcano (11,260 ft, 3,432 m)
33 miles (53 km) east of San José on the road to Cartago; the winding road up the mountain is excellent. Take a sweater and wear sturdy shoes.

Laguna de Fraijanes
Lake with nearby basketball courts, mini-soccer field, children's play and picnic areas. Located 9 miles (15 km) from Alajuela near Póas Volcano. Take a left turn at sign marked "Sabanilla" just after Corte Suprema de Justicia in Alajuela. Proceed for 19 miles (15 km), go right at the fork in the road. Admission, ¢10 for children and ¢15 for adults. Open Tuesday-Sunday, 9am-3:30pm

Lankester Gardens
Native and imported orchids and other plants in a woodsy setting, run by the University of Costa Rica. Open daily from 8am to 3pm. In March almost every orchid is blooming. Southeast of Cartago.

La Selva Biological Station
Adjoins Braulio Carrillo National Park, operated by the Organization of Tropical Studies, Apto 676, San Pedro. Tel: 236 6696. A field station for naturalists, but when space exists, tourists are welcome. Simple accommodations; three meals a day served in the cafeteria. Arrangements can be made for guided hikes and boat trips. A bus travels to and from the San José office. Two hours by car over paved roads.

Orosi Valley and Cachí Dam
South of Cartago is a beautiful valley. Go through Cartago, following the signs to Paraíso; turn right in front of the park in Paraíso. From the Mirador Orosi there is a fantastic view of the valley below. With picnic tables, a playground, and restrooms, it is a nice place for a family outing. In the town of Orosi is the Church of San José de Orosi, built by Franciscan missionaries in 1735. Recently restored, it is the oldest active church in Costa Rica and houses a small museum of colonial religious art. Continue on the unpaved but drivable road around the lake to the Cachí Dam, which provides most of the electricity for the Central Valley. Continue through town and cross the river to the Motel Río, a luncheon spot next to the Reventazón River.

Póas Volcano (9,512 ft, 2,752 m)
About a one-hour drive northwest of San José, past Alajuela. Póas volcano is still active, and constantly steaming. Its crater is among the largest in the world. Take warm clothing, arrive early (8-8.30am) as it is cloud covered most of the time. Before leaving, call the National Parks Service (Tel: 233 5473) to request weather and visibility for the summit. Films on the national parks are shown on Saturday, Sunday and holidays. On the way back visit Laguna de Fraijanes.

Ruins of Ujarrás and Paradero
Go through Cartago, following the signs to Paraíso. Turn right at the Orosi sign and watch for Ujarrás sign on the left. From the lookout (*mirador*), there is a spectacular view of the Reventazón River and the surrounding valley. See the ruins of the Church of Ujarrás. Built of limestone in 1693, it commemorates the retreat of the English pirate Morgan in 1666. Continue to the Paradero Lacustre Charrarra lakeside park on the shore of the lake formed by the Cachí Dam. Restaurant, picnicking, swimming pool, dock for motorboats and sailboats, and a camping area.

San José de la Montaña
A mountain getaway 5 miles (8 km) north of Heredia has hiking on the nearby Barva Volcano. Hotel El Pórtico is good for lunch, relaxation and hiking.

Jungle Train

Presently out of service because of landslides, and financial problems, this ancient narrow gauge train goes to Siquírres and Limón. (It is anticipated that service will be renewed in the near future. Call the ICT information office.) Sit on the right side of the train when leaving San José for the best view. Passes the Irazú Volcano and the Continental Divide, as well as coffee *fincas* and whitewater rapids. Leaves the Altantic train station (c 17 av 3) at 11am. Ride the train to Turrialba, then return to San José by bus. Swiss Travel Tel: 231 4055, has a bilingual guide going in a separate, more comfortable car. You can also take the train all the way to Limón and return to San José by airplane or bus.

The Tropical Agricultural Research and Educational Center (CATIE)

Scientists from all over the world conduct agricultural and animal husbandry research here in Turrialba, one of the major tropical research centers in the world. For information or to arrange a tour contact CATIE, Apto 7170, Turrialba. Tel: 556 6431.

Cahuita National Park

Three hours from San José, Cahuita is a long day trip and is best done on a weekend. From Limón go south for the beautiful beach and coral reef.

Chirripó National Park

Scale Costa Rica's highest peak, Mt. Chirripó at 12,500 feet (3,819 m). To get there take the Inter-American Highway to San Isidro de El General and turn north to San Gerardo.

Flamingo beach

Several private villas and hotels are located along the white beach of Flamingo, north of Playa Brasilito. Marina facililies are being expanded. A small landing field for private or chartered aircraft is an alternative to the long, bumpy road from San José.

Golfito

Situated on the southern Pacific coast is Golfito, the abandoned headquarters of the once mighty United Fruit Company. Golfito is a gorgeous sheltered natural harbor, with a hot humid, tropical atmosphere, and a free zone for shopping.

Jungle Trip/Puerto Viejo/Tortuguero/Canals

Tours leave mornings from San José by microbus, or go solo by bus or car to the port of Moín near Limón. Boats travel up the canals. Some pass through Tortuguero National Park, a wildlife preserve where green turtles lay their eggs. Chartered flights available. Overnight at lodges possible.

Lake Arenal and Tilarán

The site of Costa Rica's largest hydroelectric project and its most active volcano, Arenal, whose last major eruption was in 1968. The dam is located on an artificial lake about 24 miles (39 km) from end to end. Sailing and windsurfing are permitted on the lake, which can have waves of up to 6 feet. Driving from San José to Arenal takes about 3-4 hours.

Liberia

Capital of Guanacaste province. Just before reaching Liberia, stop for refreshments at the Hotel Las Espuelas, Tel: 66 0144, nestled under a giant Guanacaste tree. To get to the Nicoya Peninsula and beaches turn left at the traffic light in Liberia and continue on towards the town of Santa Cruz.

Limón

This tropical, hot, and steamy Caribbean coast port is a 3-hour drive from San José on a new highway. Sloths hang in the trees in the central park. Each year to commemorate Columbus Day on October 12, a week-long carnival is held and Limón is filled with a Mardi Gras atmosphere of floats, dancers, and an elaborate Grand Parade. Make hotel reservations far in advance of this date.

Marenco Biological Station

Located on the Osa Peninsula, a facility for research and recreational activities. Dormitory-style bunk beds, a combination lodge and dining hall. Tourists are encouraged and field trips can be arranged to Isla Del Caño Biological Reserve and Corcovado National Park. Reservations can also be made at Edificio Cristal, second floor, av 1, c 1-3, Apto 4025, San José. Tel: 221 1504.

Monteverde Biological Reserve and Rain Forest

This cloud forest biological reserve is located in the Sierra de Tilarán in Puntarenas province, about 4 hours drive from San José. Take the Pan-American Highway north from Puntarenas; the road is not paved. Monteverde is a community founded by Quakers. Scientists come to study tropical plants and birds. Well-marked trails, and naturalists for hire. Rubber boots, rain ponchos, and layers of clothes are highly recommended during rainy season. Souvenirs at the artisan cooperative CASEM.

Nicoya Peninsula

Can be reached by ferry leaving daily from Puntarenas at 7am and 4pm, or drive south from Santa Cruz. Santa Cruz was the center of the Chorotega tribe. A beautiful colonial church built in the 16th century still stands.

Nosara, Sámara and Garza

Located off the road south near Santa Cruz. Three beautiful white sand beaches which are very good for shell collecting. Good road until the last 12 miles (20 km). Four-wheel drive is advisable during the rainy season as small rivers and streams must be forged. SANSA airlines flies to nearby Carrillo.

Puntarenas

The port city of Puntarenas is on a long, narrow, sandy point of land which extends 3 miles (5 km) to the west into the Gulf of Nicoya. From here trips can be made to the Gulf of Nicoya, the Nicoya peninsula, and other beaches. Continuing south on the same road is the port of Caldera, where many cruise ships dock.

Quepos and Manuel Antonio National Park

Quepos, once an important banana port, is a 4-hour drive from San José. Only 4.3 miles (7 km) from Quepos are the three beaches of Manuel Antonio National Park. Drive to the first beach. Hike to the second and third. The third beach is considered one of the most beautiful in Costa Rica. Diving Safaris Inc. (Tel: 224 0033) offers dive trips and rentals. Unicorn Adventures (Tel: 777 0489) will take the traveler to a private beach, below the Mariposa Hotel, by horse through a private reserve.

Rara Avis

A private reserve encompassing over 1,500 acres (607 hectares) of primary rain forest, supporting a wide variety of wildlife. Access to Rara Avis must be arranged ahead of time. Naturalist Donald Perry's web apparatus allows observers to travel horizontally up in the forest canopy. Lodge. Tourists are welcome and an experienced biologist is available for tours. Contact: Apto 8105, San José. Tel: 253 0844.

San Gerardo de Dota

At Finca Zacatales, there is trout fishing, walking paths, simple cabins, delicious food and a good chance of seeing the elusive Resplendent Quetzal. The owners, the Chacón family, are exceptionally hospitable. Tel: 771 1732.

Santa Cruz

Santa Cruz, a cattle town, has been declared National Folklore City. Famous for its colorful fiestas. Try the Tortilla Factory Restaurant for excellent typical food.

Tamarindo

Popular Pacific coast beach, famous for deep-sea fishing, swimming and snorkeling. Papagayo Excursions. Tel: 680 0652. Sponsors tours to observe the leatherback turtles hatching.

TOUR COMPANIES

Aventuras Naturales. Tel: 225 3939. Offers 4-hour rafting trip.

Calypso Tours. av 2, c 1-3. Tel: 233 0401. Excursion boats to the islands off of Nicoya.

Club Crucero. Jungle houseboat charters on Tortuguero Canals.

Costa Rica Expeditions. c ctl, av 1-3. Tel: 222 0333. Excellent whitewater rafting, nature tour, and dirt biking. Travelers' store. Operates Tortuga

Lodge and arranges guided tours to see the green sea turtles during nesting. Recommended.

Crucero Miss Caribe. Paseo Colón, c 34-36. Tel: 233 6579. Passage on Tortuguero canals north of Limón.

Cruceros Mawamba. Tel: 233 9964. 3-day, 2-night trip leaves Friday from the Gran Hotel Costa Rica; a 50-passenger boat carries jungle visitors both ways on the Atlantic coastal canals north of Limón.

Diving Safaris Inc. av 2, c 7-9. Tel: 255 2811. Dive trips/rentals. PADI-NAUI certification.

Fantasy Tours. Lobby Hotel Irazú. Tel: 220 0042. Arranges air tours of city, volcanos, national parks, and Jacó Beach.

Geotours, S.A. Tel: 227 5868. Trips led by naturalists to Braulio Carrillo National Park on the Carribean and Carara Biological Reserve and Jacó Beach on the Pacific.

Horizontes. av 1, c 1-3, Edificio Cristal second floor. Tel: 222 2022. Arranges tours to Marenco Station and around San José.

Interviajes. c 3, av 4, Heredia. Tel: 238 1212. Scenic one-day tours in and around San José.

Isla de Pesca. Tel: 223 4560. The "River Queen" for a day-long voyage through the Tortuguero canals. Lodging at Isla de Pesca Lodge.

Miss Caribe River Boat Tour. Tortuguero Canal. Tel: 233 0155.

Orchid Travel. Tel: 238 3586. Tours to Monteverde Cloud Forest.

Pagayo Excursions. Tamarindo. Tel: 680 0652. Turtle nesting and estuary cruises.

Raravis. Apto 8105, San José 1000. Tel: 253 0844. *See* Excursions.

Río Colorado Lodge. Tel: 232 4063. Deluxe fishing lodge; operates jungle trips on the "Colorado Queen" through the canals of Tortuguero.

Ríos Tropicales. Paseo Colón c 22-24. Tel: 233 6598. Rafting and kayaking.

Saeta. Tel: 232 1474. Ten-minute airplane tours over the city of San José. Leave from Tobias Bolanos airport, Pavas. Air taxi service available to Flamingo, Jacó, and Puntarenas.

Swiss Travel. Hotel Corobicí, Hotel Amstel. Tel: 222 4622. Offers a wide variety of one-day tours in and around San José.

Tam. c 1, av ctl 1. Tel: 223 5111. Complete line of tours.

Terviajes. c 3, av 4, Heredia. Tel: 238 1212. Several scenic one-day tours in and around San José.

Unicorn Adventures. Manuel San Antonio, Quépos. Tel: 777 0489. Guided horseback tours through private reserve; sea kayaks.

Viajes Atlántico. Centro Comercial 2000, La Uruca. Tours the canals of Tortuguero. *See* Excursions.

CULTURE PLUS

Museums: *(museos)* for current listings of days and hours of operation.
 Call ICT: Tel: 222 1090 or
 General Directorate of Museums: Tel: 233 3298.

Coffee Museum: Barva, Heredia, 400 m north of the San Pedro de Barva Church. Tel: 237 1975. Built in 1834, the museum was founded in 1977 to preserve coffee traditions. Permanent exhibits include 100 pieces of machinery used in processing coffee. Admission free. Open Monday–Friday, 7am–3pm.

Costa Rican Art Museum: *(Muséo de Arte Costarricense)* Sabana Este at Paseo Colón. Tel: 222 7155. Both permanent collection and hanging exhibits of paintings and sculptures of the 19th and 20th centuries by Costa Rican artists. Open Tuesday–Sunday, 10am–5pm ¢20. Admission free on Sunday.

Crime Museum: *(Museo Criminólogico)* Organization for Judicial Investigation, middle building of the Supreme Court Complex, av 6, c 15. Tel: 223 0666 ext. 2378. The museum contains various weapons, counterfeit money, equipment to investigate accidents and unsolved crimes, and a grisly display related to violent death. Open Monday, Wednesday and Friday, 1pm–5pm. Admission free.

Entomology: *(Museo de Entomología)* Located in the basement of the school of musical arts on the campus of the University of Costa Rica, 400 m north of the San Pedro Church. Tel: 225 5555 ext. 318. Exhibits of more than 6,000 varieties of Costa Rican bugs and butterflies. Open Monday, Wednesday, and Thursday, 1pm–5pm; Tuesday, 8am–5pm. Admission free.

Ethnohistorical Museum of Limón: Located diagonal to the southeast corner of the Mercado municipal. Material related to Columbus' arrival at Port Limón and indigenous items. Monday–Friday, 9am–6pm.

Gold Museum: *(Museo de Oro)* Below the Plaza de la Cultura, av ctl, c 5. Tel: 223 0528. Excellent display of pre-Columbian gold artifacts. Open Tuesday–Sunday, 10am–5pm. Admission free.

Hotel Matama Zoo: Playa Bonita, Limón, has two jaguars, 2 apes and a pizote. Daily 8am–6pm.

Instituto Clodomiro Picado: Snake farm next to the plaza in Dulce Nombre de Coronado. Tel: 229 0344. Ten live venomous snakes on display plus maps, photos, and information on local snakes and the manufacture of anti-venom. Between 1.30 and 3pm on Friday. Watch from behind plate glass window as they milk the venom and feed the snakes. Open Monday–Friday, 1–4pm. Admission free.

Jade Museum: *(Museo de Jade)* av 7, c 9, in the I.N.S. building, 11th floor. Tel: 223 5800 ext. 2581. Exhibits of jade, pottery, and stone. Open Monday–Friday, 9am–3pm. Admission free.

Juan Santamaría Museum: Alajuela at av 3, c ctl-2. Tel: 441 4775. Features the national hero of Costa Rica, Juan Santamaría, and the period of the Costa Rican fight against William Walker and the fillibusters in 1856. Special visits may be pre-arranged including the showing of a film depicting the Battle of Rivas, in English or Spanish. Open Tuesday–Sunday, 2–9pm. Admission free.

Lankester Gardens: Paraíso de Cartago. More than 650 acres of gardens, forest, and a refuge for migratory birds. Founded in 1917 by Charles Lankester, now run by the University of Costa Rica. Best time of year to see the more than 800 species of orchids in full bloom is February and March. Park open daily 9am–3pm, ¢30. Guided tours available.

Liberia Ecomuseum: Tel: 666 0122. Guanacaste social and historical heritage including typical *sabanero* (cowboy) articles. Tuesday–Sunday, 8–12am, 2–6pm.

National Museum: *(Museo Nacional)* av ctl 2, c 17, 100 m south of Parque Nacional. Tel: 221 0295. Formerly Bellavista Fortress, headquarters of the Costa Rican Army. Features pre-Columbian ceramics, furniture, natural history specimens, colonial religious art, historical documents. Open Tuesday–Sunday, 8.30am–4.30pm. Admission ¢50.

National University Marine Zoological Museum: In the School of the National University, Heredia. Tel: 237 6363 ext 2240. Examples of marine life found in Costa Rican waters. Tuesday–Friday, 8am–4pm.

Natural Sciences Museum: *(Ciencias Naturales)* Colegio La Salle, southeast corner or La Sabana on grounds of the Ministry of Agriculture. Tel: 232 1306. Displays more than 22,500 examples of the world's animals, including some which are now extinct. The specimens are exhibited as they would appear in their natural habitat. Open Monday–Friday, 7am–3pm; Saturday, 8am–noon; March–November. Admission ¢20.

Orosí Museum of Religious Art: Adjacent to the Colonial Church of Orosi, in Cartago province. Tel: 533 3051. Religious artifacts from the colonial era. Open every day except Wednesday and Sunday 9am–5pm.

Oxcart Museum: Salitral de Desamparados. Tel: 259 7042. Display of *campesino* life, recreating activities of the last century. Tuesday–Sunday, 8am–4pm.

Parque Bolivar Zoo Barrio Amón: (north side of San José). Felines, reptiles, 132 species of birds. Not a good zoo; definitely not recommended. Tuesday-Friday. 8am–4pm, Saturday–Sunday, 9am–5pm.

Serpentarium Museum: San José, av 1, c 9, 2nd floor of Radamida Bldg. Snakes galore. Daily 10am–7pm.

Zoo Ave: La Garita de Alajuela. Tropical bird zoo. Tuesday–Sunday 8am–3pm.

MUSIC

National Lyric Opera Company *(Companía de Lírica Nacional)*. Usually two operas are presented during the season from late June to mid August. Performances are in the Teatro Melico Salazar. Tel: 222 3071.

National Symphony Orchestra *(Orquesta Sinfonía Nacional)*. The National Symphony plays a series of twelve concerts between April and November. Concerts are held in the Teatro Nacional at 8pm on Thursday and Friday evenings, and at 10.30am on Sunday morning. Tel: 222 2682.

One Hour of Music *(Una Hora de Música)*. Chamber music concerts in San José, Cartago, Alajuela, and Heredia. Tel: 232 1145.

US University Musicians Series. The Centro Cultural Costarricense Norteamericano presents concerts once a month. Tel: 225 0597.

ART GALLERIES

(Galerías de Arte)
The *Tico Times* and *La Nación* newspapers carry current exhibit listings.

Alianza Frances
av 5, c 1-3. Tel: 222 2283.
Banco de Costa Rica Gallery
In the Banco de Costa Rica downtown.
Crayons Gallery
Escazú. Centro Comercial Boulevard Rosa. Tel: 228 0257.
Expression Park
Parque España. Sunday 9am–2pm.
Facultad de Belles Artes

University of Costa Rica. Tel: 225 5555.
Galería Bellas Artes
Paseo Colón, c 38-40. Tel: 221 5159.
Galería Claus
av ctl, 25 m east of Kentucky Fried Chicken. Tel: 253 0615.
Galería Expresiva
av 2, c 30-32, 100m west of Kentucky Fried Chicken. Tel: 257 2737.
Galería de Studios Generales
University of Costa Rica, next to library.
Galería de Lazaro
Escazú, across from Los Anonos shopping center. Tel: 228 2974.
Galería de Importación del Oeste
Tel: 220 1422. La Sabana, west of Pops.
Galería Enrique Echandi
c 5, av ctl 2, behind Teatro Nacional. Tel: 222 7732.
Galería Hotel don Carlos
c 9, #779. Tel: 221 6707.
Galería Joaquin Garcia Monge
c 5, behind Teatro Nacional.
Galería José Figueres
av 2, c 3, Banco Popular.
Galería Sophia Wanamaker
Occasional exhibits in the Centro Cultural Costarricense-Norteamericano. Tel: 225 9433.
Juan Santamaría Museum
Alajuela, av 3, c ctl 2. Tel: 441 4775.
La Galería
c l, av ctl l. Tel: 221 3436.
Matiz Gallery
Plaza del Sol Shopping Center. Tel: 224 1469.
Museo de Arte Costarricense
La Sabana Park East, formerly the airport terminal building. Tel: 222 7155.
October Eight Gallery
Paseo Colón, near IBM building.
Post Argentine Gallery
Escazú. Tel: 228 4277.
Sala Jorge de Bravo
av ctl, c 13-15, on Cuesta de Moras. Tel: 233 4535.
Sala Kandinsky
Edicol Building, Sabana Sur. Tel: 231 7049.
Teatro Nacional
av 2, c 3-5. Tel: 221 1329.Exhibits in café.

LIBRARIES

(Bibliotecas)
Biblioteca Nacional
av 3, c15-17. Open to the public. Tel: 221 2436.
Biblioteca Universidad de Costa Rica
Ciudad Universitaria Rodrigo Facio. Tel: 225 7372.
Bibliomania
Escazú, 25 m west of San Rafael Church. Tel: 228 4537. Used paperbacks exchange, members only. Over 4,000 titles available.
The Bookshop
av 1, c 2-4. New (and some used) English books and magazines.

Casey's Book Exchange
ctl, av 7-9,150 m north of Hotel Europa. Tel: 221 7995. New and used paperbacks.

Mark Twain Library
The Centro Cultural Costarricense-Norteamericano, Los Yoses is 200 m north of Centro La Mufla near Los Yoses Auto Mercado, road to San Pedro. Tel: 225 9433. English language reference books and magazines, fiction, and nonfiction. Books may be checked out only by members; membership open to the public.

HOLIDAYS & FESTIVALS

1 January
New Year's Day. Week-long (Dec. 25 - Jan. 2) festivities: *Fiestas del Fin del Año*, parade of horses (*tope*); carnival; Feria de Zapote with bullfights.

2 January
Year-end holidays and fiestas. Nonviolent (for the bull) bullfights.

Second week in January
Copa del Cafe international tennis tournament.

February/March
Annual Orchid Show; also the best time to see orchids in bloom at Lankester Gardens, Cartago. National Theater Symphony season begins in March. Rodeo.

19 March
San José Day.

Mid March
National Handicraft Fair, downtown San José; Feast of St. Joseph, Patron Saint of San José. *Dia del Boyero* (Day of the Oxcart Driver) parade and blessing of the oxcarts (*carretas*), San Antonio de Escazú.

March/April
Semana Santa, Holy Week; Thursday and Friday, banks, post offices, and government offices are closed, as well as most supermarkets and restaurants; *Jueves Santo*, Holy Thursday. Start of Holy Week ceremonies. *Viernes Santo*, Good Friday. Religious processions, at 1am and 4pm. "Roman soldiers", biblical personages, and black-clad mourners, especially San Joaquín de Flores.

11 April
Juan Santamaría Day; hero of Costa Rica, died in the Battle of Rivas in action against William Walker in 1856.

21 April
Romeria, Pilgrimage of the Virgin. The English pirate Morgan expelled in 1606. End of April - Book Fair (F*eria del Libro*) in San José. International auto racing at La Guacima de Alajuela.

1 May
Labor Day.

May/June
Feast of Corpus Christi on the Thursday after Trinity Sunday.

June
Third Sunday in June is Father's Day.

29 June
Feast of Saints Peter and Paul.

25 July
Annexation of Guanacaste Province in 1824.

1 August
Pilgrims walking from San José arrive at the Basilica in Cartago, site of a miraculous appearance in 1635.

2 August
Nuestra Señora de los Angeles, Feast of Patroness of Costa Rica.

15 August
Feast of the Assumption. Mother's Day in Costa Rica.

15 September
Independence Day. Independence from Spain in 1821. All traffic in San José stops at 6.00pm on the 14th, and everyone sings the national anthem.

October
Turtles on Tortuguero and Guanacaste beaches.

12 October
Columbus Day. El Día de la Raza. Week-long Carnival in Puerto Limón with floats, dance contests, ending with an elaborate parade.

31 October
Halloween.

8 December
Feast of the Immaculate Conception. Holy Communion Day, streets are filled with girls in starched white dresses.

25 December
Christmas crowds and confetti "snow" battles. Parades.

SPORTS

Bicycling
Competitive bicycling events are listed in the sports sections of the local newspapers.
Federacion Costarricense de Ciclismo, Barrio Naciones Unidas. Tel: 223 7093.

Birdwatching
Costa Rica Expeditions. Tel: 222 0333.

Bridge
Centro Israelita Paseo Colón, c 22, across from Hospital de Niños. Tel: 233 9222. Affliated with ACBL.

Camping
Information is available in National Parks publica-

tions available at bookstores and from the ICT information office.

Fishing
Abocap. Golfito area has 22 boats across from the market.
Club Amateura de Pesca. (am only) Apdo. 33503 - 3000 San José. Tel: 232 3430. Fishing club brings all nationalities together, helps obtain licenses.
Casamar. Atlantic Coast. Tel: 441 2820.
Costa Rican Dreams. Quepos. Tel: 239 3383.
Deportes Keko. c 20, av 4-6. Tel: 223 4142.
Gilca. c 2, av 16-18. *La Casa del Pescador*. Tel: 222 1470.
Isla de Pesca. Atlantic Coast. Tel: 221 5396.
Rio Colorado. Atlantic Coast. Tel: 232 8610 (US 1 800 243 9777).
Rio Mar. Centro Comercial del Sur. Tel: 254 0840.
Sportfishing Cost Rica. Quepos. Tel: 238 4434.
Tom Bradwell. Flamingo Beach. Tel: 680 0942.
Tortuga Lodge. Atlantic Coast. Tel: 222 0333.

Golf
Cariari Country Club. Has the only 18-hole course.
Costa Rica Country Club. Escazú.
Tango Mar Surf & Saddle Club. Nicoya Peninsula near Tambor.

Horseback Riding
Many resorts rent horses and provide guides.
Club Paso Fino. Tel: 441 1466.
Escuela Nacional de Equitacion. Guachipelin, Escazú. Tel: 228 1695.
Los Inocentes. Guanacaste. Tel: 239 5482.
Hotel Cariari. Tel: 239 2248.
Unicorn Adventures. Manuel Antonio, Quepos. Tel: 777 0489.

Mountaineering
Club de Montanisno. Tel: 235 3147. Open to the public, meets monthly.

Roller Skating
Salon de Patines La Pista (*Patines*). Centro Comercial El Pueblo. Tel: 223 6077.

Sailing
Costa Rica Yacht Club. Puntarenas. Tel: 223 4224.
Catamaran Slingshot. Captain Jim Thomkins, Puntarenas.
Mar Tranquila. av 9, c 19-21. Tel: 233 4321.
Playas del Coco. Tel: 670 0229. Sailboat rentals by the day.

Tennis
Cariari Country Club. Tel: 239 2248.
Costa Rica Tennis Club. Sabana Sur. Tel: 232 1266.
Los Reyes Country Club. La Guácima.

Surfing
Asociación de Surf. Costa Rica is rated as one of the world's top five surfing spots, along with Hawaii, California, Australia, and Peru. Surfing is popular at many beaches, and international surfing competitions are held along both coasts. One place to surf nearest San José is Playa Doña Ana, at the mouth of the Río Barranca.

Rafting & Kayaking
Costa Rica is fast gaining an international reputation for its white-water excursions. Rivers Class One to Five. Everything from the calmest river ride to expert-class rapids is available with equipment and certified guides.
Aventuras Naturales, Los Yoses. Tel: 225 3939.
Costa Rica Expeditions, c ctl, av 3. Tel: 222 0333; fax: 257 1665.
Rios Tropicales, Paseo Colón. Tel: 233 6455.
Rancho Leona, Río Puerto Viejo. Tel: 710 6312.

Diving
Diving Safaries, Guana Caste. Tel: 670 0012.

BEACHES OF COSTA RICA

Beaches are very personal things. One person's dream beach is another's sandy place. Fortunately, Costa Rica has hundreds of beaches to choose from. There are talcum powder white, black, yellow and reddish sand beaches. Primeval, virginal beaches; polluted, garbage strewn silty beaches. There are beaches that offer snorkeling, beaches that have some of the best and least crowded surfing conditions in the world, beaches for walking, swimming, wading, gathering shells, and beaches which serve as embarkation points for searching for monkeys and exotic birds. There are beaches where thousands of sea turtles come every year to lay their eggs in the sand. There are quiet beaches that are perfect for greeting the sunrise, crowded beaches ideal for cold beer and loud music, and solitary beaches where yours are the only footprints on the sand.

Costa Ricans use and enjoy their beaches. Buses and cars filled with food, cold drinks, beach toys and all the family head out from the cities for weekend trips to the nearby beaches of the central Pacific, to Cahuita and Puerto Viejo on the Atlantic Coast and to the north, to the multitude of beaches in Guanacaste.

A visit to the beaches of Costa Rica yields glimpses of warm tropic seas, sunshine bouncing off the ocean and brightly illuminating the sand, trade winds fluffing tall palms, humid air encouraging the growth of coco palms, bananas, the epiphytes and orchids in the trees. There are days of intense, relentless sun that require you to follow the rhythms of the local people: long naps in the middle of the day; glorious sunsets; nights of visiting, talking... delicious sensual mornings. There are amazing, magnificent storms, tearing at the palms and flooding the roads. And then suddenly the storm is over and there is the warm, quiet calm that follows, and the renewed heat that makes the soaked plant life steam, and the people quietly lean on doorways and window sills and stare out at the sultry tropical landscape. Then there is the brilliance of the skies, impossibly blue again, after the storm. And life continues along the beaches of Costa Rica.

CARIBBEAN BEACHES

BARRA DEL COLORADO

In the Barra del Colorado National Refuge, the beach is split in two by the Río Colorado, emptying into the sea. More of a fishing spot than anything else, muddy waters and sharks make Barra del Colorado beach undesirable for swimming. You cannot get to this beach by car, but can fly in or take a boat from Muín, up the canals. Lodging available.

Tortuguero

One of Costa Rica's best beaches for green turtle watching, July through September. Sharks. Access is by jungle cruise, up the canals from Limón. Lodging available.

Portete

Near Limón; a popular beach, crowded on weekends.

Playa Bonita

Where local people swim and surf. There is a walk along the cliff with ocean views.

Isla Uvita

This small island is reached by a 20-minute boat ride from Limón. Ask any fisherman with a boat to take you there. Popular with surfers looking for a fast left break.

Westfalia

A stretch of classic coconut palm-fringed white sand beaches running along the road south of Limón and north of Cahuita. Though beautiful, there are mosquitoes and strong riptides. Water is crystalline clean.

Cahuita

Popular, beautiful Atlantic Coast beach. Excellent snorkeling on the reef. Glass-bottom boats will take you out, or you can swim from the Puerto Vargas end of the beach. White sand beach, monkeys in the palm trees, surf off the reef. Lodging, food and rental bikes available.

Puerto Vargas South of Cahuita National Park

Excellent swimming beach. Excellent camping.

Puerto Viejo

The reef surf break, dubbed "La Salsa Brava," in front of Stanford's Restaurant, explodes from December to April and again in June and July. Inside the reef is a good place to enjoy the water in calm safety. During the remaining months, the sea is quiet and is good for snorkeling. Lodging. Bicycles for rent.

Cocles

A nice beach with some dangerous currents. Good surfing. A 15-minute walk down a dirt road, south of Puerto Viejo.

Playa Chiquita

A beautiful, somewhat unknown palm tree bedecked Caribbean beach, white sand, 10 minutes south of Puerto Viejo. A lovely condo-hotel is located here. Food and lodging.

Uva

A Caribbean beach of anyone's dreams. Nearby private reserve. Extraordinary, clear water. Arguably the best, easily accessible beach along this part of the Atlantic. Can be crowded on weekends. There are bicycles for rent in Puerto Viejo, to pedal here.

Manzanillo

Twenty minutes by car south of Puerto Viejo. The rough road from Limón only recently opened up to this beach, providing driving access here. Isolated and with a fast beach break. Minimal lodging and food available.

PACIFIC COAST

PUNTARENAS PROVINCE

Puntarenas

Used for swimming by locals, but the city dumps its sewage, poorly treated, into the bay here. With all the beaches Costa Rica offers, seriously consider passing this one by. Yet the beach at sunset is a romantic place to stroll.

Boca Barranca

A stretch of beach, with some good surf, between Puntarenas and Puerto Caldera. Lodging available.

Doña Ana Recreation Area

A few hundred yards south of Boca Barranca. Good family beach; sheltered, shady, safe for swimming and has a picnic area and restaurant. No camping allowed.

Mata Limón

Beach resort on an estuary across from Puerto Caldera. Fishing is good. Cabins are available.

Playas Tivives and Valor

Good surfing beaches with long left and rights.

Playa Tárcoles

Located near the Carara Biological Reserve, the beach is gravel, but the ocean is calm and clear. Lodging, food available. Camping allowed.

Playa Escondida

A beachfront club here limits land access, but the beach can be reached by renting a boat from Jacó. (All beaches in Costa Rica are, legally, public.)

Playa Herradura

Five minutes north of Jacó. Gentler waves than in Jacó and shadier. Camping is allowed and there are trees for stringing hammocks. Black sand.

Jacó Beach

The closest major beach to San José, popular with Ticos. A party town on weekends. The beach is long and wide, but silty at times polluted. The rip currents here can be dangerous.

Playa Hermosa

Just south of Jacó, this isolated beach with access through a private ranch has very strong beach breaks. A major annual surfing contest is held here.

Playa Esterillos
A seven-mile long stretch of mostly deserted beach. At times has strong riptides. Lodging.

Playa Bejuco, Playa Palma, Playa Palo Seco
Untrammeled beaches on the drive between Jacó and Quepos.

Playa Isla Damas
Island with a long stretch of silty beach. Surfing can be good.

Quepos
Best waves in the area are found off the point here, but the beaches are funky. Wait and drive a few more miles to Manuel Antonio. Direst bus from San José. Lodging.

Playa Espadilla Norte
The first of the beaches of Manuel Antonio. One of the most popular, and most beautiful beautiful beaches in the country, but can be dangerous because of its unpredictable riptides. Four miles (7km) miles south of Quepos. Every kind of lodging. Flights from San José to Quepos are 20 minutes and under $10.

Playas Espadilla Sur and Manuel Antonio
Two exceptionally beautiful white sand beaches, location in Manuel Antonio National Park. Accessible across a sand spit which can be very submerged at high tides. Sheltered, safe wimming, good diving.

Playas Savegre, Matapalo and Baru
Seldomly-frequented beaches on the drive to Dominical. Lonely but beautiful places. Low tide is best.

Playa Dominical
Where the people of San Isidro go on weekends. Long, uncrowded beach good for swimming, at low-tide. Nearly lagoon. Currents can be dangerous. Good camping beach. Basic lodging.

Playa Dominicalito
Just south of Playa Dominical, there are good point-break waves for surfers here. Swimming is best at low tide when beaches are exposed beyond coral rocks. Beautiful views. Lodging and camping.

Playas Hermosa, Uvita, Ballena, Pinuela and Ventanas
To reach these beaches south of Playa Dominicalito, one must hike through the jungle.

OSA PENINSULA

PLAYA COLORADO
This beach on Drake Bay rewards the intrepid. Golden sands on the edge of the jungle lead to clear waters filled with tropical fish. Snorkeling is excellent. Lodging.

Playas Pira, Carbonera, Tamales and Platanares
All beaches of the Osa Peninsula, all beautiful and all difficult to get to. When you get there, they're yours.

Pavones
Across the Golfo Dulce from Osa are long empty beaches where very long waves force surfers to walk up the beach with their boards rather than paddle back out.

GUANACASTE

PLAYA PANAMA
A beautiful bay, with few signs of civilization. Swimming, camping and hunting shells. Some litter along the way.

Playa Hermosa
A partially developed beach, protected, good for swimming, diving and fishing. Kayaks and sailboards for rent. Lodging.

Playas del Coco
A funky, local resort area where fish are brought ashore from fishing boats. A wide beach, but strong riptides. Lodging.

Playa Ocotal
Site of luxury hotel. Shady cove for swimming.

Playa Pan de Azúcar
Good swimming and snorkeling. Hotel on beach.

Playa Potrero
A good beach, with camping facilities and a hotel. Fishing and diving.

Playa Blanca/Flamingo
Beautiful, extensive beach dominated by a luxury hotel and condo development. Here the Flamingo Hotel has an airstrip for private planes and parking for limos. Not the best for camping.

Playa Brasilito
A beautiful grey-sand beach, good for camping. Cabinas.

Playa Conchal
Entire beach is composed of whole and crushed shells. Very private but with riptides. Access is by foot, over and through a rocky point.

Playa Grande
From November to March, leatherback turtles, the largest reptiles in existance, come here to nest. A 20-minute walk north of Tamarindo beach, Playa Grande is a good surfing beach with long waves.

Playa Tamarindo
Headquarters for surfing in Guanacaste with three good surfing beaches in the area. This beautiful white sand beach is a nesting site for leatherback turtles. Windsurfing is becoming popular here also. Luxury hotel and many cabinas.

Playa Langosta
This beach across the estuary from Playa Tamarindo is also popular with surfers.

Playa Junquillal
Isolated, wide and quiet. A good place to walk and watch for birds. Occasional rip currents. Three nearby hotels cater to those looking for a beautiful escape.

Playa Azul
This quiet beach is on the road connecting the

small towns of Marbella and San Juanillo.

Playa Ostional

A private reserve for the protection of olive ridley turtles.

Playa Nosara

A splendid long and wide beach with white sands and good surf. The beach is backed by rolling green hills. An international community has settled near here and half of Nosara itself is a wildlife reserve. Lodging available. Road is impassable at times.

Playa Sámara

Fantasy white-sand beach with water made gentle for swimming by an offshore reef. Windsurfing is good here. Lodging available.

Playa Carrillo

Very much like Playa Samará, but not as well-known, and with less tourist infrastructure. Lodging.

Playa Bejuco and San Miguel

Beaches south of Carrillo. You must ford the Río Ora at low tide if you arrive from the north.

Playa Coyote

A long, deserted, sometimes romantic, and often windy beach.

Playas Caletas and Mal Pais

Isolated beaches south of Coyote. There are rumors of 15-foot waves at Playa Caletas. No lodging here, but one could ask around for a house with a room to let. This is four-wheel-drive country.

Cabo Blanco

At the tip of the Nicoya Peninsula, this is a lovely remote beach. Permission is needed to enter the fully protected Cabo Blanco Nature Reserve.

Montezuma

A series of beaches, tide pools and inland waterfalls. The first couple of rocky bays north of Montezuma have strong currents, Playa Grande is safe swimming. Camping and lodging available.

Bahía Ballena

Bay has nice beaches, all safe for swimming. Lodging available.

NIGHTLIFE

There's plenty to do after dark in Costa Rica, and San José is the center of late night activities.

BARS AND CLUBS

(Bares y Cantinas)

Amstel. c 7, av 1-3. Tel: 222 4622. Quiet and comfortable.

Bar Mexico. Tel: 222 7000. Opposite corner from the Barrio Mexico church. Very good *bocas*. Live mariachi bands.

Centro Comercial El Pueblo. Near Hotel Bougainvilla on highway towards Heredia. An area full of boutiques, galleries, restaurants, nightclubs, skating rink and discos.

Chelles Bar. Tel: 221 1369. av ctl, c 9. Open 24 hrs. A landmark, free *bocas*.

Chelles Taberna. Around the corner, quieter with better *bocas*.

El Cuartel. av 1, c 21-23, close to Cine California. Tel: 221 0327. Late night, after-theater crowd.

El Crocodrilo. San Pedro, across from Banco Anglo. Tel: 225 3277.

Charleston. Plaza de la Soledad. English pub, live jazz weekends.

Key Largo. c 7, av 1-3, near Holiday Inn. Tel: 221 0277. Atmosphere reminiscent of an old Bogart movie.

La Esmeralda. av 2, c 5-7. Marichi bands. Open even after 4am.

Liverpool. 600 m north of La Granja, Barrio Mexico. Motown, blues.

Los Lechones. av 4, c 11-13. Good calypso band on weekends.

Lucky Piano Bar. av ctl, c 7, next to Balmoral Hotel. Tel: 222 8385. Gringo sports on TV, piano music from 5pm daily. Prostitutes.

Mirador Ram Luna. Tel: 30 3060. Fantastic view of Central Valley.

Nashville South. Off of Parque Morazan. Bluegrass. Prostitutes.

Taberna Happy Days. Off Parque Morazan. Pop. Prostitutes.

The Place. Hotel Corobicí, Sabana Norte. Tel: 232 8122.

Shakespeare. Darts, live music.

Salon Musical de Lety. Centro Comercial El Pueblo. Tel: 234 4236.

DANCING

La Torre. c 7, off av 1. Mostly gay bar, disco, funk, rap.

Tunel del Tiempo. av Central. Lit with blinking colored lights, popular disco.

Coco Loco. Centro Comercial El Pueblo. Tel: 222 8782.

Hotel Corobicí. Sabana. Tel: 232 8122.

Infinito. Centro Comercial El Pueblo Tel: 223 2195.

Acatua. Centro Comercial El Pueblo. Tel: 233 3288. Live calypso and reggae.

La Plaza Disco Club Público. Francisco, Guadalupe. Across from Centro Comercial El Pueblo. Tel: 257 1077.

Leonardo's. Paseo Colón, Centro Colón Building. Tel: 223 7310.

CASINOS

Club Triángulo. c 7, av ctl l. Tel: 233 7081.

Club Domino. av ctl, c 7-9. Tel: 222 5022.

Hotel Cariari. Tel: 239 0022. Ciudad Cariari, on airport highway.

Hotel Corcobicí. La Sabana Norte. Tel: 232 8122.

Hotel Irazú. Tel: 232 4811. Airport highway, near Centro Comercial 2000.

Hotel Presidente. av ctl, c 7-9. Tel: 222 3022.

Hotel Sheraton Herradura. Tel: 239 0033. Next to Hotel Cariari.

Key Largo. c 7, av 1-3. Tel: 221 0277.

Le Chambourd. av 11, c 3. Private club. Tel: 233 7122.

Royal Gardens. av ctl, c ctl. Tel: 257 0022.

LATIN DANCING

Sus. Sabanilla.

Centro Social. av 2.

Salsa. 54 c 3, av 1.

LANGUAGE

SURVIVAL SPANISH

Learn a bit of Spanish before you arrive, if only the simple courtesies: "Good morning." "How are you?" "I'm well, thanks." These seemingly inconsequential phrases are an important part of daily life in Costa Rica. English is spoken by many people in San José and in the larger hotels, and one can always get by without it, but if your idea of a good trip includes some contact with local people, then speaking a bit of Spanish is the ticket. Consider spending the first week of your trip enrolled in one of the language schools. Tailored programs and schedules of all kinds, many with excursions and cultural programs available.

A pocket-sized English-Spanish dictionary is a good idea, and tiny electronic dictionaries are also available.

USEFUL WORDS & PHRASES

Numbers

1	*uno*
2	*dos*
3	*tres*
4	*cuatro*
5	*cinco*
6	*seis*
7	*siete*
8	*ocho*
9	*nueve*
10	*diez*
11	*once*
12	*doce*
13	*trece*
14	*catorce*
15	*quince*
16	*diez y sies*
17	*diez y siete*
18	*diez y ocho*
19	*diez y nueve*
20	*viente*
21	*viente y uno*
30	*treinta*
40	*cuarenta*
50	*cincuenta*
60	*sesenta*
70	*setenta*
80	*ochenta*

90	noventa
100	cien
101	ciento uno
200	doscientos
300	trescientos
400	cuatrocientos
500	quinientos
600	seiscientos
700	setecientos
800	ochocientos
900	novecientos
1,000	mil
2,000	dos mil
10,000	diez mil
100,000	cien mil
1,000,000	un millioñ

a bank	un banco
a hotel	un hotel
a restaurant	un restaurante
a restroom	un sanitario
a private bathroom	el baño
the ticket office	la oficina de billetes
a department store	una tienda
the marketplace	el mercado
What is the price?	Cuánto cuesta? or Cuánto es?
It's too expensive.	Está muy caro.
Can you give me a discount?	Me puede dar un descuento?
Do you have ____?	Tiene Usted ____?
I will buy this.	Voy a comprar eso.
Please show me another.	Muéstreme otro, por favor.

COMMON EXPRESSIONS

Good morning	Buenos días
Good afternoon	Buenas tardes
Good evening	Buenas noches
Goodbye	Hasta luego
How are you?	Cómo está Usted?
I'm well, thanks.	Muy bien, gracias.
And you?	Y Usted?
Please	Por favor
Thank you	Gracias
No, thank you	No, gracias
You're welcome.	Con mucho gusto
How kind of you.	Usted es muy amable.
I am sorry.	Lo siento.
Excuse me.	Disculpe. Con permiso. (When leaving the table or passing in front of someone.)
Yes	Si
No	No
Do you speak English?	Habla Usted Inglés?
Do you understand me?	Me entiende?
Does anyone here speak English?	Hay alguien aquí que habla inglés?
Just a moment, please.	Momentico, por favor.
This is good.	Está bueno.
This is bad.	Está malo.
Where is ____?	Dónde está ____?
the exit	la salida
the entrance	la entrada
the airport	el aeropuerto
the taxi	el taxi
the police station	la delegación de policía
the embassy	la embajada
the post office	la oficina de correos
the telegraph office	la oficina de telégrafos
a public telephone	un teléfono público

Please bring me ____.	Tráigame por favor ____.
coffee with milk.	café con leche
black coffee	café negro
tea	té
a beer	una cerveza
cold water	agua helado
hot water	agua caliente
a soft drink	un gaseoso
a menu	un menú (pronounced men-oo)
the daily special	el plato del día
May I have more beer?	Me puede dar más cerveza, por favor.
May I have the bill? (To get the attention of the waiter)	La cuenta, por favor. Oiga! Señor.
Please call a taxi for me.	Pídame un taxi, por favor.
How many kilometers is ____ from here?	Cuántos kilometros hay de aquí a ____?
How long does it take go there?	Cuánto se tarda to en llegar?
What will you charge take me to ____?	Cuánto me cobra to para llevar me a ____?
How much is a ticket to ____?	Cuánto cuesta un billete a ____?
I want a ticket to ____.	Quiero un billete a ____, por favor.
Where does this bus go?	A dónde va este bus?
Stop (on a bus)	Parada!
Please stop here.	Pare aquí, por favor.
Please go straight.	Vaya recto, por favor.
right	a la derecho
left	a la izquerda
What is this place called?	Cómo se llama este lugar?
I'm going to ____.	Me voy a ____.
Where is there an	Dónde hay un

inexpensive hotel?	*hotel económico?*
Do you have a room with ___?	*Hay un cuarto con ___?*
a bath	*un baño*
a fan	*un abanico*
air conditioning	*aire*
Where is the dining room?	*Dónde está el comedor?*
the pharmacy	*la farmacía*
the gas station	*la bomba* (the pump)
key	*la llave*
manager	*el gerente*
owner, proprietor	*el dueño* (male) *la dueña* (female)
Can you cash a traveler's check?	*Se puede cambiar un cheque de viajero?*
money	*dinero*
credit card	*tarjeta de crédito*
tax	*impuesto*
letter	*carta*
postcard	*tarjeta postal*
envelope	*sobre*
stamp	*estampilla*
bus stop	*parada del bus*
reserved seat	*asiento reservado*
reservation	*reservación*
airplane	*avión*
train	*tren*
bus	*bus*
Fill it up, please.	*Lleno, por favor.*
Please check the oil.	*Vea el aceite, por favor.*
Please fill the radiator.	*Favor de llenar el radiador.*
the battery	*la batería*
I need ___.	*Yo necesito ___.*
a jack	*un gato*
a towtruck	*una grúa*
a mechanic	*un mechánico*
a tire	*una llanta*
Help me, please.	*Ayudeme, por favor.*
Call a doctor quickly!	*Llame a un médico y prisa!*

SPEAKING TICO: TIQUISMOS

If you already speak some Spanish, learn a few Tiquismos, uniquely Costa Rican expressions. Tico Spanish is rich with them.

The familiar *"tú "* (you) is not used in Costa Rica, even with children. They often use an archaic form, *"vos."* The rules regarding the use of *"vos"* are tricky and elude even advanced students of Spanish: best to stick with *"usted,"* which is always correct.

When walking in areas outside of San José, people passing on the street greet one another with *"Adios,"* or *"'dios."* *"Hasta luego"* is used to say "goodbye."

Costa Ricans love to use *sobrenombres,* nicknames. More often than not, the nicknames used have to do with a person's physical appearance: *Macho/ Macha* if he or she is ever-so-slightly fair-skinned or fair-haired (not to be confused with *machismo,* an attribute of Latin males, used in Mexico); *China* if she has a slight slant to the eyes, or is actually Oriental; *Negro* if his skin is dark; *Gordito* for someone even slightly overweight; *Moreno* if the person is slightly dark-complexioned, and so on.

If someone asks, *"Cómo está Usted?"* it's always correct to reply, *"Muy bien, gracias a Díos,"* ("Very well, thanks to God") or *"Muy bien, por dicho,"* (Very well, fortunately") but you might want to try something a little more zippy and informal, such as: *"Pura vida,"* ("Great") or *"Con toda la pata,"* ("Terrific" – literally, with all the paw) or *"Tranquilo"* ("Relaxed").

SPANISH LANGUAGE SCHOOLS IN COSTA RICA

Costa Rica offers those who would like to learn or perfect their Spanish a number of appealing options. Whatever a student's needs, whether merely conversational or for the businessplace or to master the structure of Spanish, an appropriate language school exists. The following is an overview of what's available, what each institution offers and the current costs, all subject to change, of course.

Academia Costarricense del Lenguaje: University of Costa Rica Spanish teachers lead a monthly course of audiovisual Spanish programs. Prices vary according to the intensity of the course. For two hours two days a week the price is $96. For four hours two days a week it's $196; five hours three days a week is $360. Living arrangements with Costa Rican families are available, including 3 meals a day, private room and laundry service. Other courses include the guitar, Latin dance, tap dance and aerobics. Also available are low-price tours to the beaches and national parks. Write Apartado 336-Sabanilla, Costa Rica. Tel: 221 1624. Fax: 225 2610.

American Institute for Language and Culture: Group and individual programs blending language studies and cultural insights. Private lessons are $13 an hour. The monthly rate for 15 hours a week is $720; 20 hours a week is $960. The small group rate is $9.50 an hour. Group rates are 15 hours per week at $525; 20 hours at $700. For lodging with a Costa Rican family, add $85 to $90 per week. Educational and cultural trips available. Write P.O. Box 200-1001, San José. Tel: 225 4313. Fax: 224 4244.

Central American Institute for International Affairs: (ICAI) aims to teach students of all ages conversational Spanish in the shortest time possible with its "Total Immersion Spanish Program." Participants live with carefully selected Costa Rican families where they receive breakfast, dinner, laundry service and a private room. Courses begin every month and run for one, two, three or four weeks. Cost is $40 per day which includes homestay, tuition, registration, classroom materials, twenty hours a week of Spanish instruction and tours of San José, San Antonio Cattle Ranch, Santa Rosa National Park, Braulio Carrillo National Park, Cahuita, The Caribbean Coast, Irazú Volcano and Lankester Gardens. Write: The Language Studies Enrollment Center, PO Box 5095, Anaheim, CA 92814. Tel: 233 8571. Fax: 221 5238.

Centro Cultural Costarricense-Norteamericano: A Costa Rican institution promoting cultural exchange and understanding between citizens of Costa Rica and the United States. A five-week Spanish course of three hours daily is $250. A special course for groups of two to four students meets four to six hours a day for a minimum of forty hours. Cost is $280 per student. Individual tutorials are available for a minimum of ten hours at $15 per hour. Homestays with Costa Rican families can be arranged. The Centro also offers a library, concerts, art exhibits, theater presentations. Spanish classes for companies and organizations are also available through the Workplace Extension Program. Write APDO 1489-100, San José, Costa Rica. Tel: 225 9433. Fax: 224 1480.

Centro Linguistico Conversa: Offers six to fifteen hours of instruction per week at approximately $23 per hour. It also runs a "study farm" in the village of Santa Ana, west of San José, where a course is available including all-day instruction, meals, text materials, laundry and a host family near the school to keep the student in constant contact with the language. Cost: $1370. Write to P.O. Box 17-1007, Centro Colón, San José, Costa Rica. Tel: 221 7649. Fax: 233 2418.

Forester Instituto International: Offers a two-week language program including housing with a local family and two meals daily for $560. A more intense cultural program costs $1080, lasts four weeks with 4 hours of Spanish per day and includes housing with a family, 2 meals per day and field trips. Cost drops $100/week if students make own housing arrangements. Write: APDO 6945-1000, San José, Costa Rica. Tel: 225 3155. Fax: 225 0926. In the US, tel: (619) 943 0204.

Institute for Central American Developmental Studies: (ICADS) The focus in this Spanish learning program is on the politics, social and environmental issues in Central America. Guest lectures and discussions are part of the intensive conversation and grammar course. Students help select topics of interest. Lodging with a local family is included in the cost of the package, but is not mandatory. The one-month intensive program costs $867. Write APDO 3 Sabanilla, San José, Costa Rica. Tel: 225 0508. Fax: 234 1337. In the US write Dept. 826, PO Box 025216, Miami, FL.

Latin American Institute of Languages: (ILISA) Offers courses ranging from two to four weeks and varying in the number of hours per day. Rates are from $465 to $995. Registration fee is $125. The program includes a host Costa Rican family, 2 meals a day and laundry service, a welcome dinner in a typical Costa Rican restaurant and workbooks. Classes have a maximum of 4 students. Write: ILISA, P.O. Box 1001-2050, San Pedro, Costa Rica. Tel: 225 2495. Fax: 225 4665. In the US, contact Mega-Myers, PO Box 491036, Los Angeles, CA 90049. Tel: (310) 476 3123. Fax: (310) 476 8132.

Instituto Británico: Conducts a 3-week program combining learning Spanish with educational field trips to sites of historic, ecological and cultural importance. Cultural activities involve art exhibits, lectures and workshops. Housing with a Costa Rican family can be arranged. Write: APDO 8184-1000, San José, Costa Rica. Tel: 225 0256. Fax: (506) 253 1894.

Instituto de la Lengua Español: (The Spanish Language Institute) This institute, which is mostly for missionaries, admits others on a space available basis. It offers classes which include phonetics, grammar, conversation and translation. 15 weeks of classes at five hours daily costs $635. Write: APDO 100-2350, San José, Costa Rica. Tel: 227 7355. Fax: 227 0211.

Instituto Universal de Idiomas: Offers the "Economic Global Package," which includes a homestay with a Costa Rican family, meals and books for $570. Other offerings are 2-week classes, 3 hours a day for $145 and 4-week classes, 3 hours a day for $225. Private tutorials are $9 per hour. Write: APDO 219-2120, San Francisco de Guadalupe, Costa Rica. Tel: 257 0441.

Intensa: Offers intensive Spanish programs in classes with a maximum of 5 for 2, 3 or 4 weeks. Home stays with Costa Rican families are available and recommended. Write: PO Box 8110-1000, San José, Costa Rica. Tel: 224 6353.

Lisa Tech: Staffed by native speaking university graduates, this school is dedicated to practical methods of learning Spanish. Classes from 3 to 8 students vary from 2 to 4 weeks. Most classes are conversational but some are devoted to mechanical skills and reading. Textbooks are included in the tuition fee. Room, board and maid service are included. Write PO Box 228-4005, San Antonio de Belén, Costa Rica. Tel: 239 2225. Fax: 239 2225.

Further Reading

No evaluation intended or implied. Because reference books are often unavailable or expensive in Costa Rica, consider purchasing books before leaving home.

A Guide to the Birds of Costa Rica, Gary F. Stiles and A.F. Skutch, Cornell University Press, 1989.

A Neotropical Companion, John C. Kricher, Princeton University Press, 1989.

Above The Jungle Floor, Donald Lire Perry, New York: Simon & Schuster, 1986.

Al Calor del Togon, Marjoriee Ross de Cerdas, Promotora de Cultura y Arte Costarricense, S.A., 1986.

All Costa Rica, Ricardo Vilchez, published by author, 1988 (photographs). Available from Apartado 8033, San José.

Anthropological Bibliography of Aboriginal Costa Rica., Jorge A.Lines, Paper #7 San José: Tropical Science Center, 1967.

Area Handbook for Cosa Rica, American University, Washington, DC, US Government Printing Office, 1985.

Asi Vivimos los Ticos, Miguel Salguero, Ed. EDUCA. Berkeley and Los Angeles: Universily of California Press, 1980.

Cooking in Costa Rica, US Mission Association, Embassy of the United States of America.

Costa Rica Country Environmental Profile, A Field Study, Gary Hatshorn, et. al., Tropical Science Center, San José.

Costa Rica, Paul Glassman, Moscow, VT, Passport Press, 1985.

Costa Rica: Economic Crisis and Public Policy, Juan Diego Trejos, Latin American and Carribean Center Florida International University, 1985.

Costa Rica: Sus Hechos Políticos de 1948, Bulgarelli Aguilar, Ed. EDUCA.

Costa Rican Natural History, Daniel H Janzen, University of Chicago Press, 1983.

Costa Rican Traveler, Ellen Searby, Windham Bay Press, 1988.

Crisis in Costa Rica: The Revolution of '48, John Patrick Bell, University of Texas Press, 1971.

Don Pepe: A Political Biography of José Figueres of Costa Rica, Charles Ameringer, Albuquerque: University of New Mexico Press, 1978.

El Costarricense, Constantino Lascaris, Ed. EDUCA.

El Habla Popular en la Literatura Costarricense, Soto Arroyo, and Manuel Victor. Ed. Universida.

Historia de Costa Rica, Carlos Monge Alfaro, San José: Libreria Trejos, 1982.

Home Gardening in Costa Rica, Bernhardt, Ed, San José: The Tico Times, 1985.

In The Rainforest, Catherine Caufield, University of Chicago Press, 1984.

Investors' Guide to Cosa Rica, Costa Rican-American Chamber of Commerce, Apartado 4946 av 2, c 30-32, San José, 1000 Costa Rica. Tel: 233 2133.

La Penca: On Trial in Costa Rica, The CIA vs. the Press, Tony and Martha Avirgan, San José: Editorial Porvenir, 1987.

Let's Discover Costa Rica (for children), Avie, Betts, Andy and Jan Gingold, San José: Bandanna Republic, S.A., 1987.

Living in Costa Rica, US Mission Association, Embassy of the US, apto 920-1200, Pavas, Costa Rica.

Naturalist on a Tropical Farm, Alexander F. Skutch, *Nuestro Pensamiento Político en Sus Fuentes*, Enrique Benavides, Ed. Trejo.

Refranes y dichos Populares Usuales en Costa Rica, Hermogenes H. Hernandez, Imprenta San Martin.

South America on a Shoestring, Geoff Crowther. Lonely Planet Publications, Australia.

The Commercial Laws of Costa Rica, Juan Edgar Picado. New York, Oceana Publications, Inc.,1981.

The Costa Ricans, Richard, John, and Mavis Biesanz, Englewood Cliffs, N.J. Prentice-Hall, Inc., 1987.

The National Parks of Costa Rica, Mario Boza and Rolando Mendoza, Spain: INCAFO, 1981.

The New Key to Costa Rica, Beatrice Blake and Anne Becher, San José: Publications in English, S.A., 1988.

The Rivers of Costa Rica, Mayfield and Gallo, Manasha Ridge Press, Birmingham, NC, *El Negro en Costa Rica*, Ed. Costa Rica. Carlos Melendez and Quince Duncan.

The South American Handbook, McNally Rand.

Treasure Hunters, Carlos Liebhaber. Published by author, distributed by The Bookshop: San José.

Tropical Nature, Adrian and Miyata. K. Forsyth Scribners, 1984.

What Happen, A Folk History of Costa Rica's Talamanca Coast, Paula Palmer, San José: Ecodesarrollos, 1977.

The Tico Times (apdo. 4632, San José, Costa Rica, tel 222-8952) is the most important English newspaper in Central America. Subscriptions are mailed worldwide, and they publish a great special Tourist Edition annually. The classified section contains valuable information. They will often answer questions about the country if you write to them. US address: Dept. 717, POB 025216, Miami, FL 33102.

USEFUL ADDRESSES

CONSERVATION GROUPS

Many visitors to Costa Rica leave with the strong desire to help this small country that is trying so hard to do so much with so few resources. The following are some of the environmental organizations which are actively involved in saving and protecting Costa Rica's natural resources.

Appefloras: *Asociacion Preservacionista de Floray Fauna Silvestre* (Association for the Preservation of Wild Flora and Fauna).

This is a watchdog organization which, through volunteers, patrols areas both outside and inside the national parks, reporting illegal hunting, fishing and logging to park authorities. It is in urgent need of both volunteers and funds. Contributions are tax deductible in Costa Rica. Send donations to: Apreflofas, Apartado 1192-1007, San José, Costa Rica. Tel: 231 0792.

Areofilia: Association for the Protection of Trees.

Volunteers in this organization teach environmentally-aware land management practices to farmers in the central Pacific region, which has been ravaged by deforestation. Emphasis is on protecting watersheds and the propagation of native species of plants and animals. Visitors get tours of the operation and the chance to plant a native tree. Send specified US tax-deductible contributions to: ARBOFILIA, Audubon Society of Portland, 5151 NW Cornell Rd., Portland, OR 97210 or ARBOFILIA, Apartado 512, Tibas, 1100 Costa Rica. Tel: 235 5470.

Ascona: *Asociacion Costarricense para la Conservacion de la Naturaleza* (Costa Rican Conservation Association).

This group is concerned with, among other things, eliminating industrial pollution from Costa Rica through its investigation and lobbying work. It is currently working on rewriting a new forestry law and protecting dolphins in the tuna fishing industry. Membership is 1200 *colones* or $12 a year and allows participation in a variety of projects and committees. US constributions are tax deductible if sent through the World Wildlife Fund: ASCONA c/o World Wildlife Fund, 1250 24th St. N.W., Washington, DC 20037. Tel: (202) 293 4800. Tax-deductible contributions in Costa Rica: ASCONA Apartado 8-3790-1000, San José, Costa Rica. Tel: (506) 222 2296.

Caribbean Conservation Corporation: This group runs the green turtle tagging project at Tortuguero Beach on the Atlantic Coast, which is the largest nesting colony of this endangered species in the Western Atlantic. For the $35 annual membership fee, members receive a quarterly newsletter. Tax-deductible contributions go to: Caribbean Conservation Corp., PO Box 2866, Gainesville, FL 32602. Tel: (904) 373 6441. Or to Caribbean Conservation Corp., Apartado 448-2120 San Francisco de Guadalupe, San José, Costa Rica. Tel: (506) 224 9215.

Cedarena: *Centro del Derecho Ambiental y de los Recursos Naturales* (Envirommental and Natural Resources Law Center)

This conservation group was founded by a group of lawyers and law students to help draft model environmental laws and regulations and to educate the public and government officials on the use of the law to protect the environment. Donors are invited to a monthly luncheon to discuss issues and make suggestions. Send tax-deductible contributions to: CEDARENA Apartado 134-2050, San Pedro, Costa Rica. Tel: (506) 224 8239.

Conservation International: The goal of this US-based organization is to integrate people as part of the worldwide ecosystem. It works closely with government agencies throughout the world. In Costa Rica, it gives technical and financial support to the 200,000-acre La Amistad International Biosphere Reserve, which makes up 14 percent of Costa Rica's territory. Membership is $25 per year and entitles one to a quarterly newsletter. US tax-deductible contributions should be sent to: Conservation International, 1015 18th St. N.W., Washington DC, 20036. Tel: (202) 429 5660. In Costa Rica, send donations to Conservation International, Apartado 8-3870, San José, Costa Rica. Tel: (506) 225 2649.

Friends of Lomas Barbudal Biological Reserve: The Lomas Buarbudal Reserve in Guanacaste is constantly threatened by wildfires. This group sets up projects to establish living firebreaks to protect it. Send US tax-deductible contributions to: Friends of Lomas Barbudal, 691 Colusa Ave., Berkeley, CA 94707. Tel: (415) 526 4115.

Fundacion De Parque Nacionles (National Parks Foundation): This foundation is devoted to protecting and expanding Costa Rica's world-famous national park system. It is the leading organization for arranging debt-for-nature swaps. Send contributions to: Fundacíon Parque Nacionales, Apartado 1108-1002, Paseo de los Estudiantes, San José, Costa Rica. Tel: (506) 233 0116.

Fundacion Neotropica (Neotropica Foundation): This group works to foster "sustainable development" in communities near Costa Rica's wildlife preserves, parks, forest reserves and other protected areas. The $25 annual membership fee brings a quarterly newsletter and gives members a 10% discount on gift items from its Nature Stores and on its Heliconia Press publications. US tax-deductible contributions should be earmarked and sent to: The Nature Conservancy, 1815 North Lynn St., Arlington VA 22209, ATTN: Randy Curtis. In Costa Rica mail to: Neotropica, Apartado 236-1002, Paseo de los Estudiantes, San José, Costa Rica. Tel: (506) 255 4254.

Monteverde Conservation League: This group, a community conservation organization in Monteverde, Costa Rica, works on reforestation, environmental education and sustainable development projects. It purchases or leases land to preserve forests. It also coordinates the International Children's Rainforest Project (Bosque Eterno de los Niños). The long-range plan is to purchase 43,000 acres for a preserve. The children of Sweden have donated over one million dollars for the preserve and 18,000 acres have already been purchased. Each $100 contribution buys an acre of land. A $25 contribution entitles the donor to receive the quarterly *Tapir Tracks* magazine. Send US tax-deductible contributions for the League to The Nature Conservancy International, Children's Rainforest,1815 North Lynn St., Arlington, VA 22209.

Rainforest Alliance: This New York-based alliance helps the Monteverde Conservation League buy land for its preserve and helps the indigenous tribes of Costa Rica with their agro-forestry projects. For any contribution of over $15, the donor will receive *The Canopy* magazine, devoted to rainforest issues and notice of Alliance legislative activities in a publication called *Hot Topics from the Tropics*. Contributions go to: Rainforest Alliance, 270 Lafayette Street, Suite 512, New York, NY 10012. Tel: (212) 941 1900.

Tropical Science Centre: This ecological research organization manages the Monteverde Cloud Forest Reserve. With its donations it is purchasing land on the Pacific side of the Tilarán Mountains to protect the entire habitats of birds and animals migrating from higher altitudes within the Reserve to lower altitudes outside it. The center is dedicated to environmental education. Send earmarked US tax-deductible contributions to: Monteverde Cloud Forest, c/o National Audubon Society, 950 Third Ave., New York, NY 10012. Or in Costa Rica write Tropical Science Center, Apartado 8-3870, San José 1000, Costa Rica. Tel: (506) 253 3308.

Tsuli Tsuli (Audubon Society of Costa Rica): This US-affiliate involves itself with environmental edu-cation and lobbying the Cost Rican Legislative Assembly for an investigation of deforestation in the Tortuguero area. Basic membersip is $15 or 1,000 *colones* annually. The member receives a bimonthly bulletin. For a $30 annual fee the donor also receives a subscription to *Audubon Magazine*. Write to Tsuli Tsuli (Audubon of Costa Rica), Apartado 4910-1000, San José, Costa Rica. Tel: (506) 556 6431 ext. 237. Or to the Audubon Society of Costa Rica, P.O. Box 025216-700, Miami, FL 33102-5216.

World Society for the Protection of Animals: The Costa Rican branch of this society operates the only animal shelter and wildlife rehabilitation center in Central America, the Chompipe Biological Reserve (Tel: 506 39 7158) near Braulio Carrillo National Park. It has lobbied the Costa Rican government to adopt strict regulations on tuna fishing in to stop the slaughter of nearly 100,000 dolphins per year. Send tax-deductible contributions for Costa Rica to WSPA, 29 Perkins Street, Box 190, Boston, MA 02130. Tel: (617) 522 7000. Or to WSPA, Apartado 516-3000, San José, Costa Rica. Tel: (506) 239 7178.

OTHER INSIGHT GUIDES

Other *Insight Guides* which highlight destinations in this region include:

Insight Guide: Belize offers a full portrait of one of the world's leading "eco-tourism" destinations, whether rainforests or coral reefs.

Insight Pocket Guide: Yucatan Peninsula sifts through Mayan history and Spanish heritage to unveil the mysteries of southern Mexico.

ART/PHOTO CREDITS

INDEX

D

E

F

M

N

O

A
B
C
D
E
G
H
I
J
a
b
c
d
f
g
h
i
j
k
l